From the beginnings to the

present · sixty-nine poems

in a new presentation · ·

Edited by Stanley Burnshaw

T. Carmi, Ezra Spicehandler

NEW YORK · CHICAGO · SAN FRANCISCO

THE MODERN HEBREW POEM ITSELF

THE MODERN HEBREW POEM ITSELF

HOLT, RINEHART AND WINSTON, PUBLISHERS

Published simultaneously in Canada by Holt, Rinehart and Winston of Canada, Limited
Library of Congress Catalog Card Number: 65-14451

First Edition
81175-0315
Printed in the United States of America

··· CONTENTS ···

II

III

Appendix

THE MODERN HEBREW POEM ITSELF

TO THE READER

This book is addressed to people completely ignorant of Hebrew who wish to experience some modern poems of that language. If the career of *The Poem Itself*[1] be taken as a guide, they should be able to fulfill this wish, for both books follow the identical principle: the foreign poems are not translated into verse but, to use Robert Frost's description, "they are discussed into English." Rather than in a translation which gives the reader an experience in *English* verse, the Hebrew poem is presented both in Hebrew and in English transcription and it is accompanied with an extensive prose commentary. The commentary offers a literal rendering of the poem interwoven with an explanatory discussion.

Before turning to any of the sixty-nine "experiences" offered in this volume, the reader will want to know what to expect in the prose that accompanies each poem. The briefest summary can be given in the following sentences from my introduction to *The Poem Itself:* "Because each word of a foreign poem is unique in itself and in its order, we ask the reader to read the original along with our English approximations (set in italics, with alternative meanings in parentheses and explanations in brackets). Our comments on allusion, symbol, meaning, sound, and the like will enable him to see *what* the poem is saying and *how*, though the poem itself is an unparaphrasable totality." As to how much the reader will hear of the sound of the poem, we have assumed his total inability to read Hebrew characters; hence we have given each Hebrew word a phonetic transcription into English.

Page 155 is a representative example. The poem by Haim Gury is in Hebrew and transliterated "Odíses." How this phonetic transcription

[1] *The Poem Itself: 45 modern poets in a new presentation—the French, German, Spanish, Portuguese, Italian poems, each rendered literally in an interpretative discussion.* First published in 1960 by Holt, Rinehart and Winston, Inc., New York; American paperback edition, 1962: Meridian Books, New York; European paperback edition, with an essay on "The Three Revolutions of Modern Poetry," 1965: Penguin Books Ltd., England.

should be sounded is explained in some detail on pp. 191 ff., but to suggest at once the simplicity of the procedure, we offer the following remarks. All the consonants may be pronounced as in English except for the *r*, which is always trilled in Hebrew (roughly similar to the trilled *r* in Spanish or French), and the following two that we have marked with a dot below:—*ṣ* has the sound of *sh* (as in *shout*) to distinguish it from the undotted *s* (which is always as in *son*); and *ḥ* has the sound of *ch* in the Scottish word *Loch* to distinguish it from the undotted *h* (which is always as in *head*). We have also used an acute accent to enable the reader to make the proper stress in words of more than one syllable (as might be done with our word *demócracy*, for example). Readers with some familiarity with Spanish will have little difficulty in understanding the approximate sounds of the Hebrew vowels and diphthongs as given in our transcriptions (see p. 192). But of course the transliteration is not aimed to do more than provide a *very general* sense of the sound of Hebrew.

Readers of books of verse presumably never proceed from page 1 on but skip about, following individual habit. Though it may dismay an author who has often spent hours deciding the sequence, such caprice is recommended to the reader of our anthology, with the further suggestion that he begin toward the last third or in the middle. Plunged into this new world of poetry, he may find it more congenial to move from the more familiar to the less, from Gilboa, Sach, or Amihai to Tchernichovsky and Steinberg, rather than from Bialik onward. On the other hand, he may prefer to follow chronology (as also set forth in the essay on pp. 197 ff.), beginning with the work of the most celebrated poet, whose poems appeared in the nineties.

The thought of preparing the present work arose one evening in late 1960 while discussing *The Poem Itself* with an Israeli scholar. "Of course the method is extremely helpful with European verse," he began, "but I suppose you realize that for modern Hebrew poetry it is quite indispensable." My automatic "Why?" did not spring out of absolute ignorance. I had read all the English and French translations of modern Hebrew verse that I could lay hands on and though most of them had left me unsatisfied, I had been stirred often enough to have felt uneasy. My state differed from the one prescribed by Frost: that "for self-assurance there should always be a lingering unhappiness in reading translations." Mine was unhappiness aggravated by bewilderment. How could so many people of learning and taste speak with such warmth of these Hebrew writers whose words-in-translation had often left me cold and doubtful?

Was it only the absence of tremendously gifted translators? Was there some lack in me that had blocked my way to the poets? Or were there perhaps certain elements in the poetry of the originals that simply could not survive any carrying-over? I inclined to the last possibility, for behind the heavy clouds on the English versions, there were often "things" whose presence had excited and discomfitted me.

One such element, as in time I came to discover, was the characteristic way in which many modern Hebrew poets use referents. Taking for granted a pervasive familiarity with an immense traditional literature, they allude to words, phrases, passages—to ideas, stories, attitudes—with confidence that the originals will also resound in the reader's mind. Or so it seems to one who gradually grows aware of the breadth of the "field" that a Hebrew poet can use to "light up" with a word or a phrase: more than two thousand years of an oral and written tradition including, along with compendia such as The Bible, the Talmud (and its legends), the Midrashic commentaries, the Book of Prayer, individual works by philosophers, poets, and sages.

This evocation of traditional contexts is not, of course, unique to modern Hebrew poetry. In Western secular literature, the "method" goes back at least to Dante; in English verse, at least to Shakespeare, Marlowe, and Chaucer. And not only in specific technique, which for example sets Eliot apart, with his quotations from five languages in the last eleven lines of *The Waste Land*. Hebrew poets as a rule restrict their allusions to works of their own tradition, whereas others range at will, ignoring the frontiers of nation and culture. And modern Hebrew poets, though no longer self-excluded from Western secularism, continue in intimate relationship with their own tradition that maintained itself apart from the mainstream of European culture. Hence the difference in emotional impact made upon a reader of Hebrew poetry by an allusion to a passage in a work which he feels he "owns." The difference in responses, for example, between Eliot's insertion of Mallarmé's "Donner un sens plus pur aux mots de la tribu" as ("To purify the dialect of the tribe," in *Little Gidding*) and Ben Yitshak's line "And upon the day of our leaving [the earth] we shall stand before the gate at closing time," the last words of which echo a prayer that concludes the service for the Day of Atonement (p. 51).

Our example is one of extremes; nevertheless the difference can hardly be imaginary if for no reason other than the obvious historical one: that the Hebrew poet evokes passages from an ancient and still venerated tradition which—regardless of his private attitude toward religion—he feels to be inseparable from his own and his group's survival. In the Hebrew poetry of the last twenty to thirty years, however, the spoken language has come to play an ever enlarging role, and there has been a concomitant loss of dependence upon traditional sources. Moreover, the emotional immediacy of a great amount in the ancient Hebrew tradition is bound to diminish as new generations grow more and more remote from such works and respond to the changing cultural forces in their own countries and in the world as a whole.

For its poetic lines to embody the contexts of its allusions is as impossible for *The Waste Land* as for a verse translation from modern Hebrew. Both must resort to annotation of some kind; and the translator who rejects this help must content himself with a much different and much diminished poem—different and diminished to the extent to which the original depends on its sources, and to the manner of its reference. Often a modern Hebrew poem will light up the field to produce sharp reversals of meaning, as in Bialik's "Alone," with its biblical references in lines 8, 12, and 14 (pp. 25-27). Sometimes the evocation will amount to no more than a phrase—Bat-Miriam's association of the dimensions of the Holy Ark—"A cubit and a half is my height"—with the "plot of earth reserved, For [her] last rest" (p. 85). The poet may summon an ancient line from the Talmud—"The face of Moses is like the face of the sun and the face of Joshua like the face of the moon"—in a weirdly modern atmospheric poem about a Joshua who is both the biblical conqueror and the speaker's lost brother (pp. 143-144). To say that such poets make secular use of sacred referents may be tempting but it does not always apply and it leaves out of account complexities of mood and manner.

As the reader goes through the pages that follow, he will discover for himself the variety of ways in which modern Hebrew poets have made a new literature out of an ancient language. Contrary to widespread impression, Hebrew has never been "dead" as classical Greek is dead, nor has it been mainly sacramental as has Latin in the last centuries. Even in the darkest period of its people's history, Hebrew was used for literary prose and verse, for communal records, for personal and business correspondence, and the like. But it has not been continuously alive as English and French have been alive, and its widespread literary use did not begin till the secularist-modern movement of European Jewry had gained momentum a hundred years ago. As a vehicle in everyday living, Hebrew is one of the youngest languages in the world.

Since "poems are made of words," some additional facts about the linguistic medium will be of interest to the reader of the present book.

Alongside modern French and English, for example, the vocabulary of Hebrew looks limited, and this relatively limited range of words has been in service for centuries in writings with which educated readers of Hebrew are, to put it mildly, extremely familiar. Little surprise that such readers of modern poetry will hear all kinds of echoes from earlier contexts—or that some critics, with the passion of lexicographers, may pay more attention to the etymology than to the poetry.

The reader may wish to take account of two consequences of the "situation" of the modern Hebrew language as he makes his way into its poetry. In "To the Pomegranate," he will find, in the line addressed to the "drops" of the fruit, the phrase *adóm, adóm, adóm.* The threefold repetition, denoting "red, red, red," conveys a sonal connotation of especial charm to the reader who remembers *kadóṣ, kadóṣ, kadóṣ* ("holy, holy, holy"), for the poet mixes his praise of the pomegranate fruit with a famous anthem of praise of the seraphim (pp. 169 f.). In a different context, of images of the night sky, the verb *ṣafáḥ*, echoing Psalm 19 and meaning "to pour out," combines with the idiom *ṣafáḥ síaḥ* or *ṣafáḥ tfilá*, to suggest that the night sky "prays forth stars" (p. 51). We might add a third "consequence," pointing to extensions of meaning in ordinary words; that *lehagíd*, for example, gains power in its line (in which the moon looks down on footprints in the seawashed sand) because the word combines "tell" with "foretell, divine, prophesy" (pp. 143). But after repeated encounters of this general kind, the reader will not be surprised to find multiple meanings in a single Hebrew word. In some ways, then, the nature of their language would seem both to help and hinder modern Hebrew poets; and much of what they have made of this mixed blessing is essentially the substance of this book.

Reviewing the last five paragraphs, the reader will begin to appreciate the obstacles facing anyone who attempts to communicate the experience of a modern Hebrew poem by means of a verse translation only. We undertake to overcome these obstacles with the aid of the prose commentary that accompanies each poem, but even here we face questions not easily resolved. *How much* shall we say about each poem?—about its allusions, linguistic reverberations, formal distinctiveness, and the like? How much shall we say without giving the reader too much or too little as he undertakes to experience the poem himself? The answer is not always available—even in the case of seemingly simple poems; and frequently one has to choose among a large number of matters that demand attention. We have, of course, relied on our abilities to identify with the position of non-Hebrew-speaking readers—and since the writer of these prefatory pages also belongs to this group, we may not have gone too far off the ideal course, at least much of the time.

A large amount of critical comment already exists for the poetry of Bialik and his generation, most of it reflecting the interests of that generation. As John Keble suggested a century ago in his Oxford *Lectures on Poetry*, readers tend to seize upon those elements of a writer's work which are most congenial to their own tastes and interests and "answer" their own needs. Which is merely to say that what we as readers may find exciting in a long-dead writer, our predecessors might have missed or found dull; what they emphasized we may now regard as of small importance. Without proceeding with high self-consciousness, then, we have followed our own interests, confident that these will also reflect the interests of our readers.

This sounds uncontroversial enough, yet to "keep to one's time" calls for more audacity than some readers are likely to realize. We expect to be scolded from all sides: for saying too little or too much, but primarily for ignoring historical interpretations and allegorical meanings found by critics who could not read any writers of modern Hebrew poetry as poets first and as members of the Jewish people second. That such historical interpretation was "inevitable" at a particular time cannot be gainsaid. But our own view has been squarely focussed on the poem—on the poem itself—and anything of historical or sociological or political concern has had to take secondary importance. This by no means reflects a wish to sever the poet from his people or to disconnect him from history in the large, for we are quite aware that a poet is a human being who lives in a given time and place. It is rather our effort to free him and his poetry from interpretations growing out of a temporal situation now obsolete. Our commentaries therefore address themselves primarily to the poem in an effort to assist the reader who sets out to experience it as a poem.

A word must be said about the selection of the poets. We have undertaken the hopeless task of making a representative anthology from the founding of modern Hebrew poetry, by Chaim Nachman Bialik (1873-1934), to its multiform continuity by contemporary Israeli poets in their early maturity. Nobody but the editors can be held accountable for the choice of the poets within this volume. We make these assertions with full awareness that adverse criticism must greet any such selection made by any editor or group of editors, for ours is a choice among recent works and, as everyone knows, the closer an anthology comes to the present, the more unsatisfactory it is judged. But one qualification is perhaps worth making: the editors would have been delighted to include every modern

Hebrew poet whose work they admire, but in the limited number of pages at their disposal, they were compelled to omit several poets whose absence they themselves regret.

As for the poems themselves, the number included is no gauge whatever of the relative "importance" of their respective authors. We have had to think of the range of the entire period in terms of three overlapping[2] sub-periods—modern Hebrew verse written in Europe, in Palestine, and in Israel—and to represent the poets of each proportionately—and in every case by poems of manageable length. Here again our decisions will set off disagreement. Let it be noted, however, that the commentators also participated in choosing specific poems and that in some instances conflicting individual preferences were resolved by compromise.[3]

In presenting the literal translation of the Hebrew original at the opening of each commentary, no attempt whatever has been made to write a graceful English prose. On the contrary, we have done whatever seemed necessary in our effort to remain faithful to the original Hebrew, even to the extent of occasionally using the English language in ways that may strike some readers as deplorable. Similarly, we have used punctuation as an instrument to clarify and to assist, regarding the commas, semicolons, etc. of the originals as by no means untouchable, except in those poems where their use is as much a part of the poem as the words themselves.

Literal translations within the commentaries are set in italicized type, each line preceded by a number that corresponds to the line number of the original Hebrew poem. Included in these literal translations are occasional words and phrases enclosed either in parentheses or in square brackets. Such additions have been made whenever we could not be satisfied to render the original by a single word or phrase. Words or phrases enclosed in parentheses ( ) are for the most part alternate or secondary meanings which are likely to be "heard" by the Hebrew reader of the original. Words or phrases enclosed in square brackets [ ], however, are our own additions, and they are given for various purposes, such as—to explain, to supply words omitted but necessary for the reader's understanding, or to provide literal word-for-word equivalents of idiomatic expressions. Finally, we have begun each line of verse with a capital letter, although Hebrew makes no such distinction between upper- and lower-case type.

---

[2] as indicated by the three divisions in the Table of Contents, pp. v, vi, vii.

[3] except for the selections on pp. 92-105, whose inclusion was insisted upon by the poet.

As editors, we have taken many liberties with the materials submitted by our collaborators. We make this admission with little shame, for as initiators of the project, we consider ourselves to be more aware than our collaborators of the interests and abilities of the non-Hebrew-speaking reader. All three of us can approach modern Hebrew poetry from an "English-speaking position," despite the fact that only one—the writer of this introduction—is typical of the readers for whom this book has been prepared, since his grasp of Hebrew is too negligible to mention. Besides, many of the commentaries were originally written in Hebrew, and most of those that were written in English inevitably reflected assumptions of writers living within the world of Hebrew literature. We have therefore done a considerable amount of refocussing and of condensing, to say nothing of the rephrasing essential in maintaining a reasonable degree of homogeneity in the tone and the length of the commentaries as a whole.

The division of labors among the three editors need not be spelled out, for the interested reader of page 220 will recognize at once the differences in their respective backgrounds. And he may also appreciate the extent to which two of the editors have been dependent on the one editor who has spent the last eighteen years of his life in the milieu in which contemporary Hebrew poetry lives.

The editors acknowledge with thanks the financial assistance provided by Dr. Nahum Goldmann as a result of which it became possible to undertake the research preliminary to the writing of this volume.

The Hebrew texts are reprinted by special arrangement with Acum Ltd., Tel Aviv; Tarshish Press, Jerusalem; Avot Yeshurun, Tel Aviv.

The transliterations of the Hebrew texts were prepared by Dr. Haim Blanc, of the Hebrew University, Jerusalem.

The names of Hebrew poets which have already become somewhat familiar to English-speaking readers are spelled without regard to the system of transliteration by which the words of the Hebrew poems have been rendered. Thus, we write "Gury," rather than "Gúri;" "Shlonsky," rather than "Ṣlónski," etc. Such inconsistency also applies to certain Hebrew words well known to English readers, such as the Shekinah, the Midrash, Tarshish.

Biblical references in many of the commentaries follow the numbering of chapter and verse in the authorized Hebrew text.

January 1965 — STANLEY BURNSHAW

· · I · ·

Chaim Nachman Bialik

How does one introduce Chaim Nachman Bialik (1873-1934) to the reader interested in modern poetry? How focus attention upon the artistic achievement of a man, identified as "the National Hebrew poet," whose most personal utterances could be—and often were—read as the expression of the hopes, feelings, and despairs of the Jews of his generation? And how interpret today the body of his writing that extends beyond such "national" limits? Read on a universal level, Bialik's poetry expressed the dilemma that faced many of his Western contemporaries who, like him, had been born into a society in which religion gave meaning to life and who, like him, matured into a disrupted world which had lost its faith and with it all sense of purpose.

When two walls collapse, they sometimes meet at the moment of falling and form an arch. Bialik's poetry forms such an arch over the ruins of the traditional world into which he was born; and it reflects the collapse of that tradition. The world of faith, to which one strove to cling, revealed itself as an absurdity; the certainty of accepted ideas disintegrated into despair. It is the expression of this new despair—in more or less old poetic forms reshaped with great freedom—that gives Bialik's work its unique tension.

The measure of his contribution to the Hebrew language as an instrument for literature can hardly be appreciated today when innovation is taken for granted. Suffice it to say that in giving the classic tongue a new flexibility, Bialik enabled it to express nuances of intellectual and emotional experience which opened up a new era in poetry and diction. Unlike the authors of the secularist-modern movement begun a century before (*Haskalah*, Enlightenment, see pp. 198ff.), who were mainly concerned with introducing European literary taste and genres into Hebrew, Bialik was inclined to adapt the older forms of Hebrew literature. Unfortunately such poetic experimentation was sternly discouraged by Achad Haam, an essayist-editor of rationalistic temperament who had little taste for mysticism or symbolism—and whom Bialik regarded as his mentor. But nothing could deflect him from the main course of his linguistic innovation. Turning his back on all Hebrew brands of Euphuism, with their pastiches of biblical phraseology and related artifice, he set about refreshing the traditional language in his own original way; and when he cited scriptural idiom, he frequently gave it a reversal of meaning or worked it into new, unexpected settings.

With the growth of his reputation and influence, Bialik came to be regarded as a spokesman of the Jewish people, an embodiment of their national aspirations. He addressed the people in the second person—to him it was a living personality. He consoled and aroused it, but in the main he warned, alarmed, and flailed it. The nation's deprivation and suffering and his own were one, and their common helplessness led him to burst out in wrath or furious scorn. As a consequence, he continued to be looked to as a kind of prophet. But this public role and indeed all forms of public adulation angered and disgusted him. He was above all a lyric poet who found his life within himself. He tried to translate that life into language, perhaps out of the hope hidden in every poet that the proper words can indeed transform the world.

Though the story of his career is not essential to an appreciation of his poetry, the main facts may have interest for the reader to whom Bialik is no more than a famous name. He was born in a tree-encircled village in the southern Russian province of Volhyn. In 1878, when he was five, the family moved to a nearby suburb where his father eked out a miserable livelihood as a saloon-keeper. Soon after the father's death, the boy went to live with his grandfather, a puritanical pietist, who sent him off in his sixteenth year to prepare for the rabbinate. His fellow students at the talmudic academy had fallen under the influence of the new secularism then sweeping over the Russian-Jewish world, and it was here that Bialik discovered the works of the Hebrew Enlightenment and of Russian literature, along with the new Zionist doctrine, especially as propagated by Achad Haam. The latter's ethico-nationalist rereading of the tradition offered an answer to Bialik's growing loss of faith, enabling him to stay loyal to many of the old values. Though he considered himself a disciple, his poetry questioned many of Achad Haam's pat solutions, for it depicted the upheaval resulting from the breakdown of faith; and it often did so in desperate ways, leaving the reader little hope for a resolution of the dilemma.

Moving to Odessa, the cultural center of the Enlightenment, Bialik soon (1891) published his first poem, "To the Bird," which brought him almost instant recognition as the leading Hebrew poet. During the next two decades he composed all his major poems, each of which became an event in the Hebrew literature of his day. Pouring an immense amount of energy into editing and publishing (as well as into Zionist affairs), he wrote, in addition to verse, a few realistic short stories and literary essays; he translated Yiddish folk-poetry, *Don Quixote*, *Wilhelm Tell*, *The Dybbuk;* and he edited a compilation of rabbinic lore and the works of several medieval Spanish-Hebrew poets.

As World War I approached, Bialik's productivity as a poet diminished. After the Russian Revolution, thanks to the intervention of Maxim Gorky, he was enabled to emigrate, first to Berlin, then (1924) to Tel Aviv, where he continued his activities as writer and publisher. But Palestine had little influence on his poetry; his new homeland failed to revive his creativity. He had written almost entirely in the Ashkenazi accent; only in a few children's poems did he shift to the Israeli idiom. It is one of the paradoxes of modern Hebrew poetry that its leading exemplar wrote in meters that are now alien to it and may never be heard by the contemporary Hebrew speaker who reads them. Fortunately the biblical cadences, which Ashkenazi meters overlaid, now reemerge as the rhythm of meaning displaces metrical stress.

UPON MY RETURN · BITṢUVÁTI · בִּתְשׁוּבָתִי

Written in 1891-92, "Upon My Return" deals with a subject that recurs throughout Bialik's work: the return of the wanderer to a familiar scene. The experience always proves disillusioning, but the forms that it assumes are never the same. In the present poem, for example, the reader encounters an eerie folk-tale setting with elements reminiscent of a fairy tale. There is no moral here, no forthright interpretation. It is almost an "imagist" poem, whose artistry is all the more remarkable for having been created by a nineteen-year-old product of a small town in southern Russia who knew

UPON MY RETURN · BITSUVÁTI* · בִּתְשׁוּבָתִי

שׁוּב לְפָנַי: זָקֵן בָּלֶה,	Ṣuv lefánay: záken bále,
פָּנִים צֹמְקִים וּמְצֹרָרִים,	Pánim tsómkim umtsorárim,
צֵל קַשׁ יָבֵשׁ, נָד כְּעָלֶה,	Tsel kaṣ yáveṣ, nad keále,
נָד וָנָע עַל־גַּבֵּי סְפָרִים.	Nad vaná al-gábey sfárim.
שׁוּב לְפָנַי: זְקֵנָה בָלָה,	Ṣuv lefánay: zkéyna vála,
אֹרְגָה, סֹרְגָה פֻזְמְקָאוֹת,	Órga, sórga fuzmekáot,
פִּיהָ מָלֵא אָלָה, קְלָלָה,	Píha mále ála, klála,
וּשְׂפָתֶיהָ תָּמִיד נָעוֹת.	Usfatéha támid náot.
וּכְמֵאָז לֹא מָשׁ מִמְּקוֹמוֹ	Uḥmeáz lo maṣ mimkómo
חֲתוּל בֵּיתֵנוּ — עוֹדוֹ הֹזֶה	Ḥatúl beytéynu—ódo hóze
בֵּין כִּירַיִם, וּבַחֲלוֹמוֹ	Beyn kiráyim, uvaḥalómo
עִם־עַכְבָּרִים יַעַשׂ חֹזֶה.	Im-aḥbárim yáas ḥóze.
וּכְמֵאָז בָּאֹפֶל מְתוּחִים	Uḥmeáz baófel metúḥim
קוּרֵי אֶרֶג הָעַכָּבִישׁ	Kúrey éreg haakáviṣ
מְלֵאֵי פִגְרֵי זְבוּבִים נְפוּחִים	Mléy'ey fígrey zvúvim nefúḥim
שָׁם בַּזָּוִית הַמַּעֲרָבִית...	Ṣam bazávit hamaarávit . . .
לֹא שֻׁנֵּיתֶם מִקַּדְמַתְכֶם,	Lo ṣunéytem mikadmátḥem,
יָשָׁן נוֹשָׁן, אֵין חֲדָשָׁה; —	Yáṣan nóṣan, eyn ḥadáṣa;—
אָבֹא, אַחַי, בְּחֶבְרַתְכֶם!	Ávo, áḥay, beḥevrátḥem!
יַחְדָּו נִרְקַב עַד־נִבְאָשָׁה!	Yáḥdav nírkav ad-niv'áṣa!

nothing whatever of the modern revolution in literature.

(1) *Once again, before me: a worn old man,* (2) *A shriveling and tightened face,* (3) *[The] shadow of dry straw, shaking like a leaf,* (4) *Shaking and moving above (upon) the books.*

(5) *Once again, before me: a worn old woman* (6) *Weaving, darning stockings,* (7) *Her mouth full of oaths, curses,* (8) *And her lips perpetually moving;*

(9-10) *And as if [ever] since then, our house cat has not moved from his spot; he is still day-dreaming* (11) *By (on) the stove, and in his dream* (12) *Making a contract with mice.*

(13-14) *And as if [ever] since then, in the darkness, the cobwebs of the spider's weaving are stretched* (15) *Full of the corpses of swollen flies* (16) *There in the western corner.*

The first four stanzas compose a genre picture that is also a still-life. We are in a country cottage or in one of the homes of an East European settlement. We meet an old

* Poems marked with an asterisk were written by poets who used the traditional Ashkenazi pronunciation, which was current in Eastern Europe before the revival of Hebrew as a spoken language. See pp. 194f.

man whose face is shriveling and tightening (*tsómkim, umtsorárim:* the two *ts* sounds and the doubled *r* jar the Hebrew reader's ear). In line 3, the old man evokes a metaphor which almost cancels out his existence: he is even less than a straw: he is the shadow of dry straw. His spouse, doddering near him, is also worn—at the end of life or beyond it—and the pointlessness of her activity is expressed by the internal rime *órga sórga* ("weaving-darning," 6). She is somewhat more alive than the old man in that her mouth is full of oaths and cursing (*ála klála*), but they are uttered only from habit; they possess no actual power.

The focus then turns to the cat, motionless now as he has always been throughout the speaker's absence. He daydreams as before and his place for dreaming is the stove, for the home is also his home. Finally the picture becomes enclosed by the darkness over which the spider's web is drawn (13-14). But the spider—a frequent figure in Bialik's verse—has forgotten his spiderness: he doesn't even touch the flies.

(17) *You have not changed from what you were before* [lit. *from your long ago*]: (18) *Old oldness—no new thing.* (19) *Let me come, brothers, into your company (join you)!* (20) *Together let us rot till we stink!*

The genre painting is now completed, and its disgust possesses a superb harmony, for everything has been ordered. Internal rimes (6-7) complement the regular *abab* rimes, and they also interweave the first two stanzas: *keále* (3), *mále* (7). The same word recurs with slight variations in lines 4 and 8: *na, náot* ("moving," "to and fro"), and again in lines 7 and 15: *mále, mléy'ey* ("full"). Repetitiousness is the dominant structural feature of this poem of repetitious return. It is stressed in the parallel lines that open the first two stanzas and again in the first words of lines 9 and 13. The mechanical regularity of the trochaic meter insists upon the monotony of the living scene.

Even in this very early poem we see manifestations of the intuitive mastery with which Bialik constantly ordered the abundance of Hebrew learning and literature that flooded his mind. The "moving lips" (*sfatéha náot*, 8) of the cursing old woman are described in the identical words used in I Samuel 1:13 in picturing Hannah's urgent supplication for an offspring. The same verb was also applied to the old man's "shaking and moving" above the books (*nad vaná*). The reader of Hebrew at once recognizes this as a reversal and extended denotation of *na vanád* (Genesis 4:12), the curse of "moving and wandering (shaking)" pronounced by God upon Cain, who will find no peace anywhere.

Note how the inner order leads the reader from the old man (most significant), to the old woman (less significant), to the cat, the mice, the spider, and finally to the corpses of the flies. As we descend the scale, we might assume for a moment that in this cycle of decline the old man might also take on the aspect of a corpse. But the emotional tension, reaching its height in the summarizing stanza, closes upon a noisome exclamation. Is this the surrender of a disillusioned young rebel? Are we being told that even though it is rotten and decadent, the familiar can assure us safety? Does the speaker-wanderer who now returns from the rebuffs of the world take paradoxical comfort in degeneracy?

Or may we interpret the title more mystically: as a return in the religious sense (*tṣuvá*, the root word of the title, also means "repentance")? If we do so, we open up behind this little stock portrait, with its sociological import (the life of exile), an infinite vacuum of curses of which the old woman's is only a feeble echo.

The last two lines enforce the tragedy in identifying the speaker with all that he abhors (19). He who has been unable to escape this "home" must return to it over and over again, for there is no way out. He must stay there and rot and fill the air with the odor of his disintegration.

— TUVYA RÜBNER

Chaim Nachman Bialik

FROM THE WINTER SONGS · MIṢÍREY HAḤÓREF* · מִשִּׁירֵי הַחֹרֶף

The principle of opposing motifs operating in many of Bialik's finest poems—departure and return, innocence and defilement, separation and binding—lies at the heart of "From the Winter Songs" (1902). Here, in the first section (pp. 23f.), the tension is produced by the repression of explosive forces.

(1) *The Rock brought down to (for) us a day stronger than flint,* (2) *A powerful day, one compacted [of] frost, ice, and cold.*

(3) *The world's height (sky), the entire sphere of the earth below,* (4) *The light and the air resembling one (hammered) mass.*

(5-6) *It must be that the world had weakened and on this [preceding] night the Creator placed it upon His anvil,*

(7) *And swung His hammer and with a gigantic blow,* (8) *God summoned Force and breathed (blew): Be ye firm!*

(9) *And for a full night He pounded it between hammer and anvil* (10) *As though He sank into it as it were all His strength.*

(11) *And there emerged with the sun(rise) a fierce and adamantine day* (12) *And eternal power restrained and preserved in it.*

The winter scene is a revelation of divine action: the world that "had turned soft" has been forged into one of immense strength. Words themselves gain power: the *az* ("powerful") of line 2 becomes *áziz* ("fierce") in line 11; *mútsak* ("compacted," 2) grows into *msúmar* ("adamantine," 11). Note that the rime word at the end of line 12, *mṣúmar*, means more than "preserved," for it is the term applied to the wine that is preserved for the righteous.

(13-14) *And the flashes of brightness from God's exhalation, from the mist of His mouth [*lit. *mouth's breath], still hang in the air.*

(15) *And the morning light in its preciousness filters through [*lit. *upon] them* (16) *And [then] all its heat is removed and [only] its splendor (brightness) remains.*

(17) *And the whiteness is endless and the splendor infinite* (18) *From below up to the height and from within the house to the tree.*

(19) *And the snow strained through thirteen sieves* (20) *Coating them all like white glass.*

(21) *And the roofs have the appearance of marble hats,* (22) *Half of them glistening and half of them blue,*

(23) *And they shine in the presence [*lit. *to the eyes] of all the living and of the sun*—(24) *Only the crows blacken upon them,*

(25) *Sliding on the coating of glass and shrieking,* (26) *Pecking and scratching—and suddenly they fly off.*

(27) *And the smoke of the chimneys, like the beard of an ancient one [*lit. *an ancient of days]* (28) *Curls majestically and rises to the heavens.*

The poem becomes pure description dominated by "splendors" everywhere—*zóhar*, a key word in Bialik's poetry. The day's heat has been removed and its splendor remains (16). The light now infinite (17) points to the shining snow purified through "thirteen sieves" (19), the number in use with the grain offerings (*ómer*) at the ancient Temple of Jerusalem. The brilliance is again dispersed as it rises in the sight of the living and of the sun. Only the crows blacken the scene, shrieking, pecking, scratching. They fly off, leaving the world to its white purity,

הַצּוּר הוֹרִיד לָנוּ יוֹם חָזָק מִצֹּר,
יוֹם עָז, מוּצָק אֶחָד כְּפוֹר, קֶרַח וָקֹר.

Hatsúr hórid lánu yom ḥázak mitsór,
Yom az, mútsak éḥad kfór, kéraḥ vakór.

רוּם עוֹלָם, כָּל־כַּדּוּר הָאָרֶץ מִתַּחַת,
הָאוֹר וְהָאֲוִיר כְּעֵין מִקְשָׁה אַחַת.

Rum ólam, kol-kádur haárets mitáḥat,
Haór vehaáver keéyn míkṣa áḥat.

אֵין זֹאת כִּי נִתְרוֹפֵף הָעוֹלָם — וּנְתָנוֹ
הַיּוֹצֵר בַּלַּיְלָה הַזֶּה עַל־גַּב סַדָּנוֹ,

Eyn zot ki nitrófef haólam—untáno
Hayótser baláyla hazé al-gav sdáno,

וַיָּנֶף פַּטִּישׁוֹ, וּבְהַלְמוּת עֲנָק
אֶל קָרָא לַכֹּחַ וַיִּשֹּׁם: חֲזָק!

Vayánef patíṣo, uvhálmut anák
El kára lakóaḥ vayíṣom: ḥazák!

וְלֵיל תָּמִים בֵּין פַּטִּישׁ וְסַדָּן אוֹתוֹ רִקַּע,
וּכְאִלּוּ כָּל־כֹּחוֹ, כִּבְיָכוֹל, בּוֹ שִׁקַּע.

Veléyl támim beyn pátiṣ usdán óto ríka,
Uḥeílu ḥol-kóḥo, kivyáḥol, bo ṣíka.

וַיֵּצֵא עִם־שֶׁמֶשׁ יוֹם עַזִּיז וּמְסֻמָּר
וְכֹחַ עוֹלָמִים בּוֹ חָסוּם וּמְשֻׁמָּר.

Vayétse im-ṣémeṣ yom áziz umsúmar
Veḥóaḥ olámim bo ḥásum umṣúmar.

וְעוֹד תְּלוּיִם בָּאֲוִיר צַחְצוּחֵי הַזִּיו
מִנִּשְׁמַת אֱלוֹהַּ, מֵאֵד רוּחַ פִּיו.

Veód tlúyim baáver tsaḥtsúḥey házív
Miníṣmat elóa, meéd rúaḥ piv.

וְאוֹר בֹּקֶר מִסְתַּנֵּן עֲלֵיהֶם בִּיקָרוֹ,
וְנִטַּל כָּל־חֻמּוֹ וְנִשְׁאַר זָהֳרוֹ.

Veór bóker mistánen aléyhem bikáro,
Venítal kol-ḥúmo veníṣar zohóro.

וְאֵין סוֹף לַלַּבְנוּנִית וְלַזֹּהַר אֵין קֵץ.
מִתַּחְתִּית עַד־רוֹם וּמִבַּיִת עַד־עֵץ.

Veéyn sof lalavnúnit velazóhar eyn kets,
Mitáḥtit ad-róm umibáyit ad-éts.

וְהַשֶּׁלֶג בִּשְׁלֹשׁ־עֶשְׂרֵה נָפָה מְנֻפֶּה
כַּזְּכוּכִית הַלְּבָנָה עַל־כֻּלָּם מְצֻפֶּה.

Vehaṣéleg biṣlóṣ-esre náfa menúpe,
Kazḥúḥit halvána al-kúlam metsúpe.

וְהַגַּגּוֹת כְּכוֹבְעֵי הַשַּׁיִשׁ מַרְאִיתָם,
מַחֲצִיתָם מַבְהִיקִים וְעֵין תְּכֵלֶת מַחֲצִיתָם,

Vehagágot keḥóv'ey haṣáyiṣ mar'ítam,
Maḥatsítam mavhíkim veéyn tḥéylet [maḥatsítam,

וּלְעֵינֵי כָּל־חַי וְהַשֶּׁמֶשׁ מַזְהִירִים —
הָעוֹרְבִים לְבַדָּם עַל־גַּבָּם מַשְׁחִירִים,

Uleéyney ḥol-ḥáy vehaṣémeṣ mazhírim—
Haórvim levádam al-gábam maṣḥírim,

מַחֲלִיקִים עַל־צִפּוּי הַזְּכוּכִית וְצוֹרְחִים,
מְנַקְּרִים וְשׂוֹרְטִים — וּפִתְאֹם הֵם פּוֹרְחִים.

Maḥalíkim al-tsípuy hazḥúḥit vetsórḥím,
Menákrim vesórtim—ufít'om hem pórḥim.

וַעֲשַׁן הָאֲרֻבּוֹת, כְּזָקֵן עַתִּיק יוֹמִין,
מִסְתַּלְסֵל בְּהָדָר וְנִשָּׂא לִמְרוֹמִים.

Vaaṣán haarúbot, kizkán átik yómin,
Mistálsel behádar venísa limrómim.

וְהַקֶּרַח הַלֹּהֵט בַּכֹּל מְפַעְפֵּעַ,	Vehakéraḥ halóhet bakól mefapéa,
וּבְלֶב־כֹּל אוֹן אֵיתָן כַּמַּסְמֵר נוֹטֵעַ;	Uvlév-kol on éytan kamásmer notéa;
וּבָהִיר וּמוּצָק הָעוֹלָם! זֶה־כֹּחוֹ —	Uváhir umútsak haólam! ze-kóḥo—
שֶׁכּוֹבֵשׁ אֶת־עַצְמוֹ וְהוּא חָזָק מִתּוֹכוֹ.	Ṣekóveṣ et-átsmo vehú ḥázak mitóḥo.
מֵרֹב אַמֵּץ כֹּחַ, מֵרֹב עֹצֶר אוֹנִים	Meróv ámets kóaḥ, meróv ótser ónim
מִתְבַּקְּעִים בַּיַּעַר חֲסִינֵי אַלּוֹנִים.	Mitbák'im bayáar ḥasíney alónim.
כְּמוֹ רֻתְּקוּ בַּזִּקִּים כָּל־מְצוּקֵי הָאָרֶץ	Kmo rútku vazíkim kol-metsúkey haárets
בְּאוֹתוֹ הָרֶגַע שֶׁחִשְּׁבוּ הִתְפָּרֶץ,	Beóto haréga ṣeḥíṣvu hitpárets,
וְהֵם חוֹתְרִים וְחוֹרְגִים מִמִּסְגְּרוֹתֵיהֶם —	Vehém ḥótrim veḥórgim mimisgerotéyhem—
עוֹד מְעַט וְהִתְפּוֹצֵץ הַכַּדּוּר מִפְּנֵיהֶם!	Od meát vehitpótsets hakádur mipnéyhem!

but from now on the serenity will be disrupted.

(29) *And the flaming ice pierces within everything* (30) *And drives [*lit. *like a nail] enduring power into the heart of everything.*

(31) *And bright and solid is the world! this is its strength*— (32) *That it represses (conquers) itself and is strong from within itself.*

(33) *Out of so much tensing of force, out of so much repressing of powers,* (34) *The mightiest oaks split in the forest.*

(35) *[It is] as though all the foundations of the earth had been shackled in irons* (36) *At the very moment [that] they intended to break out,*

(37) *And they are burrowing and lunging out of their enclosures*— (38) *Any moment now the sphere wil! explode because of them [to make room for them].*

With the "flaming ice" interpenetrating everything, we enter the phases of warning against excessive containment. Too much repression of inner power brings even the mightiest of growing things to self-destruction—the oaks split apart from "so much holding back"; and if such repressing of inner force were not tempered, the sphere of the earth itself might burst apart.

The first and last parts of our selection are structured with severe and hard sounds. The opening word *hatsúr* ("The Rock," one of the appellations of God) is immediately echoed by *tsor* ("flint"). The parallel in sonality between *ḥázak* ("strong"), *az* ("powerful"), *mútsak* ("compacted"), lines 1-2, and the alliteration of *kfor* ("frost"), *kéraḥ* ("ice"), and *kor* ("cold"), line 2, intensify the effect of solidity. Note that the adjective *ḥázak* ("strong") in line 1 comes out into the open in line 8 as an imperative verb with an unmistakably biblical tone—*ḥazák*, "Be ye firm!"—and that *mútsak* ("compacted, solid," 2, 31) is reinforced by *metsúkey* ("foundations," 35). This line, coming at the high point in the poem's development, is exceptional for its harsh beauty: *kmo rútku vazikim kol-metsúkey haárets*. The amphibrachic tetrameter (∪ — ∪) that dominates the poem produces a rhythmical effect found with great frequency in Bialik's work as a whole.

— TUVYA RÜBNER

Chaim Nachman Bialik

ALONE · LEVÁDI* · לְבַדִּי

כֻּלָּם נָשָׂא הָרוּחַ, כֻּלָּם סָחַף הָאוֹר,
שִׁירָה חֲדָשָׁה אֶת־בֹּקֶר חַיֵּיהֶם הִרְנִינָה;
וַאֲנִי, גּוֹזָל רַךְ, נִשְׁתַּכַּחְתִּי מִלֵּב
תַּחַת כַּנְפֵי הַשְּׁכִינָה.

בָּדָד, בָּדָד נִשְׁאַרְתִּי, וְהַשְּׁכִינָה אַף־הִיא
כְּנַף יְמִינָהּ הַשְּׁבוּרָה עַל־רֹאשִׁי הִרְעִידָה.
יָדַע לִבִּי אֶת־לִבָּהּ: חָרֹד חָרְדָה עָלַי,
עַל־בְּנָהּ, עַל יְחִידָהּ.

Kúlam nása harúaḥ, kúlam sáḥaf haór,
Ṣíra ḥadáṣa et-bóker ḥayéyhem hirnína;
3 Vaaní, gózal raḥ, niṣtakáḥti milév
Táḥat kánfey haṣḥína.

Bádad, bádad niṣárti, vehaṣḥína af-hí
Knaf yemína haṣvúra al-róṣi hir'ída.
7 Yáda líbi et-líba: ḥárod ḥárda aláy
Al-bná, al yeḥída.

"Alone" expresses the central motif of Bialik's work: the struggle between Judaism and Western secularism; between the old and the new, faith and doubt, accepted truths and those still unexplored; between inhibition and abandon, the house and the world outside. Much like the speaker's own home in "Upon My Return" (pp. 20 f.), the setting of "Alone"—the House of Study—is a place of both desolation and refuge.

In both poems the "I" is separated from those around him but in "Alone" (1902) the speaker has never left his environment; hence the interrelationships are more complex. In the earlier lyric, he encountered the elderly couple and the house "pets," all of whom were so deeply absorbed in themselves that they didn't even look at him. But in "Alone":

(1) *The wind carried all of them away, the light swept all of them away,* (2) *A new song made the morning of their lives exult with song;* (3) *And I, a soft fledgling, was completely forgotten* [lit. *from the hearts of all*] (4) *Under the wings of the Shekinah.*

The Shekinah, one of the most beautiful expressions of Jewish mysticism, is the feminine aspect of the deity, the personification of God's love for His people. According to legend, she was exiled from heaven together with them and she wanders to and fro, an outcast from the worlds of above and below, finding her only home in the hearts of this people. Here the Shekinah, assuming her traditional embodiment as a mothering bird, struggles for the speaker's soul, but she does so without compulsion; her very passivity is her power.

(5) *Solitary, solitary I remained, and the Shekinah, too;* (6) *She fluttered her broken right wing over my head.* (7) *My heart knew (understood) her heart; she trembled with anxiety over me* (8) *Over her son, over her only* [*son*].

Lines 4-8 call to mind a popular love poem by Bialik in which the man urges his beloved: "Take me in under your wing/ And be to me a mother and a sister/ And let your bosom

כְּבָר נִתְגָּרְשָׁה מִכָּל הַזָּוִיּוֹת, רַק־עוֹד	Kvar nitgárṣa mikól hazavíyot, rak-ód
פִּנַּת סֵתֶר שׁוֹמֵמָה וּקְטַנָּה נִשְׁאָרָה —	Pínat séter ṣoméyma uktána niṣ'ára—
בֵּית־הַמִּדְרָשׁ — וַתִּתְכַּס בַּצֵּל, וָאֱהִי	Beyt-hamídraṣ—vatítkas batsél, vaéhi
עִמָּהּ יַחַד בַּצָּרָה.	Íma yáḥad batsára.
וּכְשֶׁכָּלָה לְבָבִי לַחַלּוֹן, לָאוֹר,	Uḥṣekála levávi laḥálon, laór,
וּכְשֶׁצַּר־לִי הַמָּקוֹם מִתַּחַת לִכְנָפָהּ —	Uḥṣetsár-li hamákom mitáḥat liḥnáfa—
כָּבְשָׁה רֹאשָׁהּ בִּכְתֵפִי, וְדִמְעָתָהּ עַל־דַּף	Kávṣa róṣa biḥtéyfi, vedim'áta al-dáf
גְּמָרָתִי נָטָפָה.	Gmaráti natáfa.
חֶרֶשׁ בָּכְתָה עָלַי וַתִּתְרַפֵּק עָלָי,	Ḥéreṣ báḥta aláy vatitrápek aláy,
וּכְמוֹ שָׂכָה בִּכְנָפָהּ הַשְּׁבוּרָה בַּעֲדִי:	Uḥmó sáḥa biḥnáfa haṣvúra baádi:
« כֻּלָּם נָשָׂא הָרוּחַ, כֻּלָּם פָּרְחוּ לָהֶם,	"Kúlam nása harúaḥ, kúlam párḥu lahém,
וָאִוָּתֵר לְבַדִּי, לְבַדִּי... »	Vaiváter levádi, levádi . . ."
וּכְעֵין סִיּוּם שֶׁל־קִינָה עַתִּיקָה מְאֹד,	Uḥeéyn síyum ṣel-kína atíka meód,
וּכְעֵין תְּפִלָּה, בַּקָּשָׁה וַחֲרָדָה כְּאַחַת,	Uḥeéyn tfíla, bakáṣa vaḥaráda keáḥat,
שָׁמְעָה אָזְנִי בַּבְּכִיָּה הַחֲרִישִׁית הַהִיא	Ṣám'a ózni babíḥya haḥaríṣit hahí
וּבַדִּמְעָה הַהִיא הָרוֹתַחַת —	Uvadím'a hahí harotáḥat—

be my head's refuge,/ The nest of my forsaken (exiled) dreams."

(9) *She has already been driven from every corner, only* (10) *One hidden nook, desolate and small, remained—* (11) *The House of Study—and she covered herself with the shadow, and I was* (12) *Together with her [*lit. *sharing] in the distress.*

(13) *And when my heart yearned for the window, for the light,* (14) *And when the place under her wing was [too] narrow for me,* (15-16) *She hid her head in my shoulder, and her tear dropped on my Talmud page—*

The two solitaries differ from each other. They touch and yet they do not touch. Both are forsaken and helpless as they meet in a secret, desolate corner where she huddles. For she has been "driven away" from all those places where she might have found her proper dwelling. While she, disconsolate, covers herself with shadow, he yearns impatiently for the window and its "light"—a current designation for the Enlightenment—the same light that had drawn away all the people who had once lived in this house (1). Dolefully he finds the space under her wing too narrow to contain him (14) as he thirsts for all that lies outside this window opening onto the secular world—a world far removed from the stifling confines of traditional existence.

In a poignant moment in another Bialik poem ("Before the Bookcase"), the wind (*rúaḥ*) blows out the candle when the loss of faith takes place. The wind is the new spirit abroad in the world, for *rúaḥ* means both spirit and wind. Similarly in his celebrated long poem about the diligent Talmud student ("*Hamátmid,*" 1894) as well as in other works by Bialik, terms of this type—wind, light—are used to represent secular wisdom, liberation, and love for the world of nature—whereas the constraints of the tradition are symbolized by the Talmud.

The speaker in "Before the Bookcase" had abandoned the Judaism of tradition: he returns from the "foreign isles" with "wrinkled forehead and wrinkled soul." Trying to recover his old, lost faith in the worn pages of the holy scrolls, he discovers that "no longer do open eyes look from your letters into the great depths of my soul" and "no tear trembles on [my] eyelid." The letters are "like beads of black pearls whose string has snapped." The quest to return ends with his realization that there is no return. In "Alone," written eight years earlier, no decision has been reached— and there appears to be no way out:

(17) *Silently she wept over me and enfolded me* (18) *As though shielding me with her broken wing:* (19) "*The wind carried them all away, they have all flown off* (20) *And I was left alone, alone . . .*"

(21) *And something akin to the ending of a very ancient lamentation* (22) *And something akin to a prayer, a supplication-and-trembling:* (23) *My ear heard in that silent weeping* (24) *And in that tear, boiling—*

The title word—*levádi*—appears at only one place in the poem (20). The literal translation is "my alone," and it is worth noting that this inflected possessive form is reserved for the lament of the Shekinah, a variation of the speaker's opening words.

The poet and critic Ludwig Strauss pointed out an interesting parallel in the sense of confinement between the structure of the poem and its central idea. The six stanzas seem to form three "brackets" of a closed system—1-6, 2-5, 3-4—and such bracketing appears on two levels. Note, for example, how line 21 reinvokes line 2 (to join stanzas 1-6) and how line 20 reinvokes line 5 (to join stanzas 2-5). Similarly with the use of motifs. In stanzas 1-6, we see that the speaker is both aware of the new world (1) and yet bound in the old (6). In stanzas 2-5, we observe the Shekinah's relationship to the speaker, and in stanzas 3-4 the contrast between the old and the new.

Surely no less remarkable is Bialik's way of using biblical materials. Line 12 brings a touch of surprise with its echo of Psalm 91:15, in which God says of the faithful: "I am with him in [his] trouble" and Bialik's human speaker says of God's spirit, the Shekinah: "I am with her in [her] distress." Line 14, however, brings something quite unexpected. The phrase "the place is [too] narrow for me" is drawn from Isaiah 49:20 but in Isaiah it is the many children of Israel who say this at the time of their redemption. In our poem, it is the constriction of the spirit in a world that has not yet been redeemed. Again, line 8 refers to the sacrifice of Isaac (Genesis 22: 2). In Isaac's case the story leads to a theophany promising redemption, whereas Bialik alludes to the tragic termination of the covenant. Such alterations of meaning, disrupting the traditional intent of the passages they evoke, might be taken to indicate that for the speaker of the poem his Bible no longer means what it once had meant.

He never decides either to remain or to leave the House of Study. This tormented indecisiveness is emphasized by the way in which the poem does not seem to know how to end. Stanzas 5 and 6 lack closing punctuation. Moreover, an urge to break from the control of the meter is conveyed by the many leaps between the lines within the stanzas. One has the sense of an impatience striving against bonds. At the same time, each stanza is drawn up short with a 2- or 3-stress closing line playing against the anapestic tetrameters that precede. In terms of rhythmic structure, these two forces—the urge to control (also: to remain) and the urge to break out (also: to leave)—are unequal. The pressuring force is stronger than the force that binds.

— TUVYA RÜBNER

Chaim Nachman Bialik

AT TWILIGHT · IM DIMDÚMEY HAḤÁMA* · עִם דִּמְדּוּמֵי הַחַמָּה

עִם דִּמְדּוּמֵי הַחַמָּה אֶל־הַחַלּוֹן נָא־גֹשִׁי	Im dimdúmey haḥáma el-haḥálon na-góṣi
וְעָלַי הִתְרַפָּקִי,	Vealáy hitrapáki,
לִפְתִּי הֵיטֵב צַוָּארִי, שִׂימִי רֹאשֵׁךְ עַל־רֹאשִׁי —	Lífti héytev tsavári, sími róṣeḥ al-róṣi—
וְכֹה עִמִּי תִּדְבָּקִי.	Veḥó ími tidbáki.
וּמְחֻשָּׁקִים וּדְבֵקִים, אֶל־הַזֹּהַר הַנּוֹרָא	Umḥuṣákim udvéykim, el-hazóhar hanóra
דּוּמָם נִשָּׂא עֵינֵינוּ;	Dúmam nísa eynéynu;
וְשִׁלַּחְנוּ לַחָפְשִׁי עַל־פְּנֵי יַמֵּי הָאוֹרָה	Veṣiláḥnu laḥófṣi al-pnéy yámey haóra
כָּל־הִרְהוּרֵי לִבֵּנוּ.	Kol-hirhúrey libéynu.
וְהִתְנַשְּׂאוּ לַמָּרוֹם בִּיעָף שׁוֹקֵק כַּיּוֹנִים,	Vehitnás'u lamárom bi'áf ṣókek kayónim,
וּבַמֶּרְחָק יַפְלִיגוּ, יֹאבֵדוּ;	Uvamérḥak yaflígu, yovédu;
וְעַל־פְּנֵי רְכְסֵי אַרְגָּמָן, אִיֵּי־זֹהַר אַדְמוֹנִים,	Veál-pney rúḥsey argáman, íyey-zóhar [admónim,
בִּיעָף דּוּמָם יֵרֵדוּ.	Bi'áf dúmam yerédu.
הֵם הָאִיִּים הָרְחוֹקִים, הָעוֹלָמוֹת הַגְּבֹהִים	Hem haíyim harḥókim, haolámot hagvóhim
זוּ בַּחֲלוֹמוֹת רְאִינוּם;	Zu vaḥalómot reínum;
שֶׁעָשׂוּנוּ לְגֵרִים תַּחַת כָּל־הַשָּׁמָיִם,	Ṣeasúnu legéyrim táḥat kol-haṣamáyim,
וְחַיֵּינוּ — לְגֵיהִנֹּם.	Veḥayéynu—legeyhínom.
הֵמָּה אִיֵּי־הַזָּהָב זוּ צָמֵאנוּ אֲלֵיהֶם	Héma íyey-hazáhav zu tsaméynu aléyhem
כְּאֶל אֶרֶץ מוֹלֶדֶת;	Keél éretz molédet;
שֶׁכָּל־כּוֹכְבֵי הַלַּיִל רָמְזוּ לָנוּ עֲלֵיהֶם	Ṣekól-kóḥvey haláyil rámzu lánu aléyhem
בְּאוֹר קֶרֶן רוֹעֶדֶת.	Beór kéren roédet.
וַעֲלֵיהֶם נִשְׁאַרְנוּ בְּלִי־רֵעַ וְעָמִית	Vaaléyhem niṣ'árnu bli-réya veámit
כִּשְׁנֵי פְרָחִים בַּצִּיָּה;	Kiṣnéy fráḥim batsíya;
כִּשְׁנֵי אֹבְדִים הַמְבַקְשִׁים אֲבֵדָה עוֹלָמִית	Kiṣnéy óvdim hamvákṣim avéyda olámit
עַל־פְּנֵי אֶרֶץ נָכְרִיָּה.	Al-pnéy érets noḥríya.

The six quatrains above (published in 1902) begin as a conventional love song. The mood is thoughtful, the language restrained. Unfortunately the import of some of the simple words is all but impossible to carry over into English even with the help of the most literal explanations.

(1) *At twilight* [lit. *the flickering of the sun*],

please come to the window (2) *And enfold me,* (3) *Clasp my neck firmly* [lit. *well*], *place your head upon my head—* (4) *And so be joined to me.*

(5-6) *Fastened and joined* [*together*], *we shall lift our eyes silently toward the terrible brightness (splendor);* (7) *And set free on the seas of light* (8) *All the fancies of our heart.*

(9) *And they shall rise toward the heavens in a yearning (rustling) flight like doves,* (10) *And they shall sail in the distance* [*and*] *be lost.* (11) *Upon purple mountain ridges, roseate islands of brightness (splendor)* (12) *They will descend silently in flight.*

(13) *They are the distant, the high worlds* (14) *That we saw in our dreams;* (15) *That turned us into aliens (sojourners) under the entire sky* (16) *And* [*turned*] *our lives—into hell.*

(17) *They are the islands of gold for which we thirsted,* (18) *As for a homeland;* (19) *About which all the nightstars hinted* (20) *With the light of a quivering ray.*

(21) *On them* [*the islands*] *we remained (were left) without friend or companion,* (22) *Like two flowers in a desert,* (23-24) *Like two lost ones on a foreign land forever seeking something lost.*

The union of the man and the woman takes place at twilight, when according to both Cabalistic and Hasidic tradition God's thought is especially directed toward men. It is the hour of grace: the gates of heaven are opened. Beckoning the woman to the window, the man asks her to lift her eyes with his toward "the terrible brightness"—*hazóhar hanóra.* The word "terrible"—the biblical *norá*—also denotes "awe inspiring," and *Zohar* is the title of the key work of Jewish Cabalism (literally "light, splendor"). In Bialik's phrase (*hazóhar hanóra*, 6), suggestions of awe and terror persist, foreshadowing the experience in the later part of the poem.

The images of the first stanzas body forth a land of peaceful, pleasurable calm, with seas of light, purple mountain tops, and islands of roseate brightness. But they are far off in time and place—they lie out of reach, in "the distant." Even worse, they are only to be reached in fantasy (14), projected deliberately by the mind that soon recognizes these ideal places for what they become in traitorous disenchantment. The thoughts of the heart, and the place of delight to which these "thoughts shall sail off," and upon which they will be lost—all these elements merge into a heartsickness-and-lovesickness that pervades the last half of the poem.

The two lovers have chosen to relive with their minds the cycle of hope and disillusion in which "the golden islands" for which they thirsted became a companionless desert.

Bialik's love poems are almost always overlaid with religious awareness whose character can at best be only suggested. In "Alone" (p. 25), the speaker's love experience was enmeshed with his religious feelings. Religion (to be more precise, the divine) and love both found their symbol in the "wing" that covers and protects the lonely and lost. But the wing was a broken thing; lacking wholeness, it could not give the needed protection. And the sought-for "nest" was not a refuge at all. Such overtones and undertones of disenchantment are not, however, found in Bialik's religious poems only. They invade most of his love poems and even many of his songs of airy and impersonal tone and they can be found even in some of his folk poems.

Note that the thoughts of the lovers' heart must find their ultimate rest in a far-off place, beyond sight, where they will be lost (10). The "distant," an important element in much of Bialik's verse, is not a simple symbol for an unknowable physical place beyond good and evil. On the one hand, the "distant" embodies all that is excellent; on the other, it finally reveals itself as illusion. Which is to suggest, perhaps, that its meaning could not be different in a poet who sought viable truth in the "near," the available, but failing to find it there, felt compelled to seek it in the "distant." The "distant" at first promised him all he desired, but this "home" that he thought he might reach turned out to be empty space.

Like many other personal poems by Bialik, "At Twilight" reflects to a remarkable degree the attitude of his people and, beyond that, the spiritual aspiration of Western man. The poem which began in an hour of grace ends in "eternal seeking"—seeking literally for an "object" which had been lost. The lovers' common aspiration has not been fulfilled, the "distant" did not draw near, heaven and earth have not been united. Perhaps the lovers were demanding more of human love than it can bear.

The poem, which is remarkable for its sonal beauty and nostalgic tone, is written in one of Bialik's characteristic meters—anapestic tetrameter with an unstressed final syllable. Here the alternate lines are of four and two feet, riming *abab*, with one notable exception: line 10, which is elongated in describing the sailing into the distance. Except for line 23, the flow of the anapests is modulated by an extra unstressed syllable forming a cesura after the second foot of the longer lines.

— TUVYA RÜBNER

Chaim Nachman Bialik

A TWIG FELL · TSÁNAḤ LO ZÁLZAL* · צָנַח לוֹ זַלְזַל

צָנַח לוֹ זַלְזַל עַל־גָּדֵר וַיָּנֹם —	Tsánaḥ lo zálzal al-gáder vayánom—
כֹּה יָשֵׁן אָנֹכִי:	Ko yáṣen anóḥi:
נָשַׁל הַפְּרִי — וּמַה־לִּי וּלְגִזְעִי,	Náṣal haprí—umá-li ulgíz'i,
וּמַה־לִּי וּלְשׂוֹכִי?	Umá-li ulsóḥi?
נָשַׁל הַפְּרִי, הַפֶּרַח כְּבָר נִשְׁכָּח —	Náṣal haprí, hapéraḥ kvar níṣkaḥ—
שָׁרְדוּ הֶעָלִים —	Sárdu heálim—
יִרְגַּז יוֹם אֶחָד הַסַּעַר — וְנָפְלוּ	Yírgaz yom éḥad hasáar—venáflu
אַרְצָה חֲלָלִים.	Ártsa ḥalálim.
אַחַר — וְנִמְשְׁכוּ לֵילוֹת הַזְּוָעָה,	Áḥar—venímṣeḥu léylot hazváa,
לֹא מְנוּחָה וּשְׁנָת לִי,	Lo mnúḥa uṣnát li,
בָּדָד אֶתְחַבֵּט בָּאֹפֶל וַאֲרַצֵּץ	Bádad etḥábet baófel vaarátsets
רֹאשִׁי אֶל־כָּתְלִי.	Róṣi el-kótli.
וְשׁוּב יִפְרַח אָבִיב, וְאָנֹכִי לְבַדִּי	Veṣúv yífraḥ áviv, veanóḥi levádi
עַל־גִּזְעִי אֶתָּלֶה —	Al-gíz'i etále—
שַׁרְבִיט קֵרֵחַ, לֹא צִיץ לוֹ וָפֶרַח,	Ṣárvit keréaḥ, lo tsits lo vaféraḥ,
לֹא־פְרִי וְלֹא־עָלֶה.	Lo-frí velo-ále.

One of the most celebrated of Bialik's poems, "A Twig Fell" begins with a series of simple statements:

(1) *A twig fell down upon the fence and slumbered*— (2) *So do I sleep:* (3) *The fruit dropped— and what is my stem to me?* (4) *And what is my branch to me?*

(5) *The fruit dropped, the flower is already forgotten,* (6) *The leaves survived*— (7) *One day the storm will rage—and they will fall* (8) *Dead to the earth.*

(9) *Afterwards—the nights of terror will continue,* (10) *[There will be] no rest and sleep for me,* (11) *Alone I shall flail about in the dark and smash* (12) *My head against my wall.*

(13) *And again the spring will flower and I all alone* (14) *Will hang from my stem*— (15) *A bald stalk without bud or flower* (16) *Or fruit or leaf.*

The poem begins with images of identity between the human speaker and the leafy world about him: slumbering twig, slumbering man—both man and twig outside the world of waking, both cut off from their sources of sustenance. But once "the storm will rage" (7), their paths will diverge never to come together again: what lies ahead for man, he must face alone. And whatever he may do—raging through the nights of terror (9)—will prove meaningless; his flailing about cannot undo the course of his fate.

Though the theme is hardly unfamiliar to readers of verse, "A Twig Fell" gives vividly personal embodiment to the contrasting hopes of leaf and flesh. Trees and plants live on in an endless cycle of renewal despite the winter death, but once oncoming death touches man, it does not let go. The identity of speaker and leaf ends in the hopelessness of total separation. The truth is asserted in a paradoxical shift from the opening simile (2) to the concluding metaphor (13-16) in which the man has already become a twig of death.

The especial beauty of the poem as a whole is heightened by the contrast between its graceful, uninterrupted flow and the starkness of its images and its feeling. Five of the first eight lines begin with a verb—"fell," 1; "dropped," 3; "dropped," 5; "survived," 6; "will rage," 7. The force of the verb in each case creates an initial impetus which gradually trails away into the effect of a "dying fall":—"Fell down a twig upon a fence and slumbered—/ So sleep I:/ Dropped down the fruit . . . ," etc. The word "Afterwards" (9) makes the transition from the "question" of the first half of the poem to the "answer" in the second.

"A Twig Fell" forms part of the poetry of personal withdrawal that immediately preceded Bialik's silent period. In "And When You Shall Find," written in 1910, a year before our poem, he wrote: "And when you shall find the scroll of my heart/ Rolling in the dust,/ Then will you say: there was a man innocent and simple/ And weary and weak." The same mood dominates "God Did Not Show Me" (1911): "God did not show me in night dreams/ And no sorcerer divined for me/ Where my last day will overtake me."

Bialik's preoccupation with death became even more acute in "Who Am I and What Am I That I Should Be Greeted by a Ray of Sun" (also of 1911): "Let not dream nor vision come to me, neither memory nor hope/ Without a yesterday and without a tomorrow,/ And everything shall freeze about me, an eternal silence swallow me up . . ./ A ray of sun will pass over me and not see me,/ A [the] bird's joyful cry—and it will drop dead at my feet/ Only a small cloud in the height will flutter above me/ Will look [at me]—and will float on its way silently."

Four years afterwards, with "May My Lot Be With You," Bialik fled toward anonymity and silence: "May my lot be with you/ Meek of the world/ Mute-souled who shape (embroider) their lives in secret . . . ."

— TUVYA RÜBNER

Chaim Nachman Bialik

ON THE SLAUGHTER · AL HAṢḤÍTA* · עַל הַשְּׁחִיטָה

שָׁמַיִם, בַּקְּשׁוּ רַחֲמִים עָלָי!	Ṣamáyim, bákṣu ráḥamim aláy!
אִם־יֵשׁ בָּכֶם אֵל וְלָאֵל בָּכֶם נָתִיב —	Im-yéṣ báḥem el velaél báḥem nátiv—
וַאֲנִי לֹא מְצָאתִיו —	*Vaaní* lo metsátiv—
הִתְפַּלְּלוּ אַתֶּם עָלָי!	Hitpálelu átem aláy!
אֲנִי — לִבִּי מֵת וְאֵין עוֹד תְּפִלָּה בִּשְׂפָתָי,	*Aní*—líbi met veéyn od tfíla bisfátay,
וּכְבָר אָזְלַת יָד אַף־אֵין תִּקְוָה עוֹד —	Uḥvár ázlat yad af-eyn tíkva od—
עַד־מָתַי, עַד־אָנָה, עַד־מָתָי?	Ad-mátay, ad-ána, ad-mátay?
הַתַּלְיָן! הֵא צַוָּאר — קוּם שְׁחָט!	Hatályan! he tsávar—kum ṣḥat!
עָרְפֵנִי כַּכֶּלֶב, לְךָ זְרֹעַ עִם־קַרְדֹּם,	Orféyni kakélev, leḥá zróa im-kárdom,
וְכָל־הָאָרֶץ לִי גַרְדֹּם —	Veḥól-haárets li gárdom—
וַאֲנַחְנוּ — אֲנַחְנוּ הַמְעָט!	Vaanáḥnu—anáḥnu hameát!
דָּמִי מֻתָּר — הַךְ קָדְקֹד, וִיזַנֵּק דַּם רֶצַח,	Dámi mútar—haḥ kódkod, vizánek [dam-rétsaḥ,
דַּם יוֹנֵק וָשָׂב עַל־כֻּתָּנְתְּךָ —	Dam yónek vasáv al-kutónteḥa—
וְלֹא יִמַּח לָנֶצַח, לָנֶצַח.	Veló yímaḥ lanétsaḥ, lanétsaḥ.
וְאִם יֶשׁ־צֶדֶק — יוֹפַע מִיָּד!	Veím yeṣ-tsédek—yófa miyád!
אַךְ אִם־אַחֲרֵי הִשָּׁמְדִי מִתַּחַת רָקִיעַ	Aḥ im-áḥrey hiṣámdi mitáḥat rakíya
הַצֶּדֶק יוֹפִיעַ —	Hatsédek yofíya—
יְמֻגַּר־נָא כִסְאוֹ לָעַד!	Yemúgar-na ḥís'o laád!
וּבְרֶשַׁע עוֹלָמִים שָׁמַיִם יִמַּקּוּ;	Uvréṣa olámim ṣamáyim yimáku;
אַף־אַתֶּם לְכוּ, זֵדִים, בַּחֲמַסְכֶם זֶה	Af-átem leḥú, zéydim, baḥamásḥem ze
וּבְדִמְכֶם חֲיוּ וְהִנָּקוּ.	Uvdímḥem ḥayú vehináku.
וְאָרוּר הָאוֹמֵר: נְקֹם!	Veárur haómer: nekóm!
נְקָמָה כָזֹאת, נִקְמַת דַּם יֶלֶד קָטָן	Nekáma ḥazót, níkmat dam yéled kátan
עוֹד לֹא־בָרָא הַשָּׂטָן —	Od lo-vára hasátan—
וְיִקֹּב הַדָּם אֶת־הַתְּהוֹם!	Veyíkov hadám et hathóm!
יִקֹּב הַדָּם עַד תְּהוֹמוֹת מַחֲשַׁכִּים,	Yíkov hadám ad thómot maḥaṣákim,
וְאָכַל בַּחֹשֶׁךְ וְחָתַר שָׁם	Veáḥal baḥóṣeḥ veḥátar ṣam
כָּל־מוֹסְדוֹת הָאָרֶץ הַנְמַקִּים.	Kol-mósdot haárets hanmákim.

In the spring of 1903, the civilized world was shocked by news reports of a bloody pogrom in Kishinev (Bessarabia). Bialik reacted to this event, which eclipsed all previous Russian excesses, in two poems both of which startled the world of Hebrew readers.

"In the City of Massacre"—one of a series of long poems written in the years 1902-1905—is a long, bitter, and abusive harangue directed at his people. Yet a profound spiritual struggle agitates the piled-up passages of description, reaching its climax in the lines where God calls upon man to revolt against Him: "Let them lift up their fist against Me, and demand recompense for their humiliation, / The humiliation of all the generations from their beginning to their end, / And let them shatter the Heavens and My Throne with their fist!"

The poem before us has a wholly different character. At first "On the Slaughter" seems a turbulent shrieking of pain, to which the short lines and numerous exclamation points attest. But the reader soon discovers a meticulous artistic unity. Every stanza is identical in meter and rime, composing a structure against whose confines the emotion presses and storms.

(1) *Heavens, demand mercy for me!* (2) *If there is a God in you and if the God has a path in you—* (3) *And I have not found it—* (4) *[Then] You pray for me (in my behalf)!* (5) *I—my heart is dead and there is no longer prayer on my lips,* (6) *And the hand has already weakened and there is no longer hope—* (7) *How long? until when? how long?*

The opening stanza is a prayer and a rather odd prayer at that, by one whose heart has died and who is no longer able to pray and therefore implores the heavens to pray in his stead. The prayer, however, is a questioning demand: "How long? until when? how long?" and it is based on Scripture: "How long shall the wicked, O Lord, how long shall the wicked prosper?" (Psalm 94:3) and "Until when shall you forget me, forever?" (Psalm 13:2).

(8) *Executioner! here's the neck—come and butcher (me)!* (9) *Behead me like a dog—you have the arm (power) with (and) the ax,* (10) *The whole earth is a slaughtering block to me—* (11) *And we—we are the few!* (12) *My blood is permitted* [lit. *you have the legal right to kill me*]—*Strike the skull and murder's blood will spurt,* (13) *The blood of nursling and of aged, on your garment—* (14) *It will never be erased, ever.*

(15) *And if Justice exists—let it appear at once!* (16-17) *But if Justice should appear after I am annihilated* [lit. *from*] *under the sky,* (18) *Let its throne be hurled down forever!* (19) *And let the heavens rot with eternal evil,* (20) *And you too, evil-doers, go forth in this your violence* (21) *And live in your blood and be innocent (found innocent).*

The first stanza related to heaven, the second to earth; the third unites the two domains. In line 15 the speaker again addresses the heavens, which he had commanded with his opening words, "Demand mercy for me!" But because Mercy had been unable to eliminate the executioner, he now calls out to Justice. (One should note that Jewish tradition distinguishes between Justice and Mercy as two of the "ways" of God.) But the speaker's belief in the existence of Justice is also uncertain: hence the appeal is conditional (15).

With lines 20-21, Bialik makes a reference typical of his biblical allusions. In Ezekiel 16:6, the Hebrew text announces the saving and nurturing of Israel by God: "Live in thy blood," a life-affirming statement. Addressing the perpetrators of the pogrom, Bialik condemns them with the identical phrase, closing his imprecation with the bitter command that they "be found innocent." In a world without God, how can murderers be guilty?

(22) *And cursed be he who says: Avenge!* (24) *Satan has not yet devised (created)—* (23) *A revenge such as this: the revenge for the blood of a little child.* (25) *Let the blood pierce (curse) the abyss!* (26) *Let the blood pierce into the abysses (depths) of darkness,* (27) *And let it eat away in the dark and undermine there* (28) *All the rotting foundations of the earth!*

Even Satan has not yet been able to devise a revenge adequate to atone for the murder of a child (23-24). But beyond this fact, and within the cosmic domain in which the poem operates, revenge—which is a human weakness—can hardly exist.

With the phrase "Let the blood pierce the abyss" (25) Bialik echoes the talmudic "let the law pierce the mountain" (*veyikóv hadín et hahár*) which in context means that Justice is supreme. The poem takes a terrible turn of meaning: blood, not law, will determine the world's fate. *Yikov*, however, also means "curse!" And the poem that began with a demand for heavenly mercy concludes with a curse.

For Bialik a world without God is a doomed world; hence he struggles throughout the poem to hold on to a conception of a universe having a God. And therefore the poem moves desperately between two poles: the unseen God and the abyss of darkness.

The remarkable symmetry of this poem of great violence demands some attention. In each stanza, the third line has two stresses; the first, fourth, and the last have three; and the fifth and sixth have four. (Generally the rime is *abbac-c*, with the sixth line unrimed.) Such a textured pattern of strong metrical differences might be said to mirror the stormy motion of the poem. However, the repetitive form of each stanza (even to the regular placement of exclamation points) both contrasts with and succeeds in containing the internal variations. Although at the beginning of the line, the meter is either iambic or anapestic, in line 26 it is trochaic: *Yikov hadám ad thómot maḥaṣákim.* The unexpected stress prepares the reader for the explosive curse upon which the poem ends.

As Strauss points out, Judges: 6 is almost always in the background of the poem. For example, "Go forth in this your violence" (20) is patterned on God's statement to Gideon "Go in this thy might and thou shalt save Israel" (Judges 6:14). Similarly the repeated use of the word *yeṣ* ("there is"). In lines 2, 15, 16, Bialik echoes the biblical narrative that also uses this phrase at moments of crisis (Judges 6:13, 36). In the biblical source, we find Israel in the hands of the Midianites, suffering under the cruelty of "foreign" oppressors"—the identical notion that occurred to Bialik's generation in designating the Czarist regime. Gideon, one of Israel's judges, contemplates the situation of his people only to sink into profound religious doubt. One of the men in the biblical account utters words which Bialik and his contemporaries might also have used: "There is (*yeṣ*) God with us; why, then, did all this happen to us . . . ? Where are His miracles which our fathers related to us . . . ? For now God has abandoned us and has given us into the hands of Midian" (Judges 6:13).

Gideon, who was destined to help his people, doubts both his own destiny and the possibility of help from God. He asks over and over again for "signs" and for "proofs." In the end, Gideon receives a positive response from God: the "sign" is given. Bialik and his generation cry out but receive no answer.

— TUVYA RÜBNER

Saul Tchernichovsky

Saul Tchernichovsky (1875–1943) is generally acknowledged to be the most important poet after Bialik in the generation of Hebrew writers who first became active in the Odessa of the 1890's. Among the poets of this so-called Renaissance Generation, Tchernichovsky is perhaps the one truly renaissance figure: a man of immense vitality with a voracious hunger for life. Physician, naturalist, linguist, translator, he significantly broadened the scope of Hebrew vocabulary and of its verse forms in his attempt as poet to embrace the external world in all its minute particularity.

His whole literary career constitutes a similar effort to embrace Western literature and, as it were, to transfuse it into Hebrew poetry. The astonishing variety of Tchernichovsky's activities as translator gives some indication of the diversity of literary modes which he sought to naturalize to Hebrew. Though best known for his renderings of the *Iliad* and the *Odyssey*, he translated poets from fifteen different literatures, ranging from Sophocles and Horace to Shakespeare, Molière, and Pushkin, from the *Kalevala* to *Hiawatha*. The translations also suggest that Tchernichovsky was no modernist, at least not in technique. As a contemporary of Rilke, George, Yeats, and Eliot, he chose to translate Goethe and Heine, Byron and Shelley. In many of his own poems, we find him responding to the impact of twentieth-century violence, yet the poetry to which he was continually drawn was the kind that affirmed the stirring possibilities of human achievement. He was therefore especially interested in national epics and in the literatures of the Renaissance and Romanticism. He devoted many years to rendering into Hebrew such works as the Gilgamesh cycle and large passages from the national epic of Serbia and the Icelandic Edda.

In general, both Tchernichovsky's sense of life and his experience of Hebrew culture set him apart from other Hebrew writers of his generation. He was born and reared in a prosperous village in the border region between Crimea and the Ukraine. The setting—both its fertile fields and the forbidding stretches of its great plains—loomed large in the poet's spiritual landscape throughout his life. (A poem written in 1923 begins: "Man is nothing but a little plot of land,/ Man is nothing but the image of his native landscape.") While nature often seems to be a consummation devoutly wished but rarely experienced by the ghetto-bred writers of Tchernichovsky's generation, his poetry remains more continually in touch with the rhythms and feeling of the natural world than theirs or that of any modern Hebrew verse before it.

Tchernichovsky did not undergo the induction into culture almost universal among his Jewish literary contemporaries—the one-room elementary school followed by the talmudic academy. Whereas Bialik, and virtually all European-born Hebrew writers, absorbed the language through the study of sacred texts, Tchernichovsky was taught the formal elements of Hebrew by private tutors and then was introduced to biblical and—in defiance of all tradition—modern Hebrew texts. As a result, his Hebrew lacks some of the indigenous quality of Bialik's. The sources of its vocabulary and the models for its syntax are sometimes foreign. This degree of independence from traditional precedents may have made it easier for Tchernichovsky to adapt Hebrew to so great a variety of European prosodic forms. Because of the remarkable continuity of ancient and modern Hebrew literary experience, all Hebrew poetry tends to be allusive—but this is far less true of Tchernichovsky's work than of Bialik's. As one critic has observed, the poetry of Bialik brilliantly recapitulates all the successive historical stages of Jewish experience and fuses them into the poet's own deepest needs of expression. Compared to Bialik, Tchernichovsky was only superficially acquainted with the Talmud, the Midrash, the medieval commentators, and the mystic writers. The only Hebrew literary past to which his early poetry alludes with any imaginative richness is the Bible.

Circumstances forced Tchernichovsky to be even more of a wanderer than Bialik. Because of the restrictions against admitting Jewish students, he had to study medicine outside Russia, first in Heidelberg, then in Lausanne. After working within Russia as a doctor during the trying years of war and revolution, he discovered—as did everyone else connected with the Odessa literary group—that there could be no future for Hebrew writers under the Soviet regime; and he left Russia in 1922. An unsuccessful attempt to get a medical post in Palestine led to a nine-year stay in Germany, interrupted by several temporary moves in the hope of finding more satisfactory positions elsewhere in Europe. Like Bialik, Tchernichovsky managed to settle in Palestine for only the final decade of his life.

But while the dark experience of exile—personal, national, and metaphysical—remains central to Bialik's poetry, Tchernichovsky's work generally conveys a sense of being at home in a natural world despite the physical uprootings and personal difficulties experienced by the man himself. It is not really surprising that Tchernichovsky was able to acclimatize himself poetically in many ways to the Palestinian setting after his arrival there in 1931. Unlike Bialik, he strove to adopt the Sephardic accent for his serious poetry, and some of the best work of his last years is a response to the physical presence of the Land of Israel and to the human effort of its rebuilders.

Saul Tchernichovsky

MY ASTARTE · AṢTÓRTI LI* · עַשְׁתָּרְתִּי לִי

עַשְׁתָּרְתִּי לִי, הֲלֹא תָּסִיחִי לִי: מֵאָן
הַגַּיְא אֵלֵינוּ בָּאת? הַאִם בְּיַד כְּנַעֲנִי צִידוֹן
מֵעִיר לְמָעוֹז יָם, בֵּין גַּלֵּי שְׁבוֹ וְכַלְצִידוֹן?
4 הֶאָרְבוּ לוֹ בָּהָר וְעִם־לֵיל אַלּוּפֵי דָן?

Aṣtórti li, haló tasíḥi li: meán
Hagáy eyléynu vat? haím beyád knáani [tsídon
Meír lemáoz yam, beyn gáley ṣvo [veḥaltsídon?
4 Heárvu lo bahár veím-leyl alúfey dan?

The pagan world exercised a continuing fascination over Tchernichovsky. He spent much of his life imaginatively exploring the pagan roots of many cultures: Egypt, Babylonia, Greece, Russia, even Finland. But it was to the ancient Canaanite cult that he gave the greatest place in his poetry, for it offered him a clear alternative image of what the later Hebrew-speaking inhabitants of Canaan could have been if freed from the limitations imposed by Judaism and the God of the Jews. Tchernichovsky, then, sometimes uses the pagan gods for strictly polemic purposes in protest against Jewish tradition. Thus, in "Before the Statue of Apollo" (1899), the first important statement of his pagan "program," he describes the Jewish people as rebels against a Nietzschean god of life, a "God, Lord of the wondrous deserts,/ God, Lord of the conquerors of Canaan by storm—/ And they bound him in phylactery thongs."

But paganism is more than an ideological drumbeat in Tchernichovsky's poetry. Like his younger English contemporary, D. H. Lawrence, Tchernichovsky had an unusual gift of imaginative response to the idea of a free life of the instincts. And for him, as for Lawrence, the pagan world was a vivid embodiment of the natural existence men supposedly had led before they were maimed by repression and inhibition.

"My Astarte," subtitled "an idyll," is in a quieter mood than most of his pagan poems. The speaker is a woman, praying to the fertility goddess Astarte. Apparently a village-dweller, she addresses a newly acquired statuette of Astarte which has been brought from afar:

(1) *My Astarte, won't you tell me: from where* (2) *Did you come to us in the valley? Was it in the hand of a merchant (Canaanite) of Sidon* (3) *From [the] city stronghold of the sea, through waves of agate and chalcedony?* (4) *Did the chieftains of Dan lie in ambush for him [the merchant] on the mountain (and) at night?*

הַאִם בִּצְרוֹרוֹת בַּד עַל דַּבְּשׁוֹת גְּמַלֵּי דְדָן
וּנְאָקוֹת מַעֲלוֹת חוֹל הַפָּז בְּנִיעָן וְנִידָן
נִשֵּׂאת עִם אֹרְחַת שְׁבָא, נוֹשֶׁקֶת רוֹמָה כִּידוֹן,
8 וְלִפְנֵיהֶם מְטַרְטֵר קוֹל רִמּוֹנִים וְסַהֲרוֹן רָן?

נִפְלָאוֹת לִי, מַה־נִּפְלָאוֹת עֵינַיִךְ אִסְמָרַגְדִים,
אַף כֻּלָּךְ עָשׂוּךְ שֵׁן, יְצוּרַיִךְ כֹּה מִתְלַכְּדִים.
11 וְאֵין אִישׁ מְגַלֶּה סוֹד, מִי נְתָנֵךְ לִי — אֵין אִישׁ!

סַלְסִלַּת תְּאֵנִים לָךְ — חָפַנְתִּי קֶמַח סָלְתִּי,
13 מִשֶּׁמֶן זֵיתִי לֹג — — — אֵלַיִךְ הִתְפַּלָּלְתִּי:
« נַהֲגִיהוּ, נַעַר צַח, אֵלַי תְּבִיאִיהוּ חִישׁ! »

Haím bitsrórot bad al dábṣot gmáley dedán
Uneákot máalot ḥol hapáz benían venídan
Nisét im órḥat ṣva, noṣéket róma kídon,
8 Velifnéyhem metárter kol rimónim [vesáharon ran?

Nifláot li, ma-nifláot eynáyiḥ ismarágdim,
Af kúlaḥ ásuḥ ṣen, yetsuráyiḥ ko mitlákdim.
11 Veéyn iṣ megále sod, mi netáneḥ li—eyn iṣ!

Salsílat teéynim laḥ—ḥafánti kémaḥ sólti,
13 Miṣémen zéyti log — — — eyláyiḥ hitpalálti:
"Nahagíhu, náar tsaḥ, eyláy teviíhu ḥiṣ!"

(5) *Was it with (in) bundles of linen on the humps of Dedanite camels* (6) *And she-camels raising the golden sand with their swinging and swaying* (7) *[That you] were borne with a Sheban caravan, armed with spears lifted high,* (8) *And before them the sound of pomegranate [bells] tinkling and singing crescent [ornament]?*

(9) *Wondrous to me, how wondrous to me are your eyes that are emeralds,* (10) *Indeed all of you they have made of ivory, your limbs link together so.* (11) *And no one reveals the secret, who gave you to me—no one [*lit. *no man]!*

(12) *A little basket of figs for you—I have scooped up my best flour,* (13) *A log* [a biblical measure] *of my olive oil— — —I have prayed to you:* (14) "*Lead him, a shining (pure) lad, bring him to me swiftly.*"

Tchernichovsky seems to have deliberately set this poem as a challenge to his own virtuosity. He wrote many idylls both early and late in his career, but the form as he used it was expansive and narrative; typically, he would take many hundreds of hexameter lines to give a leisurely, detailed account of the pleasures of village life. Here, on the other hand, he tries to convey the idyllic sense of broad, sun-warmed vistas through the rigorously restricted form of a Petrarchan sonnet. And while he observes the Petrarchan conventions scrupulously, he also seeks to endow his Canaanite woman with convincingly dramatic speech.

Her first words sound naturally direct in the Hebrew, though the language is, appropriately, biblical rather than modern. (The vocabulary in general evokes the more exotic and archaic usages of the Old Testament, although there are a few post-biblical words in the poem.) Enjambment is used in at least half the lines of the octave, and all pauses are dictated by the dramatic sense, so that the sonnet form is not felt as an impediment to the speaking voice which dramatically questions Astarte. The sestet is more symmetrically formal. As the speaker moves from questioning to fervent praise and supplication, the lines are all strongly end-stopped, with a cesura occurring regularly after the third foot, suggesting the choreographic rhythm of ecstatic ritual.

The poem selects its "idyllic" details with the greatest effectiveness. The speaker wonders (1-4) whether the Astarte originally came by sea from Sidon in the north, or overland from Sheba in the far south (5-8). Thus the octave calls forth a whole ancient

Near Eastern world, where after disembarking Tyrian merchants run the danger of attack from Danite—significantly, Israelite—marauders, and where armed caravans cross the Arabian desert, to the tinkle of pomegranate-bells (suggesting fertility) and crescent-shaped ornaments (again associated with Astarte, often thought of as a moon-goddess).

The general effect the poem aims at is to crystallize the magic lights of an exotic world. There is a cultivated quality of strangeness in the vocabulary—"chalcedony," "she-camels" (*nákot*, derived from the Arabic), the biblical epithet "stronghold of the sea" for Sidon.

Until the final tercet, almost everything is seen as artifact: the sea is a jewelled surface, the sand is gold, the caravan is a parade of finely wrought ornaments. Astarte, of course, is literally an artifact (9-10), but the poem establishes an equation that works both ways. The Canaanite woman, we sense, is addressing the real Astarte, not just a piece of carved ivory, and the real Astarte is as exquisitely beautiful as the statuette which represents her. The poem has captured a distinctive mode of ancient Near Eastern poetry in rendering the work of nature in terms of the splendor of art. Compare the description of the lover in the Song of Songs, 5:14-15: "His hands are rods of gold set with beryl; his body is polished ivory overlaid with sapphire; his legs are pillars of marble set upon sockets of fine gold." At the same time, the sexual images are inescapable—the undulating female camels, the pomegranate shapes, and the intertwined limbs.

Only the last tercet places the idea of artifact in the background. Here the poem passes from visual and auditory images to taste and smell as the woman enumerates the items of her simple sacrifice—fine flour and olive oil (a standard offering prescribed in the Pentateuch), and figs, associated with fertility. The change in sensory focus is appropriate, for this is the most humanly immediate moment of the poem. The woman prays for a "shining" (*tsaḥ*) lad, like the "shining and ruddy" lover of the Song of Songs 5:10.

— ROBERT ALTER

Saul Tchernichovsky

TO THE SUN: 7,8 · LAṢÉMEṢ* · לַשֶּׁמֶשׁ

בְּעָמְדִי בֵּין הַחַי וּבֵין הַגּוֹסֵס כְּבָר (אָמָּנוּת מַה־נּוֹרָאָה!) וְאִזְמֵל חַד בְּכַפִּי, יֵשׁ בּוֹכֶה מִתּוֹךְ גִּיל וְיֵשׁ מְקַלֵּל בְּאַפִּי, סָפַגְתִּי אַחֲרוֹן אוֹר תּוֹךְ אִישׁוֹן גּוֹסֵס זָר.	Beómdi veyn haḥáy uvéyn hagóses kvar (Umánut ma-noráa!) veízmel ḥad beḥápi, Yeṣ bóḥe mítoḥ gil veyéṣ mekálel beápi, 4 Safágti áḥaron or toḥ íṣon góses zar.
אֶל רַעַם תּוֹתְחֵי־אוֹן מִתְגַּלְגְּלִים בַּכָּר, לְאֵשׁ נוֹצְצָה בְּאֶשּׁוּן מִנְהַרְתִּי לִי בְּגַפִּי הִתְוֵיתִי אַחֲרוֹן־קָו, מָחַקְתִּי חַי מִדַּפִּי, מִסַּף מְשֹׁהָם כָּךְ תֵּעָקֵר אֶבֶן־יְקָר.	El ráam tótḥey-on mitgálgelim bakár, Leéṣ nótsetsa veéṣun minhárti li vegápi Hitvéyti áḥaron-kav, maḥákti ḥay midápi, 8 Misáf meṣóham kaḥ teáker éven-yekár.
וְאוּלָם בְּאוֹתוֹ זִיק בָּעַיִן הָעוֹמֶמֶת, בָּאוֹר הַסּוֹפֵג אוֹר וּבְטֶרֶם קָם לָעַד; וְאוּלָם בְּאוֹתוֹ בְּרַק אֵשׁ קוֹדְחָה וְצוֹרֶמֶת,	Veúlam beóto zik baáyin haomémet, Baór hasófeg or uvtérem kam laád; 11 Veúlam beóto brak eṣ kódḥa vetsorémet,
בָּאֵשׁ הַקּוֹרְאָה לְאֵשׁ, הַמְצַוָּה אֵיד וּשְׁמַד, — הָיִיתָ אַתָּה בָּם; זֶה הוֹדְךָ הֲמָמָנִי; — הַאִם קִדַּמְתִּי בֹא אוֹ אֵחַר צוּר בְּרָאָנִי?	Baéṣ hakór'a leéṣ, hamtsáva eyd uṣmád,— 13 Hayíta áta vam; ze hódḥa hamamáni;— Haím kidámti vo o éḥar tsur braáni?

The sonnet has almost as long a history in Hebrew poetry as it does in Italian; it was introduced to Hebrew literature in the 14th century by Immanuel of Rome, a contemporary of Dante. But for all the venerability of the Hebrew sonnet, no poet had put it to so wide a variety of uses or displayed such virtuosity in handling the form as Tchernichovsky. He published in Berlin in 1922 *The Notebook of Sonnets*, a volume of verse which also included a historical essay on the sonnet and a poetic tribute "To the Hebrew Sonnet." In both the essay and the tribute, Tchernichovsky makes clear that he turned to the sonnet partly in response to the neglect of formal beauty which he felt was encouraged by critics of modern Hebrew verse.

"To the Sun," the first and most impressive section of the *Notebook*, is composed in a particularly demanding form: the sonnet corona. A corona is a cycle of fifteen Petrarchan sonnets in which the last line of each poem is repeated as the first line of its successor; the fourteenth sonnet ends with the first line of the first poem and is followed by a concluding sonnet made up of the first lines of all the previous poems, in sequence. The cumulative power that can be generated by this difficult form with its virtuoso conclusion is extraordinary; one understands Tchernichovsky's pride in reminding us, in his dedicatory note, that "this sonnet corona [is] the first in our literature."

Ideally the first cycle should be read with

"On the Blood," a corona completed the year after the publication of "To the Sun." The two titles, in fact, are in a sense interchangeable, for "To the Sun" develops an equation between sun and blood, or fire and blood: "You Who are present in the hiding-place of being, I beseech You, guard the blood for me./ Do not put out Your fire, which You kindled in me, with Your compassion," (Sonnet 5). "On the Blood" wrestles with history while the poet of "To the Sun" wrestles with his own soul. But it should be kept in mind that the historical foreground of the later corona is a dramatic background for the earlier one: Russia and Europe from 1914 to 1922, world war, revolution, pogroms, civil anarchy, a widening circle of uninhibited violence. "On the Blood," in proposing art as the answer to the madness of history, suggests one possible reason for the adoption of the difficult corona form in both cycles: the poet is trying to shore up his sense of beauty against the moral chaos around him with an artistic convention that demands restraint, control, balance, complex interweaving.

One of several themes that is repeated with fugal intricacy in "To the Sun" is the speaker's vacillating sense of himself as a sun-blessed creature rooted in the earth's timeless life-energies, and as an outcast in time, engulfed by the violence and heartlessness of an alien age. This double sense of self is perhaps hinted at in the opening line of the cycle: "I was like a hyacinth and a mallow to my God, . . ." Mallow, according to the Talmud, is a flower that turns and opens to the sun; the hyacinth, according to Greek legend, springs from the blood of murder, and its petals bear the letters AI AI, the syllables of woe. Sonnets 7 and 8 of the corona present an exciting transition from lamentation to sun-fired song. The speaker of Sonnet 7 is an army doctor, working by lantern light in a makeshift underground operating room. (Tchernichovsky saw considerable frontline action as a medical officer in the Russian army from 1914 to 1918.)

(1) *As I stood between the living and the already dying* (2) *(What a terrible craft!) and a sharp scalpel in my hand,* (3) *Sometimes weeping for joy and sometimes cursing in anger,* (4) *I soaked up the last light from the pupil [of the eye] of an alien (stranger) dying man.*

(5) *By the thunder of mighty cannons [*lit. *cannons of might] rolling through the meadow,* (6) *By the fire flashing (flickering) to me alone in the darkness of my tunnel* (7) *I marked the last line, I wiped out a living creature from my page,* (8) *So from an onyx threshold a precious stone is ripped out.*

(9) *And yet in that spark in the fading (dulling) eye,* (10) *In that light soaking up light and before it goes blind;* (11) *And yet in that flash of scorching and screeching fire,*

(12) *In the fire calling to fire, commanding disaster and destruction—* (13) *You, You were in [all of] them; this glory of Yours stunned me;* — (14) *Have I come too early or was the Rock [God] late in creating me?*

To the reader familiar with the reference in line 1 (to Numbers 17:13), the poem begins on a note of great breadth and grandeur: "And he [Aaron] stood between the dead and the living and the plague was stayed." The underground operating room of the octave is a kind of grave. The doctor's craft is terrible because futile: he is forced to be a macabre parody of God, helplessly crossing out lives from his book. But the "darkness of the tunnel" is punctuated with images of light—the dying light in the eye, the lantern, the flashes of artillery, the hardened flame of the jewel—which will flare up in the sestet.

The turning from despair to affirmation is signaled by the initial "And yet" of the sestet. Lines 9-12, as the progression of images indicates, should be read in a crescendo, reaching a peak in line 12, with its heavily accented long-*ey* sounds and final thud of *eyd uṣmád* ("catastrophe and destruction"). Lines 13-14 bring a marked rhythmic change. The sound and sense of line 13, with stressed alliteration of *h*'s and *m*'s, force us to read it

הַאִם קִדַּמְתִּי בֹּא אוֹ אֵחַר צוּר בְּרָאָנִי?
׳אֱלֹהִים׳ סָבִיב לִי וּמְלֵאִים כָּל הַיְקוּם.
כּוֹכָבִים אֱלֹהַי, אֶתְפַּלֵּל לָמוֹ, קְסוּם־
פְּנֵיכֶם, מְאוֹר־יוֹם וְסַהַר חִוַּרְיָנִי.

כִּי בִלְתְּךָ אֵין כְּלוּם, הוֹי שֶׁמֶשׁ חִמְּמָנִי!
בְּנֵי־שֶׁמֶשׁ אַתֶּם לִי, הַגְּלָמִים תְּלוּיִם רוּם,
בְּנֵי־שֶׁמֶשׁ — עֵץ הַפִּיל וּקְלִפּוֹת כָּל הַשּׁוּם,
גִּלְגּוּלֵי אוֹר וָחֹם — הַפֶּחָם הָרַתְּחָנִי.

וְהָיָה כָּל הַיְקוּם קוֹל תְּפִלָּה, תְּפִלַּת־כֹּל:
לְךָ קוֹרְאוֹת אִמּוֹת־תַּנִּים, גּוּרֵיהֶן כִּי תְפַלַּחְנָה,
לְךָ יָרֹן שׁוֹפַר־קְרָב עִם הָנֵץ אוֹר בַּמַּחֲנֶה,

הַשְּׁמָשׁוֹת בְּגַלְגַּל־עָל, כִּי יִגְרְפֵם הַקּוֹל.
בְּמַקְהֵלַת אֵין־הַסּוֹף אָרְנָּה וְלֹא אֶדֹּם:
עוֹד בְּלִבִּי לָן הַטַּל, הַיּוֹרֵד עַל שְׂדֵה־אֱדוֹם.

Haím kidámti vo o éḥar tsur braáni?
'Elóhim' sáviv li umléim kol haykúm.
Koḥávim elóhay, etpálel lámo, ksum-
4 Pnéyḥem, meór-yom vesáhar ḥivaryáni.

Ki vílteḥa eyn klum, hoy ṣémeṣ ḥimemáni!
Bney-ṣémeṣ átem li, haglámim tlúyim rum,
Bney-ṣémeṣ—ets hapíl uklípot kol haṣúm,
8 Gilgúley or vaḥóm—hapéḥam harathḥáni.

Veháya ḥol haykúm kol tfíla, tfílat-kol:
Laḥ kórot ímot-tánim, guréyhen ki tefaláḥna,
11 Laḥ yáron ṣófar-krav im hánets or bamáḥne,

Haṣmáṣot begálgal-al, ki yígrefem hakól.
13 Bemakhélat eyn-hasóf aróna veló édom:
Od belíbi lan hatál, hayóred al sde-édom.

much more slowly, at a lower pitch, than the preceding line. "Stunned me" (*hamamáni*) implies a physical blow, and one hears a kind of muffled thunder in the whole line. Despite the dominance of death, the presence of light—even dying and destructive light—avows the existence of vital, inexhaustible energy. The cannon fire calls for answering fire and it also calls to the fire or light in the dying eye (9), and, echoing the "abyss calling to abyss" of Psalm 42, it imposes itself in the poem as a force of cosmic dimensions.

The speaker concludes the sonnet with a sudden, and for the moment, enigmatic, question. As the child of an age to whom fire means only destruction, should he have been born in a much earlier period when the vital principle of fire (or sun) was worshipped? Or perhaps he has come to the world too early, before the fulfilment of the vision when "a generation will create . . . its next god, and we shall worship Him in exultation" (Sonnet 10). Standing "between the living and the dying," is not only dramatic but symbolic as well. The speaker finds himself between a moribund age and the eternal sources of life which were accessible in the past and, hopefully, will be so again in the future. Sonnet 8 repeats the question which ends the previous sonnet, then goes on with the affirmation of life:

(1) *Have I come early or was the Rock [God] late in creating me?* (2) *"Gods" are around me and fill the whole universe.* (3) *Stars are my gods, I pray to them, bewitched* (4) *By your faces, light of day and pale moon.*

(5) *For there is nothing without (except) You, O Sun that has warmed me!* (6) *You are children of the sun (sun-creatures) to me, [you cloud] masses hung on high,* (7) *Children of the sun (sun-creatures)—the elephant tree and all the garlic skins,* (8) *Avatars of light and heat—the combustible coal.*

(9) *And the whole universe will be a voice of prayer, the prayer of all*: (10) *To You, mother-jackals call as they give birth to their whelps,* (11) *To You, the battle horn sings as light breaks in the camp,*

(12) *[To You] the suns in the sphere above, as the sound (voice) sweeps them.* (13) *In the choir*

of infinity I shall sing and I shall not be still: (14) *In my heart the dew still reposes that descended [*lit. *descends] on the field of Edom.*

Many of the English equivalents offered here are inadequate. The diction and grammar of the poem are more elevated, more biblically poetic, than our version can indicate. Note also that the Hebrew here for "gods" (*elóhim*), which the speaker, living in a post-pagan world, feels compelled to enclose in quotation marks, does not suggest an absolute cleavage between polytheism and monotheism, for this plural noun is used in the singular sense for God throughout the Bible.

After the credo of the first quatrain, the poem runs up and down the scale of sun-saturated creation in two series—5-8, 9-13—culminating in the "choir of infinity" (13). Everything that exists is an "embodiment of light" (8), containing seeds of the sun's life-energy, from the cloud masses (*glámim* implies formlessness) and the aromatic elephant tree down to the garlic skin, a proverbial equivalent in Hebrew for something worth next to nothing.

The second series, which ends in a sun-worshipper's version of the music of the spheres, is appropriately more elevated in style than the first. It begins (9) with the verb "to be" in prophetic future, as if the speaker were setting out to say, "And it shall come to pass on that day . . ." The poem's vision of unity becomes so intense that its language approaches the language of eschatology. The epiphany of the sun-god came, we remember, in the blast of cannons. The vital energy that is praised in the poem exists beyond all moral categories: the same force is present in the dimming eye of the dying man and in the first trumpet of war.

Line 14—like many of the terminal lines in the corona—is a sudden reversal in tone and perspective. Line 13 triumphantly ends with a jubilant trumpet-blare: *aróna veló édom* ("I shall sing and I shall not be still"). Line 14, by contrast, is a still, gentle voice. From the celestial grandeur, the speaker turns to his own heart; from fiery cosmic power to the dew on a Near Eastern desert; and from a vision of life-present to a fantasy of life-past. The "field of Edom" is the desert through which Moses led the ancient Israelites. In the next sonnet the speaker will identify his own religious consciousness with that of his desert-dwelling ancestors, whom he imagines as having lived close to the primitive vital forces of nature.

— ROBERT ALTER

Saul Tchernichovsky

EAGLE! EAGLE OVER YOUR MOUNTAINS · ÁYIT! ÁYIT AL HARÁYIH

עַיִט! עַיִט עַל הָרַיִךְ

עַיִט! עַיִט עַל הָרַיִךְ, עַיִט עַל הָרַיִךְ עָף!
אַט וָקַל, — נִדְמֶה כְּאִלּוּ רֶגַע — אֵינוֹ אֶלָּא צָף,
צָף־מַפְלִיג בְּיָם שֶׁל תְּכֵלֶת, עֵר לְרֶנֶן־גִּיל בְּלֵב
הַשָּׁמַיִם — הָרָקִיעַ, חָג אִלֵּם בְּאוֹר צוֹרֵב.

עַיִט! עַיִט עַל הָרַיִךְ, עַיִט עַל הָרַיִךְ עָף!
יְשַׁר־גֵּו וְכֶבֶד אֵבֶר, שְׁחוֹר־נוֹצָה וּרְחַב־כָּנָף;
טָס מָתוּחַ (חֵץ מִקֶּשֶׁת), עַיִט עָג עוּגִיּוֹת חוּגָיו;
תָּר עִקְּבוֹת טַרְפּוֹ מִמַּעַל בָּאֲפָר וּבַחֲגָו.

עַיִט! עַיִט עַל הָרַיִךְ, עַיִט עַל הָרַיִךְ עָף!
טָס גּוֹלֵשׁ־גּוֹלֵשׁ וּבְמַגַּע פֶּלֶא אֵבֶר לֹא נָקָף.
רֶגַע קַל – קָפָא, מִשְׁנֵהוּ – נִיד־לֹא־נִיד בְּאֶבְרוֹתָיו,
רֶטֶט כָּל־שֶׁהוּא לְפֶתַע — וְעוֹלֶה לִקְרַאת הָעָב.

עַיִט! עַיִט עַל הָרַיִךְ, עַיִט עַל הָרַיִךְ עָף!
אַט וָקַל, — נִדְמֶה כְּאִלּוּ — רֶגַע אֵינוֹ אֶלָּא צָף...
אֶרֶץ, עַיִט עַל הָרַיִךְ, — עַל פָּנַיִךְ חַשְׁרַת צֵל,
מֵאֶבְרוֹת עֲנָק חוֹלֶפֶת, מְלַטֶּפֶת הַרְרֵי־אֵל...

Áyit! áyit al haráyiḥ, áyit al haráyiḥ af!
At vakál,—nidmé keílu réga—eynó éla tsaf,
Tsaf-maflíg beyám ṣel tḥélet, er lerénen-gil [belév
Haṣamáyim—harakía ḥag ilém beór tsorév.

Áyit! áyit al haráyiḥ, áyit al haráyiḥ af!
Yeṣár-gev veḥéved éver, ṣḥor-notsá [urḥáv-kanáf;
Tas matúaḥ (ḥets mikéṣet), áyit ag ugiyót [ḥugáv;
Tar ikvót tarpó mimáal baafár uvaḥagáv.

Áyit! áyit al haráyiḥ, áyit al haráyiḥ af!
Tas golés-golés uvmagá péle éver lo nakáf.
Réga kal—kafá, miṣnéhu—nid-lo-níd [beevrotáv,
Rétet kol-ṣehú leféta—veolé likrát haáv.

Áyit! áyit al haráyiḥ, áyit al haráyiḥ af!
At vakál,—nidmé keílu—réga éyno éla tsaf...
Érets, áyit al haráyiḥ,—al panáyiḥ ḥaṣrát tsel,
Meevrót anák ḥoléfet, melatéfet hárerey-el...

The "eagle" (*áyit*) of the title, a word popularly confused in Hebrew with "vulture," is a far more ominous bird than its English counterpart. It is the "bird of prey" in Genesis 15:11 that swoops down on the sacrifice in the moment of Abraham's midnight covenant with God. The opening repetition of "Eagle" vividly recalls the first line of Blake's "The Tiger," a poem Tchernichovsky undoubtedly knew. His poem, like Blake's, tensely evokes a wild creature of fearful symmetry. The feminine "you" whom the speaker addresses is the Land (15). The mountains over which the eagle circles are the bare, stony Judean hills.

(1) *Eagle! eagle over your mountains, an eagle*

is flying over your mountains! (2) *Slow and light—it seems as if for a moment—it is merely floating,* (3) *Floating, sailing in a sea of blue, alert to the song of delight in the heart* (4) *Of the heavens—of the sky, circling mutely in searing light.*

(5) *Eagle! eagle over your mountains, an eagle is flying over your mountains!* (6) *Straight of body, heavy-pinioned, black of feather and broad of wing;* (7) *Soaring taut—arrow from a bow—an eagle makes the rings of its (sweeping) circles;* (8) *Tracking from above the signs of its prey in meadow and in rock-crevice.*

(9) *Eagle! eagle over your mountains, an eagle is flying over your mountains!* (10) *Soaring, gliding-gliding, and with wondrous touch did not move a wing.* (11) *For an instant—it froze, then—the barest movement* [lit. *movement-no-movement*] *in its wings,* (12) *The slightest tremble suddenly—and it rises toward the cloud.*

(13) *Eagle! eagle over your mountains, an eagle is flying over your mountains!* (14) *Slow and light—it seems as if—for a moment it is merely floating . . .* (15) *[O] Land (earth), [an] eagle [is] over your mountains—over your face, a massing of shadow* (16) *From the giant wings passes, caresses the mountains of God.*

The first line of the poem, repeated as a musical theme at the beginning of each stanza, is one of the most impressive lines of modern Hebrew poetry for its fusion of image and sonality. The impact of the stress pattern, the skillful variation of masculine and feminine arrests of the breath groups, the many monosyllabic verbs and adjectives propel the poem with force and grace. One cannot read the Hebrew without being aware of the repetitions—of lines, words, consonants, and vowels—which produce the effect of incantation.

The double nature of the poem's sounds—chant-like regularity of rhythm and reiterated harshness—echoes the speaker's contradictory sense of what the eagle is. In the first stanza, the eagle appears as a thing of breathtaking beauty, the beauty of pure effortless power, beyond all limit or restraint. But the last word of the stanza, "searing," introduces the idea of pain and possible destructiveness. This idea becomes prominent in the next stanza when we see the eagle's lovely movement as the flight of an arrow, and when we are reminded that the circling eagle is circling in for the kill. Yet the speaker's awed admiration in no way diminishes: the third stanza is a study in the beauty of perfect movement, with no hint that the movement is one that brings violent death. The verb tenses shift briefly from present to past (10-11) as the eagle descends from its timeless world to earth and then soars up again, while the verse rhythm adroitly imitates glide, poised stillness, then swift flight.

The final stanza closes the circle of incantation, adding a cry of warning to the Land. But even in the ominous image of the eagle's shadow, with which the poem concludes, there is something curiously attractive; the shadow "caresses" the mountains of God. The speaker has been confronted with a vision of primal power in (or above) nature: his feelings toward it are ambivalent.

In any case, the language of the last two lines clearly suggests the mythic dimension of the poem. *Ḥaṣrát* (15), a word which occurs only once in the Bible (2 Samuel 22:12), describes the clouds "thick" with water that the Creator massed around Himself in darkness. The "gathering of shadow," then, together with the substitution of "giant" for "eagle," indicates that "mountains of God" is not just an epithet for the hills of Judea, but that it retains the cosmic force of its original biblical usage in which it is paired with "the great abyss" (Psalms 36:6): "Thy righteousness is like the great mountains; thy judgments are the great abyss . . ."

— ROBERT ALTER

Saul Tchernichovsky

THREE ASSES · ṢALÓṢ ATONÓT · שָׁלֹשׁ אֲתוֹנוֹת

שָׁלֹשׁ אֲתוֹנוֹת מְשָׂרְכוֹת אֶת דַּרְכָּן,		Ṣalóṣ atonót mesarḥót et darkán,
שָׁלֹשׁ אֲתוֹנוֹת — מִבְּאֵר־שֶׁבַע לְדָן:	2	Ṣalóṣ atonót—mib'er-ṣéva ledán:
חוּמָה וּשְׁחוֹרָה וּצְחוֹרָה, — לְאִטָּן.		Ḥumá uṣḥorá utsḥorá,—leitán.
עָבְרוּ הַשָּׁלֹשׁ עַל־יַד צְרִיחַ מִסְגֵּד,		Avrú haṣalóṣ al-yad tsríaḥ misgéd,
כָּרְעָה הַשְּׁחוֹרָה, כִּי קָרְאוּ לַמּוֹעֵד.	5	Kar'á haṣḥorá, ki kar'ú lamoéd.
עָבְרוּ הַשָּׁלֹשׁ עַל־יַד פֶּתַח מִנְזָר,		Avrú haṣalóṣ al-yad pétaḥ minzár,
צָנְחָה הַחוּמָה מוּל אִיקוֹנִין מְשֻׁזָּר.		Tsanḥá haḥumá mul ikónin moṣzár.
עָבְרוּ הַשָּׁלֹשׁ עַל חָרְבָּה קְדוֹשָׁה,	8	Avrú haṣalóṣ al ḥurbá kedoṣá,
עָמְדָה הַצְּחוֹרָה מַרְכִּינָה אֶת רֹאשָׁהּ.		Amdá hatsḥorá markiná et roṣá.
עַל־גַּב הַשְּׁחוֹרָה, עַל גַּבָּהּ, סַיִף רָב;		Al-gáv haṣḥorá, al gabá, sáyif rav;
עַל־גַּב הַחוּמָה, עַל גַּבָּהּ, מֻטָּל צְלָב;	11	Al-gáv haḥumá, al gabá, mutál tslav;
עַל גַּב הַצְּחוֹרָה אַךְ שְׁטִיחַ זָהָב.		Al-gáv hatsḥorá, aḥ ṣtíaḥ zaháv.
אֵין כְּלוּם עַל גַּבָּהּ בִּלְתִּי אִם־הַשָּׁטִיחַ — —	13	Eyn klum al gabá biltí im-haṣatíaḥ—
בִּמְהֵרָה בְיָמֵינוּ יִרְכַּב עָלֶיהָ מָשִׁיחַ.		*Bimherá beyaméynu yirkáv aléha maṣiaḥ.*

Folk literature and folklore play an important role in Tchernichovsky's poetry. He was often attracted to the ballad and, through his use of it, helped make it an accessible means of expression for modern Hebrew poets. "Three Asses," written toward the end of his life, is subtitled "a legend." Though the poem is not really a ballad, it attempts to reproduce both the symmetrical simplicity of folk imagination and the lilting music of ballad versification.

The obvious source of this original legend is the reference to the Messiah in Zechariah 9:9 as "a poor man and riding on a donkey." That text is imaginatively fused with another one from the Song of Deborah (Judges 5:10) which describes the princes of Israel "riding on white asses, sitting on rich cloths." The three asses of the poem make their way from Beersheba in the South to Dan in the North, the proverbial limits of the land that is holy to all three western faiths.

(1) *Three asses are threading their way (amble),* (2) *Three asses—from Beersheba to Dan:* (3) *A brown one and a black one and a white one—slowly.*

(4) *The three passed by the minaret of a mosque,* (5) *The black one kneeled, for they had called the appointed time [for prayer].* (6) *The three passed by the entrance of a monastery,* (7) *The brown one slumped down before a braided ikon.* (8) *The three passed by a holy ruin,* (9) *The white one stood lowering its head.*

(10) *On the back of the black one, on her back*

[is] a great sword. (11) *On the back of the brown one, on her back a cross rests.* (12) *On the back of the white one, only a golden rug.*

(13) *There is nothing on her back except for the rug*— — (14) SPEEDILY IN OUR DAYS MAY THE MESSIAH RIDE UPON HER.

Much of the ballad's charm depends on its sound—the regular march of anapests echoes the steady clatter of the asses' hooves, while the rimed couplets and triplets blend musically, suggesting a distinct sense of folktale or fairytale reality. A triplet introduces the three asses, appropriately ambling slowly because history—and the Redemption—bides its time. The three asses are identified through three symbolic acts (4-9), one couplet allotted to each. Then the three characteristic stances toward history appear in the second triplet (10-12). The poem upsets this perfectly symmetrical structure by adding a concluding couplet which places the white ass and its destined rider at the center of attention.

Though many of Tchernichovsky's poems express rebellion against Jewish tradition, others reflect a finely sympathetic understanding of its world view. His legend of the three asses is deeply rooted in a Jewish folk conception of the role of Judaism among the western faiths. The two dark asses kneel before the material, temporal symbols of their faiths; the white one (*tsḥorá* in Hebrew suggests purity) merely bows her head reverently before the ruins of a structure erected by faith in the past. The brown and black asses bear the symbols of their churches militant in history; the white ass carries a shining symbol of expectation for the resolution of history in peace.

"Speedily in our days" (*bimherá beyaméynu*) is a phrase from the often repeated *kadíș*, which is really a prayer for the coming of the Messiah. The phrase also occurs in a popular hymn about the prophet Elijah, who, according to a well-known tradition, is the herald of the Messiah. A fifth foot, added to the rhythm of the last line, sets its supplication apart from the rest of the poem: *bimherá beyaméynu yirkáv aléha maṣíaḥ*. This idea of Judaism as the faith of expectation is rounded out by the concluding couplet with its deft riming of *ṣatíaḥ* ("rug") with *maṣíaḥ* ("Messiah")—one might almost think of *maṣíaḥ* as the "destined" rime that the golden cloth (*ṣatíaḥ*) has been waiting for patiently throughout unredeemed history.

— ROBERT ALTER

Jacob Fichman

MIDNIGHT · ḤATSÓT · חֲצוֹת

הָאוֹת יֻתַּן, וְלֵב נֵעוֹר יִרְאֶה		Haót yután, velév neór yir'é
כַּף אֵשׁ שְׁלוּחָה מִתַּחַת כָּל חֻפָּה.		Kaf eṣ ṣluḥá mitáḥat kol ḥupá.
אַךְ קַלֵּי־דָם נִקְשַׁב לְקוֹל מַתְרֶה.		Aḥ káley-dam nikṣáv lekól matré.
וְשָׁוְא הִזְהִיר הַקּוֹל. וְשָׁוְא נִבָּא.	4	Veṣáv hizhír hakól. Veṣáv nibá.
הַבֹּקֶר נְכָאָיו יַרְנִין הוֹזֶה,		Habóker neḥaáv yarnín hozé,
וְיוֹם צְמוּד־פֶּה אֶל חֵיק שִׁמְשׁוֹ נֶחְבָּא;		Veyóm tsmud-pé el ḥeyk ṣimṣó neḥbá;
רַק בְּרַק חֲצוֹת יִקְרַע אֶת כָּל מִכְסֶה;		Rak brak ḥatsót yikrá et kol miḥsé;
וְכַת רוּחוֹת נִנְעֶרֶת מֵאָרְבָּהּ.	8	Veḥát ruḥót nin'éret meorbá.
הוֹי, לֵב נִדְהָם, אַל נָא תָּשׁוּב תִּשְׁקַע		Hoy, lev nidhám, al na taṣúv tiṣká
בְּחֶזְיוֹנוֹת טִפְּחוּךְ: עֵת קַדֵּם		Beḥezyonót tipḥúḥa: et kadém
אֶת הַצְּלָלִים. וְאֵין לְהֵרָדֵם.	11	Et hatslalím. Veéyn leheradém.
וְאֶת הַתְּהוֹם חוֹנֵן. מֹד כָּל עָמְקָהּ.		Veét hathóm ḥonén. Mod kol omká.
מֹץ כָּל אֵימֶיהָ עַד לְשִׁכָּרוֹן —	13	Mots kol eyméha ad leṣikarón—
אוֹ אָז תִּפְתַּח אֶת פִּיהָ וְתָרֹן.		O az tiftáḥ et píḥa vetarón.

Jacob Fichman followed a pattern found so often in the biographies of Hebrew writers of the period that it seems to have been almost mandatory. Born (1881) in a small town in southern Russia and educated in a traditional one-room elementary school (*ḥéder*), he felt drawn to the broader cultural world, and at a young age ran away from home. Struggling to maintain himself, he moved from odd to odder jobs until finally he reached Odessa, where he joined the circle of Jewish writers. As a professional man of letters, he eked out a difficult existence, editing various publications while producing work of his own. For a short time (1913) he edited a journal in Palestine. Returning to Europe, he sat out World War I but went back to Palestine in 1925 and lived there till his death in 1958.

A lover of nature, which he came to know in his childhood, Fichman is a lyric poet in the traditional Romantic mold. Though he produced a large amount of creative and critical writing, his best work is found in his many short, controlled lyrics. "Midnight" is fairly typical, though this sonnet is more densely textured than most of his poems. Sounding a traditional Romantic note, it extols night as the time of revelation and of terrible truth.

(1) *The sign (signal) will be given and [the] awakened heart will see* (2) *A palm [hand] of*

flame extended under every canopy. (3) *But unheeding* [lit. *light-bloodedly*] *we listen to the warning voice.* (4) *And in vain the voice warned. In vain it prophesied.*

(5) *Morning dreamily sings its sorrows* [lit. *makes its sorrows sing*], (6) *And the day with pressing lips* [lit. *clinging mouth*] *hides in the bosom of its sun;* (7) *Only midnight's lightning tears every covering;* (8) *And a band of spirits shakes loose from its ambush.*

(9) *O heart confounded, do not sink again* (10) *Into the visions that nurtured (reared) you:* [*it is*] *time to greet (meet)* (12) *The shadows. And not to sleep.* (12) *And favor (choose) the abyss. Measure its entire depth.* (13) *Suck to intoxication all its terrors—* (14) [*Only*] *then will she* [*the abyss*] *open her mouth and sing.*

Like so many other writers of his generation, Fichman drew heavily on traditional phrases and images, and their associations lend color to his poem. The allusions are too numerous to be cited and some of them are mainly linguistic echoes. Line 4, for example, repeats the well-known "In vain did the seers prophesy" (Lamentations 2:14). Line 5 couples "morning" and "makes sing" from Psalms 65:9. The image in line 8, in which the spirits shake loose to move upon the poet, recalls the Cabalistic belief in a group of spirits that wait to pounce on the unwary as well as the folk-belief, also recorded in the Talmud, that spirits move abroad at midnight.

The "palm of flame" introduced in the second line reappears in the seventh as the "lightning of midnight." Similarly the "canopy" (2) anticipates the "covering" (7). And *neór* ("awakened," 1) reemerges in the form of *nin'éret* ("arises, shakes out from," 8), two derivations from the same root.

The sestet continues the tone of struggle as the speaker warns the heart against escape into sleep and urges it not to give way to the day's false dreaming (10). When terrifying shadows fall over the world, it is time to go out—to embrace the deep darkness, plumb its depths—to drink in all the terrors of the night until they intoxicate him, for only then will the abyss open its mouth and let *its* song be heard. Day deceives, truth belongs to the night. The poet becomes the instrument of the night rather than the singer of his own song.

To some readers the sonnet will call to mind a passage in the Babylonian Talmud: at midnight a north wind would begin to blow through King David's palace and touch the strings of the harp above his bed. David would awake to the sound of the harp and would compose his psalms till dawn.

The play of light and darkness, apparent in the second quatrain, occupies an important place in Fichman's poetry. To be sure he is drawn to write rapturously about the wash of sunlight on the countryside of the homeland; he extolls the beauty of its hot blue sky and burning sun as symbols of the ancient land reborn. But he displays the persistent Romantic yearning to wrap himself in the velvety softness of night. One has the feeling that his poems in praise of noon are an almost rationalized and expected reaction to the beauties of the new homeland whereas his poems extolling the night arise spontaneously—they are his "natural" songs.

— DAVID MIRSKY

Avraham Ben Yitshak

THE LONELY SAY · BODEDÍM OMRÍM · בּוֹדְדִים אוֹמְרִים

יוֹם לְיוֹם יַנְחִיל שֶׁמֶשׁ דּוֹעֶכֶת	Yom leyóm yanḥíl ṣémeṣ doéḥet
וְלַיְלָה עַל לַיְלָה יְקוֹנֵן	Veláyla al láyla yekonén
וְקַיִץ אַחַר קַיִץ יֵאָסֵף בַּשַּׁלֶּכֶת	Vekáyits aḥár káyits yeaséf baṣaléḥet
וְעוֹלָם מִצַּעֲרוֹ מִתְרוֹנֵן.	Veolám mitsaaró mitronén.
וּמָחָר נָמוּת וְאֵין הַדִּבֵּר בָּנוּ	Umaḥár namút veéyn hadibér bánu
וּכְיוֹם צֵאתֵנוּ נַעֲמֹד לִפְנֵי שַׁעַר עִם נְעִילָה	Uḥyóm tseténu naamód lifnéy ṣáar im neilá
וְלֵב כִּי יַעֲלֹז הֵן אֱלֹהִים קֵרְבָנוּ	Velév ki yaalóz hen elohím kervánu
וְהִתְנֶחָם — וְחָרַד מִפַּחַד הַמְּעִילָה.	Vehitneḥám — veḥarád mipáḥad hameilá.
יוֹם לְיוֹם יִשָּׂא שֶׁמֶשׁ בּוֹעֶרֶת	Yom leyóm yisá ṣémeṣ boéret
וְלַיְלָה אַחַר לַיְלָה יִשְׁפֹּךְ כּוֹכָבִים	Veláyla aḥár láyla yiṣpóḥ koḥavím
עַל שִׂפְתֵי בּוֹדְדִים שִׁירָה נֶעֱצֶרֶת:	Al siftéy bodedím ṣirá neetséret:
בְּשֶׁבַע דְּרָכִים נִתְפַּלֵּג וּבְאֶחָד אָנוּ שָׁבִים.	Beṣéva draḥím nitpalég uveeḥád ánu ṣavím.

A native of Galicia (Poland), Avraham Ben Yitshak (1883-1950) studied in Vienna and Berlin, residing for the most part in Vienna. He had made two trips to Palestine before taking up final residence there in his fifty-sixth year.

An extremely conscientious artist, Ben Yitshak wrote little and published less: only eleven poems appeared during his lifetime, nine of them before World War I (his entire literary output had been lost during that war). Readers and critics rediscovered him only after his death, when a few additional poems were published along with the now-famous eleven.

In its use of image and color, in its loose pattern and elliptical statement, his verse shows an affinity with Austrian and German Post-symbolism. But Ben Yitshak's tone is distinctly his own, combining a biblical vocabulary with individual freshness of figure and sound. Although most of his verse dates from a time when Sephardic (Israeli) pronunciation was not yet the rule, it would seem that he had already anticipated it.

(1) *Day to day bequeathes (leaves) a glimmering sun* (2) *And night laments for night* (3) *And summer after summer is gathered (up) in leaf fall* (4) *And the world sings from (rejoices in) its sorrow.*

The first two lines call to mind Psalm 19:2: "Day unto day uttereth speech, and night unto night showeth knowledge." The pattern continues with "and summer to summer," but where the Psalmist's is a joyous celebration ("The heavens declare the glory of God . . ."), Ben Yitshak's poem opens with a dirge. Line 4 makes a momentary shift in tone, with *mitronén* ("sings out"), but the dirge-like mood recovers as earth "sings from its sorrow" in the cycle from death to the return: the statements continue to be linked by "and" (prefixed *ve*) without a single "but" or "yet":

(5) *And tomorrow we shall die speechless (not*

having utterance within us) (6) *And upon the day of our leaving [the earth] we shall stand before the gate at closing time* (7) *And when the heart rejoices [that] indeed God has brought us close [to Him]* — (8) *It will then repent [from joy] and will tremble in fear of treachery (betrayal).*

Encompassed by the cosmic cycle, the speaker and his silent fellows know that they await finality. In line 6, *uḥyóm tseténu*, which usually denotes "as upon the day of going forth," is generalized: "now, upon leaving this world." Such a reading is confirmed by "before the gate at closing time," which echoes a famous prayer that concludes the Day of Atonement service—"Open to us the gate at the time of the closing of the gates, for the day has turned"—which Ben Yitshak considered one of the finest lyrical poems in Hebrew. But note how the hopefulness of the prayer is converted into the speaker's consciousness of approaching finality (8). Even if he should rejoice for an instant, he might soon regret it: "trembling" (*ḥarád*) combines "anxiety" and "trembling," arising out of the tragic human flaw that might reject the consolation of a friendly, welcoming God.

A sudden modulation into the major key occurs with the last stanza: (9) *Day to day bears a burning sun* (10) *And night after night pours out stars;* (11) *Upon the lips of the lonely (the few), song comes to a halt:* (12) *Into seven paths we divide (part), and by one we return.*

The darkling image of the first stanza has now become a vision of splendor. The sun, which barely glimmered in line 1, is now aflame with light, and the darkness that was filled with lamentation has grown abundant with stars. But it is not because he is departing from the world that the speaker becomes aware of its beauty. It is because he suddenly perceives the inexorable truth of the human condition: he is now entering into a realm of silence from which there can be no return. And so his song of rejoicing at God's having brought him close to Himself (7) now halts upon his lips (11). The line recalls verse 3 of the same Psalm, which speaks of the silent praise of the heavens: "their voice is not heard." The silent praise of the lonely speaker of the poem expresses his ultimate recognition that man sets out, from birth, in many different directions but returns by one (12).

The key word is *eḥád* ("one"), which is stressed by being flanked by two pauses. In contrast to the usual memento-mori motif, here the "one" way is not the way to the tomb's emptiness; rather it conveys a "way" of hopefulness, for it is the end of loneliness and of dispersion upon the "seven paths" ("seven" in biblical Hebrew suggests "many"). "One" (*eḥád*) is also emphasized by its interesting grammatical use here. Hebrew numerals agree in gender with the nouns they designate, and *déreḥ* ("way, path") is one of the very few nouns that may be used as either masculine or feminine. At first, line 12 qualifies "ways" by the feminine *ṣéva* ("seven, many"), as would be expected; but then, surprisingly, the line retains the masculine form for "one" (*eḥád*). This divergence in gender serves to oppose the "one" way to the "many" ways. Ben Yitshak is probably alluding here to the familiar invocation *ṣmá Yisraél* ("Hear, O Israel!") in which God is also designated by the masculine *eḥád*. In English the word should perhaps be capitalized: "Into seven paths we divide, and by One we return."

The reader familiar with the Hebrew of Psalm 19 cannot fail to hear in the 10th line of our poem an added overtone. "Day unto day uttereth speech, and night unto night showeth knowledge"—the second line of the Psalm is reshaped by Ben Yitshak with images of heavenly bodies; but the verb *ṣafáḥ* not only means "to pour out" but is also used in the idiom *ṣafáḥ siaḥ* or *ṣafáḥ tfilá* "to pour out prayer," perhaps suggesting (with *yiṣpóḥ*) that the night "prays forth stars."

If the deceptively simple poem reveals a wealth of meaning, it would seem to rise from the poet's insistence upon silence as the only possible means of self-expression.

— DAN PAGIS

Avraham Ben Yitshak

HAPPY ARE THEY WHO SOW · AṢRÉY HAZOR'ÍM · אַשְׁרֵי הַזּוֹרְעִים

אַשְׁרֵי הַזּוֹרְעִים וְלֹא יִקְצֹרוּ
כִּי יַרְחִיקוּ נְדוֹד.

אַשְׁרֵי הַנְּדִיבִים אֲשֶׁר תִּפְאֶרֶת נְעוּרֵיהֶם
הוֹסִיפָה עַל אוֹר הַיָּמִים וּפִזְרוֹנָם
וְהֵם אֶת עֶדְיָם הִתְפָּרְקוּ עַל אֵם הַדְּרָכִים.

אַשְׁרֵי הַגֵּאִים אֲשֶׁר גַּאֲוָתָם עָבְרָה גְּבוּלֵי נַפְשָׁם
וַתְּהִי כְּעַנְוַת הַלֹּבֶן
אַחֲרֵי הֵעָלוֹת הַקֶּשֶׁת בֶּעָנָן.

אַשְׁרֵי הַיּוֹדְעִים אֲשֶׁר יִקְרָא לִבָּם מִמִּדְבָּר
וְעַל שְׂפָתָם תִּפְרַח הַדּוּמִיָּה.

אַשְׁרֵיהֶם כִּי יֵאָסְפוּ אֶל תּוֹךְ לֵב הָעוֹלָם
לוּטֵי אַדֶּרֶת הַשִּׁכְחָה
וְהָיָה חֻקָּם הַתָּמִיד בְּלִי אֹמֶר.

Aṣréy hazor'ím veló yiktsóru
Ki yarḥíku nedód.

Aṣréy handivím aṣér tif'éret neuréyhem
Hosífa al or hayamím ufizronám
Vehém et edyám hitparáku al em hadraḥím.

Aṣréy hageím aṣér gaavatám avrá
Vatehí keanvát halóven [gvuléy nafṣám
Aḥaréy healót hakéṣet beanán.

Asréy hayod'ím aṣér yikrá libám mimidbár
Veál sfatám tifráḥ hadumiyá.

Aṣreyhém ki yeasfú el toḥ lev haolám
Lutéy adéret haṣiḥeḥá
Vehayá ḥukám hatamíd bli ómer.

This poem, completed in 1928, was the last one published by Ben Yitshak. It appeared after a twelve-year silence and twenty years before his death. The poet would seem to have considered it his farewell to his art.

The "lonely" souls of our preceding selection are now the "generous" and the "proud," who act but never think of being rewarded; their reward is in their acts, in their very existence. Serene and silent, humble but proudly so, they withdraw from the world unheard and unremembered—like the thirty-six legendary saints of Jewish lore who remain forever unrecognized.

In the earlier (1925) manuscript drafts of this poem, Ben Yitshak tended to attribute to these generous and proud souls some possibility of utterance and of reconciliation with the world—"their speech shall not be bitter . . . and the memory of days is their banner." One of the drafts is even entitled "In Memoriam." But with his final version, as printed above, the poet rejected all such compromise:

(1) *Happy (blessed) are they who sow and shall not reap* (2) *For they shall wander afar.*

(3) *Happy are the generous, the glory of whose youth* (4) *Has added to the light and extravagance of the days,* (5) *And they [the generous ones] shed their ornaments at the crossroads.*

(6) *Happy are the proud whose pride overflowed [surpassed] the banks (limits) of their souls* (7) *And became like the humility of whiteness* (8) *After the rainbow rises in the cloud.*

(9) *Happy are they who know that their hearts cry out from the wilderness* (10) *And on their lips silence blossoms.*

(11) *Happy are they, for they shall be gathered into the heart of the world* (12) *Wrapped in the mantle of oblivion* (13) *And their everlasting lot shall be silence [without utterance].*

As in "The Lonely Say," the opening line is an evocation of biblical passages: "They who sow in tears shall reap in joy" (Psalms 126:5), and "Blessed are ye that sow beside all waters" (Isaiah 32:20). But the poem reverses the biblical meaning and builds itself upon a series of paradoxes:—the sowers' joy issues from the fact that they shall *not* reap, and their glory and beauty (also reversing traditional passages) reside in their total renunciation of their ornaments. Their pride is humility. The cry of their heart blossoms into silence. And, finally, their blessing lies in attaining to oblivion. Line 11—they will be "gathered into the heart of the world"—echoes a Hebrew idiom for death: "gathered unto his fathers." But in the context of the poem, the "heart" of the world may suggest transcendental love.

The conclusion is especially rich in connotations. The word *ḥukám* (13) means "their law" (which they impose upon themselves) as well as "their lot, portion," in which latter connection it carries a slight overtone of "fate." The adjectival *hatamíd* qualifies this "lot" or "portion" without losing its character as a substantive. Thus *hatamíd* is literally "the eternal," "the constant," suggesting an aura of holiness and being translatable as "eternity, constancy, continuity." However, the daily (and continual) offering and sacrifice is sometimes referred to simply as *tamíd.* If *tamíd* is read as a noun, the meaning would be: "their lot shall be a constant sacrifice accompanied by speechlessness." Clearly the poet had this in mind, for in one of the manuscript drafts of the poem, the word appears as a richly connotative noun: "for theirs is the *Tamíd.*"

Unlike some of the works of the so-called Decadence, with which Ben Yitshak was intimately acquainted—von Hofmannsthal's "Letter from Lord Chandos," for example—the present poem's renunciation of expression does not imply any despair over language or the fate of poetry. "Happy Are They Who Sow," on the contrary, affirms the poet's conviction and confidence in silence as the only mode of true self-expression. It brings us rather toward the reaches of Mallarmé with their celebration of "silence" and of the purity of the page's whiteness unsoiled by words.

The last words of the poem *bli ómer* ("without speech, without words") recall the silent praise of the heavens in Psalm 19. If in the preceding poem this was largely a connotation, here it may be taken as a firm resolution to *adhere* to silence.

In this farewell poem, Ben Yitshak renounced rime and regular stanza patterns. Four of the five stanzas begin with *aṣréy* ("happy, blessed are they who"); and the last, opening with a variation of the phrase (*aṣreyhém*), conveys a tone of finality and summation. Indeed, the last stanza gathers up the earlier images of proud humility to give expression to their essential quality: the bliss of oblivion and of silence.

— DAN PAGIS

Jacob Steinberg

NOT AN ENCLOSED GARDEN · LO GAN NÁUL* · לֹא גַן נָעוּל

לֹא גַן נָעוּל הָעוֹלָם; בְּיוֹם צַר לְעֵת שֵׂיבָה
שֶׁבַע שְׂמָחוֹת יָצֵרוּ אֶת תּוּגָתְךָ הַשְּׁלֵוָה.

שֶׁפִי תִּצְעַד הַזִּקְנָה; גַּם בִּנְאוֹת הַמַּזְקִינִים
שׂוֹרֵץ שֶׁפֶק אַכְזָרִי עִם עַקְרַבֵּי הַמִּינִים.

דּוּמָם תֵּשֵׁב וּתְהַרְהֵר: שָׁבְתָה דַּרְכֵּי הַסְּלוּלָה —
וּמֵעֵבֶר לָהּ יַעַל הֲמוֹן־עָם בַּהֲמֻלָּה.

בֹּקֶר תָּקִיץ וְתָחוּד: תְּקוּפָה אַחַת נִגְלָה —
וּבְנֵי־עָשׁ בְּשׁוּלֶיהָ כְּבָר נִנְעָרִים שְׁאוֹלָה.

אַךְ בִּשְׁקֹט עֶרֶב בָּהִיר רַנִּים יַחַד מַזָּלוֹת,
וּבֵין מַזָּל לְמַזָּל רַק כִּגְבוּל הַנִּמְשָׁלוֹת.

אָז אֵין נִבְדָּל וָשָׁב; וַאֲשֶׁר נִשְׁפַּט לָרָקָב —
רוֹאֶה קֶבֶר וּמַחֲרִישׁ וּמִתְאַפֵּק אֶל שְׁחָקָיו.

Lo gan nául haólam; beyóm tsar leét séyva
Ṣéva smáḥot yatséru et tugátḥa haṣléyva.

Ṣéfi títs'ad hazíkna; gam bin'ót hamazkínim
Ṣórets séfek aḥzári im akrábey hamínim.

Dúmam téyṣev uthárher: ṣávta dárki haslúla—
Umeéyver la yáal hamón-am bahamúla.

Bóker tákits vetáḥud: tkúfa áḥat nagóla—
Uvnéy-aṣ beṣuléha kvar nin'árim ṣeóla.

Aḥ biṣkót érev báhir ránim yáḥad mazálot,
Uvéyn mázal lemázal rak kigvúl hanimṣálot.

Az eyn nívdal vaṣáv; vaaṣér níṣpat larákav—
Róe kéver umáḥariṣ umit'ápek el ṣḥákav.

Jacob Steinberg, born 1887 in the Ukraine, was a youthful member of Bialik's circle in Odessa. Prior to World War I, he moved to Warsaw, where he wrote for Hebrew and Yiddish journals. Coming to Palestine in 1915, he remained there a few years, then rejoined Bialik in Berlin in 1922. He returned to Palestine two years later and died there in 1947.

As early as 1907, Bialik acclaimed him as one of the heralds of the new trend in Hebrew verse, with its individual lyricism as opposed to national and social rhetoric. Steinberg's poetry reveals a strongly individual and reflective quality, holding in balance a rational drive to define reality with an insistent belief that the enigma of being cannot be adequately expressed. Abstract concepts —truth, pride, future, regret-and-consolation —are often personified by his verse but not in purely allegorical terms.

Although Russian and French Symbolism left their mark on him, the changing character of Hebrew poetry failed to affect the work of his last twenty years. He clung to the Ashkenazi Hebrew; his rime scheme remained simple and traditional; his prosody regular, symmetrical. At the same time, however, his syntax grew more and more involved. The work of his last period, from which our selections are taken, is especially compact.

Our first poem opens as if to refute an accepted opinion: for those approaching death the world is not the "enclosed garden" (Song of Songs 4:12). (1) *The world is not an enclosed (locked) garden; on a narrow (sorrowful, hostile) day at the time of aging* (2) *Seven (many) joys will lay siege to (harass) your serene grief.*

(3) *Old age would [*lit. *will] walk calmly; [but] even in the oases of the aging* (4) *Cruel doubt and scorpions of heresy [*lit. *heretics].*

(5) *Silently you will sit and think: my paved road has stopped [is deserted]*— (6) *And beyond it crowds of people rise noisily.*

(7) *In the morning you will awake and speak riddles (poesy): One era has been rolled up* (8) *And the young moths on its margins are already being shaken into the netherworld.*

(9) *But when a clear evening quiets (down), the constellations (fates, destinies) sing together.* (10) *Between constellation and constellation there is only a boundary [separation] like that between things likened.*

(11) *Then no one is separated and returns [from his destined course]: and whoever has been condemned (judged) to decay*— (12) *Sees the grave, and is silent and restrains himself facing [*lit. *toward] his heavens.*

In days of sorrow and trouble, old age seems to find some consolation in a quiet sadness, but this sadness is intruded upon by many unspecified delights. The assault comes not only from without but also from within: the constant danger of doubt and of heresy. The word *gam* ("even," "also," 3) seems to imply that they were natural accompaniments of youth. An earlier draft of the poem reads *náḥaṣey haséfek* ("snakes of doubt") paralleling the image at the conclusion of line 4: the doubts, the heresies, swarm like snakes or scorpions.

Stanza 3 returns to the aging speaker who now comments on what he *thinks:* "My paved road is at rest," the last word (*ṣávta*) also meaning "abandoned". It is a picture of stark loneliness, far from the noise of the vital, active crowds (*hámon*, 6, means both "clamor" and "crowd").

The opening of the next stanza parallels line 5, and at once we get to a key concept. *Táḥud* means "you speak riddles"; in biblical Hebrew, *ḥidá* (derived from the same root as *taḥúd*) sometimes conveys "parable" or "fable" or "poetry in general." In Steinberg's work, this word *ḥída* carries all these meanings, for poetic utterance, an enigma in itself, strives to illuminate the enigma of reality (in some of his poems *ḥída* is even personified). Line 7, then, asserts that in the morning, old age wakes and asks the riddle, and it imagines that an era has been rolled up like a scroll and that the moths eating away its margins are already scattering into oblivion. So, at least, old age thinks.

With line 9, the poem abandons its earthbound images—scorpions, crowds, moths—to turn upward, to the sky. *Mázal* means not only "planet" but "fate" and "luck" as well. The pessimism and loneliness now dissolve into growing unity—the heavenly bodies begin to sing together as when "the morning stars sang together" in the famous passage in Job (38:7). But the next line (10) introduces a simile that is difficult to interpret.

Here, at the axis of the poem, we find the word *nimṣálot*, an adjective used as a noun, which usually denotes things which are likened or compared for qualities they hold in common. It comes from the biblical *maṣál*, meaning "parable" and sometimes "poetry in general"—a recurring word in Steinberg's verse, which cannot be given only one interpretation. Calling himself, elsewhere, the "teller of fables from Judah" (*memáṣel hamṣálim mihúda*), he identifies his poetic method as self-expression through parable. And he now asserts (10) that distinctions between things kindred enough to be "likened" to one another blur when a man attains a synoptic view of the universe. Indeed, they almost disappear, for, as the last stanza declares, when life is seen in such terms, "no one is isolated" from existence as a whole or can lift himself out of his fated course (11). Aging and death are divided by only a thin boundary from living itself. The boundaries are inessential. The overall unity of "likened things" becomes the more cogent consideration. Hence they who will soon die are silent about the coming of death. The elliptical language of the last line suggests that the speaker "restrains himself toward his heavens" because all reason for complaint has dissolved in his feeling of *virtual* unity.

The closed couplets throughout accord with the restrained atmosphere and with the pervasive tone of finality. Anapestic tetrameters appear throughout, with two added unstressed syllables in each line: one at the end, the other after the first two feet. The resulting cesura in each line creates a conspicuous division which is sustained by the syntactical structure of the poem.

— DAN PAGIS

Jacob Steinberg

CONFESSION · VÍDUY* · וִדּוּי

וְעוֹד מְעַט וּמוֹתַר חַיַּי יִתַּם
בְּמַעֲשֵׂי חֵן, הַקְּטַנִּים וְהַיְקָרִים;
3 וּכְזָקֵן שָׂשׂ אֶל רִיק — אֶת עֵינַי אָרִים
לַגָּדוֹל וְלָרָם, שֶׁאֵחֲרָה עִתָּם.

וְחֵרוּת זוּ נִבְחָרָה, אוֹר הָרוּחַ,
בָּהּ נִגְלָה לִי בְּעוֹד־עֵת כָּל רִיק לִי אָרַב,
7 בָּהּ רָחַב לִי הָעוֹלָם גַּם בִּמְצָרָיו, —
הִיא תְּהִי לְאַט לְאוֹר עָצְבִּי הַזָּרוּחַ.

וּכְאִישׁ לֹא יִבְחַר שָׁוְא — אָז אֶבְחַר שֶׁבֶת
וּרְאוֹת בִּידֵי אַלְמוֹנִים כָּל יְקָרָם;
11 וְחֵן לִי זָר, הַזְּמַן עַל אֵלֶּה קָרַם,
אֶרְאֶנּוּ שַׂי לִתְקוּפָה מִתְקָרֶבֶת.

Veód meát umótar ḥáyay yítam
Bemáasey ḥen, haktánim vehaykárim;
3 Uḥzáken sas el rik—et éynay árim
Lagádol velarám, ṣeéyḥara ítam.

Veḥéyrut zu nivḥára, or harúaḥ,
Ba nígla li beod-ét kol rik li árav,
7 Ba ráḥav li haólam gam bimtsárav,—
Hi tehí leát leór ótsbi hazarúaḥ.

Uḥeíṣ lo yívḥar ṣav—az évḥar ṣévet
Ur'ót bidéy almónim kol yekáram;
11 Veḥén li zar, hazmán al éyle káram,
Er'énu ṣay litkúfa mitkarévet.

Like the preceding poem by Steinberg, "Confession" is built on a series of contrasts and veiled paradoxes. Within the deceiving sonal simplicity of the three rimed quatrains (*abba*) lies a complex elusiveness. This is a poem of old age—and a confession of altered preferences.

In the opening line, the word *mótar*, literally "remainder," inescapably summons its meaning in Ecclesiastes 3 : 19, "so that a man hath no preeminence [*motár*] above a beast." The ironical implication here is that the speaker's remaining years will be anything but "preeminent."

(1) *And soon the remainder of my life will end* (2) *In charming (beautiful) deeds, small and dear (precious).* (3) *And like an old man hastening toward futility (vainly rejoicing)—I shall raise*

my eyes (4) *Toward the great and the exalted [things] whose time* [for him] *has passed [*lit. *is late].*

The speaker, now conscious of how little time remains in his life, implies his preference for the little gracious deeds over those of heroic dimensions. He raises his eyes to grand and exalted things, not in awe, but with cruelly honest awareness that for him they have lost their relevance and value. This knowledge has liberated him:

(5) *And this chosen freedom—the light of the spirit—* (6) *Within which every vanity that lay in wait for me was uncovered (revealed) to me in time,* (7) *Within which the world even in its straits widened for me—* (8) *It* [this chosen freedom] *will slowly become the light of my shining sadness.*

Stanza two elaborates the central paradox of the opening stanza as the word *rik* (3)—"vanity," "nothingness"—recurs in line 6. The Small and Unexalted had broadened and augmented his existence, and, in the moments of his distress, sustained him. They shall now become "the light of his shining sadness" or, if one prefers, "the glowing light of his sadness" (8). "Shining light" (*or zarúaḥ*) carries an obvious overtone of "Light is sown [*or zarúa*] for the righteous" (Psalms 97:11). His "chosen freedom" enables the speaker to attain complete detachment.

(9) *And like a man who does not choose worthlessness—I shall then choose to sit* (10) *And see others possessing all things precious to them [*lit. *view in the hands of nameless ones all their preciousness];* (11) *And [this] charm (beauty)—foreign to me—with which time has encrusted them* [nameless men] (12) *I shall view as a gift to an approaching era.*

Note the difference in lines 6 and 11: the speaker's recognition of emptiness is not shared by the "nameless others" of the new generation. He views what these men hold dear as a "gift" to the era to come. Will it also, in time, prove to be a will-o'-the-wisp? Or does the poem suggest that this gift, after its surface covering will have been shed, may usher in for men of the future the same light of the spirit (5) that has endowed him with freedom? Such freedom, detached and sure, is also proud: "I prefer to sit and see..." (9-10).

The poem is remarkable for the often baffling nature of its many abstractions and the differing value judgments sometimes but not always attached to them as the poem develops (for example: *ḥen* "charm, beauty," 2, 11). The rich textural play appears in the many alliterations—for example: *árav* (6), *ráḥav* and *bimtsárav* (7), *ṣav* (9)—and in the manipulation of idiomatic change. It is perhaps most evident in its insistence upon sonal repetition (for example, *uḥeiṣ lo yívḥar ṣav—az évḥar ṣévet,* line 9).

The preoccupation with time (notably in lines 4, 6, 11) brings to mind the wisdom literature of the Bible. Much of the vocabulary echoes Ecclesiastes, which is generally regarded as a meditation of old age. But for all such apparent similarities and concern with vanity, "Confession" moves in a quite different world. Its feeling tone is as complex as the modes of its poetic idiom, which often resists paraphrase. — DAN PAGIS

· · II · ·

Uri Zvi Greenberg

WITH MY GOD THE BLACKSMITH · IM ÉYLI HANÁPAḤ* · עִם אֵלִי הַנַּפָּח

כְּפִרְקֵי נְבוּאָה בּוֹעֲרִים יְמוֹתַי בְּכָל הַגִּלּוּיִים
וְגוּפִי בֵּינֵיהֶם כְּגוּשׁ הַמַּתֶּכֶת לְהִתּוּךְ.
וְעָלַי עוֹמֵד אֵלִי הַנַּפָּח וּמַכֶּה בִּגְבוּרָה:
כָּל פֶּצַע, שֶׁחָתַךְ הַזְּמָן בִּי, פּוֹתֵחַ לוֹ חִתּוּךְ
וּפוֹלֵט בִּגְצֵי רְגָעִים הָאֵשׁ הָעֲצוּרָה.

זֶהוּ גּוֹרָלִי־מִשְׁפָּטִי עַד עֶרֶב בַּדָּרֶךְ.
וּבְשׁוּבִי לְהָטִיל אֶת גּוּשִׁי הַמֻּכֶּה עַל עֶרֶשׂ,
פִּי — פֶּצַע פָּתוּחַ.
וְעֵירוֹם אֲדַבֵּר עִם אֵלִי: עָבַדְתָּ בְּפָרֶךְ.
עַתָּה בָּא לַיְלָה; תֵּן — שְׁנֵינוּ נָנוּחַ.

Kefírkey nevúa bóarim yemótay
[beḥól hagilúyim
2 Vegúfi veynéyhem kegúṣ hamatéḥet lehítuḥ.
Vealáy ómed éyli hanápaḥ umáke bigvúra:
4 Kol pétsa, ṣeḥátaḥ hazmán bi, potéaḥ lo ḥítuḥ
Ufólet begítsey regáim haéṣ haatsúra.

Zéhu goráli-miṣpáti ad érev badáreḥ.
7 Uvṣúvi lehátil et gúṣi hamúke al éres,
Pi—pétsa patúaḥ.
9 *Veéyrom* adáber im éyli: avádta befáreḥ.
Áta ba láyla; ten—ṣnéynu nanúaḥ.

Born in 1895 in Galicia, Uri Zvi Greenberg began his literary career with a volume of Yiddish verse published in 1915. After serving in the Austro-Hungarian army during World War I, he joined the Zionist pioneers in Palestine. His earliest book of Hebrew poetry (*Anacreon at the Pole of Melancholy*, 1928) is strongly marked by the influence of German Expressionism, but at the same time foreshadows his subsequent work in its total identification of personal experience with an impersonal Jewish-Messianic destiny.

In his poetic manifesto *Against the Ninety-Nine* (published in the same year) he violently attacks the "99 citizen-writers" who are trying to produce in Hebrew a literature nourished by cosmopolitan, "extra-territorial" influences rather than by their real life as individuals within the unique revival of Hebrew nationhood. These "melancholy esthetes, sneezing at the scent of lilacs in the twilight," long for the "idyllic ride upon camels under the beautiful, melancholy sky, behind fast trains . . ." He calls for a volcanic "Literature of Destinies" as opposed to the "Literature of Talents," for a poetry that will embody in the idiom of the tribe a "Jewish answer from the blood," a prophetic cry springing from the "dynamic principle of Israel." All his subsequent work has been in the very deepest sense political, a *cri de cœur* springing from national tribulations and victories.

During the 1936 riots of the Arabs against the settlers, for example, Greenberg published *The Book of Denunciation and of Faith*, calling for revenge and denouncing the complacency of his generation in failing to see the eternal enmity borne by "the cross and the crescent" against the messianic destiny of the Jews. During Israel's struggle for independence, Greenberg was involved in the underground activities of the Irgun, and in 1949 he was elected to Parliament. His poetic production has since 1928 been consistently extremist in content and tone, drawing on the tradition of biblical prophecy.

(1) *Like chapters of prophecy, my days burn*

in all the revelations, (2) *My body among them like a lump of metal to be forged.* (3) *And over me stands my God the blacksmith and hammers with might:* (4) *Each wound [which] time has cut in me opens like a crack for Him* (5) *And emits in sparks of moments the pent-up fire.*

(6) *This is my destiny-sentence till evening [come] upon the road.* (7) *And when I return to throw my beaten lump on the bed,* (8) *My mouth is a gaping wound.* (9) *And* NAKED *I speak to my God: "Yours has been hard labor.* (10) *Now night has fallen; come—let us both rest."*

Readers who find this poem reminiscent of "Holy Sonnet XIV," in which John Donne asks his God the artisan to "breake, blowe, burn and make [him] new," may rest assured that Uri Zvi Greenberg was not familiar with Donne when this poem appeared in 1928. The similarities, however, are not superficial. As in Donne's sonnet, the deity is presented as entirely human; the implied relationship with Him is extremely intimate; the imagery far-fetched; the diction alive and direct; the tone ranging from the rhetorical to the personal. Greenberg's sources are exclusively biblical here. The prophetic chapters referred to in the first line, for example, are, among others: "Is not my Word like as fire? saith the Lord; and like a hammer that breaketh rock in pieces?" (Jeremiah 23:29). But the Bible is used only as background, for the dominant note of the poem points to a personal experience and an acquaintance with God which are unbiblical, culminating in the ironic friendliness of the conclusion—"come, let us both rest!" By contrast, the stern biblical echoes serve to sharpen the irony.

The metaphors of the first stanza are richly mixed. The "fire" of the poet's days, which is his prophetic destiny, burns both miraculously and painfully while the divine blacksmith hammers at the red-hot bar of metal which is the speaker's body. (The root idea appears in Ezekiel 22:20: "As they gather silver, and brass, and iron, and lead, and tin, into the midst of the furnace, to blow the fire upon it, to melt it; so will I . . . melt you.") In lines 4-5, Time is both within and without: it cuts open wounds out of which "sparks of minutes" are emitted from "pent-up fire." The last phrase (*haéṣ haatsúra*) is also a biblical echo ("His word was in mine heart as a burning fire shut up in my bones," Jeremiah 20:9).

This identification of violent prophetic destiny with violent ravages of time carries the primary sense of the stanza. In the visible effects of time upon his body, the speaker sees his fate, the fact of his election, and his kinship with the prophets. This is expressed in imagery of great precision. As anyone knows who has seen a blacksmith at work, the hammered red-hot iron seems to receive new bloody wounds with each blow, and the sparks come out of these wounds.

Stanza 2 opens in a matter-of-fact way. The heat, pain, and violence are accepted as inevitable, a "destiny-sentence," a way of life. When evening comes, the speaker lays his "beaten lump" on the bed and sees himself rather grotesquely, his open mouth a gaping wound. It is a wound because it is red and also an opening of his body. This image has a tie to Greenberg's view of specifically Jewish destiny. In his poetic manifesto noted above, he wrote: "Our body is very wild. It is a wandering body of symbols. And is our nerve-system in any way like that of the Gentiles? The Hebrew mouth is more like a wound; behind the Hebrew forehead an eagle screams."

The conclusion of the poem gains its effect from the deliberately stressed *éyrom* ("naked") and the short phrases addressed to the blacksmith. Lines 9-10 bring the speaker and his God into complete sympathy. God has been working hard, making the poet suffer; the poet has been suffering the violence of time and destiny because God has chosen him: now they both deserve respite. The state of *éyrom* in which the poet now speaks expresses this intimacy and also his human defenselessness. The word harks back to I

Samuel 19: 23-4, where Saul found David in the company of the prophets: "the spirit of God was upon him also . . . And he stripped off his clothes also, and prophesied before Samuel in like manner, and lay down naked all that day and all that night."

"With My God the Blacksmith" is one of the few Hebrew poems of the twenties to have withstood the great changes that have occurred in literary taste and in the language itself. It reads as if it had been written yesterday. To realize its full sonal value, however, the reader should make the Ashkenazi stresses as indicated by the acute accents in our transliteration. The rime scheme is appropriately irregular: *abcbc defdf.* The formal meter, a traditional amphibrach (∪ — ∪) with slight variations, merely gives shape to what is strikingly rare in the Hebrew poetry of its period: out of the printed page a living voice, dramatically modulated, speaks. — ARIEH SACHS

Uri Zvi Greenberg

ON A NIGHT OF RAIN IN JERUSALEM · BELÉYL GÉṢEM BIRUṢALÁYIM

בְּלֵיל גֶּשֶׁם בִּירוּשָׁלַיִם

This poem was published in 1954. As in all of Greenberg's work, "Jerusalem" implies divinely appointed national destiny.

(1) *The few trees in the yard moan like forest trees,* (2) *Heavy-rivered [are] the thundered clouds,* (3) *The angels of peace [are] at the head of my children's bed,* (4) *In the moaning of the trees and the thickness of the rain.*

(5) *Outside—Jerusalem: city of the father's glorious trial,* (6) *The binding of his son upon one of the mountains,* (7) *The fire-from-dawn still burns on the mountain,* (8) *The rains have not put it out: fire between the* [ritual] *pieces.*

(9) *"If God commands me now as He commanded* (10) *My ancient father—I shall surely obey,"* (11) *My heart and my flesh sing on this night of rain;* (12) *And the angels of peace [are] at the head of my children's bed!*

(13) *What of glory? What is like unto this miraculous feeling* (14) *Alive ever since the ancient dawn until now [and] toward the mountain of myrrh [Moriah]?* (15) *The blood of the Covenant in [this] father's prayer-full body sings,* (16) *Ready to make the sacrifice on the Hill of the Temple at dawn.*

(17) *Outside—Jerusalem . . . and the moaning of God's trees* (18) *Cut down there by enemies in all generations . . .* (19) *Heavy-rivered clouds: within them lightnings* (20) *And thunderings, that to me on a night of rain [are] tidings* (21) *From the Mouth of The Might until the end of generations.*

That this rainy night is charged with manifestations of Providence is made clear in line 4. *Haṣrát gṣamím* ("thicknesses [or] dark densenesses of rains") harks back to David's song of thanks for deliverance: "And he made dark pavilions round about him, dark waters [*haṣrát máyim*] and thick clouds of the skies . . ." (2 Samuel 22:12). The "moaning forest" in the storm, the violent "rivers" of rain, are the divine messengers of the life that is connected with the "few trees" in the yard and with the day-to-day continuity of the speaker's family life. Line 3 establishes the theme, for it is as a loving father, awake in the stormy night while his children lie safe in sleep, that he experiences a revelation of his essential relation to God.

Stanza 2 derives its force from the rich texture of biblical allusions. "One of the

עצי מעט בחצר הומים כעצי יער,	Atséy meát beḥatsér homím kaatséy yáar,
כבדי נהרות עננים מרעמים,	Kivdéy neharót ananím mor'amím,
מלאכי השלום למראשות ילדי	Mal'aḥéy haṣalóm limraaṣót yeladáy
בהמית העצים וחשרת הגשמים.	Behemyát haetsím veḥaṣrát hagṣamím.
בחוץ — ירושלים: עיר מסת הוד האב	Baḥúts—yeruṣaláyim: ir masát hod haáv
ועקדת בנו באחד ההרים:	Vaakeydát bnó beaḥád heharím:
האש־משחרית עוד דולקת בהר	Haéṣ-miṣaharít od doléket bahár
הגשמים לא כבוה: אש בין הבתרים.	Hagṣamím lo ḥibúha: eṣ beyn habtarím.
'אם אל יצוני כעת כשצוה	'Im el yetsavéni ḥaét keṣetsivá
לאבי הקדמון — אציית בודאי',	Leaví hakadmón—atsayét bevadáy'
רן לבי ובשרי בליל הגשם הזה	Ran libí uvsarí beléyl hagéṣem hazé
ומלאכי השלום למראשותי ילדי!	Umal'aḥéy haṣalóm limraaṣotéy yeladáy!
מה מהוד מה משל לזה רגש פלאי	Ma mehód ma maṣál lezé régeṣ pil'í
חי מקדם שחרית עד כעת אל הר מור:	Ḥay mikédem ṣaḥarít ad kaét el har mor:
מתרונן דם הברית בגוף אב תפלי	Mitronén dam habrít begúf av tfilí
נכון לקרבן הר הבית עם אור!	Naḥón lekorbán har habáyit im or!
בחוץ — ירושלים .. והמית עצי יה	Baḥúts—yeruṣaláyim . . vehemyát atséy ya
שכרתום האויבים בה מכל הדורות..	Ṣekratúm haoyvím ba mikól hadorót . .
עננים כבדי נהרות: בם ברקים	Ananím kivdéy neharót: bam brakím
ורעמים, שהם לי בליל גשם — בשורות	Ureamím, ṣehém li beléyl géṣem—bsorót
מפי הגבורה עד סוף הדורות.	Mipí hagvurá ad sof hadorót.

mountains" (6) comes from the account in Genesis 22 of God's challenge and Abraham's unquestioning obedience in offering Isaac. But "one of the hills" is at the same time Jerusalem, a city built upon and surrounded by hills. Thus the "glorious trial" (5) of Abraham becomes the archetype of the rainy Jerusalem night that is the poem's actual setting.

Throughout Greenberg's poetry, fire is a central symbol for divine Jewish destiny (cf. "With My God the Blacksmith," p. 60) and in this poem the "fire-from-dawn" (7) has especially rich resonances. It appears in the passage from Genesis noted above ("he took the fire in his hand," etc.); at the same time, it recalls the miraculous fire in Abraham's earlier vision of God when the Covenant was first renewed ("And it came to pass, that, when the sun went down, and it was dark, behold . . . a burning lamp [*lapíd eṣ*, "a torch of fire"] passed between those pieces" (Genesis 15:17). The "fire-from-dawn," then, is both the fire that now appears in the poet's raging vision and the fire which Abraham at the dawn of the race saw: *beyn habtarím* ("between the pieces") of the animals and birds he had sacrificed to God on the fateful night of the Covenant. But *btarím* has still another touch here. Line 8 echoes the Song of Songs' "many waters cannot extinguish love," which is strengthened by the further allusion to *hárey váter*—the "cleft mountains," also from the Song of Songs (2:17).

If the speaker is Abraham, his children, guarded by the angels of peace, are like Isaac, the seed of future glory. And so the rainstorm becomes the occasion for a renewed Covenant, in which the speaker realizes that his own faith is no smaller than that of his primordial father's. Like Abraham, he can say "I shall surely obey." His entire being, his "heart and his flesh," rejoice with the knowledge, induced by the storm, that he too is ready to sacrifice his own children. The drama of his imagined sacrifice is intensified in line 12 by the repeated reference, now concluded by an exclamation point, to his children's angelic sleep.

The ecstatic faith of stanza 3 is followed by an attempt at analyzing it (in stanza 4). But the ecstasy is beyond analysis (13). As in many other poems, Greenberg makes observations frequently found in mystical writers: that the poem itself is only a weak reflection of the ineffable experience from which it sprang; that faith is miraculous and the moment of revelation beyond time. Here (14) the image of *har hamór* richly sums up the miracle, for it means both "the hill of myrrh" and divine love (Song of Songs 4:6; 5:1) as well as the "Hill of Moriah" to which Abraham brought his son as a sacrifice—and on which Solomon's Temple was subsequently built (2 Chronicles 3:1). In addition, it is the hill on which the temple will be rebuilt when the ancient covenant is millenially fulfilled.

The various strains of imagery in the first three stanzas—the inextinguishable flame atop the sacred mountain, the sacrificial shedding of blood, the national destiny that transcends all temporal events—converge in *korbán har habáyit* (16): literally, "the sacrifice on the mountain of the temple."

— ARIEH SACHS

Uri Zvi Greenberg

UNDER THE TOOTH OF THEIR PLOUGH · TÁḤAT ṢEN MAḤARAṢTÁM

תַּחַת שֵׁן מַחֲרַשְׁתָּם

The Streets of the River (*Reḥovót Hanahár*, 1951), from which our poem is taken, is Greenberg's passionate lament for the loss of European Jewry. The expression of horror, hatred, and sorrow in this poetry is shatteringly direct, unweakened by self-conscious doubt or aesthetic sophistication.

(1) *The snows have melted again there . . . and the murderers are now farmers.* (2) *They have gone out to plough their fields there, those fields that are my graveyards (fields of my graves).* (3) *If the tooth of their plough digs up and rolls over on the furrow* (4) *One of my skeletons, the ploughman will not be saddened or shocked.* (5) *He will smile . . . recognize it, recognize in it the mark [*lit. *hit] of his tool.*

The entire poem draws bitterly on the pastoral mode in its portrayal of the beautiful Polish countryside: "snows melting . . . farmers ploughing . . . birds singing . . . herds by the shining stream . . . flourishing trees . . . church bells tolling." Simultaneously, it points to the reality that this pastoral scene disguises. The farmers are the murderers, the fields are graveyards, the trees suck blood.

This tension between pastoral and real is present even in the title, for the ploughshare,

שׁוּב הִפְשִׁירוּ שְׁלָגִים שָׁם.. וְהַמְרַצְּחִים הֵם עַכְשָׁו — אִכָּרִים.		Ṣuv hifṣíru ṣlagím ṣam . . . vehamratsḥím [hem aḥsáv—ikarím.
הֵם יָצְאוּ שָׁם לַחֲרשׁ שְׂדוֹתֵיהֶם, שְׂדוֹת קִבְרֵי הַשָּׂדוֹת הֵם!		Hem yats'ú ṣam laḥaróṣ sdoteyhém, [sdot kvaráy hasadót hem!
אִם בְּשֵׁן מַחֲרַשְׁתָּם יְחֻפַּר וִיגֻלְגַּל עַל הַתֶּלֶם	3	Im beṣén maḥaraṣtám yeḥupár [vigulgál al hatélem
אֶחָד מִשְּׁלָדַי, לֹא יֶעְגַּם הַחוֹרֵשׁ, לֹא יָחְרָד.		Eḥád miṣladáy, lo yeegám haḥoréṣ, [lo yoḥrád.
יְחַיֵּךְ.. יַכִּירֵהוּ.. אֶת מַכַּת כֶּלְיוֹ הוּא יַכִּיר בּוֹ.		Yeḥayéḥ . . yakiréhu . . et *makát kelyó* [hu yakír bo.
שׁוּב אָבִיב שָׁם בַּנּוֹף: פְּקָעִים וְלִילָךְ וְצִפְצוּף צִפֳּרִים.		Ṣuv avív ṣam banóf: pkaím veliláḥ [vetsiftsúf tsiporím.
מִרְבַּץ עֲדָרִים עֲלֵי נַחַל נוֹצֵץ וּמֵימָיו רְדוּדִים..	7	Mirbáts adarím aléy náḥal notséts [umeymáv redudím . .
אֵין־עוֹד יְהוּדִים עוֹבְרֵי־אֹרַח זְקָנִים וּפֵאוֹת.		Eyn-od yehudím ovréy-óraḥ zkaním ufeót.
בַּקְרֶצְ׳מִיס אֵינָם בְּטַלִּית־וְצִיצִית עַל כֻּתֹּנֶת;		Bakrétṣmis eynám betalít-vetsitsít al kutónet;
וְאֵינָם בַּחֲנֻיּוֹת הַסִּדְקִית אֲרִיגִים וּמַכֹּלֶת;	10	Veeynám baḥanuyót hasidkít arigím [umakólet;
אֵינָם בְּבָתֵּי מְלַאכְתָּם, אֵינָם בָּרַכֶּבֶת;		Eynám bevatéy melaḥtám, eynám barakévet;
אֵינָם בַּשְּׁוָקִים, אֵינָם בְּבֵית כְּנֶסֶת;		Eynám baṣvakím, eynám bevéyt knéset;
הֵם מִתַּחַת לְשֵׁן מַחֲרַשְׁתָּם שֶׁל נוֹצְרִים.	13	Hem mitáḥat leṣén maḥaraṣtám ṣel notsrím.
פָּקַד אֱלֹהִים אֶת גּוֹיָיו בְּרֹב חֶסֶד — —		Pakád elohím et goyáv beróv ḥásed— —

which connotes rural peace and honest toil, has a "tooth" and is therefore a kind of burrowing cannibal. The tension is heard in the sound of the language formed in lines 1-5 by two alliterative elements that are in complete contrast: the recurrent *ṣ* from the opening words on— *ṣuv hifṣíru ṣlagím ṣam* . . . —reflecting the hushed peace of the countryside, and the gutturonasal and gutturopalatal *gool, gal, tel, kel.* The word *vigulgál* (3) literally means "will be rolled over" but is very close in sound to *gulgólet*—a skull. The black irony of the stanza is most apparent in line 5, where the farmer appears as a kind of retired artisan accidentally coming across one of his *œuvres* and smiling with pleasurable recognition and pride: it was done with his own "instrument"—an axe or a knife (as opposed to his plough).

(6) *It is springtime again there in the landscape: bulbs and lilac and twittering birds,* (7) *[Where] herds lie down by the shining stream whose waters are shallow.* (8) *No more wandering Jews, beards and side-curls.* (9) *No [more] in the inns [krétṣmis:* a Yiddish word] *(with) talis and tsisis* [prayer-shawl and fringes] *over their shirt;* (10) *And no longer in the trinket, clothing and grocery shops;* (11) *No longer in their workshops, no longer on the train;* (12) *No longer in the markets, no longer in the synagogue;* (13) *They are under the tooth of the plough of Christians.* (14) *God has remembered (visited) His Gentiles with abounding grace.*

אֲבָל אָבִיב הוּא אָבִיב — וְהַקַּיִץ אַחֲרָיו מְדֻשָּׁן.		Avál avív hu avív—vehakáyits aḥaráv [meduṣán.
דְּשֵׁנִים גַּם עֲצֵי־יַרְכְּתֵי־הַדְּרָכִים כִּבְגַנִּים.	16	Deṣeyním gam atséy-yarketéy-hadraḥím [kivganím.
מִיְּמֵיהֶם לֹא הָיוּ אֲדֻמִּים הַפֵּרוֹת כַּאֲשֶׁר הֵם		*Mimeyhém* lo hayú adumím haperót [kaaṣér hem
אַחֲרֵי שֶׁאֵינָם הַיְּהוּדִים — —		Aḥaréy ṣeeynám hayhudím— —
לַיְּהוּדִים לֹא הָיוּ פַּעֲמוֹנִים לְצַלְצֵל לֵאלֹהִים,		Layhudím lo hayú faamoním letsaltsél [lelohím,
בְּרוּכָה הַנַּצְרוּת, כִּי לָהּ יֵשׁ פַּעֲמוֹנִים בַּגְּבֹהִים!	20	Bruḥá hanatsrút, ki la yeṣ paamoním [bagvohím!
וְקוֹלָם הַהוֹלֵךְ בַּמִּישׁוֹר בְּאָבִיב־שָׁם עַכְשָׁו,		Vekolám haholéḥ bamiṣór baavív-ṣam aḥsáv,
בִּכְבֵדוּת זְרֻמָּה בְּמֶרְחֲבֵי נוֹף זִיו וְנִיחוֹחַ,		Biḥvedút zrumá bemerḥavéy nof ziv [veniḥóaḥ,
הוּא אַדִּיר וְשַׁלִּיט עַל הַכֹּל: אֵין עַל מָה עוֹד לִפְסֹחַ,	23	Hu adír veṣalít al hakól: eyn al ma od [lifsóaḥ,
כַּאֲשֶׁר פַּעַם פָּסַח עַל גַּגּוֹת יְהוּדִים — —		Kaaṣér páam pasáḥ al gagót yehudím— —
בְּרוּכָה הַנַּצְרוּת, כִּי לָהּ יֵשׁ פַּעֲמוֹנִים בַּגְּבֹהִים!		Bruḥá hanatsrút, ki la yeṣ paamoním [bagvohím!
לִכְבוֹד אֱלֹהִים הַמֵּיטִיב לַנּוֹצְרִים וְהַכֹּל..		Liḥvód elohím hameytív lanotsrím vehakól . .
וְכָל הַיְּהוּדִים תַּחַת שֶׁן מַחֲרַשְׁתָּם מֻנָּחִים;	27	Veḥól hayhudím táḥat ṣen maḥaraṣtám [munaḥím;
אוֹ תַּחַת עִשְׂבֵּי הַמִּרְעֶה;		O táḥat isvéy hamir'é;
אוֹ בְּקִבְרוֹת הַיַּעַר!		O vekivrót hayáar!
אוֹ עַל גְּדוֹת נְחָלִים וְאִם בָּם..	30	O al gdot neḥalím veím bam . .
אוֹ בְּצִדֵּי דְרָכִים.		O vetsidéy draḥím.
הַלְלוּ לְיֶזוּנְיוּ בְּפַעֲמוֹנֵי הַכֹּבֶד: בִּים־בָּם!		Halelú leyezunyú befaamonéy hakóved: [bim-bam!

(15) *But springtime is springtime—and the summer that follows is fat (thriving).* (16) *The roadside trees are fat as [trees] in gardens.* (17) *The fruit has never been so red as it is* (18) *Now that the Jews are no more—*

The pastoral *mirbáts adarím* ("the herds lying down," 7) has many biblical antecedents whose echoes deepen the sarcasm. The shining stream has a special poignancy in Greenberg's verse, which often uses the image of clear, flowing water as a symbol of his happy childhood in Poland.

In lines 8-14 it is ostensibly the *goyím* ("Gentiles") who are exulting, but at the same time it is the poet himself lamenting: *eynám . . . eynám . . . eynám . . .* ("they are no more") 9,10,11,12. The relationship between the two simultaneous voices changes in line 14, and from now on it is the poet only who speaks. By joining *goyáv* ("His Gentiles")—

here a contemptuous use of the word—to a lofty biblical phrase *berôv ḥésed* ("with abounding grace"), line 14 almost turns the tone of benediction into an oath. A similar discordant effect is achieved by the other allusions to and quotations from the Book of Prayer, twisted with bitter irony (notably lines 9, 14, 26).

The tone of contained rage carries over into the third stanza. The fact that spring returns, heedless of catastrophe, is seen as an insult to the dead. And the summer that follows is *meduṣán*, "overfat," stupefied with abundance. The uncared-for trees by the roadside are as *deṣeyním* ("fattened," 16) as the trees in cultivated gardens, because their roots have found secret sources of nourishment in the corpses lying under the roadside. All nature is now cannibalistic.

(19) *The Jews had no bells with which to ring to [summon] God.* (20) *Blessed is Christianity, for it has bells in the heights!* (21) *And (their)* [bells'] *voice goes over the plain now, in the springtime* (22) *Flowing heavily over the breadth of a landscape of brightness and fragrance,* (23) *It is mighty and the master of everything: there is nothing more to [be] pass[ed] over* (24) *As once He passed over the roofs of Jews — —* (25) *Blessed is Christianity, for it has bells in the heights!* (26) *To honor a God who does good to the Christians and to all . . .* (27) *And all the Jews are laid under the tooth of their plough;* (28) *Or under pasture grass;* (29) *Or in graves in the forest!* (30) *Or on the banks of rivers, or within them . . .* (31) *Or on the roadsides*

(32) *Praise ye Yézunyu with the heavy bells: Bim-Bam!*

In the irony of the last section the Chosen People are the Cursed People who have no bells with which to summon God. The mournful tolling of *eynám* ("they are no more," 9,10,11,12) which pervaded the second stanza, is, as it were, defined by the bells (19) which now become the dominating symbol and sound. The poem which follows "Under The Tooth Of Their Plough" is entitled "Under Bells" and contains the line "In the ringing-roaring-of-bells it is announced: that they are no longer" (*ṣeeynám*). Note that the sound of church bells has always struck religious Jews as a desecration and blasphemy.

Sarcasm is everpresent in the language employed: The bells toll (22) *biḥvedút zrumá*, "with flowing solemnity," and the word *zrumá* echoes the account in Ezekiel (23:20) of the Egyptian paramours, "whose issue [*zirmá*—"seminal emission"] is like the issue of horses."

The poem closes with a burst of mortal contempt: Praise ye "Yézunyu"—the Polish affectionate diminutive for Jesus. *Bim-bam*—doubling the sound of *veím bam* (30)—sounds the final note of meaningless, self-satisfied, bestial stupidity.

— ARIEH SACHS

Uri Zvi Greenberg

MARTYRS OF SILENCE · KDOṢÉY DUMIYÁ · קְדוֹשֵׁי דוּמִיָּה

בְּלֵילוֹת הַלְּבָנָה אוֹמֶרֶת אִמִּי הַקְּדוֹשָׁה
לְאָבִי הַקָּדוֹשׁ:
כְּשֶׁנּוֹלַד לִי הַבֵּן אִיקְלְעָה הַלְּבָנָה בַּחַלּוֹן,
4 מִיָּד הוּא פָּקַח אֶת עֵינָיו וְהִבִּיט בָּהּ; מֵאָז
רוֹנֵן זֶה זִיוָהּ בְּדָמוֹ עַד הַיּוֹם
וּלְבָנָה מְהַלֶּכֶת מֵאָז בֵּין שִׁירָיו — —

הַרְבֵּה כֶּסֶף־אַלְדָּמִי הָיָה בְּאָבִי
אֲבָל רֶכֶב הַנְּדוֹד לֹא עָמַד לְעֵת כֶּסֶף
9 סָמוּךְ לְבֵיתוֹ..
לָכֵן הוּא יָדַע דּוּמִיָּה וְנִגּוּן,
וְאָהַב־בְּעֵינָיו כַּנְפֵי צִפֳּרִים.
‘— בִּרְצוֹתָן לָעוּף, הֵן עָפוֹת לָהֶן.. כָּךְ.’

אַךְ אִמִּי.. רִתְמַת רֶכֶב נְדוֹד לְהָסְפָּהּ:
14 לְפִי דֹּפֶק הַלֵּב יָדַע כָּל יֶשְׁהָּ גַּם לֵילֵךְ
בְּרַגְלַיִם מַמָּשׁ עַל הַיָּם:
לְפִי מִשְׁעוֹל־הַלְּבָנָה־עַל־גַּלִּים
אֵלַי, אֶל הַבֵּן, בְּצִיּוֹן —
18 אַךְ לֹא מְצָאַתְנִי יוֹשֵׁב עַל הַחוֹף מְחַכֶּה־לָהּ
וְחָזְרָה עִם מִשְׁעוֹל־הַלְּבָנָה־עַל־גַּלִּים:
עֲיֵפַת נְדוֹד, חֲמַת רֹאשׁ, מֻכַּת יָם.

עַכְשָׁו — גַּם אִמִּי כְּאָבִי: קְדוֹשֵׁי דוּמִיָּה.
22 יֵשׁ מִשְׁעוֹל־לְבָנָה עַל גַּלִּים נוֹצְצִים;
וְיֵשׁ הַבֵּן הַיָּחִיד
הַשָּׂרִיד
בָּעוֹלָם — —

Beleylót halvaná oméret imí hakdoṣá
Leaví hakadóṣ:
Kṣenolád li habén ikleá halvaná vaḥalón,
4 Miyád hu fakáḥ et eynáv vehibít ba; meáz
Ronén ze zivá bedamó ad hayóm
Ulvaná mehaléḥet meáz beyn ṣiráv— —

Harbé ḥósef-aldomí hayá veaví,
Avál réḥev handód lo amád leét kósef
9 Samúḥ leveytó . .
Laḥén hu yadá dumiyá venigún,
Veaháv-beeynáv kanféy tsiporím.
‘—birtsotán laúf, hen afót lahén . . kaḥ.’

Aḥ imí . . ritmát réḥev nedód leḥospá:
14 Lefí dófek halév yadá kol yeṣá gam leyléḥ
Beragláyim mamáṣ al hayám:
Lefí miṣ’ól-halvaná-al-galím
Eláy, el habén, betsiyón—
18 Aḥ lo metsaátni yoṣév al haḥóf meḥaké-la
Veḥazrá im miṣ’ól-halvaná-al-galím:
Ayefát nedód, ḥamát roṣ, mukát yam.

Aḥṣáv—gam imí ḥeaví: kdoṣéy dumiyá.
22 Yeṣ miṣ’ól-levaná al galím notsetsím;
Veyéṣ habén hayaḥíd
Hasaríd
Baolám— —

"Martyrs of Silence" is one of a series of four poems entitled "At the Rim of Heaven," and indeed the conversation in the first stanza appears to take place in an imaginary world somewhere between eternity and time. It is reported in the present tense, yet both parents are dead. They are *kdoṣím:* "holy, sacred" and also "sainted, martyred" in the sense of "dead for the Sanctification of the Name of God" (*kidúṣ haṣém*). The poet overhears his mother talking about his birth, in which she perceives something miraculous, for as a newborn baby he was fascinated by the moon shining through the window, the very moon whose radiance still "sings in his blood" and "walks among his poems."

(1) *On nights of the moon says my sacred mother* (2) *To my sacred father:* (3) *When the son was born (to me) the moon happened by in the window,* (4) *At once he opened his eyes and looked at her* [the moon]; *since then* (5) *This radiance of hers sings in his blood, until this day,* (6) *And since then the moon goes walking among his poems.*

(7) *Much never-stilled longing was there in my father,* (8) *But the Chariot of Wandering was not there* [lit. *did not stand*] *at the time of longing* (9) *By his house . . .* (10) *That is why he knew stillness and melody* (11) *And loved-with-his-eyes the wings of birds* (12) "*—When they want to fly, they just fly off . . . so.*"

(13) *But my mother . . . her longing had* [*was harnessed to*] *a Chariot of Wandering:* (14) *By the heart's beat, her whole being even knew how to walk* (15) *With* [*her*] *feet actually upon the sea* (16) *By the path-of-the-moon-on-the-waves* (17) *To me, to the son, in Zion — —* (18) *But she did not find me sitting on the shore awaiting her* (19) *And* [*she*] *returned with the path-of-the-moon-on-the-waves:* (20) *Weary (of) wandering, feverish* [lit. *head hot*], *seastruck.*

(21) *Now—my mother too, like my father:* [*they are*] *martyrs of silence.* (22) *There is a moon path on the sparkling waves:* (23) *And there is the only son* (24) *The remnant* (25) *In the world — —*

Stanza 2, speaking of the father, explains that his soul's restless longing (7) was fixed upon "silence and melody" (*nigún*, 10, refers to Hasidic melody, hence to religious dedication). When the son left home and settled in Zion, the father saw him as a fledged bird constrained to leave the nest, and though, as the son says, the father "loved-with-his-eyes" the wings of the birds that want to fly off, he accepted the separation. The "Chariot of Wandering" (8, 13) is a common figure in medieval Hebrew verse, signifying "parting" or "departure on a long journey."

The mother's reaction to the son's departure was of a different order (stanza 3). The very passion of her longing was a mystical attachment which enabled her to "follow" in her son's paths (13-17). And it was the son who failed her by failing to await her on the shore (18-20).

But now that both parents are "martyred and silenced" (21), the mother's longing has been stilled. And all that is left is the memory of her longing when she was still alive (the moon's path on the sparkling waves, 22) and the poet's desolation.

The moon, the central symbol of the poem, provides the setting at the rim of heaven. It epitomizes the poet's unique destiny—the moon "happened by" in the window—the word is the Aramaic *ikleá* rather than the Hebrew *nikleá*, and it implies something akin to the annunciation made to Abraham or to Samson's father, Manoah. The moon embodies the speaker's world of poetry and imagination (5-6) and it "provides" the path for the mother's impassioned longing (stanza 3). It is also connected with the present silence of the parents, and with their different "longings" when alive, for *kósef* ("longing," 7, 8, 13) is strongly related by sound in this context to *késef* ("silver"), hence the "silvery" moonlight.

The recurring phrase "moon's-path-on-the-waves" (16, 19, 22) has an extremely musical quality in Hebrew, achieved by the counterpoint of the anapestic beat and the alliterated *ol* and *al: miṣ'ól-halvaná-al-galím.* The sea-that-separates appears frequently in Greenberg's poems on his mother, and the variation on "moonstruck" in line 20—*mukát yam*, "seastruck"—is both novel in its use of language and meaningful in its context.

The economy and concentration throughout the poem are remarkable. Elaborating a tightly knit set of symbols (the magical moon, the chariot of parting, the separating sea), the poet presents his triple portrait with highly dramatic intensity. The successive shortening of the final three lines and the rime *yaḥíd-saríd* (23-24)—the first rime in the entire poem—combine to slow down the reading. Compelling the voice to dwell upon each word, they stress the desolation of the scene.

— ARIEH SACHS

Uri Zvi Greenberg

AMPUTATION OF THE WING · KRITÁT KANÁF · כְּרִיתַת כָּנָף

לְפֶתַע וּלְפִתְאוֹם בְּבֹקֶר לֹא עָבוֹת		Leféta ulfit'óm bevóker lo avót
וְרֵיחַ כָּל הַצּוֹמֵחַ נָדַף		Veréaḥ kol hatsoméaḥ nadáf
וְכָל הַצִּפֳּרִים עָפוֹת בְּמִין כָּנָף אַחַת..	3	Veḥól hatsiporím afót bemín kanáf aḥát . .
אַלְלַי לְכָל רוֹאָן בְּכָךְ וְהוּא לֹא נָטַל בְּיָדָיו		Aleláy leḥól roán beḥáḥ vehú lo natál
אֶת עִנְּבֵי עֵינָיו וְלֹא סָחַט!		Et invéy eynáv veló saḥát! [beyadáv
גַּם הַצִּפֳּרִים עַצְמָן אֵינָן יוֹדְעוֹת מִי קִצֵּץ לָהֶן כָּנָף		Gam hatsiporím atsmán eynán yod'ót [mi kitséts lahén kanáf
לְפֶתַע וּלְפִתְאוֹם הֵן עָפוֹת כָּךְ בָּאֲוִיר		Leféta ulfit'óm hen afót kaḥ baavír
נוֹטוֹת אֶל צַד..	8	Notót el tsad . .
וְאַף דָּם אֵינוֹ נוֹטֵף וְאֵין הֶכֵּר כִּי לְכָל צִפּוֹר		Veáf dam eynó notéf veéyn hekér ki
הָיוּ שְׁתֵּי כְנָפַיִם לְהַעֲבִיר		Hayú ṣtey ḥnafáyim lehaavír [leḥól tsipór
לְבָבוֹת דִּכְסִיפִין מֵהָכָא לְהָתָם —		Levavót diḥsifín mehaḥá lehatám— —
עַכְשָׁו אֵין יוֹתֵר לְהָתָם.	12	Aḥsáv eyn yotér lehatám.
בִּדְבַר אֱלֹהִים כְּמוֹ בַּחֲלוֹם נֶחְתְּכָה כָּנָף		Bidvár elohím kemó vaḥalóm neḥteḥá ḥanáf
וְעַל מְקוֹם הַחִתּוּךְ חָתַם.		Veál mekóm haḥitúḥ ḥatám.

This lyric appeared in 1955 in "At a Time When the Face Is Covered," a series of poems whose theme is estrangement, "the Face" referring both to God's and the speaker's. In the stark title poem of the series, the soul, "covering itself" paradoxically with the "autumn of its summer," tells how "God has bestowed-forsaken the earth to men:/ Do with it what you will, I shall hide my face from you—/ He said as He entered His heavens and became silent." The predominant note of these poems is a bitter lyricism quite different from the rage of Greenberg's earlier, "prophetic" poems. The directness is muted and the imagery works largely through allusion and symbolism.

(1) *All of a sudden one cloudless morning* (2) *And the fragrance of all growing things spread (about)* (3) *And all the birds flying with a sort of single wing . . .* (4) *Woe to him who saw them thus and did not take in his hands* (5) *The grapes of his eyes and did not press (them)!*

(6) *Even the birds themselves do not know who cut off their wing* (7). *All of a sudden they fly thus through the air* (8) *Inclining to [one] side . . .* (9) *And no blood at all drips and there is no sign that each bird* (10) *[Once] had two wings with which to transport*

(11) *Longing hearts from over-here to over-there — —* (12) *Now that there is no longer any over-there.* (13) *By the Word (command) of God as if in a dream a wing has been severed* (14) *And the place of the severing He has sealed.*

Two kinds of meaning, that of nightmare and that of waking reality, are interfused. At first reading, all we perceive is an intensely visual rendering of some ineffably horrible experience, in terms as untranslatable and inexplicable as those of a dream. Line 13 may suggest that the surreal landscape portrayed in the preceding lines has indeed been witnessed in a nightmare or vision. Yet the opening of the poem gives the setting as a "clear morning," thus creating the deliberate opposition between dream and reality that gives the entire poem the strange vividness of something seen simultaneously with the inner and the outer eye.

The shocking appearance of the single-winged birds (3) creates a visceral tremor; the horror of the sight is beyond words, making the viewer wish to pull out and crush "the grapes of his eyes" (5). The final word—*ḥatám* ("sealed")—makes of the entire experience a sacrament of irrevocable loss.

But if the immediate impact of the poem depends on the appeal of its surrealistic imagery to primordial fears of mutilation, it does lend itself to more discursive discussion as well. Many of the migratory birds which seasonally pass through Israel originate in Europe. In lines 10-11 we learn that each bird "once had two wings with which to transport/ Longing hearts from over-here to over-there." The birds, then, that before the annihilation of the people in Europe had been viewed with nostalgia and yearning (cf. "Martyrs of Silence," p. 68), suddenly appear one "clear morning" as horribly and senselessly mutilated. The amputated wing itself symbolizes the murdered kin, and in line 12 we learn that the "over-there," once the land of the heart's desire, no longer exists. The birds' grotesque flight is completely aimless now: they have nowhere to go.

Line 11, except for the word *levavót* ("hearts"), is in Aramaic. This transition from Hebrew to Aramaic and the riming of the repeated (11-12) Aramaic *hatám* ("there") with the Hebrew *ḥatám* ("sealed") in line 14 is both striking and natural, and gives great finality to the conclusion. The varying length of the lines effectively counterpoints the natural pauses of the speaking voice throughout the poem.

Rimed lines, for the most part couplings through identical or similar sound of differently spelled words (e.g., *nadáf-beyadáv*), alternate with unrimed lines, to create a subtle rhetorical pattern. The rimes are: *áf* and *áv* endings—2, 4, 6, 13; *at* and *ad* endings —3,5,8; *avír*—7,10; *atám*—11, 12, 14.

— ARIEH SACHS

Simon Halkin

TO TARSHISH · TARṢÍṢA · תַּרְשִׁישָׁה

Born in White Russia in 1899, Simon Halkin emigrated to the United States in his fifteenth year. Following his university studies in New York and Chicago, he came to Tel Aviv in 1932 where he remained as a teacher until 1939. He returned to America for a decade. In 1949 he was called to the Hebrew University to succeed the late Joseph Klausner as Professor of Modern Hebrew Literature. Halkin is well known to readers of English for his *Modern Hebrew Literature: Trends and Values*, and to readers of Hebrew for his verse, novels, criticism, and his translations of Whitman and Shakespeare in particular.

The trained reader will see in Halkin's poetry a confluence of various traditions experienced and grasped deeply. Moral and mystical concepts of Judaism clash with a European intellectual heritage as well as

אֱלֶגְיָה לֹא תַעְגֵּם קוֹלָהּ בְּשֶׁפֶךְ אוֹר דְּרוֹמִי,	Elégya lo tagém kolá beṣéfeḥ or dromí,
לוּ גַּם לוּט עָב תָּחוּחַ, דַּק כָּאֵפֶר הַדָּלִיל.	Lu gam lut av taḥúaḥ, dak kaéfer hadalíl.
מַה־כֵּן אֵפוֹא נִרְעַשְׁתָּ בִּי, לִבִּי, בִּנְטוֹת יוֹמִי	Ma-ken eyfó nir'ásta bi, libí, bintót yomí
וְשַׁוַּע שִׁיר תִּדְרֹשׁ צָעִיר, יִבְקַע, יֵבְךְּ כֶּחָלִיל?	Veṣéva ṣir tidróṣ tsaír, yivká, yevk keḥalíl?
בַּמֶּרְחַקִּים, בִּקְצֵה הָאָרֶץ, יָשֹׁקוּ אֳרָנִים,	Bamerḥakím, biktséy haárets, yaṣóku oraním,
בַּמֶּרְחַקִּים, בִּקְצֵה הָאָרֶץ, תַּמּוּ הַשָּׁנִים.	Bamerḥakím, biktséy haárets, támu haṣaním
מָה הֱקִיצוֹתָ, לֶב־לִבִּי, עַד לֹא תִדְמֶה כָּלִיל?	Ma hekitsóta, lev-libí, ad lo tidmé kalíl?
שְׁרַב־סִיוָן הִרְתִּיעַ יָם חוֹלֶה אֲחוֹרַנִּית	Ṣrav-siván hirtía yam ḥolé aḥoranít
וְנֶחְשְׂפָה הַיְרוֹקָה עַל שֶׁן־צוּק נַעֲוֶה.	Veneḥsefá hayeroká al ṣen-tsok naavé.
בְּאוֹר־עַרְבַּיִם מְכֻשָּׁף פֹּה אָץ מְעֹדַנִּית	Beór-arbáyim meḥuṣáf po ats meodanít
יוֹנָה אֶל הַסְּפִינָה מֵאֵל מַצְמִיא וְלֹא יְרַוֶּה,	Yoná el hasfiná meél matsmí veló yeravé.
גַּם הוּא לַיָּם עָרַג, דָּג הֶעֱלַתּוּ הַחַכָּה,	Gam hu layám arág, dag heelátu haḥaká,
וְאֶת רֹאשׁוֹ יָגֵּעַ אֶל הַסֶּלַע לֹא בָקַע:	Veét roṣó yagéa el haséla lo vaká:
תַּרְשִׁישָׁה, לֵב פּוֹתֶה, עַל פִּי הַתְּהוֹם עוֹד יְקַוֶּה!	Tarṣíṣa, lev poté, al-pi hathóm od yekavé!
תַּרְשִׁישׁ שֶׁלִּי, הֲלֹא יֵשֵׁךְ עַתָּה, בְּרֶגַע זֶה,	Tarṣíṣ ṣelí, haló yeṣéḥ atá, beréga ze,
וְיַעַר־אֳרָנַיִךְ בְּרֶגַע זֶה לִי יְפַלֵּל.	Veyáar-oranáyiḥ beréga ze li yefalél.
בְּחֹרֶף שְׁחוֹר־כְּנָפַיִם, בְּעַב־הַשֶּׁלֶג, זְאֵב רָזֶה	Beḥóref ṣḥor-knafáyim, beáv haṣéleg, zeév [razé
בְּמִדְרוֹנֵי הָרַיִךְ נָע, נוֹאָשׁ גַּם מְיַלֵּל.	Bemidronéy haráyiḥ na, noáṣ gam miyalél.
וְקַיִץ כִּי יָנוּב בָּךְ, עַגְמוּמִי תָּמִיד וָזָר,	Vekáyits ki yanúv baḥ, agmumí tamíd vazár,
אָשׁוּב אֶל קֹר חֵיקֵךְ עִם עֵדֶר עֲגוּרִים, חָזַר	Aṣúv el kor ḥeykéḥ im éder agurím, ḥazár
בַּהֲרִיחוֹ רָחוֹק סוּף־אֲגַמַּיִךְ הַמְמַלֵּל.	Behariḥó raḥók suf-agamáyiḥ hamemalél.

with a somewhat pantheistic conception of pure sensation and pure "being" rooted in nature, such nature being conceived as both private and universal. The attempt at synthesizing these many elements finds expression in a number of Halkin's poems, but these elements are never presented as such or in allegorical masquerade. "To Tarshish" (from *On the Island*, 1946) is not, as one might expect, a variation on a biblical theme. It is a modern lyric, its speaker faces a contemporary situation. But the emotive background of the poem gains significance from its relation to the bewildering career of the prophet Jonah.

We are familiar with the story. At a certain moment in his life, the prophet decides to evade his destiny, to renounce his role as mediator between God and men. He plans to remove himself to the farthest point on earth known to his countrymen—to Tarshish. Presumably the voice of his relentless God will not be able to reach him there. The reader knows his attempt is doomed to failure. Tarshish becomes to the poet the realm of Nature, the haven of the concrete, where being is its own reason and does not have to be justified by "values"—moral, spiritual, or intellectual. God-seekers have usually gone to the south, to the desert. Thus it seems appropriate for Tarshish to be situated in the opposite direction, in the pine-covered regions to the north.

Standing on the sandy seashore of Joppa (Jaffa), on a hot summer day, the speaker feels that (1) *No elegy will sadden its voice in a cataract of southern light,* (2) *Although [the light is] shrouded by a crumbly cloud, thin as flaky ash.* The aridity is stressed by comparing the clouds, carriers of moisture, to heaps of ashes. There is a subtle irony in these opening lines. In his own eyes the speaker seems old and tired, unequal to his task in this climate which is so antagonistic to the nature of his poetic temperament. He should have been resigned to muteness. But deep within him a voice is alive, and he asks himself in surprise: (3) *Why then have you stirred within me, my heart, as my day declines (sets)* (4) *Demanding an outburst of young song piercing, crying like a flute?* These stirrings project before his eyes a vision of a country where such a song would be most natural: (5) *In the distance, at the edge of the earth, pine trees swish (yearn)* (6) *In the distance, at the edge of the earth, the years have ended.* There the temporal as experienced by a time-conscious human being loses its meaning. Returning from this vision, the speaker continues to wonder at himself: (7) *Why have you wakened, my heart-of-hearts, just before you fell completely silent?*

At the beginning of the next stanza, present surroundings become dominant again. Another sight appears, out of the distant past—picturing the prophet who found himself in a predicament somewhat similar to that of the speaker. (8) *The burning heat of June [*lit. the month *Siván] drove back a sick sea* (9) *And the weeds (moss) on the jagged rock were bared.* The strong pines of the north are contrasted with the sickly green algae exposed by the retreating sea. Tarshish is throughout associated with health, virility, and coolness, but Joppa, with sickness, heat, and despair. (10-11) *Here, in the bewitched twilight, Jonah stumbling, hastened to the boat from a God who causes thirst but does not slake.* The word *meodanít,* that describes the fleeing prophet's stumbling gait, is a modification of *maadanót,* "shackled," "fettered." Jonah's similarity to the speaker is now stressed. Jonah also was out of his element, distraught, and unable to commit the ultimate act of despair; he also hoped for deliverance in a far-off country: (12) *A fish brought up by the rod, he* [Jonah] *too longed for the sea* (13) *And did not crack his wearied head against the rock:* (14) *[O] foolish heart, still longing for Tarshish on the brink of the depths!*

(15) *[O] my Tarshish, you do exist now, at this very moment.* There is a deep affinity between the speaker and this land; in a certain sense just as much as he longs for it, the land longs for him: 16) *And at this very moment your pine forests pray for (expect) me.* It is not a land of roseate happiness. It knows cruelty and hunger and sadness, but it exerts a powerful fascination over its devotees even now— (17) *In a black-winged winter, in the cloud of the snow, a thin wolf* (18) *Moves on your mountain slopes, too despairing to howl.* But the speaker envisages its summer: (19-20) *And when summer blooms within you, I, ever melancholy and foreign, shall return to the coldness of your breast with a flock of cranes coming back* (21) *When from afar they scented the muttering reeds of your lakes.*

The seven-line stanza, riming *ababccb,* tends to emphasize its developing theme with the closing lines. The metrical base of the line is composed of 7 iambic feet, frequently with a cesura after the fourth or third stress. The rhythmic feeling has breadth and amplitude yet the language is extremely compact within an intricate syntactical structure.

In the remaining three sections, "To Tarshish" elaborates the foregoing themes and introduces a number of new ones. Our selection sets the stage for a complex of lyric contemplations, too extensive to be included in this commentary. At the climax of the poem, the speaker who believed himself to be prophet and ascetic, rooted in the contemplation of God, is carried away by the exciting sensuousness of Tarshish. He is swallowed up by the eternal eroticism of nature, as Jonah was by the whale. And he is in danger of being caught and ground in the "mortar of continuous existence," at once betrayer and betrayed.

— ABRAHAM HUSS

Abraham Shlonsky

TOIL · ÁMAL* · עָמָל

הַלְבִּישִׁינִי, אִמָּא כְּשֵׁרָה, כְּתֹנֶת־פַּסִּים לְתִפְאֶרֶת	Halbiṣíni, íma kṣéyra, któnet-pásim letif'éret
וְעִם שַׁחֲרִית הוֹבִילִינִי אֱלֵי עָמָל.	Veím ṣáḥarit hovilíni eléy ámal.
עוֹטְפָה אַרְצִי אוֹר כַּטַּלִּית.	Ótfa ártsi or katálit.
בָּתִּים נִצְּבוּ כַּטּוֹטָפוֹת.	Bátim nítsvu katotáfot.
וְכִרְצוּעוֹת־תְּפִילִּין גּוֹלְשִׁים כְּבִישִׁים, סָלְלוּ כַּפַּיִם.	Veḥirtsúot-tfílin gólṣim kvíṣim, sálelu [kapáyim.
תְּפִלַּת שַׁחֲרִית פֹּה תִּתְפַּלֵּל קִרְיָה נָאָה אֱלֵי בּוֹרְאָהּ.	Tfílat-ṣáḥrit po titpálel kírya náa éley bór'a.
וּבַבּוֹרְאִים	Uvabór'im
בְּנֵךְ אַבְרָהָם,	Bneḥ avráham,
פַּיְטָן סוֹלֵל בְּיִשְׂרָאֵל.	Páytan sólel beyisráel.
וּבָעֶרֶב בֵּין הַשְּׁמָשׁוֹת יָשׁוּב אַבָּא מִסִּבְלוֹתָיו	Uvaérev beyn haṣmáṣot yáṣuv ába misivlótav
וְכִתְפִלָּה יִלְחַשׁ נַחַת:	Veḥitfíla yílḥaṣ náhat:
הֲבֵן יַקִּיר לִי אַבְרָהָם,	Havén yákir li avráham,
עוֹר וְגִידִים וַעֲצָמוֹת.	Or vegídim vaatsámot.
הַלְלוּיָהּ.	Halelúya.
הַלְבִּישִׁינִי, אִמָּא כְּשֵׁרָה, כְּתֹנֶת־פַּסִּים לְתִפְאֶרֶת	Halbiṣíni, íma kṣéyra, któnet-pásim letif'éret
וְעִם שַׁחֲרִית הוֹבִילִינִי	Veím ṣáḥarit hovilíni
אֱלֵי עָמָל.	Eléy ámal.

Born in Poltava (Ukraine) in 1900, Abraham Shlonsky belongs to the group of innovators who brought to Hebrew literature the revolutionary verve, experimental audacity, and inconoclasm typical of the new century. His father, a true product of the changing East European Jewish world, gave his son a secular Hebrew as well as a religious education, sending him off in his thirteenth year to study in Jaffa's newly founded suburb of Tel Aviv. Unlike earlier Hebrew poets, Shlonsky learned spoken Hebrew in childhood and for a short period lived in the exciting milieu of the pre-war Tel Aviv *gymnasium* that was to give Israel many of its leaders and intellectuals. After the outbreak of World War I, he was forced to return to Russia, where he completed his high school work and lived through the crucial years of the Revolution. In 1922 he emigrated to Israel as a young pioneer and worked as road-builder and farmer.

A prolific writer, Shlonsky has published many volumes of verse, seventy translations (among them *Hamlet, Eugen Onegin, Tyl Eulenspiegel*), and an anthology, *Russian*

Poetry, co-edited with Lea Goldberg, which affected younger writers deeply. As editor and mentor, he headed the literary Left, an extremely productive force during the first decade of the new nation. As leader and spokesman of the anti-classicists, he challenged the authority of Bialik and in his own poetry he reflected the influence of Blok's symbolism and the experimentalism and wild imagery of Mayakowsky and Yesenin. A great innovator in language, Shlonsky introduced the raciness of the newly spoken idiom into the verse and where words were lacking he coined them. (Many have since become an accepted part of the language.)

"Toil" appears in a sequence named for Mt. Gilboa, a hill dominating the Valley of Jezreel in whose fields Shlonsky worked. All the poems of this era (1927) mirror a landscape which had been a nostalgic dream in Russia and which, after it became real, lost none of its festive appeal. Shlonsky presents the new Palestinian earth in an ecstatic, quasi-religious light. The building of the homeland and the tilling of its soil are transformed into acts of worship. And the modernist influences of Blok, Yesenin, and other Russian poets are absent from the "Gilboa" poems: they follow the style and language of the Bible and Prayerbook. The lines have the undefined rhythms of the Psalms, varying in length and seemingly arbitrary in shape; but read aloud, they reveal an orderliness indicative of Shlonsky's inclination toward symmetry even in free verse:

(1) *Dress me, good (pious) mother, in a glorious coat of many colors* (2) *And with dawn lead me to toil.*

(3) *My country wraps itself in light as in a prayer shawl.* (4) *Houses stand out [*lit. *stood] like phylacteries.* (5) *And like phylactery straps, the highways that palms have paved glide down.*

(6) *Here [now] the beautiful town prays matins to its creator* (7) *And among the creators* (8) *[Is] your son, Abraham,* (9) *A hymn-writer (poet)—road-paver in Israel.*

(10) *And in the evening, at sunset, father shall return from his labors* (11) *And like a prayer, he will whisper with contentment:* (12) *My darling son Abraham,* (13) *Skin and veins and bones.* (14) *Hallelujah!*

(15) *Dress me, good (pious) mother, in a glorious coat of many colors* (16) *And with dawn lead me* (17) *To toil.*

Each word in the first stanza is loaded with associations and symbols. The speaker addresses not his own but the generic "mother" common to Yiddish folk-poetry. In the new life, detached from the recent past, nostalgia turns "mother" into a symbolic figure who can give both a blessing and a sacrifice. The "coat of many colors" is of course an allusion to Genesis 37:3, where Jacob makes his gift of love to Joseph. But the Bible reader knows that the coat will be soaked in blood, and line 2 recalls the Isaac story, where sacrifice is also an act of love to be done with "your only son, which you love." Love and sacrifice become one. The pioneer-speaker is a beloved son and the altar is toil. Toil has become an act of worship.

Stanza 2 is a composite of allusions: to Psalm 104:2 (describing God as "wrapped in light as with a cloak"); to the prayer shawl (*tálit*); to phylacteries (*tfílin*), which are part of daily worship. The latter consist of boxes called "houses" and of leather straps. The square houses perched on the hills are like phylactery boxes worn on the head, and the roads gliding into the valley like the phylactery straps. The land is now a worshipper standing at his morning prayer.

The words *gólṣim kviṣim* make a striking synthesis of old and new. In the Song of Songs, the hair of the beloved descends (*galṣú*) like a flock of mountain goats. *Kviṣim*, however, is a modern term ("roads") associated with the new homeland. The lines also speak of labor, and *kapáyim* ("palms") reinforces the image of worship: the roads are being paved by "palms" of young pioneers, many of whom as members of the intelligentsia had never worked with their hands.

Kirya (6) in old Hebrew usually designates Jerusalem but in modern usage, a new town or settlement. The town prays to the creator, but it is not God, creator of the old world, but man the creator of the new. This Abraham is a new Abraham: poet, road-builder. *Páytan* (6) traditionally refers to a writer of medieval hymns but here Shlonsky celebrates his grand role as worker-poet in the tradition of the early poets of the Russian Revolution. The meter here has a "boastful" lilt. If we ignore the printed form, lines 6-7-8 become a quatrain of trochaic tetrameters.

The penultimate stanza makes the son's act not a sacrifice but a recompense for the father's suffering, as the father whispers contentedly: "My darling son," echoing "Ephraim, my darling son" (Jeremiah 31:19). And it is not the spiritual Ephraim-Abraham whom the poem celebrates but an Abraham of "skin and veins and bones." With the last stanza repeating the opening lines, toil is exalted while at the same time recognized as a necessary daily burden. The secular days have become a prolonged sacrifice and a prolonged festival.

— LEA GOLDBERG

Abraham Shlonsky

THREE OLD WOMEN · ṢALÓṢ ZKEYNÓT · שָׁלשׁ זְקֵנוֹת

This poem comes from the last section of *Stones of Chaos* (*Avnéy Bóhu*, 1934). In contrast to the intimate, nostalgic tone of the 1927 volume in which "Toil" appeared, *Stones of Chaos* is permeated by the sense of crisis that pervaded Europe and Palestine in the thirties. The book contains Shlonsky's Paris poems (he had spent much time in that city), poems about building the homeland which are now darkened by the foreshadowing catastrophe, short introverted lyrics, and odes of an apocalyptic mood. For all of Shlonsky's meticulous riming, constructing, and skillful playing with verbal meanings, one senses a disrupting world. Then suddenly, in the last section, one finds poems of childhood that speak of the poet's growth as an artist in a milieu in which Jewish and non-Jewish influences interplay: ". . . Maimonides looks upon the portrait of Bakunin."

Placed between two autobiographical poems, "Three Old Women" seems out of context. Its atmosphere and its terms of reference are universal whereas the other poems move between the poles of childhood and old age. Our poem seems to be unique in balancing an epic-like sweep with immediate observation:

(1) *In the gray evening, by the white house,* (2) *Three old women sit, looking (out) before them.* (3) *And silence (is all) around.* (4) *As though the hawk suddenly froze in (his) flight.* (5) *Three old women sitting by the house.*

The first impression recalls a Dutch genre painting and line 3—*vehás savív* ("silence all around")—confirms the static quality. But with the introduction of the hawk, the silence becomes charged with a sense of terror—the verb "froze" is hardly reassuring. Line 5 makes an effort to restore the quietude, repeating the first impression.

(6) *Above their heads, someone is silently knitting* (7) *A stocking of blue in the old style.* (8) *A skein of gold unrolls on the horizon.* (9) *Three old women suddenly saw a boy.*

Leaving the real setting, the poem extends the picture to the universe. The sky is now an old-fashioned "stocking of blue" (7) that

בָּעֶרֶב הָאָפֹר עַל יַד הַבַּיִת הַלָּבָן
יוֹשְׁבוֹת שָׁלֹשׁ זְקֵנוֹת וְצוֹפִיּוֹת אֶל נִכְחָן.
וְהָס סָבִיב.
כְּאִלּוּ בִּמְעוּפוֹ קָפָא פִּתְאֹם הָעַיִט.
שָׁלֹשׁ זְקֵנוֹת יוֹשְׁבוֹת עַל יַד הַבַּיִת.

וּמִי־שֶׁהוּא דוּמָם סוֹרֵג מֵעַל רֹאשָׁן
פֻּזְמָק כָּחֹל בְּנֹסַח הַיָּשָׁן.
צְנֵפַת זָהָב בָּאֹפֶק מִתְגּוֹלֶלֶת.
שָׁלֹשׁ זְקֵנוֹת רָאוּ לְפֶתַע יֶלֶד.

שָׁלֹשׁ זְקֵנוֹת הִתְעוֹרְרוּ פִּתְאֹם
וְנֶאֶנְחוּ: מִסְכֵּן... וַדַּאי יָתוֹם...
וְאַחַר־כָּךְ נִגְּשׁוּ. לִטְפוּהוּ עַל הַלֶּחִי.
הַיֶּלֶד הִתְבּוֹנֵן — וְהִתְפָּרֵץ בִּבְכִי.

וְאַחַר־כָּךְ בָּא לַיִל, כְּיֶלֶד לֹא־מוּבָן.
שָׁלֹשׁ זְקֵנוֹת חָמְקוּ אֶל תּוֹךְ הַבַּיִת הַלָּבָן.
וְהָס סָבִיב.
רַק אֵיזֶה עֶלְבּוֹן עוֹד הִתְחוֹגֵג כְּעַיִט
מֵעַל לְדַף סַפְסָל, שֶׁנִּתְרוֹקֵן עַל־יַד הַבַּיִת.

Baérev haafór al yad habáyit halaván
Yoṣvót ṣalóṣ zkeynót vetsofiyót el niḥeḥán.
Vehás savív.
Keílu bim'ufó kafá pit'óm haáyit.
Ṣalóṣ zkeynót yoṣvót al yad habáyit.

Umí-ṣehú dumám sorég meál roṣán
Puzmák kaḥól banúsaḥ hayaṣán.
Tsnefát zaháv baófek mitgolélet.
Ṣalóṣ zkeynót raú leféta yéled.

Ṣalóṣ zkeynót hit'orerú pít'óm
Veneenḥú: miskén . . . vadáy yatóm . . .
Veaḥár-kaḥ nigṣú. Litfúhu al haléḥi.
Hayéled hitbonén—vehitparéts bevéḥi.

Veaḥar-káḥ ba láyil, keyéled lo-muván.
Ṣalóṣ zkeynót ḥamkú el toḥ habáyit halaván.
Vehás savív.
Rak éyze ilavón od hitḥogég keáyit
Meál ledáf safsál, ṣenitrokén al-yád habáyit.

"Someone" is knitting. Shlonsky hardly dares utter his name, but the Unknown Someone who reappears in many of his poems testifies to the writer's deep-rooted religious feeling. Someone carries on the knitting for the old women who, for the moment, have stopped. The stocking image is succeeded by the sunset whose "golden skein unrolls" to brighten the gray evening (8). Then a boy is seen and his sudden arrival brings the stanza to a close. We may learn something of his "meaning" only after finishing the poem. Is he the incomprehensible childhood—the "child who is not understood" (14)? Or, since the lyric appears among the autobiographical verses describing childhood, is the boy having his first, frightening encounter with old age?

(10) *Three old women suddenly awoke* (11) *And sighed: Poor thing . . . probably an orphan . . .* (12) *And afterwards [they] went [to him]. Caressed his cheek.* (13) *The boy stared—and burst into tears.*

The static picture has come alive. Perhaps the old women have been stirred out of their own need to pity someone weaker than themselves. Readers of other poems by this writer are aware that, under the influence of Ivan Karamazov's moving speech, Shlonsky often uses childhood to represent not joy but the tears of children which have turned the world into the proverbial vale of tears. One of the poems actually uses some of Ivan's words: "This, your world, is like Sodom/ So long as one child sobs."

(14) *And afterwards night came, like a child who is not understood.* (15) *Three old women slipped away into the white house.* (16) *And silence (is all) around.* (17) *Only a kind of shame-wretchedness-insult circles still like a hawk* (18) *Above the wooden bench that was emptied near the house.*

The old women caress the boy but he stares at them and sobs—the poem does not indicate why—perhaps out of fear, perhaps out of repulsion as he looks upon old age. In any event, the love-need of the old women fails to obtain his response. Life's beginning and life's end are anything but a perfect cycle.

The child is not understood and the night is like that child: they darken the poem. The old women slip away, leaving the scene to a stillness which is interrupted and defined by the hawk's circling of another sort: it is no longer merely terror but an inexplicable failure of meeting, of understanding. The failed encounter ends in a symbol of its meanings that the Hebrew *ilavón*—a typical Shlonsky recasting: "shame-wretchedness-insult"—suggests but does not define.

Old age has frightened childhood, tries to caress it, meets with sobs, and turns its back on it—and yet the poem also contains a sense of resignation. This is conveyed largely through the form: four stanzas, two of which (2,3) are the traditional quatrains, riming *aabb*. Placed in the center of the poem, these four-line stanzas contrast with the five-line stanzas, which rime as *aa-x-bb*, the repeated words *vehás saviv* ("and silence all around," 3, 16) breaking the pattern. In these stanzas the rimes are almost identical. First: *halaván/ nihehán—haáyit/ habáyit;* the second: *muván/ halaván—keáyit/ habáyit.*

This formal quality of the poem gives it stability and balance. The intervening middle lines of the first and last "framing" stanzas do not disrupt. They act as a cesura to underscore the suggestion of the lines.

— LEA GOLDBERG

Abraham Shlonsky

END OF ADÁR · KETS ADÁR · קֵץ אֲדָר

Though Shlonsky has written few poems about nature, his verse is by no means devoid of nature imagery. Natural phenomena have had a deep and always symbolic effect upon him, as for example in the leaf-fall image that recurs throughout his work. But the leaf-fall (*ṣaléḥet*) and other such figures are essentially symbolic or mood motifs; he uses them as Dostoevsky uses the description of "the slanted rays of the setting sun" throughout his novels.

Shlonsky's verse of the thirties and early forties contained many elements indicating a "return to nature," but they reflected rather the poet's effort to hold onto the world about him—to preserve it by the vestigial optimism to which a man of his generation might cling. His deliberate hopefulness enabled him to believe in the world's future by linking it to its distant, primeval past: to unchanging tree, hill, millstone; to the simplest of rural occupations: water-drawer, miller. This period of the poet's striving is reflected memorably in the two cycles "An Other Genesis" and "Songs of Bread and Water."

In the early twenties, when "End of Adár" was written, Shlonsky's encounter with the landscape of the Valley of Jezreel and of Mt. Gilboa was like a new encounter with himself. He was intoxicated; the experience carried him into exotic metaphors. But in those places and in those days the exotic was an everyday experience. The image of

כְּאֶצְעֲדוֹת־הַזָּהָב אֲשֶׁר לִזְרוֹעוֹת הַבֶּדְוִיָּה,		Keets'adót-hazaháv aṣér lizroót habedviyá,
יַעַנְדוּ הָרֵי הַגִּלְבֹּעַ לְעֵמֶק יִזְרְעֶאל		Yaandú haréy hagilbóa leémek yizreél
אֶת צְמִידֵיהֶם	3	Et tsmideyhém
בִּשְׁעוֹת הַזָּהָב אֲשֶׁר לְעַרְבֵי קֵץ־אֲדָר.		Biṣ'ót hazaháv aṣér learvéy kets-adár.
אָז תֵּצֶאןָ הַשֹּׁאֲבוֹת הָעַיְנָה,		Az tetséna haṣoavót haáyna,
וְהָיוּ הַכַּלָּנִיּוֹת כְּאֶצְעָדוֹת לְרַגְלֵיהֶן.	6	Vehayú hakalaniyót keets'adót leragleyhén.
הַטִּי, הַטִּי־נָא אֶת כַּדֵּךְ,		Hatí, hatí-na et kadéḥ,
וְנִשְׁתֶּה מֵימֵי־עַיִן קָרִים, נוֹזְלִים,	8	Veniṣté meyméy áyin karím, nozlím,
וְהָיוּ לְחִכֵּנוּ כַּיַּיִן הַטּוֹב.		Vehayú leḥikéynu kayáyin hatóv.

the Bedouin grew out of the Palestinian soil as naturally as palm tree, terebinth, and thornbush. Moreover, Hebrew as an ancient oriental tongue was the bearer of this exoticism. Shlonsky achieved a special style for fusing the experience and language of an oriental country with the world-view of a man of basically European education and thought. Even today the poems of this idiom have an *avant-garde* ring. One is fascinated to discover how with the aid of biblical verse and "oriental" metaphors a poem can emerge that is so close to Expressionism. Shlonsky's uniqueness in achieving such poems explains why many critics date the "New Hebrew Poetry" with his work.

The stanzas before us make up the first part of "End of Adár." Adár is the month that roughly corresponds to our February-March— in Israel it is the spring month that also foreshadows summer drought. It is the "moment" of saturated earth, of bursting, of the almost splendid efflorescence that must soon die. With the burnt-out browns and yellows of Adár's end, the flowering land seems to forecast drought and sun-blast. But the speaker seizes the moment of blooming and speaks of it as men do about the exaltation of love, aware that all such moments cannot last long.

(1) *Like the golden bangles on the arms of a Bedouin woman* (2) *Gilboa's hills adorn the Valley of Jezreel* (3) *With their bracelets* (4) *In the golden hours [that belong to] the evenings of Adár's end.* (5) *Then do the women who draw water go out to the well.* (6) *And the anemones become like bangles to (on) their legs.*

The ornament of the Bedouin woman is *ets'adót* ("bangles") but that of Gilboa's hills *tsmidím* ("bracelets"). To modern speakers of Hebrew, *ets'adót* is an exotic word for a piece of oriental jewelry but *tsmidím* is a common term today. As he refers to the bracelet, the speaker associates the hill-landscape with the world-view of modern man, confining the exotic bangle to the Bedouin woman.

The obsolete orthography of *tetséna* ("then they go out," 5) deliberately used here by Shlonsky ties the new world to the biblical world, only to be followed by a neologism—*kalaniyót*, "anemones," 6—a flower's name that every Israeli knows. Hebrew verse written in the Diaspora rarely used the names of flowers; hence *kalaniyót* is a key word for indicating the new relationship between the people and the soil. Trained Hebrew readers take delight in the ease with which the poet shifts from this modern term to the almost archaic *ets'adót* in the same line.

(7) *Incline, pray incline your pitcher* (8) *And let us drink the cold flowing waters of the well* (9) *And they shall be like good wine to our palates.*

כִּי יָרַד הָאֲדָר לִגְווֹעַ מִתְּנוּבָה,		Ki yarád haadár ligvóa mitnuvá,
כַּאֲשֶׁר יָמוּתוּ הַבֶּדְוִים אֲשֶׁר לְשֵׁבֶט עַזְרָא	11	Kaaṣér yamútu habedvím aṣér leṣévet ázra
מִנִּי אַהֲבָה.		Miní ahavá.
אָז הָיִינוּ שְׁמֵי־הַשְׁקִיעָה	13	Az hayínu ṣmey-haṣki'á
אֲשֶׁר לְעַרְבֵי קֵץ־אֲדָר.		Aṣér learvéy kets-adár.

One almost thinks that a love-poem is about to begin—and that it will bring the biblical response "And I will also water your camels" (Genesis 24:19). But who is to incline the pitcher? the woman? the earth itself, filled with the waters of Adár's end? Without identifying the one addressed by the speaker, the poem takes a sudden turn:

(10) *For Adár has descended to die from produce* [lit. *ripeness, yield*] (11) *Like the Bedouin of the Asra tribe* [*who*] *die* (12) *From love.*

The allusion to Heine's lyric "Der Asra," part of the repertory of every European young lady, attains curious freshness and significance in the context of this poem of the Palestinian world: *ich bin aus Jemen,/ Und mein Stamm sind jene Asra,/ Welche sterben, wenn sie lieben.* "I am from Yemen,/ And my kinsmen are those Asra/ Who die when they love." The produce of the Palestinian spring which is condemned to die is love. Note that *tnuvá* ("produce," 10) and *ahavá* ("love," 12) form the only rime. Throughout the lyric the softness of these "v" sounds is echoed by *bedviyá* ("Bedouin woman," 1), *zaháv* ("gold," 4), *ṣoavót* ("women who draw water," 5), *ligvóa* ("to die," 10), and *arvéy* ("evenings of," 4, 14). The allusion to Heine's Asra is framed by the two rime words (10,12) and the line is long—the death heavy and ripe.

(13) *Then we became the sunset skies* (14) [*that belong to*] *the evenings of Adár's end.*

The first 12 lines, for all their allusions, might have been no more than a richly metaphorical landscape poem. But the closing couplet breaks the frame unconditionally: man unites with nature; unexpectedly he "becomes" the universe. This is the kind of poetic leap that eludes commentary but is felt and accepted instantly by the sensitive reader, without questioning or theorizing. He simply knows that something has taken place which has brought the poem to a higher and a different level. —"Then we became the sunset skies [that belong to] of the evenings of Adár's end." Such a passage helps one understand what Keats meant when he said that "poetry should surprise by a fine excess."

— LEA GOLDBERG

Abraham Shlonsky

MR. X SPEAKS ABOUT HIS NEIGHBORHOOD · NEÚM PLONÍ AL ṢḤUNATÓ

נְאֻם פְּלוֹנִי עַל שְׁכוּנָתוֹ

Readers unfamiliar with Hebrew can hardly appreciate the masterful dexterity with which Shlonsky uses the language. In our preceding commentaries, we have pointed to words and lines that indicate some of his many innovations and characteristic phrasings; but to convey an adequate idea of his contribution, we should have to add more than is possible in this volume. Drawing from the various levels and periods of the language, he has developed not only new words but new grammatical forms; he has created fresh nuances and new concepts.

Shlonsky is often considered "difficult," and it is true that his style does not always lend itself to facile deciphering. But his syntax invariably remains faithful to the logic and spirit of Hebrew and he does not strain words to fit the needs of rhythm or rime.

Occasionally the reader may meet difficulties in following the structure of an entire poem rather than of a sentence. In this respect his style reminds one of Baudelaire's where the lucidity of individual sentences seems to dissipate when they are joined to form a poetic whole.

Shlonsky often seems to seek out complicated techniques. He delights in playing with pattern, rhythm, and rime. Actually he tends to use precise and traditional meters but he breaks them up, sometimes making each word a separate line, in the manner of Mayakowsky's indented verses (which the Russians refer to as "ladder" poems).

The foregoing remarks apply to Shlonsky's work prior to the fifties. His latest book, *Stones of Parchment* (1960), from which our poem is taken, is quite different in style. "Mr. X Speaks About His Neighborhood" impresses one as simple, controlled, almost prose-like. Emphasizing words which report a day-to-day existence, Shlonsky avoids the decorative and the festive—in vocabulary and in tone.

The subject is the title: Mr. X speaking about the section where he lives in the new Tel Aviv, which hardly resembles the dynamic, expanding town of Shlonsky's earlier poems. At this period in its evolution, the city is static. Residential neighborhoods are now established, taken for granted: a monotonous stability regulates the lives of their inhabitants. Boredom is the poem's motif. But though as boredom it is close to the Symbolists' *ennui*, the feeling is different. This is the urban boredom of straight roads and well-ordered streets—of a man living in a modern city built in uniform style. Neither buildings nor streets are described, for the style of the poem is the description.

However, the ironical dissonance of the poem is already present in the title. *Neúm* in ordinary usage means "speech," "lecture." In biblical usage it generally refers to the word of God in the mouth of His prophets. By using the biblical spelling of the word and coupling it with a familiar rabbinical formula (*neúm ploní* etc., employed in the signature of verdicts, contracts, writs), Shlonsky immediately establishes the tone of the poem: "Thus spake Mr. So-and-so . . . ."

בֵּית־מְגוּרַי הוּא בֶּן 5 קוֹמוֹת, —	Bet-meguráy hu ben ḥaméṣ komót,—
וְכָל חַלּוֹנוֹתָיו מְפֻהָקִים אֶל שֶׁכְּנֶגֶד,	Veḥól ḥalonotáv mefohakím el ṣekenéged,
כִּפְנֵי הַנִּצָּבִים אֶל מוּל רְאִי.	Kifnéy hanitsavím el mul reí.
70 קַוֵּי אוֹטוֹבּוּסִים בְּעִירִי,	Ṣiv'ím kavéy otobúsim beirí,
וְכֻלָּם עַד מַחְנָק וְעַד סִרְחוֹן הַגּוּפִים.	Veḥulám ad maḥnák veád sirḥón hagufím.
הֵם נוֹסְעִים	Hem nos'ím
הֵם נוֹסְעִים	Hem nos'ím
הֵם נוֹסְעִים אֶל לֵב הַכְּרָךְ,	Hem nos'ím el lev hakráḥ,
כְּאִלּוּ אִי־אֶפְשָׁר לִגְווֹעַ מִשִּׁעֲמוּם גַּם כָּאן, —	Keílu i-efṣár ligvóa miṣiamúm gam kan,—
בִּשְׁכוּנָתִי שֶׁלִּי.	Biṣḥunatí ṣelí.
שְׁכוּנָתִי שֶׁלִּי הִיא קְטַנָּה מְאֹד,	Ṣḥunatí ṣelí hi ktaná meód,
אַךְ יֵשׁ בָּהּ כָּל הַלֵּדוֹת וְהַמִּיתוֹת,	Aḥ yeṣ ba kol haleydót vehamitót,
וְכָל שֶׁבֵּין לֵדָה לְמָוֶת	Veḥól ṣebéyn leydá lemávet
שֶׁיֵּשׁ בִּכְרַכֵּי הָעוֹלָם, —	Ṣeyéṣ biḥrakéy haolám,—
אֲפִילוּ תִּינוֹקוֹת, הַמְסוֹבְבִים לְהַפְלִיא צַלַּחַת־מְעוֹפֶפֶת,	Afílu tinokót, hamesovevím lehaflí [tsaláḥat-meoféfet,
וּ־3 בָּתֵּי־קוֹלְנוֹעַ.	U-ṣloṣá batéy-kolnóa.
לוּלֵא הִסְתַּפַּקְתִּי בַּשִּׁעֲמוּם שֶׁיֵּשׁ לִי בְּבֵיתִי,	Luléy histapákti baṣiamúm ṣeyéṣ li beveytí,
הָיִיתִי הוֹלֵךְ לְאֶחָד מֵהֶם.	Hayíti holéḥ leeḥád mehém.
בֵּית־מְגוּרַי הוּא בֶּן 5 קוֹמוֹת, —	Bet-meguráy hu ben ḥaméṣ komót,—
זוֹ שֶׁקָּפְצָה מִן הַחַלּוֹן שֶׁכְּנֶגֶד	Zo ṣekaftsá min haḥalón ṣekenéged
נִסְתַּפְּקָה בְּ־3 בִּלְבַד. —	Nistapká be-ṣalóṣ bilvád.—

(1) *The building I live in has 5 floors* (2) *And all its windows are yawned to what's opposite (across)*, (3) *Like the faces of those who stand before the mirror.* We have already been deposited in the neighborhood, surrounded by its dry, functional surface. The floors are written "5"—"five" would be wasteful and inefficient. At the same time, *mefohakím* ("are yawned," 2) breaks the rule of normal usage. Shlonsky puts the verb in the passive to coin a new image, one that is markedly depersonalized. In boredom the windows are yawned out "to" the buildings across the street—which are the same as the buildings on this side, ad infinitum.

(4) *There are 70 bus lines in my city*, (5) *All of them up to [the point of] choking and up to [the point of] the stinking of bodies.* (6) *They travel* (7) *They travel* (8) *They travel to the heart of the city* (9) *As if it were impossible to die from boredom here also*—(10) *In my own neighborhood.* Line 5 deliberately omits "are filled with" or "are packed with" to produce a shock of terseness—in contrast to the weary, thrice-repeated verb in 6,7,8. But "they travel" does not convey motion or change. It is

rather another fact that enforces sameness.

(11) *My neighborhood is very small,* (12) *Yet it contains all the births and deaths,* (13) *And whatever [there is] between birth and death* (14) *That is in the world's cities—* (15) *Even children, who spin "flying saucer" disks marvelously,* (16) *And 3 movie theatres.* (17) *If I did not find the boredom that I have in my own home quite enough,* (18) *I would go to one of them.*

We are in a specific neighborhood—but specific neighborhoods do not really exist. They are all the same, for all their modernity. Even the entertainments offer the same sameness. Note how these emporia have been reduced and neutralized by the spelling-out here of the number "one" (18).

Except for the one simile in line 3, the language of the entire poem is as festive as a business report. The closing lines continue in the same depersonalized tone:

(19) *The building I live in has 5 floors—* (20) *That woman* [lit. "one," feminine demonstrative pronoun] *who leaped from the window opposite* (21) *Found 3 to be quite enough.*

The verse is unrimed and its rhythms free, yet a certain symmetry persists in the structure. The first and last stanzas, for example, are each three lines long, and the opening line of each is identical.

— LEA GOLDBERG

Yocheved Bat-Miriam

A CUBIT AND A HALF · ÁMA VAḤÉTSI KOMÁTI* · אַמָּה וָחֵצִי קוֹמָתִי

אַמָּה וָחֵצִי קוֹמָתִי,
אַמָּה וָחֵצִי אַף הִיא —
הַהִיא כִּבְרַת־אֶרֶץ הַשְּׁמוּרָה
לִמְנוּחָה אַחֲרוֹנָה שֶׁלִּי.

וְצוֹפֶה כְּחַלּוֹן פָּתוּחַ
לְרוּחוֹת מֶרְחַקִּים וָרוֹם —
כָּל יוֹם שֶׁבּוֹקֵעַ וְעוֹלֶה,
כְּאִלּוּ הוּא תָּלוּי עַל תְּהוֹם.
וְהוֹמָה מִתְיַפְּחָה בְּיָדַי
בְּבִרְכַּת הַפְּרִידָה לָעַד —
כָּל יָד הַמּוּשָּׁטָה לְשָׁלוֹם
וּנְבוֹכָה נֶחֱלֶצֶת מִיָּד.

וְנָבוֹךְ מִזְדַּקֵּר כָּל צַוָּאר,
כְּתִינוֹק מִזְּרוֹעוֹת הָאֵם,
שֶׁנֶּעֱצַב לֹא־חֻמַּל, לֹא־רֻחַם,
אֵין־אוֹנִים, חָדֵל וְאִלֵּם.

אֵיךְ אֶאְטֹם אָזְנִי מִקּוֹלָם,
אֵיךְ אַעְלִים עֵינַי מִזֶּה —
וְקוֹרֵן כָּל מֵצַח זוֹרֵחַ
בְּנֹגַהּ מֵעֵבֶר מִזֶּה!

וְרוֹעֵד כָּל צַעַד כְּכוֹשֵׁל,
כְּבוֹכֶה מִתְעַלֵּם בְּלִי קוֹל,
וּסְלִיחָה דוֹמַעַת הִנְּנִי,
מֵהַכֹּל מְבַקְּשָׁה עַל כֹּל.

Áma vaḥétsi komáti,
Áma vaḥétsi af hi—
Hahí kívrat-érets haṣmúra
Limnúḥa aḥróna ṣelí.

Vetsófe keḥálon patúaḥ
Lerúḥot merḥákim varóm—
Kol yom ṣebokéa veóle,
Keílu hu táluy al thom.
Vehóma mityápḥa beyádi
Bevírkat haprída laád—
Kol yad hamuṣáta leṣálom
Unvóḥa neḥlétset miyád.

Venávoḥ mizdáker kol tsávar,
Ketínok mizróot haém,
Ṣenéetsav lo-ḥúmal, lo-rúḥam,
Eyn-ónim, ḥadél veilém.

Eyḥ étom ózni mikólam,
Eyḥ álim éynay mizé—
Vekóren kol métsaḥ zoréaḥ
Benóga meéver mizé!

Veróed kol tsáad keḥóṣel.
Kevóḥe mitálem bli kol,
Uslíḥa domáat hinéni,
Mehákol meváksa al kol.

Born in Russia in 1901, Yocheved Bat-Miriam—like Shlonsky, Alterman, and (Goldberg p. 74, 106, 120)—assimilated the techniques of contemporary Russian poets, first of the Symbolists and then of the various modernists generally referred to as "Futurists." Among all these, she is clearly closest to Boris Pasternak. Beginning her literary career in 1923, she published her first book of verse (*Meraḥók*) in 1929 in Palestine, having emigrated there three years earlier, following a brief stay in Paris. Though she published steadily throughout the thirties and forties, she has written no poetry since

1948, the year of her son's death in the War of Independence. Her collected verse appeared in 1963.

Bat-Miriam has produced the kind of dense poetry which rarely commands a wide audience and often defies the facile critic and challenges the thoughtful one. The unique difficulty of her verse arises from the tension between her Futuristic idiom and her personal background—she was reared in an atmosphere of traditional Jewish piety. The childhood spent in her parental home glows steadily at the center of her imagination.

Reading a Bat-Miriam poem, particularly of a later date, one always feels a vibrant tension between daring syntax and astonishing metaphorical leaps, on the one hand, and artful, conservative prosody, on the other. Each poem beats with a major force of will to capture an intense emotional experience, with its varied associations. When the poetry succeeds in striking the balance between emotion and intellect, the commonest themes—yearning for childhood innocence, sanctity of home, love for a person or a landscape, fear of death, alienation—burst forth with fresh light. Almost every clause, even those that escape logical discourse, evokes an emotional response.

In "A Cubit and a Half," an early poem, the point of departure is the reference to the dimensions of the Holy Ark (Exodus 25:10): "And they shall make an ark of acacia wood: two cubits and a half shall be the length thereof, and a cubit and a half the breadth thereof, and a cubit and a half the height thereof."

(1) *A cubit and a half is my height;* (2) *A cubit and a half is also she—* (3) *That plot of earth reserved* (4) *For my last rest.*

The contrast between the significance of the Holy Ark and the insignificance of the speaker's imagined grave energizes the ordinary imagery associated with the fear of death. The diction is meaningfully familiar, but the fact that death is unavoidable emerges as a spectre of horror encountered, as it were, for the first time, since the dimension "a cubit and a half" links spiritual immortality with the nothingness of material death. The plot of earth, looming now menacingly, begins to infuse otherwise commonplace acts and objects with ominous import.

The reader of the Hebrew text at once becomes aware of two inversions which both wrench the syntax and place the words *hi* ("she") at the end of line 2 and *hahi* ("that") at the beginning of line 3.

(5) *And [there] looks out (awaits), like an open window,* (6) *To the winds of distances and height,* (7) *Each day which bursts forth and rises* (8) *As if hung over an abyss.* (9) *And [there] moans, sobbing in my hand* (10) *With the blessing of eternal farewell,* (11) *Every hand extended in greeting* (12) *And perplexed immediately withdraws.*

(13) *And perplexed each neck cranes,* (14) *Like a baby from a mother's arms,* (15) *Who sorrowed: unpitied, unconsoled,* (16) *Powerless, inert, voiceless.*

(17) *How shall I shut my ear to their cry,* (18) *How shall I avert my eyes from [all] this—* (19) *And each shining brow radiates* (20) *With an effulgence from beyond (this).*

The structure is cyclical: we move from a hushed statement of situation (stanza 1) through a series of anguished musical periods (stanzas 2,3), and back again to a sigh of submission (stanza 5). We are propelled through the middle section by the repetition of the conjunctive "and" (*ve*) prefixed to a verb.

The feeling generated by this simple plot of earth in the first stanza pervades the next three. Every sign of hope, of longing—the first symbolized by the Holy Ark but then repeated in the open window, the distance and height, the day bursting forth and rising, the extended hand, the craning neck, the radiant brow—accentuates the tragedy of inevitable death and thereby almost emerges by antithesis as an emblem of death itself.

(21) *And each step trembles like one who stumbles,* (22) *Like one who weeps, vanishing voiceless,* (23-24) *And I seek from all a tearful forgiveness for all.* Hemmed in on all sides by

the presence of death, the poet ends her lament in quiet humility—not in rage against the order of the universe.

Though this is an early poem (written in Ashkenazi), Bat-Miriam's confident mastery of her art is unmistakable. She takes liberties precisely where the context either allows or demands it. Only the even lines rime, but since the odd lines are always feminine and the even always masculine, the ear feels an accentual pattern throughout. And in the one instance of insufficient rime (2-4) the reduction in the end-of-line resonance is compensated for by the repeated *iy* sounds within the stanza.

Note also that each instance of syllable dropping (e.g., 1,2,16,17,18) has its semantic justification. Lines 1 and 2 are based on the biblical phrase which is the point of departure of the poem. In 16 the syllable dropped from the second foot is added to the third to break the monotony of the catalogue of adjectives describing the "baby" that we all are. In 17-18 the syllable dropped in the same place in each line calls our attention to *ózni* ("my ear) and *éynay* ("my eyes"). Such variations avoid the monotony that might otherwise result from the regular amphibrachic pattern.

Obviously working on the principle that the first word of a phrase is the one most emphasized (in this poem in particular where each word carries unusual force), Bat-Miriam achieves astonishing effects by jarring the expected syntactic ordering. *Hahí* (3, already mentioned) sets the shock pattern, but *vetsófe* (5), *vehóma* (9) are even more striking here since the verb precedes its subject by two lines, a phenomenon rarely found in Hebrew. — ARNOLD BAND

Yocheved Bat-Miriam

CRANES FROM THE THRESHOLD · AGURÍM MEHASÁF · עֲגוּרִים מֵהַסַּף

Written in Palestine and in the Israeli accent, this poem is the first of thirteen composing a cycle, "Cranes from the Threshold," a work inspired by the poet's memories of childhood in the landscape of southern Russia. Unlike many other poets of her generation uprooted from Europe who could not relate with equal intimacy to the country of their childhood and the Palestine of their maturity, Bat-Miriam attuned her sensibilities to both. With its further development of syntactical originality and its intensely personal referents, the work could not possibly be mistaken for that of any other poet.

The cranes seen from the threshold—the central image—emerge as an obsessive private symbol throughout the cycle. Memories of childhood, of home, of the surrounding countryside, all focus within it. Often the threshold becomes the window, the cranes, the rain, the sun, the wind. Even in the poet's adult imagination these various elements are combined, as they might have been seen in her childhood's mind.

(1) *Behind me you remained on the road,* (2) *And my footstep exults (sings) remembering.* (3) *A golden, pensive sheaf,* (4) *Cranes, cranes on the meadow.*

מֵאַחֲרַי אַתְּ נִשְׁאַרְתְּ עַל הַדֶּרֶךְ,	Meaḥaráy at niṣ'árt al hadéreḥ,
וְרוֹנֵן צַעֲדֵי הַנִּזְכָּר.	Veronén tsaadí hanizkár.
אֲלֻמָּה זְהֻבָּה וּמְהֻרְהֶרֶת,	Alumá zehubá umhurhéret,
עֲגוּרִים, עֲגוּרִים עַל הַכָּר!	Agurím, agurím al hakár!
אֶכָּשֵׁל בְּעָנָן כִּבְאֶבֶן,	Ekaṣél beanán kiveéven,
אֶכָּשֵׁל בְּיוֹמִי כִּבְחֵטְא.	Ekaṣél beyomí kiveḥét.
יִשָּׂאֵנִי בֵּין כָּחוֹל וְכוֹכֶבֶת	Yisaéyni beyn kḥol veḥoḥévet
תֹּם גִּמְגּוּמֵךְ הַמְרַטֵּט!	Tom gimguméḥ hamratét!
כִּי הָיִית, כִּי הִקְרַנְתְּ מִבֶּכִי,	Ki hayít, ki hikránt mibéḥi,
כִּי גָּחַנְתְּ עַל גַּל מְצֻיָּר,	Ki gaḥánt al gal metsuyár,
נוֹשְׁמָה, מַפְלִיגָה וְהוֹלֶכֶת	Noṣmá, mafligá veholéḥet
נִשְׁמַת חוֹף לֹא־נִרְאֶה וְנִסְעָר.	Niṣmát ḥof lo-nir'é venis'ár.
מְטַפְּחִים אֵלָיו וְאֵלַיִךְ	Metapḥím eyláv veeyláyiḥ
(הַסְּגוּרָה בְּמֶרְחַקּוֹ הַזָּהֹב!),	(Hasgurá bemerḥakó hazahóv!),
מְטַפְּחִים מִשְׁתַּפְּכִים יָמַי לִי	Metapḥím miṣtaphím yamáy li
וְשָׁרִים חֲלוֹמֵךְ הָאָהוּב.	Veṣarím ḥaloméḥ haahúv.

The unnamed feminine singular "you" (*at*, 1), to whom the poem is addressed, is evidently the landscape of the childhood that the speaker left behind. The "golden" hue will flicker like a leitmotif throughout the poem (11, 14, 23). Is the pensiveness the poet's own pensiveness? Is the sheaf also a sheaf of memories? The reader at once feels the presence of multiple reverberations whose relationships will make up the poem's "method." Flying in the sky, the wild cranes convey the feeling of unfettered nature. Together with the "golden sheaf" they somehow seem to elevate—even to redeem—the speaker, who is no longer the child, as her mind flits from one element to another in the internal landscape of memory.

(5) *I falter [shall keep faltering] on a cloud as on a stone.* (6) *I falter on my day as on a sin.* (8) *The purity (innocence) of your quivering stammer* (7) *Carries me between blue and a star.*

(9) *Because you* ["at," 1] *were, because you were radiant in your weeping,* (10) *Because you bent over a painted wave,* (11) *Breathing [as] you sailed on and on,* (12) *The breath (spirit) of an unseen and stormy shore.*

The relationship between the poetess and her landscape becomes human; the landscape becomes an intimate friend or even begins to fuse with the speaker. It is this fusion which suffuses and justifies the vividness, the felt presence of the stormy outpouring in the stanza.

(13) *My days* [line 15] *are pounding, beating toward it* [the shore] *and toward you* (14) *(Who are enclosed within its golden distance!)* (15) *Are beating [and] are pouring themselves out for me* (16) *And [they] are singing your beloved dream.* The present days are beating out their song of memories—waves

זְהָרִים וּדְמִי לְלֹא־שַׁחַר,		Zeharím udmí lelo-ṣáhar,
זְהָרִים וּתְכֵלֶת אֵין־שֵׁם;		Zeharím utḥélet eyn-ṣém;
יְחִידָה הַשָּׁעָה הַצּוֹמַחַת	19	Yeḥidá haṣaá hatsomáḥat
וּמֵעֵבֶר לְעֵינַי תֵּעָצֵם.		Umeéver leeynáy teatsém.
יְחִידָה אֶל הַסַּף וְהָאֶבֶן,		Yeḥidá el hasáf vehaéven,
שֶׁבָּדוּ אַגָּדָתֵךְ בְּרֹן,		Ṣebadú agadatéḥ berón,
יוֹלִיכוּנִי כְּאוֹת הַזּוֹהֶבֶת,	23	Yoliḥúni keót hazohévet,
כְּשֵׁם עַל דַּפֵּךְ הָרִאשׁוֹן.		Keṣém al dapéḥ hariṣón.

pounding toward the golden shores of the past.

(17) *Splendors and silence without meaning (dawn)*, (18) *Splendors and azure without name;* (19) *Unique (solitary) is the hour that grows* (20) *And that will be closed beyond my eyes*. The ineffable moment of splendor has come. It is "without meaning," inexplicable, because it cannot be named in words (18).

(23) *They* [splendors] *will lead me like a goldening letter*, (24) *Like a name on your first page*, (21) *Solitary to the threshold and the stone* (22) *That devised your legend with (exultant) song*. The poem ends upon the threshold of the house, of childhood, of memory. The remembered "splendors" (17, 18, 23) are magnificently alive. The goldening letter and the exultant song of the last stanza close the circle begun by the "golden sheaf" and the "exulting footstep" of the first.

Each stanza has a rocking motion, as the sudden shifts are made between past and present. The images of the past are alive and nurture her present. They bear her "between blue and a star." And the very act of recollection becomes an hour of ecstasy (stanza 5). The only note of diminution intrudes with the knowledge of the transitoriness of this "unique hour"—which "will be shut beyond my eyes" (20).

Some of the passages strike the "outsider" as reflections of purely personal import to the poet—hence the impossibility of offering discursive statements of the "meaning" of every line and every image, without recourse to the body of Bat-Miriam's poetry. One must read—and reread—the poem from a different stance. The violation of normative syntactical order and the fusion of planes of consciousness and of time limits may suggest a Mallarmean mode of evocation. It is within such a frame that the poem asks to be experienced.

— ARNOLD BAND

Avot Yeshurun

IN THE CITY OF THE JUDGES · BEÍR HAṢOFTÍM · בְּעִיר הַשּׁוֹפְטִים

Born in 1904 in the western Ukraine, Avot Yeshurun spent his childhood in his grandfather's home in Poland, where he was deeply affected by its traditional Hasidic atmosphere. He came to Palestine in 1925 (". . . the first Arab I met in the country, a man with a black beard, reminded me of my father"). For many years he roamed the country's Jewish-Arab villages, working as a building-hand, swamp-dredger, fruit-picker, as well as a laborer in a brick-factory and a print-shop. His first book of poetry—remarkable for its harsh oriental sonalities and its evocation of the Arab milieu—appeared in 1942.

The Jewish patriarch of Eastern Europe and the Arab native of Israel—"this man with the camel"—are the key figures in Yeshurun's poetry. Both represent well-defined worlds of tradition, morality, and language, deeply rooted in their respective landscapes. And both have "disappeared," both have been the victims of tragedy. The identification between these two figures underlies much of Yeshurun's verse, which is often baffling and inaccessible though it treats of "public" themes and sometimes carries didactic, moralistic overtones.

Many of the poems of Avot Yeshurun (the literal meaning of his adopted name is "the fathers are looking [at us]") are studded with expressions in Yiddish and Arabic, bilingual (Hebrew-Arabic) puns, Hebrew slang, portmanteau words; the syntax is often wrenched, seemingly arbitrary; the rimes are unconventional in the extreme. But these stylistic idiosyncrasies do not stem from a desire to shock the reader or to camouflage the poet's intent. They are the outcome of his attempt to bridge the gap between two conflicting worlds; to define his spiritual and emotional heritage and his moral position in relation to the new land and new people he encountered upon coming to Palestine (". . . it was not Herzl or Weizmann who brought me to the land of Israel but the Arab docker who transported me from the ship to the shore of Jaffa . . ."). His poetry bears the marks of his unusual struggle to wield a Hebrew idiom which would be powerful enough to overcome the pull of his rich mother-tongue, Yiddish, while at the same time expressing his deep attachment for those in the old home whom he "sentenced to the hard labor of endless longing." And it is in the name of his Yiddish-Hebrew heritage—expressed in a wealth of intimate detail—that he celebrates the nobility of the Arab, mourns his absence from the Israeli landscape, and attacks a morality which condones or ignores acts of injustice.

"In the City of the Judges" (1949) is composed of two sections. The first describes the conflict between powerful childhood allegiances and the attraction of a strange, compelling present; the second appeals to the "judges" for a verdict.

The opening line calls forth a familiar image of synagogue life: the child enveloped in the fragrance of his father's prayer-shawl, *talít*. But *krumá* (2, literally "overlaid with skin" or "covered as if by skin") implies an element of coercion which is reinforced by "talisman." The child cannot release himself from the "charm" of his father's prayer-shawl, which has become part of his flesh. At the same time, he is drawn to the "prayer-shawl" of the Arab: the visual reference here is to the *'abáya*, cloak of the Arab, which, like

רֵיחָנִית טַלִּית אַבָּא,		Reyḥanít talít ába,
קְרוּמָה עָלַי כְּמִין טַלִּיסְמָא.		Krumá aláy kemín talísma.
וְרוּחַ יִשְׂרָאֵל סָבָא	3	Verúaḥ yisraél sáva
בְּטַלִּיתוֹ שֶׁל כָּל « תַּעַל אִשְׁמַע! »		Betalitó ṣel kol *"ta'ál ísma'!"*[1]
אַדִּירִים טַלִּית אַבָּא,		Adirím talít ába,
פְּרוּעָה עָלַי, מִי לֹא שׁוֹמֵעַ.		Pruá aláy, mi lo ṣoméa.
פֶּן אֲנִי לַכַּעְבֶּה,	7	Pen aní *laká'be*,[1].
פֶּן אֲנִי מִצְחִי טוֹבֵעַ...		Pen aní mitsḥí tovéa . . .
אַבָּא מוֹרְאִי,		Ába mor'í
שְׁלַח יָדְךָ לְצַוָּארִי...	10	Ṣlaḥ yadḥá letsavarí . . .
תְּמוֹל מָצָאתִי קֶרֶן אַיִל,		Tmol matsáti kéren áyil,
הַרְחֵק בַּנֶּגֶב מִדְבָּרוֹ.		Harḥék *banégev* midbaró.
שִׁפְטוּ אַתֶּם בִּירוּשָׁלַיִם,	13	Ṣiftú atém biruṣaláyim,
אִם לֹא הָיִיתִי צַוָּארוֹ...		Im lo hayíti tsavaró . . .
תְּמוֹל מָצָאתִי קֶרֶן אַיִל,		Tmol matsáti kéren áyil,
אוּלַי הַקֶּרֶן עֲבוּרִי.	16	Uláy *hakéren* avurí.
שִׁפְטוּ אַתֶּם בִּירוּשָׁלַיִם,		Ṣiftú atém biruṣaláyim,
אִם לֹא מָצָאתִי שׁוֹפָרִי.		Im lo matsáti ṣofarí.

the *talít*, is often black and white. The word *talísma*, in echoing the Yiddish or Ashkenazi form *(tális)* for "prayer-shawl," strengthens the poignancy of the clash between the two cultures.

(1) *Fragrant is father's prayer-shawl*, (2) *Sheathing me like a talisman.* (3) *And the spirit of ancient Israel* [lit. *grandfather-Israel*] (4) *[Is] in the prayer-shawl of every* "TA'ÁL ÍSMA'! [lit. in Arabic: "Come, listen!" the common form of address is here changed into an epithet].

(5) *Mighty is father's prayer-shawl*, (6) *Wild upon me, who cannot hear [it].* (7) *For fear that I [submit] to* KÁ'BE, (8) *For fear that I [and] my forehead drown. . . .*

The father's prayer-shawl hovers wildly about him, like a flag or a storm (6). It is *adirím* (the plural form of *adír*, "lord" or "lordly"), a biblical expression which here also recalls the Yiddish usage of *ádir* for "a person of great authority." The violation of grammatical usage—*adirím*, a masculine plural, here modifies *talít*, a feminine singular—serves to magnify the prayer-shawl's power.

The *ká'ba* is the famous black stone in the Great Mosque at Mecca. Again Yeshurun ignores formal grammar and even forfeits a rime (*ába*, 5; *ká'ba*, 7) in order to keep the colloquial pronunciation: *ká'be*.

The fear that he might worship the "calf" of Islam—that "I [and] my forehead" (a plural qualified by a verb in the singular) might "sink" into the holy stone (a reversal of I Samuel 17:49, "the stone sunk into his forehead")—prompts him to address his father directly:

[1] The symbol ' stands for the Arabicised or gutteral pronunciation of the letter *áyin* which, in these Arabic words, is always thus pronounced.

(9) *[My] father my fear,* (10) *Lay your hand upon my neck . . .*

The first section ends on an outcry of guilt: *ába mor'i,* "[my] father-my-terror" (patterned on *aví-morí,* "my father, my teacher"), if this attraction constitutes guilt in your eyes, if I betray you by seeing the two peoples as one, then—as Abraham did to Isaac—"lay your hand upon my neck . . ." (a paraphrase of Genesis 22:10-12). The introduction of the sacrifice motif has already been hinted at by the mention of the *Ká'ba,* for, according to Moslem tradition, it was Abraham who built the stone and it was there that he sacrificed Ishmael (Isaac's brother).

The uneven rhythms and dramatic outbursts of the first section now give way to an almost lilting narrative, which develops the Isaac-Ishmael theme:

(11) *Yesterday I found a ram's horn,* (12) *Far away in the* SOUTH *[was] his [Abraham's] desert.* (13) *You in Jerusalem (,you) judge,* (14) *If I was not his* [the horn's] *neck . . .*

(15) *Yesterday I found a ram's horn,* (16) *Perhaps (it is) the* HORN *(ray of light) for me (in my behalf).* (17) *You in Jerusalem (,you) judge,* (18) *If I have not found my trumpet (ṣofár).*

The Judges of Jerusalem—"the city of justice"—are called upon to determine who is right: he or his father. The son was already sacrificed once; he was the ram (14). Must the act of sacrifice now be repeated?

Perhaps the ram's horn—which testifies to the common past of the inhabitants of the land—can become the ray of hope (*kéren,* "horn," also means "ray of light" or "ray of hope" as well as "strength"), the source of spiritual and emotional unity. The doubt implied by "perhaps" is almost dispelled in the last line where the *kéren* becomes a *ṣofár*—the horn used by the ancient Hebrews as a trumpet in battle or upon sacred festivals, and still used in synagogues, notably on the Day of Atonement.

The poem comes full circle, returning to its synagogue setting; but now the tension of the two opposed worlds is resolved in the symbol of the *ṣofár,* which represents both cultures, the past as well as the present, atonement and redemption.

— T. CARMI

Yonatan Ratosh

IN PURPLE · BAARGAMÁN · בָּאַרְגָּמָן

לֹא יָנַקְתָּ שְׁדֵי אִמִּי, אַחָא,
וְלֹא שֶׁמֶן אֶחָד מְשָׁחָנוּ.
וְרַק הַבּוֹר — אֶחָד הוּא וְרָחָב
אֵלָיו יִפֹּל כּוֹכָב אַחַר כּוֹכָב.
אִישׁ וָאִישׁ וְשֶׁבֶר כּוֹכָבוֹ
אִישׁ וָאִישׁ וְגֹבַהּ לְבָבוֹ
— כִּי בַּיָּמִים הָהֵם אֵין מֶלֶךְ
וְאִישׁ הַיָּשָׁר בְּעֵינָיו יַעֲשֶׂה.

Lo yanákta ṣdéy imí, áḥa,
Veló ṣémen eḥád meṣaḥánu.
Verák habór—eḥád hu veraḥáv
Eyláv yipól koḥáv aḥár koḥáv.
Iṣ vaíṣ veṣéver koḥavó
Iṣ vaíṣ vegóva levavó
—Ki bayamím hahém eyn méleḥ
Veíṣ hayaṣár beeynáv yaasé.

וְאִישׁ וָאִישׁ — יְשַׁלֵּם בְּדָמָיו.
וְאִישׁ וָאִישׁ — יִסָּפֶה עַל אֶחָיו.
וְאִישׁ וָאִישׁ: לַדֶּרֶךְ פְּעָמָיו —
וְהֹלֵם גִּבּוֹרִים עַל פִּי אָבְדָן.
וְאִישׁ וָאִישׁ יְרַפֵּד בַּעֲצָמָיו
אֵם הַדֶּרֶךְ הָעוֹלָה בָּאַרְגָּמָן.

Veíṣ vaíṣ—yeṣalém bedamáv.
Veíṣ vaíṣ—yisafé al eḥáv.
Veíṣ vaíṣ: ladéreḥ peamáv—
Vehólem giborím al pí ovdán.
Veíṣ vaíṣ yerapéd baatsamáv
Em hadéreḥ haolá baargamán.

* *

לֹא יָנַקְתָּ שְׁדֵי אִמִּי, אַחָא,
וְלֹא מָוֶת אֶחָד מְצָאָנוּ.
וְרַק הַכֶּתֶר — אֶחָד הוּא וְרָחוֹק.
אֵלָיו יִשַּׁח כָּל רֹאשׁ וָרֹאשׁ כַּחֹק.
אִישׁ וָאִישׁ וְלַהַט חֲמָתוֹ
אִישׁ וָאִישׁ וְחֶרֶב מִשְׁפָּטוֹ
— כִּי בַּיָּמִים הָהֵם אֵין מֶלֶךְ
וְאִישׁ הַיָּשָׁר בְּעֵינָיו יַעֲשֶׂה.

Lo yanákta ṣdéy imí, áḥa,
Veló mávet eḥád metsaánu.
Verák hakéter—eḥád hu veraḥók.
Eyláv yiṣáḥ kol roṣ varóṣ kaḥók.
Iṣ vaíṣ veláhat ḥamató
Iṣ vaíṣ veḥérev miṣpató
—Ki bayamím hahém eyn méleḥ
Veíṣ hayaṣár beeynáv yaasé.

וְאִישׁ וָאִישׁ — יְשַׁלֵּם בְּדָמָיו.
וְאִישׁ וָאִישׁ — יִסָּפֶה עַל אֶחָיו.
וְאִישׁ וָאִישׁ: לַדֶּרֶךְ פְּעָמָיו —
וְהֹלֵם גִּבּוֹרִים עַל פִּי אָבְדָן.
וְאִישׁ וָאִישׁ יְרַפֵּד בַּעֲצָמָיו
אֵם הַדֶּרֶךְ הָעוֹלָה בָּאַרְגָּמָן.

Veíṣ vaíṣ—yeṣalém bedamáv.
Veíṣ vaíṣ—yisafé al eḥáv.
Veíṣ vaíṣ: ladéreḥ peamáv—
Vehólem giborím al pi ovdán.
Veíṣ vaíṣ yerapéd baatsamáv
Em hadéreḥ haolá baargamán.

* *

Yonaton Ratosh was born (1908) and reared in Russia but his only language was Hebrew. His parents educated their children in virtual isolation and it was not until after their emigration to Palestine, in 1921, that Ratosh could as it were enter the "world." In time he more than made up for the deprivation, for not long after entering political and cultural affairs, he became a controversial figure; and if his recognition as a poet came late, it was less because of his poetic innovations than of his doctrinal views.

Convinced that the future Hebrew nation would have to lead in a common fight for national liberation of all the peoples living in the Fertile Crescent, Ratosh published a series of articles in the newspaper he edited, calling for the expulsion of the British. He was dismissed from his position as editor. Not long after, he attempted to win a following among the non-socialist of the paramilitary organizations, and though he failed, he was in part responsible for the decision of Abraham Stern to establish a "terrorist" underground (Irgun). The Irgun disintegrated and in 1942, Stern was shot down by the British police.

It is against this background that one must read "In Purple," a lament for a man whom the poet cannot accept as a kindred spirit and whose ideals he cannot share (Stern never accepted Ratosh's program). Yet he calls him his brother: he has chosen the fighter's road that leads not only to death but also to glory.

(1) *You did not suck at my mother's breasts, brother,* (2) *And not one [the same] oil anointed us.* (3) *Only the grave is one and wide* (4) *Into which star after star falls.* (5) *Each man and the breaking-up of his fate [*lit. *star]* (6) *Each man and the pride of his heart* (7) *—For in those days there was no king* (8) *And each man would do (does) what was (is) right in his own eyes.*

(9) *And each man shall pay with his blood.* (10) *And each man shall perish with his brothers.* (11) *And each man sets forth [*lit. *his steps] upon the road* (12) *And the [foot]beat of heroes [is] on the brink of annihilation [*lit. *perdition].* (13) *And each man shall pave with his bones* (14) *The crossroads that go up in purple.*

The key word is *iṣ*, meaning not merely the male of the species (which would be *adám*) but man as noble striver and fighter. It is originally a "lord," and *eḥáv* (10) are not necessarily his brothers but his retainers who follow him in battle. For Ratosh as for many modern Hebrew poets, the original shadings and meanings of biblical Hebrew persist behind the derived sense in which the words are used today: "anointed" (2) brings to mind not only the newborn infant but the anointment of a king; "pride" (6) is literally "tallness of the heart." Again *ovdán* (12) means "loss" or "perdition," but originally the chasm into which a man falls when he misses his footing on the narrow mountain road.

Line 7-8, a direct quotation from Judges, exploits a built-in ambiguity of the Hebrew language. The tense is undetermined—*eyn méleḥ* means "there is no king" or "there was no king"—thus linking the present of the poem with a past political chaos.

(15) *You did not suck at my mother's breasts, brother,* (16) *And not one [*lit. *the same] death has found us.* (17) *Only the crown—is one and distant* (18) *Before which each head bows as is due.* (19) *Each man and the fire of his anger,* (20) *Each man and the sword of the judgment he makes* (21) *For in those days there was no king* (22) *And each man would do what was right in his own eyes.*

Lines 23-28 repeat lines 9-14, and the quotation from Judges (7-8) which serves as a subrefrain (21-22). But the second stanza has substituted the note of death (16) for the note of royalty (2).

אַתָּה רִאשׁוֹן — כַּכֶּלֶב הַמּוּמָת.	29	Atá riṣón—kakélev hamumát.
אַתָּה רִאשׁוֹן — בַּדֶּרֶךְ הָאַחַת:		Atá riṣón—badéreḥ haaḥát:
הַדּוֹרֵךְ עַל בָּמוֹתָיו — לְבַדּוֹ		Hadoréḥ al bamotáv—levadó
הַחוֹצֵב לוֹ קֶבֶר בְּיָדוֹ.	32	Haḥotsév lo kéver beyadó.
אַתָּה רִאשׁוֹן לְשֶׁפֶךְ הַדָּמִים		Atá riṣón leṣéfeḥ hadamím
אַתָּה רִאשׁוֹן לְרֵאשִׁית הַיָּמִים		Atá riṣón lereṣít hayamím
— כִּי בַּיָּמִים הָהֵם אֵין מֶלֶךְ	35	—Ki bayamím hahém eyn méleḥ
וְאִישׁ הַיָּשָׁר בְּדָמָיו יַעֲשֶׂה.		Veíṣ hayaṣár bedamáv yaasé.
וְאִישׁ וָאִישׁ יִכָּתֵב בְּדָמָיו		Veíṣ vaíṣ yikatév bedamáv
וְאִישׁ וָאִישׁ יֵאָסֵף אֶל עַמָּיו		Veíṣ vaíṣ yeaséf el amáv
וְאִישׁ וָאִישׁ — וְהֹלֶם פְּעָמָיו	39	Veíṣ vaíṣ—vehólem peamáv
שׁוֹפָר בַּגִּבּוֹרִים עַל פִּי אָבְדָן.		Ṣofár bagiborím al pi ovdán.
וְאִישׁ וָאִישׁ יְצַבַּע בִּשְׁחוֹר דָּמָיו		Veíṣ vaíṣ yetsabá biṣḥór damáv
סוּת הַדֶּגֶל בִּתְכֵלוֹ אַרְגָּמָן.	42	Sut hadégel bitḥoló argamán.

(29) *You are the first to be butchered like a dog.* (30) *You are the first—on the one road:* (31) *Treading on your high places—alone* (32) *Hewing yourself a grave with your (own) hand.* (33) *You are the first spilling of the blood* (34) *You are the first in the beginning of the days* (35) *—For in those days there was no king* (36) *And each man would do what was right in his blood.*

(37) *And each man is recorded by [what] his blood [does]* (38) *And each man shall be gathered to his ancestors* (39) *And each man—and the beat of his footsteps* (40) *A ram's horn (call) of heroes on the brink of annihilation [*lit. *perdition]—* (41) *And each man dyes with the black of his blood* (42) *The flag-cloak's blue in purple.* The "high places" (31) are where the sacrifice was made to the gods and where—as a special sacrifice—prisoners of war were killed. "Hewing a grave" (32) suggest the monumental stone for generations to come. The *ṣofár* is the ram's horn (40) originally used to call men to battle.

If the main motif of the first stanza is death and that of the second, glory, the third declares their identity. "Pay with his blood" (9,23) is modulated to "recorded in blood" (37); and so forth. The entire poem is constructed of correspondences, modulations, and substitutions. The earlier "Each man" (5,6,19,20) serves to revoke the non-identification of the opening and to replace it with the deeper "You and I, we are men."

The last two lines make for difficult paraphrase. "Black of the blood" is Hebrew for "lifeblood," and the "flag-cloak" is, of course, the flag in which the body of the dead soldier is wrapped for a hero's burial—a modern image, but Ratosh is fond of mixing his periods. As for purple, the proverbial color of glory, the crossroads "go up in purple," as in flame.

As a poetic structure, the work has the aspect of a triple sonnet, but it would be misleading to take it as such. In structure, the form corresponds to the thought: a sequence of thesis, antithesis, synthesis. The same structural relationship may be found in every corresponding pair of lines, with the further complication that some of the theses-antitheses are also identities.

Rimes are paired throughout, with deliberate departures from simple regularity. Lines 7-8 are repeated as 21-22 and 35-36; 1 rimes with 15, 2 with 16. Punctuation violates the usual pattern, being stopped where words would be expected to continue and left unmarked where a stop insists. Words are used obliquely, the rimes are heavy and the effect is hypnotic.

— DAVID SARAPH

Yonatan Ratosh

THE SOUL OF · ET NIṢMÁT · אֶת נִשְׁמַת

צֶדֶק לְפָנָיו יְהַלֵּךְ		Tsédek lefanáv yehaléḥ
יְפַלֵּס אָרְחוֹ מִישׁוֹר		Yefalés orḥó miṣór
צֶדֶק בַּמָּגֵן לְפָנָיו בָּאַשְׁמַנִּים	3	Tsédek bamagén lefanáv baaṣmaním
צֶדֶק לְפָנָיו יְהַלֵּךְ		Tsédek lefanáv yehaléḥ
אֶל אֱלֹהֵי רוּחוֹת יָם		El elohéy ruḥót yam
קֶרֶב אֲפִיק תְּהוֹמוֹתַיִם		Kérev afík tehomotáyim
אֲשֶׁר בִּכְנָפוֹ מַעֲרִיב עֲרָבִים	7	Aṣér biḥnafó maarív aravím
שֵׂיבַת זְקָנוֹ עוֹלָה קָצֶף		Seyvát zekanó olá kátsef
עִם נֵרַת אֵלִים עָלִיתָ		Im nerát eylím alíta
גַּם תָּבוֹא	10	Gam tavó
עִם נֵרַת אֵלִים הַשָּׁמֶשׁ		Im nerát eylím haṣámeṣ
בַּמָּבוֹא		Bamavó
אֶל סוֹף כָּל מַיִם רַבִּים	13	El sof kol máyim rabím
אֶל רֹאשׁ עַפְרוֹת כָּל אֶרֶץ		El roṣ afrót kol árets
רֹאשׁ כָּל דֶּרֶךְ הוֹלֶכֶת שָׁמַיִם		Roṣ kol déreḥ holéḥet ṣamáyim
רֹאשׁ כָּל דֶּרֶךְ יוֹרֶדֶת שְׁאוֹל		Roṣ kol déreḥ yorédet ṣeól

Of essential importance in Ratosh's poetry is his predilection for the ancient "Canaanite" world and its mythology. This note runs throughout his work, whether, as in *Laṣaléḥet* (c. 1948), he reconstructs an old ritual of deification through self-sacrifice, or, as in his last poem published in book-form (*Ḥavá*, 1963) he reinterprets the story of the Fall as a coronation of a rain-god.

Ratosh's poetry involves a well-defined, controversial political and historical theory, one part of which often makes little sense without some knowledge of the other. Ratosh rejects both the Jewish religion and Zionism as highly undesirable for the development of the new nation. Israel must, he believes, detach itself completely from the countries in which its settlers lived for centuries and recreate its character wholly in accordance with the linguistic, cultural, and historical heritage of the "Land of the Euphrates." This is the territory of which Israel has always been a part. Despite the waves of invaders and conquerors, the peoples of the Land of the Euphrates have maintained a continuous pastoral-agrarian-urban culture of their own. And this cultural-linguistic-literary heritage has been Hebraic—but Hebraic in a sense quite different from what is generally understood. It is the heritage of Hebrew when it was still a living language and not merely, as Ratosh maintains, the sacred tongue of a religion codified by one group of the peoples of this region, the Judeans, when they lived in the Babylonian and Persian capitals around the 7th century B.C.

The Judeans in time spread out all over the world and they spoke whatever language happened to be used in their country of residence. They continued to pray and to read their sacred books in Hebrew and to venerate Jerusalem as their holy city. As a result of their purely cultic use of the original language, says Ratosh, the main extant body of the old Hebrew literature has been preserved not in its original form but in a much-edited version—edited, as he would say, for the purpose of transforming the specific deity of a confederation of cities into the exclusive, single, and jealous "God of the Jews" as we know him. What the pre-exilic parts of the Old Testament were like can therefore only be reconstructed, largely with the aid of such rediscovered remains of the same culture as the Ugaritic epics.

To the contemporary revival of Hebrew, then, the Jewish religion must be held irrelevant. Instead of utilizing the cultural forces that this religion exerts, references must be made to the older Hebrew world. That is why Ratosh's poems, when they pray, invoke Báal and Aṣeyrát; when they sacrifice, they sacrifice "on every high mountain and under every green tree"; and when their dead go on the last journey, from the town on the cliff to the burial place in the dunes, this is the hymn that the pall-bearers must chant:

(1) *Justice walks before him* (2) *Makes level his path* (3) *Shield-bearing Justice before him in the darknesses* (4) *Justice walks before him*

(5) *To the God of the winds of the sea (spirits of the West)* (6) *Within the bed of the twin abysses* (7) *Who with his wing makes [the] evenings,* (8) *The white of his beard rises in foam* With a beat as slow as the funeral procession in which it is chanted, the poem tells us how the dead man is taken to the palace of the Gods of the seawinds, far in the west, where earth and heaven, the twin abysses, meet. The title as well as some of the lines (e.g. 19,20, 41-44) come from Jewish religious literature, with which Ratosh is intimately familiar and on which he does not hesitate to draw. "*Et Nişmát*", from the Jewish prayer for the dead, literally means "the soul of" in the accusative case and can no more stand alone than the Latin accusative "Requiem." Line 1 is Psalms 85:14 but by line 4, Justice has become a personification, and by 5-8, we have entered a different world, whose images and attributes are expressed in terms of Ugaritic lore. *Tsédek* ("Justice," 1) and *mişór* ("a plain," 2) may be conducting the soul to its western elysium, for a man's life is seen in terms of the sun's path, with birth at sunrise and death at sunset.

(9) *With the lamp of the Gods you have risen* (10) *And shall also sink* (11) *With the lamp of the Gods, the Sun,* (12) *At sunset* (13) *To the end of all the many waters* (14) *To the head of the soil of all land* (15) *Head of every road that leads up to heaven* (16) *Head of every road that leads down to hell*

This western elysium is the palace of El, ruler of the winds and the sea, Father of Gods and men, who reigns as patriarch over the ancient Hebrew pantheon. His spouse Aṣeyrát-Yam, his children Báal and Anát, with Coṣár and Báal's twin rival Mot, who is Death. The pantheon is much like the Greek: El: Kronos; Aṣeyrát-Yam: Aphrodite Ourania; Báal: Zeus; perhaps Mot: Prometheus; Anát: Athena, the war maiden; and Coṣár: Hephaistos, the smith, lame legs and all. Here among these gods is the eternal home that awaits the good man when his time comes to die.

אֶל אֱלֹהֵי רוּחוֹת יָם	17	El elohéy ruḥót yam
קֶרֶשׁ מֶלֶךְ אַב שָׁנִים		Kéreṣ méleḥ av ṣaním
אֲשֶׁר בְּיָדוֹ נֶפֶשׁ כָּל בָּשָׂר		Aṣér beyadó néfeṣ kol basár
לִפְעָמָיו יִשְׁתָּחוּ כָּל חַי		Lif'amáv yiṣtáḥu kol ḥay

זֶה הַגֶּבֶר		Ze hagéver
רָאָה עֹנִי וְשִׁבְטוֹ	22	Raá óni veṣivtó
זֶה הָאִישׁ חָדַל מִמַּעַשׂ		Ze haíṣ ḥadál mimáas
— — לְבֵיתוֹ		— —Leveytó

צֶדֶק לְפָנָיו יְהַלֵּךְ		Tsédek lefanáv yehaléḥ
יְפַלֵּס אָרְחוֹ מִישׁוֹר	26	Yefalés orḥó miṣór
צֶדֶק בַּמָּגֵן לְפָנָיו בָּאַשְׁמַנִּים		Tsédek bamagén lefanáv baaṣmaním
צֶדֶק לְפָנָיו יְהַלֵּךְ		Tsédek lefanáv yehaléḥ

קֶרֶב אֲפִיק תְּהֹמוֹתַיִם		Kérev afík tehomotáyim
קֶרֶשׁ מֶלֶךְ אַב שָׁנִים	30	Kéreṣ méleḥ av ṣaním
אֲשֶׁר מִיָּדוֹ נֵזֶר בַּעַל		Aṣér miyadó nézer báal
אֲשֶׁר מִיָּדוֹ עֹז עֲנָת		Aṣér miyadó oz anát
אֲשֶׁר מִיָּדוֹ חָכְמַת כּוֹשָׁר		Aṣér miyadó ḥoḥmát koṣár
אֲשֶׁר מִיָּדוֹ טוּב אֲשֵׁרָת		Aṣér miyadó tuv aṣeyrát
אֲשֶׁר מִימִינוֹ קֶרֶן בַּעַל	35	Aṣér miyminó kéren báal
אֲשֶׁר מִשְּׂמֹאלוֹ כֹּבֶד מוֹת		Aṣér mismoló kéved mot

אֵל אַדִּיר אֲבָרוֹת		El adír avarót
מֵצֵל כַּנְפֵי עוֹלָם		Metsél kanféy olám
הָעוֹשֶׂה מִשְׁפָּט בִּתְהוֹמָיו	39	Haosé miṣpát bithomáv
בָּרֵךְ אֶת הַבָּא אֶל עַמָּיו		Baréḥ et habá el amáv

אֶת נִשְׁמַת		Et niṣmát
עַבְדְּךָ		Avdeḥá
שֶׁהָלַךְ	43	Ṣeheláḥ
לְעוֹלָמוֹ —		Leolamó—

צֶדֶק לְפָנָיו יְהַלֵּךְ		Tsédek lefanáv yehaléḥ
יְפַלֵּס אָרְחוֹ מִישׁוֹר		Yefalés orḥó miṣór
צֶדֶק בַּמָּגֵן לְפָנָיו בָּאַשְׁמַנִּים	47	Tsédek bamagén lefanáv baaṣmaním
צֶדֶק לְפָנָיו יְהַלֵּךְ		Tsédek lefanáv yehaléḥ

(17) *To the God of the winds of the sea* (18) *To the timbered [house] of the King, Father of the years* (19) *In whose hand is the breath of all flesh* (20) *At whose feet all the living bend*

El's palace is the last destination of (21) *This [is the] man* (22) *Who has seen affliction (poverty) and its rod* (23) *This [is the] man who has ceased from striving (action)* (24) — — *To his home (for his household)*

(25) *Justice walks before him* (26) *Makes level his path* (27) *Shield-bearing Justice before him in the darknesses* (28) *Justice walks before him*

(29) *Within the bed of the twin abysses* (30) *The timbered [house] of the King, Father of the years* (31) *From whose hand [is given] the crown of Báal* (32) *From whose hand [is given] the might of Anát* (33) *From whose hand [is given] the wisdom of Coṣár* (34) *From whose hand [is given] the bounty of Aṣeyrát* (35) *From (on) his right hand the horn (strength) of Báal* (36) *From (on) his left hand the heaviness (liver) of Mot*

And as the dead man draws nearer the cemetery, the house-priest invokes a last blessing: (37) *El, mighty-winged,* (38) *Who shades (covers) the corners of the world* (39) *Who deals justly in his abysses [in both heaven and earth]* (40) *Bless him who comes to his fathers* (41) *(Bless) the soul of [et niṣmát]* (42) *Your servant* (43) *Who has gone* (44) *To his world [rest]* . . . Bless him with the blessing he deserves—and here the first stanza is repeated and, as Ratosh observes, the entire litany should be repeated again and again, until the procession arrives at the grave. The poem, written for the poet's father, is to be read as a lament, whose extremely powerful incantatory effect depends on repetitions of the basic three-beat line of both Old Testament and Canaanite verse.

— DAVID SARAPH

Yonatan Ratosh

DREAM · ḤALÓM · חֲלוֹם

הַחֲלוֹם	Haḥalóm
אַדִּיר הָאֲבָרוֹת —	—Adír haavarót
הַצּוֹרֵר אוֹתָנוּ	Hatsorér otánu
בִּכְנָפָיו הָאַדִּירוֹת	Biḥnafáv haadirót
בָּשָׂר וְדָם וָנֶפֶשׁ	Basár vadám vanéfeṣ
וּסְדוֹר כָּל דִּבְרֵי נְכֹחָה —	Usdór kol divréy neḥoḥá—
נָתוֹן כָּל מַאֲמַצֵּי	Natón kol maamatséy
שְׁרִיר וָלֵב	Ṣrir valév
כְּכָל אֲשֶׁר יוּכַל	Keḥól aṣér yuḥál
שׂוּם שִׂכְלֵנוּ הַדַּל	Sum siḥléynu hadál
לְהַשִּׂיג —	Lehasig—
הוּא מַשֶּׁהוּ	Hu máṣehu
שֶׁאָנוּ נִלְחָמִים עָלָיו —	Ṣeánu nilḥamím aláv—
בִּדְבֵקוּת —	Bidvekút—
בְּזַעַם —	Bezáam—
בְּחֵמָה שְׁפוּכָה —	Beḥemá ṣfuḥá—
בְּשַׁעְבֵּד אֶת כָּל כֹּחוֹת הָרוּחַ	Beṣaabéd et kol koḥót harúaḥ
וְהַגּוּף —	Vehagúf—
נוֹפְלִים	Noflím
וּגְלוּיֵי עַיִן —	Ugluyéy áyin—
הִתְנַבֵּא עֵירֹם —	Hitnabé eyróm—
פָּרֹץ כָּל גָּדֵר דְּחוּיָה	Paróts kol gadér deḥuyá
וְעוֹמְדָה אֵיתָן —	Veomdá eytán—
הִסְתָּעֵר עַל כֹּל	Histaér al kol
בִּזְרוֹעַ נְטוּיָה —	Bizróa netuyá—
בְּמוֹרָא גָּדוֹל	Bemorá gadól
וּבְשִׂמְחַת שִׁקּוּל הַדַּעַת	Uvsimḥát ṣikúl hadáat
הַמָּתוּן־מָתוּן	Hamatún-matún
הַנָּהִיר־נָהִיר	Hanahír-nahír
הַצָּלוּל מִכָּל צָלוּל	Hatsalúl mikól tsalúl
— כַּדָּם	—Kadám
— כַּמַּיִם הַחַיִּים	—Kamáyim haḥayím
— כַּשַּׁיִשׁ	—Kaṣáyiṣ

In "Dream," as in most of his later work, Ratosh has divested himself of the formal prosodic apparatus that plays so important a role in his early poems. There is no longer any strict meter. The rhythm together with the rime—which is now very largely internal rime and alliteration—have become the nervous system rather than the skeleton of the poem.

(1) *The dream* (2) *—Mighty of wings* (3) *That enwraps us* (4) *In its mighty wings* (5) *Flesh and blood and soul* (6) *And ordering all that is true—* (7) *Giving (making) all efforts* (8) *Of muscle and heart* (9) *To the extent that* (10) *The grasp of our poor intellect* (11) *Can attain—*

The dream is envisaged as a huge hovering bird or angel which holds the dreamer tight and carries him along; not a bubble thrown off by a brain too active to come to rest in sleep but a power which forces body and mind to make the utmost effort of which they are capable. *Avarót* ("wings," 2) has the same denotation as *knafáyim* (the base form of *biḥnafáv*, 4, "wings") but it is far more solemn in tone. A similar effect of exaltation is obtained by the use of such forms as *natón* ("giving," 7), *paróts* ("crashing," 22), *histaér* ("changing," 24), and *sdór* ("ordering of," 6), rather than the more common inflections.

The dream (12) *Is something* (13) *For which we fight—* (14) *Fervently—* (15) *Angrily—* (16) *With outpoured wrath—* (17) *Subjugating all powers of the mind* (18) *And the body—* (19) *[for which we] Fall* (20) *And with open eyes—* (21) *Prophesy nakedly—* (22-23) *Crashing through every tottering and firmly standing fence—* (24) *Charging upon everything* (25) *With outstretched arm—* (26) *And great terror* (27) *And [also] with the joy of (calm) deliberation* (28) [which is:] *patient* [lit. *patient-patient*], (29) *Lucid* (30) *More limpid than limpid [most limpid]:* (31) *—As blood* (32) *—As the living waters* (33) *—As marble*

The dream, says Ratosh—without repeating the word, for the whole poem is one sentence of which each stanza is a different clause, advancing the argument step by step toward the conclusion—is the motivation of our striving and of all we do in the course of striving: act against our better judgment, defy convention, revolt in a surge of emotion, or, on the other hand, fight with that cold, pitiless exaltation of one who has considered everything and has irrevocably chosen his path and his objective. Lines 25-26 are from Deuteronomy 26:8, but here the terrors are as much in our own minds as in the enemy's. Blood and marble (31,33) are in the physical sense anything but limpid, yet the poem associates them with "living water" (32): they are made to reflect the quality of something pure and single-minded.

The dream is what man fights for, for it

אֲשֶׁר נֵדַע כִּי הוּא	Aṣér nedá ki hu
בּוֹרֵא־חַיִּים —	Boré-*ḥayím*—
אֵלִים וַאֲנָשִׁים	Elím vaanaṣím
וְלוֹ נַקְרִיב	Veló nakrív
בְּלֵב חָפֵץ וּמְהַסֵּס,	Belév ḥaféts umhasés,
בְּצַעַר וְחֶדְוָה,	Betsáar veḥedvá,
חִנָּם,	Ḥinám,
אֶת כָּל הַמְעַט הַזֶּה	Et kol hameát hazé
אֲשֶׁר מָצָאנוּ —	Aṣér matsánu—
אֲשֶׁר נֵחַנּוּ בּוֹ —	Aṣér neḥánu bo—
הוּא הוּא מוֹתַר	Hu hu motár
כֹּל הָאָדָם	Kol haadám
מִן הָאָדָם —	Min haadám—
שֶׁאֵין לוֹ חֵקֶר	Ṣeéyn lo ḥéker
וְתִכְלָה לוֹ אָיִן —	Vetiḥlá lo áyin—
וְלֹא יִמַּד	Veló yimád
וְלֹא יִשָּׁקֵל	Veló yiṣakél
וְאֵין אִישׁ אֲשֶׁר	Veéyn iṣ aṣér
לֹא יוּכַל	Lo yuḥál
לְמָצְאוֹ	Lemots'ó
בְּתֻמּוֹ	Betumó
בְּהִתְמַכֵּר	Behitmakér
צָלוּל צָלוּל —	Tsalúl tsalúl—
בִּצְלוֹל	Bitslól
— הַרְפֵּה מִכָּל גָּדָה —	—Harpé mikól gadá—
אֶל תּוֹךְ תְּהוֹמוֹת נֶפֶשׁ	El toḥ tehomót néfeṣ
וְאָדָם	Veadám
וְעוֹלָמוֹ —	Veolamó—
בַּעֲשׂוֹתוֹ אֶת חֲלוֹמוֹ	Baasotó et ḥalomó
בְּמוֹ חַיָּיו —	Bemó ḥayáv—

is that (34) *Which we know* (35-36) *Creates gods and men* ALIVE (37) *And to which we will sacrifice* (38) *With willing and hesitant heart* (39) *With sorrow and rejoicing,* (40) *Gratis,* (41) *All the (this) little* (42) *That we have found—* (43) *With which we have been endowed—*

The dream (44-45) *Is that which gives Everyman preeminence above a man*—and which gives the lie to Ecclesiastes when he says that "a man has no preeminence over a beast." The dream is that (47) *Which cannot be probed* (48) *And has no limit* (49) *And cannot be measured* (50) *And cannot be weighed*—all of these attributes being traditionally those of God.

And here our poem-sentence comes to its conclusion: (51) *And there is no man who* (52) *Cannot* (53) *Find it [dream]* (54) *In its entirety*

—but here *betumó* can also be taken to refer to man, in which case line 54 means "In his innocence-simplicity-sincerity." (55) *By surrendering* (56) *With complete possession of his faculties* [see line 30]— (57) *And diving—* (58) *—Letting go of every shore—* (59) *Into the abysses of soul* (60) *And of man* (61) *And of his universe—* (62) *Making his dream* (63) *With his very own life—*

To control the syntax of this involved sentence, Ratosh uses a favorite device of his: an intricate and highly individual pattern of indentation which he will permit no compositor to change by so much as a hair-space and which he claims to be much more elastic than the conventional punctuation system.

In this recent poem by Ratosh the modulations of meaning have become increasingly subtle, though there is obvious play on two meanings of a single root in lines 56-57: *tsalúl-tslol* ("transparent-diving"). For the most part, however, the manipulations are on the level of connotation, alerting the reader to the contradictory qualities of man, who is raised here to the image in which he has been created by the power of the dream —which, supreme paradox, he himself has made "with his own life."

— DAVID SARAPH

Yonatan Ratosh

SANDS · ḤOLÓT · חולות

קֶסֶם מְהַלֵּךְ עַל הַמַּיִם הָרַבִּים	Késem mehaléḥ al hamáyim harabím
קֶסֶם עַל תְּהוֹם תְּהוֹמוֹתַיִם	Késem al tehóm tehomotáyim
הַיּוֹם הַזֶּה אֶשְׂתָּרֵךְ	Hayóm hazé estaréḥ
עַל מֵימֵי יָם הַתִּיכוֹן	Al meyméy yam hatiḥón
כְּשַׁכְשֵׁךְ	Keṣaḥṣéḥ
בְּמֵי אַפְסַיִם	Beméy afsáyim
הַיּוֹם הַזֶּה אֲטַפֵּס בַּטּוּחוֹת	Hayóm hazé atapés batuḥót
בְּאַפִּרְיוֹן	Beapiryón
בְּתוֹךְ קֶצֶף נוֹסֵס	Betóḥ kétsef nosés
בִּמְגַפַּיִם —	Bemagafáyim—
כָּל הָעוֹלָם נִקְסַם בִּמְחִי שָׁפְכוֹ	Kol haolám niksám bimḥí ṣofhó
בַּקֶּצֶף הָרוֹגֵעַ	Bakétsef harogéa
עַד רַךְ	Ad raḥ
כָּל הָעוֹלָם נִצָּב אֵי כָּךְ אֵיתָן	Kol haolám nitsáv ey ḥaḥ eytán
בְּהִפּוּכוֹ	Behipuḥó
וַאֲנִי אֶנָּשֵׂא	Vaaní enasé
בַּסֻּלָּם הָרוֹפֵס	Basulám harofés
עַד אֶפֶס אֶרֶץ וְשָׁמַיִם —	Ad éfes érets veṣamáyim—
כָּל הַיָּמִים חָמְדָה נַפְשִׁי	Kol hayamím ḥamdá nafṣí
אֶת הַמַּיִם הָרַבִּים	Et hamáyim harabím
כָּל הַלֵּילוֹת בְּתֹם לֵבָב יַחְדָּו	Kol haleylót betóm leváv yaḥdáv
עַכְשָׁו	Aḥṣáv
כָּל הָעוֹלָם בְּאִדְוָה יֵחַד	Kol haolám beidvá yeḥád
כָּל הָעוֹלָם יִרְעַד בְּחֶדְוָה	Kol haolám yir'ád beḥedvá
כָּל הַחֲלוֹמוֹת בִּמְחִי אֶחָד	Kol haḥalomót bimḥí eḥád
כָּל הָעוֹלָמוֹת בְּאֶפֶס יָד	Kol haolamót beéfes yad
וּדְכִי הַיָּם וְקִצְפּוֹ	Udḥí hayám vekitspó
בְּיַחַד	Beyáḥad
עַל פִּי תְהוֹם בַּכָּף	Al pi tehóm bakáf
בָּהִיר —	Bahír—
בְּאֶפֶס יָד	Beéfes yad
וּמְחִיר	Umḥír
וְעַכְשָׁו —	Veaḥṣáv—

בָּרוּךְ סוֹהֵר סְהָרִים חִנָּם	Barúḥ sohér seharím ḥinám
לְכָל נֶפֶשׁ אָדָם יַחְדָּו	Leḥól néfeṣ adám yaḥdáv
פֹּה —	Po—
וְעַכְשָׁו —	Veaḥṣáv—
עַל שְׂפַת הַיָּם הַבָּהִיר —	Al sfat hayám habahír—
עֶרֶב עֶרֶב	Érev érev
אִתָּנוּ בָּעִיר —	Itánu vaír—

"Sands"—Ratosh in a lighter mood—is also about a dream; perhaps not about the dream that makes man more than man, but about one of those wishes quite unimportant in themselves which will haunt you all your life, until one magical day when (1) *An enchantment walks over the many waters* (2) *An enchantment over the twin abysses*—and the spell is wound up, for *késem* ("enchantment, charm,") also means "sorcery" and "attractiveness"—And you say: (3) *This very day I shall stroll* (4) *On the waters of the Middle Sea* [a play on the Hebrew word for "Mediterranean"] (5) *Like one who paddles* (6) *In ankle-deep water* (7) *This day I shall confidently climb* (8) *Into a palanquin* (9) *Surrounded by rising spray* (10) *In (high) boots.*

(11) *All the world is enchanted in the suddenness of [*lit. *in the blow] pouring itself out* (12) *In foam relaxed* (13) *To [the point of] softness* (14) *All the world stands somehow firm* (15) *In its inversion* (16) *And I shall be carried up* (17) *On the unsteady ladder* (18) *To where land and sky come to an end.*

(19) *All the days (always) my soul has longed* (20) *For the many waters* (21) *All the nights together in the innocence (fullness) of my heart.* (22) *Now* (23) *All the world will be one in the water rings [spreading rings on the water]* (24) *All the world will tremble in joy* (25) *All the dreams in one single stroke* (26) *All the worlds without any effort* (27) *And the sea's fall and foam* (28) *All together* (29) *On the brink of the abyss in the palm [of the hand]* (30) *Bright—* (31) *Without effort* (32) *Or cost* (33) *And Now—*

The whole world will be put right today, your dream will come true. It costs you nothing, not even your effort. You could have done it any day, and you don't know why you haven't done it until now, for it comes to you as a gift. For: (34-35) *Blessed be he who makes moons shine free [*lit. *moons moons] for all people alive [*lit. *every soul of man together]* (36) *Here* (37) *And now* (38) *On the beach of the bright sea* (39) *Night after night* (40) *With us in the town.*

The poem is filled with internal rimes. Each of stanzas 1, 2, and 3 is treated as a unit held at the end by a dash—as sections of a single sentence which are all resolved and anchored in the closing stanza, with its blessing and declaration . . . Note the repetition of *kol* ("all") followed by *olám* ("world," 11, 14, 23, 24), by *yamím* ("days," 19), *leylót* ("nights," 21), *ḥalomót* ("dreams, 25), *olamót* ("worlds," 26). Note also the repetition of forms of words denoting "together": *yaḥdáv* (21), *yeḥád* (23), *eḥád* (25), *beyáḥad* (28), and *yaḥdáv* (35).

— DAVID SARAPH

Nathan Alterman

A SUMMER NIGHT · LEYL KÁYITS · לֵיל קַיִץ

דּוּמִיָּה בַּמֶּרְחָבִים שׁוֹרֶקֶת.	Dumiyá bamerḥavím ṣoréket.
בֹּהַק הַסַּכִּין בְּעֵין הַחֲתוּלִים.	Bóhak hasakín beéyn haḥatulím.
לַיְלָה. כַּמָּה לַיְלָה! בַּשָּׁמַיִם שֶׁקֶט.	3 Láyla. Káma láyla! Baṣamáyim ṣéket.
כּוֹכָבִים בְּחִתּוּלִים.	Koḥavím beḥitulím.
זְמַן רָחָב, רָחָב. הַלֵּב צִלְצֵל אַלְפַּיִם.	Zman raḥáv, raḥáv. Halév tsiltsél alpáyim.
טַל, כְּמוֹ פְּגִישָׁה, אֶת הָרִיסִים הִצְעִיף.	Tal, kemo pgiṣá, et harisím hits'íf,
בְּמַגְלֵב זָהָב פַּנָּס מַפִּיל אַפַּיִם	7 Bemaglév zaháv panás mapíl apáyim
עֲבָדִים שְׁחוֹרִים לְרֹחַב הָרָצִיף.	Avadím ṣḥorím leróḥav haratsíf.
רוּחַ קַיִץ שָׁטָה. עֲמוּמָה. רוֹגֶשֶׁת.	Rúaḥ káyits ṣáta. Amumá. Rogéṣet.
עַל כִּתְפֵי גַּנִּים שְׂפָתֶיהָ נִשְׁפָּכוֹת.	Al kitféy ganím sfatéha niṣpaḥót.
רֹעַ יְרַקְרַק. תְּסִיסַת אוֹרוֹת וָחֶשֶׁד.	11 Róa yerakrák. Tsisát orót vaḥéṣed.
רְתִיחַת מַטְמוֹן בַּקֶּצֶף הַשָּׁחֹר.	Retiḥát matmón bakétsef haṣaḥór.
וְהַרְחֵק לַגֹּבַהּ, בִּנְהִימָה מְרֻעֶבֶת,	Veharḥék lagóva, binhimá mur'évet,
עִיר אֲשֶׁר עֵינֶיהָ זֹהַב מְצֻפּוֹת,	Ir aṣér eynéha zóhav metsupót,
מִתְאַדָּה בְּזַעַם, בְּתִמְרוֹת הָאֶבֶן,	15 Mit'adá bezáam, betimrót haéven,
שֶׁל הַמִּגְדָּלִים וְהַכִּפּוֹת.	Ṣel hamigdalím vehakipót.

Nathan Alterman, for a time the most influential Hebrew poet since Bialik, was born in Warsaw in 1910. The son of a Hebrew educator, he was reared in Kishinev, arriving in Palestine in 1925 where he completed his studies at a Tel Aviv *gymnasium*. Somewhat later he went to France to study agronomy.

A disciple of Shlonsky (see pp. 74 ff.), Pasternak, and of French Symbolism, he became the most prominent exponent of the "imagistic" trend in Hebrew poetry. His brilliant wit and fantastic imagery, his mastery of language and meter, the seemingly "spoken" flavor of his charged rhetoric, brought him two generations of admirers and imitators. It was only natural, then, for his "line" to become the main target of attack in the 1950's when a new trend, influenced by Anglo-American poetry, proclaimed the virtues of understatement, irony, prosaic diction, and free verse.

Alterman's writing is extremely rich and varied. Besides his four volumes of lyric poetry, he is the author of a large collection of satirical, topical verse and songs, two plays (one in verse), children's books, and translations from English, French, Yiddish, and Russian. (Shakespeare's *Othello*, *Julius Caesar*, *The Merry Wives of Windsor*, *Antony and*

Cleopatra; a collection of *Ballads and Songs of England and Scotland;* Racine's *Phaedra;* Molière's *Le Misanthrope, Le Malade Imaginaire,* etc.).

Almost from its beginnings, Alterman's work was marked by two distinct strains which occasionally intermingle. On the one hand—his often brilliant, ballad-like topical verse published weekly under the heading "The Seventh Column"; these became a running "poetic" commentary on the turbulent thirties and forties and played a remarkable role in expressing and shaping the mood of a people caught up in the birth of a country and the death of its European communities. On the other hand—his lyrical, hermetic, and "literary" poetry, which made no overt references to actual events or to personal biography. His first book, *Koḥavím Baḥúts* (*The Stars Outside,* 1938), with its neo-romantic themes, highly charged texture, and metrical virtuosity, immediately established him as a major force.

Our selection from his first volume is a poem characteristic in mood and technique. A mysterious atmosphere surrounds the speaker who waits as if lost in time and space. No other people, no specific events, yet something is happening around him in the warm summer night. The setting of the poem spreads out between two fields of light: the "innocent" stars far above in the quiet sky (stanza 1) and the fuming stones of a distant city evaporating in the "rage" of its illuminated towers and cupolas (stanza 4).

(1) *Silence whistles in the (wide) spaces.* (2) *Glitter of a knife in the eye of cats.* (3) *Night. How much night! In the skies: quiet.* (4) *Stars in swaddling clothes.*

(5) *Wide, wide time. The heart rang two thousand.* (6) *Dew, like an encounter, veiled the eyelashes,* (7) *With a golden whip a street-lantern throws down (prostrate)* (8) *Black slaves across the width of the platform.*

(9) *A summer wind roams (floats). Muted. Agitated.* (10) *Her* [the wind's] *lips are poured out upon shoulders of gardens.* (11) *[A] greenish malice. Fermentation of light and of suspicion.* (12) *Boiling of a treasure in the black foam.*

(13) *And far, toward the height, with famished growl,* (14) *A city whose eyes are plated with gold,* (15) *Evaporates in rage, in the stone billows* (16) *Of the towers and the cupolas.*

Dimensions of time and of space overlap. The lone speaker feels that time is motionless and almost unreal. It is a matter of "How much night!" (3) and of "wide, wide time" (5)—*raḥáv* ("wide") repeats the root of *merḥavím* ("spaces," 1), literally meaning "widenesses."

The silence is so overpowering that one can hear it. *Dumiyá* (patterned on the stock oxymoron *hadmamá zoéket,* "silence shrieks") is a more unusual word for "silence"; and *ṣoréket* ("whistles") suggests a silence roaming like a wind whistling over the plains.

Line 2 is a typical Alterman device: creating abstract qualities by manipulating concrete elements. The cats—a traditional accesory in magical circumstances—are not individualized; they are endowed with one collective, menacing eye. The "glitter of a knife"—later echoed by "greenish evil" (11) —is at once contrasted with the "quietude" of the skies.

This quiet is almost idyllic, so that the stars are seen as innocent, sleeping children swaddled in diapers (4). The concrete image of a hazy halo surrounding the stars on a hot southern night is presented by its implication for the speaker: the stars, traditionally a symbol of eternity, appear as new-born.

Time is not old but "large" (5). Only the heart marks the passage of time by its fateful "ringing." The number "two thousand," which refers to the span of the Diaspora, is an extremely hackneyed phrase in Israel—linked with *keóreḥ hagalút* ("as long as the Diaspora"), a proverbial expression for interminable duration. Hence, for the heart, the length of time seems unreal, immeasurable.

The sudden "encounter" (6), answering, as it were the heart's expectancy (5), is introduced by an inverted simile—a method often found in Alterman's verse: instead of comparing the less known to the better known, he does the reverse. Thus even the encounter is not explicitly embedded in the setting but merely hinted at by means of a simile. With line 9 the emotional tone intensifies, as the detached adjectives body forth the feeling. But the erotic element (10) is not individualized: the lips (feminine in Hebrew) pour out upon the gardens (masculine). The entire setting is suffused with wind and with unreal imagery: greenish malice, seething of lights and suspicion, foam that is black, a boiling treasure. The strangeness is reinforced in Hebrew by the use of a neologism (*ḥéṣed*, "suspicion") and less common forms *róa* ("evil") and *yerakrák* ("greenish"). Moreover, the sonal effect of lines 11-12 is remarkable for its onomatopoeic quality and for its intricate orchestration of groups of consonants in changing orders which are echoed in neighboring lines. The closely related sounds of *r*, *ḥ* and of *t*, *k* occur 18 times in obvious interplay with 5 sibilants.

Though the setting in the first 3 stanzas is specific, there are hardly any concrete details. Everything around the man on the platform is caught in motion, yet there is neither succession nor development. This effect of "timelessness" is emphasized by the predicateless sentences (2-5, 11-12) and the preponderance of nouns (almost five times as many as verbs or adjectives). Though the sensuous elements are present, they are generally divorced from their normal environments. Thus each introduces a realm of its own, rich with overtones, but the resulting images are vague in outline, emphasizing the diffused haziness of this summer night and the unexplicated feeling of something vague, strange, ominous.

The traditional quatrains, riming *abab* and alternating feminine with masculine rimes, have a slow movement of trochaic hexameter (with the exception of lines 1, 4, 12) but only line 5, where time is being "measured," has all 6 stresses. The final stanza, with its single inverted sentence and the cesuras after unstressed syllables, is in strong contrast to the segmented movement of the preceding lines—as though one breathless sweep were carrying the strong finale of the poem. The last line is the only one where two consecutive stresses are skipped; the whole line is reduced to two major stresses.

The rimes, when not identical, are compensated for by preceding sounds. Thus in *mur'évet-haéven* (13-15) the identical sound is *éve* but the sounds *m*, *r*, *t* of the first rime-word appear in the word preceding the second rime: *betimrót;* and the *h*, *n* sounds of the second rime-word are present in the word preceding the first: *binhimá* (*binhimá mur'évet —betimrót haéven*). Actually all consonants of both pairs are involved in the riming, but in changed order. Such sonal patterns linked to rime often run through entire stanzas in Alterman's first book.

— BENJAMIN HRUSHOVSKI

Nathan Alterman

THIS NIGHT · HALÁYLA HAZÉ · הַלַּיְלָה הַזֶּה

הַלַּיְלָה הַזֶּה.		Haláyla hazé.
הִתְנַכְּרוּת הַקִּירוֹת הָאֵלֶּה.		Hitnakrút hakirót haéyle.
מִלְחֶמֶת שְׁתִיקוֹת בְּחָזֶה מוּל חָזֶה.	3	Milḥémet ṣtikót beḥazé mul hazé.
חַיָּיו הַזְּהִירִים		Ḥayáv hazhirím
שֶׁל נֵר הַחֵלֶב.		Ṣel ner haḥélev.
רַק שְׁמוּעָה שֶׁל אֵין־נֹחַם, כְּרוּחַ קְרִירָה,		Rak ṣmuá sel eyn-nóḥam, kerúaḥ krirá,
פֹּה הֶחֱלִיקָה לְאֹרֶךְ גְּדֵרוֹת הֲרוּסוֹת	7	Po heḥlíka leóreḥ gdeyrót harusót
וְלִטְּפָה רְצִיפִים נְטוּלֵי הַכָּרָה		Velitfá retsifím netuléy hakará
וְהֵנִיעָה גְּשָׁרִים כְּשׁוּרַת עֲרִיסוֹת.		Veheynía gṣarím keṣurát arisót.
בַּכִּכָּר הָרֵיקָה צֵל עוֹבֵר. נֶעֱלָם.	10	Bakikár hareyká tsel ovér. Neelám.
הֲמֻלַּת צְעָדָיו לְבַדָּהּ עוֹד הוֹלֶכֶת.		Hamulát tseadáv levadá od holéḥet.
אַל תִּשְׁכַּח, אַל תִּשְׁכַּח־נָא, עֲפַר הָעוֹלָם,		Al tiṣkáḥ, al tiṣkáḥ-na, afár haolám,
אֶת רַגְלֵי הָאָדָם שֶׁדָּרְכוּ עָלֶיךָ.		Et ragléy haadám ṣedarḥú aléḥa.
הַלַּיְלָה הַזֶּה.	14	Haláyla hazé.
מְתִיחוּת הַקִּירוֹת הָאֵלֶּה.		Metiḥút hakirót haéyle.
קוֹל נֵעוֹר וְשׁוֹאֵל. קוֹל מֵשִׁיב וּמְהַסֶּה.		Kol neór veṣoél. Kol meysív umhasé.
לְטִיפָה מוּזָרָה. אוֹר חִיּוּךְ מְעֻשֶּׂה.		Letifá muzará. Or ḥiyúḥ meusé.
חַיָּיו וּמוֹתוֹ	18	Ḥayáv umotó
שֶׁל נֵר הַחֵלֶב.		Ṣel ner haḥélev.
אָז יָרֵחַ מַלְבִּישׁ מַסֵּכוֹת שַׁעֲוָה		Az yaréaḥ malbíṣ maseḥót ṣaavá
עַל חַלּוֹן, עַל עֵינַיִם קָרוֹת, עַל נוֹפִים,		Al ḥalón, al eynáyim karót, al nofím,
עַל הַשּׁוּק הָעוֹמֵד מְאֻבָּן בַּשָּׁבָץ,	22	Al haṣúk haoméd meubán baṣaváts,
בִּידֵי גֹּלֶם שְׁלוּחוֹת שֶׁל קְרוֹנוֹת וּמְנוֹפִים.		Bidéy gólem ṣluḥót ṣel kronót umnofím.

"This Night," from Alterman's first volume, brings us into a world of metonymy in which man is expressed by the objects surrounding him, without any direct defining of his feelings:

(1) *This night.* (2) *The estrangement of these walls.* (3) *War of silences in chest (breast) confronting chest (breast).* (4) *The cautious life* (5) *Of the tallow candle.*

(6) *Only a rumor of non-consolation, like a cool*

wind, (7) *Glided here along ruined fences* (8) *And caressed unconscious quays* [lit. *which fainted*] (9) *And rocked bridges as [though they were] a line of cradles.*

(10) *A shadow passes in the empty square. Disappears.* (11) *The tumult of its* [lit. *his*] *steps still walks on by itself.* (12) *Don't forget, please don't forget, dust of the world,* (13) *The feet of the man that trod on you.*

(14) *This night.* (15) *The tenseness of these walls.* (16) *A voice awakes and asks. A voice answers and hushes.* (17) *A strange caress. Light of an artificial smile.* (18) *The life and death* (19) *Of the tallow candle.*

(20) *Then the moon clothes in masks of wax* (21) *A window, cold eyes, landscapes,* (22) *[And] the market that stands petrified in a stroke* (23) *[Closed] in the extended hands of a monster, (golem), [hands] of wagons and levers.*

The objects that "fix" the emotions of the participants are introduced by means of demonstrative pronouns and definite articles (literally "The night this one," "The estrangement of the walls these ones"). It is a specific night with specific walls and a specific candle yet the total effect is indefiniteness, estrangement, mystery.

As in the preceding poem, the unidentified voice does not describe the setting directly. It is the unmaterial objects and spiritual qualities that hold the stage: alienation, silence fighting silence, the cautious breath of a candle (stanza 1); rumor roaming like a cold wind, an anonymous shadow, the independent noise of steps (stanzas 2-3); tension, a disembodied voice, a weird caress, the unspecified light of a deceptive smile (stanza 4). Such non-material things, or rather the relations between them (the silences of a heart, the ghostlike steps and voice), populate Alterman's poetic world. As Leo Spitzer pointed out, the grotesque effect of Christian Morgenstern's verse is dependent on the relational nouns detached from their normal relational framework—e.g., *Ein Knie geht einsam durch die Welt,* "A knee goes by itself through the world." Alterman uses this same device, much as Rilke does, to elevate spiritual and non-material elements above specific events and objects—which are seen as adventitious. Moreover, there is often a pronounced element of horror in these non-material nouns, detached from their normal framework, from any chain of events. The noise of steps (11-12) lives on after the shadow of a man has disappeared from the square—and perhaps from life.

The emotional appeal to "the dust of the world" (*afár haolám,* 13-14) after the disappearance of the footsteps, is rich with connotations; for *ṣoḥén afár* ("the dweller in the dust") is a traditional figure for the dead, but *olám* ("world") also means "eternity."

The fourth stanza is patterned on the first. The "estrangement" becomes "tenseness"; the "silences" are replaced by detached voices; and the "cautious life of the tallow candle" is now the "life and death" of the candle. The candle is "cautious" because the winds of tension are about to break out. The menace is everpresent and the talk (16), the strange caress, and the artificial smile usher in its death. A recurrent symbol in Alterman's poetry, the candle bears overtones of a poor and simple setting, folk superstitions, fatal circumstances. Here the death of the candle is an omen for the death of whatever lived between the opposed personae in the scene.

The poem moves from the "interior" (stanza 1) to images of weird motion in the "exterior" (stanzas 2-3) and back again to the room (stanza 4) where the "strange caress" echoes the "caress" of "despair" (6-7). Though the poem has come full circle with the repetition of its initial pattern, it does not end at this point. The fifth stanza now "freezes" the external world. Even the "market-place"—which in Alterman's poetry represents colorful, dynamic life—is here petrified (like the quays of line 8); the "cold eyes" become but another item in a list of external objects. Thus, though the point of departure was intimate, and the external setting (stanzas 2-3) seemed to be an extension of the human situation, the finale reverses the point of view, placing the poem in the larger context of "nature." Both domains, the human and the natural, the internal and the external, echo each other and *both* are frozen in a "mask of wax" (20)— recalling death and the eternity of a wax museum.

The anapestic flow of the poem is constantly interrupted in stanzas 1 and 4 by frequent full stops, feminine rimes, and missing syllables (thus line 1 is amphibrachic; *ṣel ner haḥélev*— "of the tallow candle," 5—lacks an unstressed syllable after *ner*, which slows down the reading).

The halting movement of stanzas 1 and 4 is counterpointed by the stanzas that follow them (2 and 5): here the 4-beat anapestic line is intact, running through the stanza in one complex sentence without interruption of missing syllables or feminine rimes.

Stanza 3, at the poem's center, is a kind of mediate member. It begins with the curt, factual tone of the first stanza, then passes to a longer 2-line sentence which suddenly introduces the direct appeal of a human voice.

— BENJAMIN HRUSHOVSKI

Nathan Alterman

THE FOUNDLING · HAASUFÍ · הָאֲסוּפִי

הִנִּיחַתְנִי אִמִּי לְרַגְלֵי הַגָּדֵר,	Hiniḥátni imí leragléy hagadér,
קְמוּט פָּנִים וְשׁוֹקֵט. עַל גָּב.	Kmut paním veṣokét. Al gav.
וָאַבִּיט בָּהּ מִלְּמַטָּה, כְּמוֹ מִן הַבְּאֵר, —	Vaabít ba milmáta, kmo min habeér,—
עַד נוּסָהּ כְּהִנָּס מִן הַקְּרָב.	Ad nusá kehanás min hakráv.
וָאַבִּיט בָּהּ מִלְּמַטָּה, כְּמוֹ מִן הַבְּאֵר,	Vaabít ba milmáta, kmo min habeér,
וְיָרֵחַ עָלֵינוּ הוּרַם כְּמוֹ נֵר.	Veyaréaḥ aléynu hurám kemó ner.
אַךְ בְּטֶרֶם הַשַּׁחַר הֵאִיר, אוֹתוֹ לֵיל,	Aḥ betérem haṣáḥar heír, otó leyl,
קַמְתִּי אַט כִּי הִגִּיעָה עֵת	Kámti at ki higía et
וָאָשׁוּב בֵּית אִמִּי כְּכַדּוּר מִתְגַּלְגֵּל	Vaaṣúv beyt imí keḥadúr mitgalgél
הַחוֹזֵר אֶל רַגְלֵי הַבּוֹעֵט.	Haḥozér el ragléy haboét.
וָאָשׁוּב בֵּית אִמִּי כְּכַדּוּר מִתְגַּלְגֵּל	Vaaṣúv beyt imí keḥadúr mitgalgél
וָאֶחֱבֹק צַוָּארָהּ בְּיָדַיִם שֶׁל צֵל.	Vaeḥevók tsavará beyadáyim ṣel tsel.
מֵעֲלֵי צַוָּארָהּ, לְעֵינֵי כֹּל יָכוֹל,	Mealéy tsavará, leeynéy kol yaḥól,
הִיא קְרָעַתְנִי כְּמוֹ עֲלוּקָה.	Hi kraátni kemó aluká.
אַךְ שָׁב לַיְלָה וְשַׁבְתִּי אֵלֶיהָ כִּתְמוֹל,	Aḥ ṣav láyla veṣávti eyléha kitmól,
וַתִּהְיֶה לָנוּ זֹאת לְחֻקָּה:	Vatihyé lánu zot leḥuká:
בְּשׁוּב לַיְלָה וְשַׁבְתִּי אֵלֶיהָ כִּתְמוֹל	Beṣúv láyla veṣávti eyléha kitmól
וְהִיא לַיְלָה כּוֹרַעַת לַגְּמוּל וְלָעֹל.	Vehí láyla koráat lagmúl velaól.
וְדַלְתוֹת חֲלוֹמָהּ לִי פְּתוּחוֹת לִרְוָחָה	Vedaltót ḥalomá li ptuḥót lirvaḥá
וְאֵין אִישׁ בַּחֲלוֹם מִלְּבַדִּי.	Veéyn iṣ baḥalóm milvadí.
כִּי נוֹתְרָה אַהֲבַת־נַפְשׁוֹתֵינוּ דְּרוּכָה	Ki notrá ahavát-nafṣotéynu druḥá
כְּמוֹ קֶשֶׁת, מִיּוֹם הִוָּלְדִי.	Kemó késet miyóm hivaldí.
כִּי נוֹתְרָה אַהֲבַת נַפְשׁוֹתֵינוּ דְּרוּכָה	Ki notrá ahavát nafṣotéynu druḥá
וְלָעַד לֹא נִתֶּנֶת וְלֹא לְקוּחָה.	Velaád lo nitének veló lekuḥá.
וְעַל כֵּן עַד אַחֲרִית לֹא הֵסִיר אוֹתִי אֵל	Veál ḳen ad aḥarít lo hesír otí el
מֵעַל לֵב הוֹרָתִי הַצּוֹעֵק	Meál lev horatí hatsoék
וַאֲנִי — שֶׁנִּתַּקְתִּי מִבְּלִי הִגָּמֵל —	Vaaní—ṣenutákti miblí higamél—
לֹא נִגְמַלְתִּי וְלֹא אֶנָּתֵק.	Lo nigmálti veló enaték.
וַאֲנִי שֶׁנִּתַּקְתִּי מִבְּלִי הִגָּמֵל	Vaaní ṣenutákti miblí higamél
נִכְנָס אֶל בֵּיתָהּ וְהַשַּׁעַר נוֹעֵל.	Niḥnás el beytá vehaṣáar noél.

הִיא זָקְנָה בְּכִלְאִי וַתִּדַּל וַתִּקְטַן
וּפָנֶיהָ קֻמְּטוּ כְּפָנַי.
אָז יָדַי הַקְּטַנּוֹת הִלְבִּישׁוּהָ לָבָן
כְּמוֹ אֵם אֶת הַיֶּלֶד הַחַי.
אָז יָדַי הַקְּטַנּוֹת הִלְבִּישׁוּהָ לָבָן
וָאֶשָּׂא אוֹתָהּ בְּלִי לְהַגִּיד לָהּ לְאָן.

Hi zakná beḥil'í vatidál vatiktán
Ufanéha kumtú kefanáy.
Az yadáy haktanót hilbiṣúha laván
Kemó em et hayéled haḥáy.
Az yadáy haktanót hilbiṣúha laván
Vaesá otá bli lehagíd la leán.

Each of Alterman's books marks a distinct phase in his poetic development. The overloaded imagery, rich dissonant rimes, and leaping, elliptic composition of *The Stars Outside* (1938) were followed by the relatively controlled language and composition of the poems in *The Joy of the Poor* (1941), a cycle regarded by some as his major work. He achieved even greater simplicity of language and imagery in a series of ballad-like poems written in the early forties (subsequently published in *The City of the Dove*, 1958). The poems of this period are concerned with themes of enlarged scope, often of a moral or existential nature. They are less involved in complicated and unrealistic metaphors. The images are basic, often "universal"; the composition symmetrical; the rimes exact. There is a folklore-like, semiballadic strain in the tone and in the symbolism of the verse.

The monologue of the dead "Foundling" is in many ways characteristic of Alterman's work at this period:

(1) *At the foot of the fence my mother placed me,* (2) *[My] face creased and still. On [my] back.* (3) *And I looked at her from below, as from a well,—* (4) *Until she fled as one flees from a battle.* (5) *And I looked at her from below, as from a well,* (6) *And a moon was raised over us like a candle.*

(7) *But before the dawn lighted, that same night,* (8) *I got up slowly, for the time had come* (9) *And I returned to my mother's home like a rolling ball* (10) *Which comes back to the feet of the one who kicked it.* (11) *And I returned to my mother's home like a rolling ball* (12) *And I embraced her neck with hands of shadow.*

(13-14) *In the sight of the Almighty she tore me off her neck like a leech.* (15) *But when night returned, I returned to her as on the day before,* (16) *And this became our custom (law):* (17) *When night returns I return to her as on the day before* (18) *And night after night she bows to the recompense (retaliation) and to the yoke.*

(19) *And the doors of her dream are wide open to me,* (20) *And there is nobody in that dream but me.* (21) *For the love of our souls has remained taut* (22) *As a bow, from the day of my birth.* (23) *For the love of our souls has remained taut* (24) *And it can never be given nor taken.*

(25) *And therefore until the (very) end, God did not remove me* (26) *From my parent's screaming heart.* (27) *And I—who had been pulled away without being weaned—*(28) *Have not (ever) been weaned (found release) and shall not (ever) pull away.* (29) *And I who had been pulled away without being weaned* (30) *Enter her house and lock the gate.*

(31) *She grew old in my prison and (grew) lean and (grew) small* (32) *And her face became creased as my face.* (33) *Then my small hands clothed her in white* (34) *Like a mother clothing her living child.* (35) *Then my small hands clothed her in white* (36) *And I carried her (off) without telling her where.*

וְאַנִּיחַ אוֹתָהּ לְרַגְלֵי הַגָּדֵר	Vaaníaḥ otá leragléy hagadér
צוֹפִיָּה וְשׁוֹקֶטֶת, עַל גָּב.	Tsofiyá veṣokétet, al gav.
וַתַּבִּיט בִּי שׂוֹחֶקֶת, כְּמוֹ מִן הַבְּאֵר,	39 Vatabít bi soḥéket, kmo min habeér,
וַנֵּדַע כִּי סִיַּמְנוּ הַקְּרָב.	Vanedá ki siyámnu hakráv.
וַתַּבִּיט בִּי שׂוֹחֶקֶת כְּמוֹ מִן הַבְּאֵר,	Vatabít bi soḥéket kmo min habeér.
וְיָרֵחַ עָלֵינוּ הוּרַם כְּמוֹ נֵר.	Veyaréaḥ aléynu hurám kemo ner.

(37) *And at the foot of the fence I placed her* (38) *Watchful and still, on (her) back.* (39) *And she looked at me laughing, as from a well,* (40) *And we knew that we ended the battle.* (41) *And she looked at me laughing, as from a well.* (42) *And a moon was raised over us like a candle.*

There are immutable ties such as those between mother and child, which "can never be given nor taken" (24). A mother may abandon her infant, helpless, "on its back" (2), at the foot of a fence (1), but it will live on in her imagination and rule her dreams: so long as she is alive, she will carry her unweaned baby within her.

In Alterman's ballad, this basic psychological situation is dramatically inverted: it is the dead foundling who is the active participant in the relationship. He who was never weaned (28) imprisons her in his world, punishes her for having transgressed elementary, superhuman laws. He who was never a *gamúl*, "a weaned child," inflicts the *gmul*, the "punishment" or "recompense" (18).

The nightly "yoke" (12) is forcibly expressed in the unrelenting repetition of the infant's return, in simile after simile, stanza after stanza. And the "recompense" (18) is fully realized in the total reversal of roles (stanzas 6, 7): the mother becomes creased and small until she assumes the attributes of the infant of the first stanza—white shrouds instead of white swaddling clothes (33-34). Now she too is released: she looks at him "laughing" (39)—and the battle is ended.

The vocabulary of this forceful ballad is extremely simple. (In fact, most of the words appear in a list of basic Hebrew, and about half of them belong to the 400 words most commonly used in contemporary Hebrew.) Syntactic units and lines are parallel in each stanza. The anapestic pattern is unusually regular and it is emphasized by the absence of feminine rimes. The variation usually achieved in Hebrew by alternating feminine and masculine rimes is replaced here by alternating the length of the line: 4-3-4-3-(4-4) anapests—a common device of folk songs.

"The Foundling" relies upon direct, elementary similes (there are hardly any metaphors), simple diction, conventional meter and rime. But the fantastic realism of the framework and the paradox and fatality of the dramatic situation endow the basic images with the value of symbols, in the best tradition of folk poetry.

— BENJAMIN HRUSHOVSKI

Nathan Alterman

THE MOLE · HAḤÓLED · הַחֹלֶד

One of the major works of modern Hebrew poetry, *The Joy of the Poor* is a complex of 31 poems, loosely linked by a developing pattern of motifs, basic symbolic situations, and related elements of language and of imagery. Although the total effect is kaleidoscopic (recalling the genre of Eliot's *Waste Land* or Rilke's *Duino Elegies*), the settings are restrained in color and detail, the vocabulary simple and suggestive, often echoing familiar word-patterns in the Bible (especially Ecclesiastes and Lamentations) and in the Prayerbook. An almost imperceptible thread of plot runs through the work, which is extremely varied in strophic and metrical forms.

Though it would be of course impossible to give an idea of the impact of *The Joy of the Poor* as a whole, a few remarks may serve to outline the background of "The Mole," which is taken from the first sequence.

The book opens with a series of poems spoken by a dead lover to his living beloved. He is at first characterized as "the poor one who is like a dead one"—*aní kemét*, patterned on a well-known proverb: *aní ḥaṣúv kemét*, "the poor are (as good) as dead." He is "poor" in his lack of materiality. The unreal setting, which endows the most conventional themes with remarkable resonance, establishes the book's central ideas: the indestructibleness of spiritual values, especially of those non-rational ties between lovers and friends, parents and children, that subsist beyond death.

As in "The Foundling" (p. 112), the metaphor of the dead being alive in the thoughts of the living is dramatically realized and the situation inverted: it is the dead, no longer destructible, who voice the "joy of the poor." In a later poem, when the city is besieged, the dead man is the only one who, in the guise of the "alien," can pass through the gates. He is "the witness" and he is the guardian of memory.

The relationship between the dead lover and his living beloved is extremely complex. On the one hand, he urges her to join him, which means to die: the "Day of Joy," as he says in the opening poem, will be the day of her burial. On the other hand, he wants her to continue to live; it is he who "defends" her from hunger and poverty in the besieged city.

The image of the dead lover undergoes constant transformations. The persistent lover, who awaits her in death, becomes the "alien," the "foreigner"—the only one who can care for her in the besieged city, "for the living cannot save the living." The lover who swears to avenge her upon her enemies, as he listens to her sobbing through the window panes, becomes the "vulture," the "man of eyes," crazed with jealousy, forever shouting "My wife, my wife!" In "The Mole" he comes even closer: he is present in her room,

לֹא לַהֶבֶל נִשְׁבַּעְתִּי לָךְ אֹמֶן.		Lo lahével niṣbáti laḥ ómen.
לֹא לַשָּׁוְא עֲקֵבַיִךְ אָשׁוּף.		Lo laṣáv akeváyiḥ aṣúf.
עִם הַחֹלֶד חָתַרְתִּי מֵעֹמֶק,	3	Im haḥóled ḥatárti meómek,
וְכָמוֹהוּ עִקֵּשׁ וְכָשׁוּף.		Veḥamóhu ikéṣ veḥaṣúf.
אַתְּ עַצֶּבֶת רֹאשִׁי הַמַּקְרִיחַ,		At atsévet roṣí hamakríaḥ,
אַתְּ יְגוֹן צִפָּרְנַי הַגְּדוֹלוֹת,		At yegón tsipornáy hagdolót,
אַתְּ שִׂמְעִינִי בְּנֶפֶץ הַטִּיחַ,	7	At ṣim'íni benéfets hatíaḥ,
בְּחֵרוּק הָרִצְפָּה בַּלֵּילוֹת.		Beḥerúk haritspá baleylót.
מוּל מַרְאָה מְשֻׁבֶּצֶת בִּנְחֹשֶׁת,		Mul mar'á meṣubétset binḥóṣet,
מִתְנוֹעֵעַ נֵרֵךְ הָאֶבְיוֹן.		Mitnoéa neréḥ haevyón.
הַהוֹלְכִים אֶל פָּנַיִךְ בַּחֹשֶׁךְ,	11	Haholḥím el panáyiḥ baḥóṣeḥ,
בָּךְ צָפוּ מִכְתָּלִים וְחֶבְיוֹן.		Baḥ tsafú miktalím veḥevyón.
וּבְצֵאתִי לְגָנְבֵךְ כְּשִׁבֹּלֶת,		Uvtsetí legonvéḥ keṣibólet,
סִנְוְרַנִי הַנֵּר בְּהִלּוֹ,		Sinveráni hanér behiló,
וְנוֹתַרְנוּ אֲנִי וְהַחֹלֶד	15	Venotárnu aní vehaḥóled,
חֲשֵׁכִים וּסְמוּרִים לְמוּלוֹ.		Ḥaṣeḥím usmurím lemuló.
* *		* *
לֹא לַהֶבֶל נִשְׁבַּעְתִּי לָךְ אֹמֶן		Lo lahével niṣbáti laḥ ómen
וּבַצַּר לִי גֵּו־אֶרֶץ אָשׁוּף.		Uvatsár li gev-érets aṣúf.
אֶל חַיַּיִךְ כָּלִיתִי מֵעֹמֶק,	19	El ḥayáyiḥ kalíti meómek,
כִּי הַחַי הוּא כִּשּׁוּף עַל כִּשּׁוּף.		Ki haḥáy hu kiṣúf al kiṣúf.
תִּמְהוֹנִי אַתְּ! רְאִי מַה נִּלְעַגְתִּי		Timhoní at! reí ma nil'ágti
מַה שִּׁנַּנְתִּי לֶכְתֵּךְ וְעָמְדֵךְ.		Ma ṣinánti leḥtéḥ veomdéḥ.
גַּם עַל קַט וְטָפֵל לֹא דִּלַּגְתִּי,	23	Gam al kat vetafél lo dilágti,
גַּם חָרַדְתִּי מִגִּיל בַּעֲדֵךְ.		Gam ḥarádti migíl baadéḥ.
מִסְּבִיבֵךְ מַחֲשַׁבְתִּי מְהַלֶּכֶת,		Misvivéḥ maḥṣavtí mehaléḥet,
מַחֲשַׁבְתִּי מְסַמֶּרֶת הָעוֹר,		Maḥṣavtí mesaméret haór,
עַל נְזִיד־הַפָּרוּר וְהַלֶּחֶם	27	Al nezíd-haparúr vehaléḥem
וְהַנֵּר שֶׁיַּסְפִּיק לְמָאוֹר.		Vehanér ṣeyaspík lemaór.

blind but stubbornly striving to reach her from the depths:

(1) *Not for naught (for vanity) have I vowed to be faithful to you [*lit. *faithfulness].* (2) *Not in vain do I assault your heels.* (3) *With the mole I burrowed (strove) from the deep,* (4) *And, like him, stubborn and charmed (enchanted).*

The opening words, *lo lahével*, link the first and last lines of the book, paraphrasing and insistently denying the dictum of Ecclesiastes: *havél havalím, hakól hével*, "Vanity of vanities; all is vanity." Obviously this denial, coming from the mouth of a dead speaker, is more than ambiguous. Moreover, the atmosphere of violence and destruction in which the book is steeped, and the lover's longing for a "joy of doom" and for her death, give his repeated negation a very special significance. The second line of "The Mole," using the rare verb *aṣúf* ("I shall oppress [bruise]"), reinforces the motifs of darkness-death, vigilance-vengeance, by alluding to God's curse upon the serpent, in Genesis 3:15 ("it shall bruise *[yeṣufḥá]* thy head, and thou shalt bruise *[teṣufénu]* his heel"), and to the verse in Psalms 139:11 (surely the darkness shall cover *[yeṣuféni]* me").

The setting of the poem is now established and the major "characters" are introduced: the dead lover is like a mole (4) and he also burrows and strives with the mole (3). The two are interchangeable. The second stanza evokes both the changes taking place in the body of the dead and the physical appearance of a mole:

(5) *You are the sorrow of my balding head,* (6) *You are the grief of my big (finger) nails,* (7) *(You,) listen to me in the cracking of plaster,* (8) *(In) the creaking of the floor at night.*

The inverted reality of the poem is now supported by a scene from folklore and folk-belief: (10) *Your poor (humble) candle sways* (9) *Facing a mirror inlaid with copper.* (11) *Those going toward your face in the dark,* (12) *Watched you from walls and from hiding (-place).*

The woman is absorbed in an act of divination: she is summoning the dead. But the light of the candle defends her from the darkness and is also a symbol of her life. Elsewhere the lover, in the guise of the "alien," says: "And on the verge of doom, I shall extinguish you like a candle." This is the paradox underlying the image of the candle in the last stanza of the prelude to "The Mole":

(13) *And when I went forth to steal you as [if you were] an ear of wheat* (14) *The candle blinded me with its brightness,* (15) *And we remained (alone), the mole and I,* (16) *Dark and bristling against it [the candle].*

In the next section, the various motifs are developed and almost all the lines of the prelude are repeated, in different order and in contexts which transform their meaning:

(17) *Not for naught (vanity) did I vow to be faithful to you* (18) *And in my distress I assault the body of the earth.* (19) *For I longed for your life from the deep,* (20) *For the living is (a) spell upon spell (charm upon charm).*

(21) *You are my amazement! See how ludicrous I became,* (22) *How I rehearsed (learned by heart) your walking and your standing.* (23) *Nor did I skip (even the) trifling and (the) paltry,* (24) *(And) I also trembled with joy for you.*

(25) *Roundabout you my thought (concern) stalks,* (26) *My thought which bristles the skin,* (27) *[My thought of] the pottage of the pan and the bread* [idiomatic for "a modest meal"], (28) *And the candle that should suffice for light.*

וַאֲנִי הַגּוֹחֵן אֶל יָדַיִךְ,		Vaaní hagoḥén el yadáyiḥ,
מְיֻגָּע וְזָקֵן כְּאִמֵּךְ.		Meyugá vezakén keiméḥ.
וְנוֹשֵׂא אֶת עָנְיֵךְ וּמְרוּדַיִךְ	31	Venosé et onyéḥ umrudáyiḥ
בְּלִי מִפְלָט וּמָנוֹחַ מִמֵּךְ.		Bli miflát umanóaḥ miméḥ.
אַתְּ עַצֶּבֶת רֹאשִׁי הַמַּקְרִיחַ,		At atsévet roṣí hamakríaḥ,
אַתְּ יְגוֹן צִפָּרְנַי הַגְּדוֹלוֹת,		At yegón tsipornáy hagdolót,
טִרְדָּתִי הַכְּבֵדָה מֵהַשְׁכִּיחַ,	35	Tirdatí hakvedá mehaṣkíaḥ,
מוּעָקַת הִרְהוּרַי בַּלֵּילוֹת.		Muakát hirhuráy baleylót.
כִּי נִשְׁבֶּרֶת הִנָּךְ כְּשִׁבֹּלֶת		Ki niṣbéret hináḥ keṣibólet
וְצָרֵינוּ עוֹמְדִים עַל תִּלָּם,		Vetsaréynu omdím al tilám,
וְנוֹתַרְנוּ אֲנִי וְהַחֹלֶד	39	Venotárnu aní vehaḥóled
חֲשֵׁכִים וּסְמוּרִים לְמוּלָם.		Ḥaṣeḥím usmurím lemulám.
וּבְמַרְאָה מְשֻׁבֶּצֶת בִּנְחֹשֶׁת		Uvmar'á meṣubétset binḥóṣet
מִתְנוֹעֵעַ הַנֵּר הַלּוֹחֵךְ.		Mitnoéa hanér haloḥéḥ.
אַתְּ רוֹאָה אֶת פָּנֵינוּ מֵחֹשֶׁךְ,	43	At roá et panéynu meḥóṣeḥ,
וְיוֹדַעַת כִּי לֹא נִשְׁכָּחֵךְ.		Veyodáat ki lo niṣkaḥéḥ.
כִּי חָצוּי הָעוֹלָם, כִּי הוּא שְׁנַיִם,		Ki ḥatsúy haolám, ki hu ṣnáyim,
וּכְפוּלָה הִיא הֶמְיַת מִסְפְּדוֹ,		Uḥfulá hi hemyát mispedó,
כִּי אֵין בַּיִת בְּלִי מֵת עַל כַּפַּיִם,	47	Ki eyn báyit bli met al kapáyim,
וְאֵין מֵת שֶׁיִּשְׁכַּח אֶת בֵּיתוֹ.		Veéyn met ṣeyiṣkáḥ et beytó.
וּבְלִי קֵץ אֶל עָרֵי נְכָאֵינוּ		Uvlí kets el aréy neḥaéynu
יוֹשְׁבֵי חֹשֶׁךְ וָתֵל נִבָּטִים.		Yoṣvéy ḥóṣeḥ vatél ṇibatím.
נִפְלָאִים, נִפְלָאִים הֵם חַיֵּינוּ,	51	Niflaím, niflaím hem ḥayéynu,
הַמְּלֵאִים מַחֲשָׁבוֹת שֶׁל מֵתִים.		Hamleím maḥṣavót ṣel metím.

(29) *And I (am the one) who stoops over your arms,* (30) *Tired and old like your mother.* (31) *And I [am the one] who carries your poverty and wretchedness* (32) *Without refuge or respite from you.*

(33) *You are the sorrow of my balding head,* (34) *You are the grief of my big (finger)nails,* (35) *My anxiety (burden)—too heavy to be forgotten,* (36) *The distress (oppression) of my meditations (thoughts) at night.*

(37) *Because you break like an ear of wheat* (38) *And our enemies persist [*lit. *stand on their mound]* (39) *And (only) the mole and I remained* (40) *Dark and bristling facing them.*

(41) *And in a mirror inlaid with copper* (42) *The flickering candle sways.* (43) *You see our faces from the dark* (44) *And you know that we shall not forget you.*

The point of view has changed. Now it is not the dead (4) who is "enchanted" *(kaṣúf)* but the living who weaves an unbreakable spell *(kiṣúf)*. The pursuer (3-4) becomes first a protector (21-30) and then one who is pursued (31-36). Whereas he was dark and bristling (16), now it is his unrelenting concern, his "thought," that makes the woman's flesh bristle (26). The lover-mole went forth to steal her as though she were a stalk of wheat (13); but the stalk of wheat is fragile and must now be protected from the powerful unnamed enemies (33-34).

The last 2 stanzas formulate one of Alterman's basic themes: (45) *For the world is split, for it [the world] is two* (46) *And the clamor of its lament is double,* (47) *For there is no home without a dead [one] on [its] arms,* (48) *And there is no dead [one] who forgets his home.*

(49-50) *And endlessly, the dwellers of darkness and mound look out at the cities of our sorrows.* (51) *Wonderful, wonderful are our lives,* (52) *Which are full of the thoughts of the dead.*

When *The Joy of the Poor* was written Europe was occupied, the first signs of the approaching holocaust were reaching Palestine. The German army was on the threshold of Egypt. The book does not refer directly to these events, but their presence is clearly felt, especially in the second part, where the personal situation is enlarged and transformed into a social one. In "The Mole" there is only the barest intimation of the larger, perhaps national, ramifications of the theme: there is no force to oppose the "enemies" other than the imaginary forces of darkness—the dead lover and the mole. The seeds of the larger metaphor are, however, already present. "The Underground" that will defy the enemy later in the book is already hinted at in the attributes of the unreal figures here burrowing in the deep (the verb *ḥatárti*, "I burrowed, strove," [3] becomes the noun *maḥtéret*, "underground," which serves as the title of a poem toward the climax of the volume.

— BENJAMIN HRUSHOVSKI

Lea Goldberg

AFTER TWENTY YEARS · AḤARÉY ESRÍM ṢANÁ · אַחֲרֵי עֶשְׂרִים שָׁנָה

א

עֶשְׂרִים שָׁנָה — וּכְמוֹ שֶׁנּוֹהֲגִים לוֹמַר
« כֵּן, מַשֶּׁהוּ קָרָה בֵּינְתַיִם בָּעוֹלָם » —
וְרֶגֶשׁ זֶה אֵינֶנּוּ יַיִן מְשֻׁמָּר:
הוּא לֹא נִהְיָה חָרִיף יוֹתֵר, אַף לֹא יוֹתֵר מֻשְׁלָם.

לֹא, הַאֲמֵן, לֹא שֵׁיבָתְךָ הִיא זֹאת —
אוּלַי רַק מַבָּטְךָ אָדִישׁ וְלֹא נִכְלָם,
רַק בּוֹ הֵן מְגִלּוֹת חַיֵּינוּ הַגְּנוּזוֹת
וְכָל אֲשֶׁר « קָרָה בֵּינְתַיִם בָּעוֹלָם ».

שְׁנֵי אֲנָשִׁים, אָכֵן, שְׁנֵי אֲנָשִׁים זָרִים
מִשְּׁנֵי עֶבְרֵי הַתְּהוֹם שֶׁל הֶרֶס וְאֵימָה.
אֲפִלּוּ עַל קִבְרֵי מֵתֵינוּ הַיְקָרִים
לֹא עוֹד נֹאמַר הַיּוֹם אוֹתָהּ תְּפִלָּה עַצְמָהּ.

I

Esrím ṣaná—uḥmó ṣenohagím lomár
"Ken, máṣehu kará beyntáyim baolám"—
Veréges ze eynénu yáyin meṣumár:
Hu lo nihiyá ḥaríf yotér, af lo yotér muṣlám.

Lo, haamén, lo seyvatḥá hi zot—
Uláy rak mabatḥá adíṣ veló niḥlám,
Rak bo hen megilót ḥayéynu hagnuzót
Veḥól aṣér "kará beyntáyim baolám".

Ṣney anaṣím, aḥén, ṣney anaṣím zarím
Miṣnéy evréy hathóm ṣel héres veeymá.
Afílu al kivréy meytéynu haykarím
Lo od nomár hayóm otá tfilá atsmá.

The poetry of Lea Goldberg shows strong affinities for the Symbolists of both Eastern and Western Europe. Born in Kovno, Lithuania, and educated at the Universities of Kovno, Bonn, and Berlin, she became thoroughly familiar with Russian and German literatures. (She has also done a great deal of translating from these languages and from Italian, English, and French as well.) She settled in Israel early in her career, joining Shlonsky's circle (see p. 75) soon after her arrival in 1935.

Although associated with the modernist movement of the thirties, Lea Goldberg uses traditional verse forms. Her modernism is reflected in the conversational style of her work and in her rejection of both the rhetoric of her predecessors and the bombast of some of her contemporaries. A taste for simplicity leads her to limit her symbolic vocabulary to the familiar, investing everyday words, images, rhythms, and even rimes with astonishing freshness.

She is one of the few poets of her generation to eschew ideological versifying. She writes about such universal matters as childhood, nature, love (especially mature love), aging, and death. And her poems are highly personal and introspective.

"After Twenty Years" is an encounter between two estranged lovers. The point of view is the woman's, and the first part of the poem is conversational in the extreme. The lines are long and for the most part hexameters, but the predominant iambic meter is varied sufficiently to give the illusion of living speech. The opening is a carefully executed pastiche of clichés:

(1) *Twenty years—and as it's customary to say* — (2) *"Yes, something has happened meantime in the world"*— (3) *And this feeling isn't preserved (aged) wine:* (4) *It doesn't gain in strength or perfection* [lit. *become stronger or more perfect*]. With the unobtrusive reference to "preserved wine" (3), the religious symbolism that will soon dominate the poem is introduced. The *yáyin hameṣumár* is that wine which, before the earth was created, had been prepared for the righteous to enjoy in the world to come.

European poets, before the rise of secularism, could write about love as they would of a religious sacrament, and in Romantic poetry love would become a substitute for the sacred. But with the collapse of such "secular religion," love lost its eternal dimension: the metaphor broke down. And yet the fact that love is now seen as ephemeral cannot deprive it of emotional poignancy: (5) *No, believe* [*me*], *it's not your aging hair*— (6) *Perhaps only your indifferent and unembarrassed expression,* (7) *Only in it are the hidden scrolls of our lives* (8) *And all that "has happened meantime in the world."*

(9) *Two people, yes, two strange people* (10) *On either side of the abyss of destruction and terror.* (11) *Even over the graves of our dear dead* (12) *Today we'll no longer recite the very same prayer.* There is only one repository for the memory of the lovers and of their tragic history that followed: the "indifferent and unembarrassed expression" of his face. And the memories themselves are "hidden scrolls"—apocrypha rather than the authentic thing. Personal tragedy, moreover, is connected with the European tragedy common to both (11), but, ironically, time and history (10) have drawn an everwidening gulf between them.

With the second part of the poem, the

ב	II
שְׁנֵי מִנְיָנִים שֶׁל שָׁנִים	Ṣney minyaním ṣel ṣaním
לִגְיוֹנוֹת שֶׁל יָמִים לְבָנִים,	Ligyonót ṣel yamím levaním,
שְׁנֵי מִנְיָנִים שֶׁל שָׁנִים	Ṣney minyaním ṣel ṣaním
שֶׁהָיוּ לְמִדְבַּר־שְׁמָמָה.	Ṣehayú lemidbár-ṣmamá.
אַל תַּתְחִיל, לְמַעַן הַשֵּׁם!	Al tatḥíl, lemáan haṣém!
אֵין לָדַעַת מִי הָאָשֵׁם.	Eyn ladáat mi haaṣém.
כְּתָמִיד: אַתָּה אָשֵׁם	Ketamíd: atá aṣém
וַאֲנִי אֲשֵׁמָה.	Vaaní aṣemá.
כָּךְ מֻטָּל בֵּינֵינוּ הַזְּמַן,	Kaḥ mutál beynéynu hazmán,
הַשָּׁנִים אֲשֶׁר זָב דָּמָן,	Haṣaním aṣér zav damán,
הַמֵּת הַיָּקָר, הַזְּמַן,	Hamét hayakár, hazmán,
תְּהֵא נִשְׁמָתוֹ צְרוּרָה...	Tehé niṣmató tsrurá . . .
וַאֲנַחְנוּ מִשְּׁנֵי עֲבָרָיו	Vaanáḥnu miṣnéy avaráv
כְּאוֹיְבִים אַחֲרֵי הַקְּרָב,	Keoyvím aḥaréy hakráv,
וּמֵתֵינוּ בִּשְׂדֵה הַקְּרָב	Umeytéynu bisdé hakráv
וְאֵין כַּפָּרָה.	Veéyn kapará.

conversational hexameters shift into a ritualistic three-beat staccato which can barely contain the swell of emotion. The lines grow clipped, short; the rime pattern (*abab*), which was unobtrusive in the first part, now drums a funereal tempo (*aaax, bbbx, cccy, dddy*); and religious imagery takes over:

(13) *Two tens of years [minyaním],* (14) *Legions of white days,* (15) *Two tens of years [minyaním]* (16) *Which have become a desolate desert.* The image of the *minyaním* (13, 15), the synagogal quorum, calls up memories of swaying men wrapped in white prayer-shawls: white shawls, white shrouds, white days, merging into a desolate desert as faith disappears.

(17) *Don't start now, for God's sake!* (18) *There's no knowing who's to blame.* (19) *As always: you're to blame (guilty)* (20) *And I'm to blame (guilty).*

(21) *Thus, between us, is time laid out:* (22) *The years whose blood has flowed,* (23) *Time, the dear dead one,* (24) *May He Rest in Peace . . .*

(25) *And we are on either side of him* (26) *Like enemies after battle,* (27) *And our dead [lie] in the battlefield* (28) *And there is no atonement.*

Our "dear dead" have been destroyed. Line 24 repeats a key fragment from the requiem "*El malé raḥamim,*" which in its full form means "May his soul be bound up in the bond of (eternal) life." The "victim" of the battle of love is Time, the personification of the lovers' estrangement. And there is nothing that can be done to atone for this crime of estrangement.

— EZRA SPICEHANDLER

Lea Goldberg

ḤAMSÍN OF NISÁN · ḤAMSÍN ṢEL NISÁN · חַמְסִין שֶׁל נִיסָן

אָכֵן אֵדַע, זֶה יוֹם לְלֹא תְּמוּרָה
וְלֹא נָפַל דָּבָר וְלֹא אֵרַע
וְלֹא יַבְדִּיל בֵּינוֹ לְבֵין יָמִים
צִיּוּן וָאוֹת אֲשֶׁר מִטּוֹב עַד רַע.

וְרַק לַשֶּׁמֶשׁ רֵיחַ שֶׁל יַסְמִין,
וְרַק לָאֶבֶן קוֹל שֶׁל לֵב פּוֹעֵם,
וְרַק לָעֶרֶב צֶבַע שֶׁל תַּפּוּז,
וְרַק לַחוֹל שְׂפָתַיִם מְנַשְּׁקוֹת.

Aḥén edá, ze yom leló tmurá
Veló nafál davár veló erá
3 Veló yavdíl beynó levéyn yamím
Tsiyún vaót aṣér mitóv ad ra.

Verák laṣémeṣ réaḥ ṣel yasmín,
Verák laéven kol ṣel lev poém,
7 Verák laérev tséva ṣel tapúz,
Verák laḥól sfatáyim menaṣkót.

In an enthusiastic essay on Avraham Ben Yitshak (pp. 50ff.), whose views had deeply impressed her, Lea Goldberg recalls the older poet's description of an arrested flash of perception: "I remember standing at the entrance of a house, on a staircase. The house was built of wood and painted green. The sand that covered the porch steps was made up of small bits of colored glass . . . They possessed the magic of a summer's evening and I knew that only once in my life would I see such a sight."

For Lea Goldberg such a moment of insight contains the essence of youth in the ever flowing stream of time. It arises out of ordinary phenomena—an orange, a peasant girl, a fragment of memory—to flash upon the dark screen of human consciousness in a sudden moment of grace. Such a moment, flashing upon the poet quite without warning, and on a day that was only "anonymous and drab" (9), is celebrated in the present poem.

"Ḥamsín," the name given to the hot desert wind that frequently lashes Israel, is an Arabic word meaning "fifty," folk meteorology insisting that there are fifty *ḥamsinim* a year. This Israeli equivalent of the sirocco is often gritty with sand. Its devastating heat tries the temper and nerves; the bright haze intensifies the nuances of color and light. A combination of restlessness and acute sensitivity pervades the lines of this lyric about the *ḥamsín* in the month of *Nisán*, which is approximately April.

(1) *Indeed I know this is a day without [any] change (counterpart)* (2) *And nothing fell (took place) and [nothing] happened.* (4) *And no mark, no omen [*lit. *ranging from good to evil]* (3) *Separates it from [other] days.* The word *tmurá* (1) means both "change" and "counterpart." Thus the entire poem is present in the opening line with its double resonance.

A regular iambic pentameter and a somewhat rigid rime scheme (*aaba*) produce an overtone of weariness. The first words *aḥén edá* ("truly I know") have a sighing quality.

(5) *And only that the sun has the scent of jasmine,* (6) *And only that the stone has the sound of a throbbing heart,* (7) *And only that the evening has the color of an orange,* (8) *And only that the sand has kissing lips.* The rime has been abandoned but the meter remains strict. Each

אֵיךְ אֶזְכְּרֶנּוּ, אַלְמוֹנִי, סְתָמִי,	Eyḥ ezkerénu, almoní, stamí,
אֵיכָה אֶשְׁמֹר חַסְדּוֹ הַפִּתְאוֹמִי,	Eyḥá eṣmór ḥasdó hapit'omí,
אֵיךְ אַאֲמִין שֶׁיּוֹם אֶחָד הָיָה	Eyḥ aamín ṣeyóm eḥád hayá
כָּל נִיד וְרֵיחַ עֶצֶם מֵעַצְמִי?	Kol nid veréaḥ étsem meatsmí?
כִּי כָּל אִילָן הָיָה מִפְרָשׂ רוֹטֵט,	Ki kol ilán hayá mifrás rotét,
וְלִדְמָמָה עֵינַיִם שֶׁל יַלְדָּה,	Velidmamá eynáyim ṣel yaldá,
וְלִדְמָעוֹת נִיחוֹחַ הַלִּבְלוּב,	Velidmaót niḥóaḥ halivlúv
וְשֵׁם הָעִיר כְּשֵׁם אַהֲבָתִי.	Veṣém haír keṣém ahavatí.

line begins with *verák*, which has the literal force of "and only the fact that," and is followed by the preposition *la* ("to") joined to the second word. In a straightforward word-for-word translation, line 5 would read: "And only to the sun is there the scent of jasmine."

The *la* sounds that begin the second word in lines 5, 6, 7, 8 tie in with the *lo* sounds in 1, 2, 3. Note also that the first three of the words prefixed by *la* (5, 6, 7) have two *e* sounds, the first of which is stressed. This penultimate stress (*laṣémeṣ, laéven, laérev*) plays against the normal last-syllable stress of most Hebrew words, to produce an emphatic impact. The force is felt especially in line 7, where two such penultimate stresses follow each other (*laérev tséva*).

(9) *How can I remember it [the day], anonymous [and] vague,* (10) *How can I guard (preserve) its sudden grace,* (11) *How shall I believe that on one [this] day* (12) *Every flutter and scent was of my very essence [*lit. *bone of myself*, a play on *bone of my bone].*

The third stanza has resumed the rime scheme of the first. And lines 9, 10, and 11 each begin with *eyḥ* and *eyḥá* (two forms of "how") to recall the *aḥén* of line 1. The enjambment of lines 11-12 emphasizes the central idea, coming as it does after the questioning of 9 and 10. The final rime in 12 ties the whole statement together—as Mayakowsky once put it, "rime is the tightening nail."

As the poem draws to its close, it picks up some of the symbols frequently found in the work of Lea Goldberg:

(13) *For every tree was a trembling sail,* (14) *And silence [had] a little girl's eyes,* (15) *And tears [had] the aroma of blooming,* (16) *And the name of the city [was] like the name of my love.* We shall find, for example, images of little girls' eyes and of blooming in the "River Poems" that follow. In "Ḥamsín of Nisán" these and other such images acquire unity in a sudden moment of grace. To the Hebrew reader, the word *eyḥá* has a markedly elegiac tone. Even the city, which in other poems by Lea Goldberg is associated with alienation, here takes on the intimate identity of the speaker's love.

— EZRA SPICEHANDLER

Lea Goldberg

THE TREE SINGS TO THE RIVER

HAÉTS ṢAR LANÁḤAL · הָעֵץ שָׁר לַנַּחַל

אֲשֶׁר נָשָׂא אֶת סְתָוִי הַזָּהוּב,	Aṣér nasá et staví hazahúv,
אֶת דָּמִי בְּשַׁלֶּכֶת גָּרַף,	Et damí beṣaléḥet garáf,
אֲשֶׁר יִרְאֶה אֲבִיבִי כִּי יָשׁוּב	Aṣér yir'é aviví ki yaṣúv
עִם תְּקוּפַת הַשָּׁנָה אֵלָיו,	Im tkufát haṣaná eláv,
אָחִי הַנַּחַל, הָאוֹבֵד לָעַד,	Aḥí hanáḥal, haovéd laád,
הֶחָדָשׁ יוֹם־יוֹם וְאַחֵר וְאֶחָד,	Heḥadáṣ yom-yóm, veaḥér veeḥád,
אָחִי הַזֶּרֶם בֵּין שְׁנֵי חוֹפָיו	Aḥí hazérem beyn ṣney ḥofáv
הַזּוֹרֵם כָּמוֹנִי בֵּין אָבִיב וּסְתָיו.	Hazorém kamóni beyn avív ustáv.
כִּי אֲנִי הַנִּצָּן וַאֲנִי הַפְּרִי,	Ki aní hanitsán vaaní haprí,
אֲנִי עֲתִידִי וַאֲנִי עֲבָרִי,	Aní atidí vaaní avarí,
אֲנִי הַגֶּזַע הָעֲרִירִי,	Aní hagéza haarirí,
וְאַתָּה — זְמַנִּי וְשִׁירִי.	Veatá—zmaní veṣirí.

Our two lyrics are from five "River Songs" which bear the superscription "The Choir of Small Voices," a literal rendering of line 6 of the first of Verlaine's "Ariettes Oubliées." The first poem distinguishes the river from the stone. "I," sings the river, "am the ephemeral and she [the stone] is the permanent (existent). She is the mysteries of creation, and I their revelation . . ." We are presented with a "masculine" and a "feminine." Dynamic and everchanging, the river is the masculine element of "Becoming," in contrast to the stone, which in its stability suggests "Being." The poet is equated with the river—with change and becoming. In the verse before us, however, a new speaker appears: the tree. The tree addresses the river:

(1) *[He] who carried my golden autumn,* (2) *Swept away my blood with the leaf fall,* (3) *[He] who shall see my spring when it returns* (4) *To him with the turning of the year,*

(5) *My brother the river, who is forever lost,* (6) *New each day and different and one (one and the same),* (7) *My brother the stream between his two shores,* (8) *Who streams as I do between spring and autumn.*

(9) *For I am the bud and I am the fruit,* (10) *I am my future and I am my past,* (11) *I am the solitary tree trunk,* (12) *And you—are my time and my song.*

The river is not changed by the seasonal cycles as the tree is changed, for the river is an external phenomenon which reflects what goes on within the tree, carrying away the leaves that the tree casts off. The river, then, is process: it is movement and time; and yet, though in constant flux ("new each day and different"), it remains a unity ("one and the same").

The tree experiences the cyclic changes to bud and to fruit: it is its own future and past (9, 10). But future and past can reflect themselves only upon the river and they express themselves by means of the river. Thus, the river is the poem. The tree is the internality that creates, the process, that makes itself known on the river of time.

The reader will find much of interest in the rhythm of the poem. Though the meter is predominantly anapestic, the first two feet of lines 1, 3, 5, 7, 11 are iambic. And the stress is placed upon (1) *He who carried*, (3) *He who shall see*, (5) *My brother the river*, (7) *My brother the stream*. Then a shift of stress occurs in line 8, where the word *kamóni* ("like me") breaks the regular meter of the anapest.

The complete omission in 8 of the strong *ḥ* sounds that pervaded lines 5, 6, 7 draws attention to the sonal softness and flow of *hazorém kamóni beyn avív ustáv* ("Who streams as I do between spring and autumn.").

The rhythm of the last stanza quickens into a staccato close. The single rime, the assonance, and the vowel brevity contribute to the clipped gait. And again, the break in the regular anapest of line 12 stresses the summarizing remark: *Veatá—zmaní veṣirí*, "And you—are my time and my song."

THE GIRL SINGS TO THE RIVER

HAYALDÁ ṢARÁ LANÁḤAL · הַיַּלְדָּה שָׁרָה לַנַּחַל

לְאָן יִשָּׂא הַזֶּרֶם אֶת פָּנַי הַקְּטַנִּים?	Leán yisá hazérem et panáy haktaním?
לָמָּה הוּא קוֹרֵעַ אֶת עֵינַי?	Láma hu koréa et eynáy?
בֵּיתִי הַרְחֵק בְּחֹרְשַׁת אֳרָנִים,	Beytí harḥék beḥorṣát oraním,
עֲצוּבָה אִוְשַׁת אֳרָנַי.	Atsuvá ivṣát oranáy.
פִּתַּנִי הַנַּחַל בְּזֶמֶר־גִּיל,	Pitáni hanáḥal bezémer-gil,
רִנֵּן וְקָרָא בִּשְׁמִי,	Rinén vekará biṣmí,
הָלַכְתִּי אֵלָיו אַחֲרֵי הַצְּלִיל,	Haláḥti eyláv aḥaréy hatslíl,
נָטַשְׁתִּי אֶת בֵּית אִמִּי.	Natáṣti et beyt imí.
וַאֲנִי יְחִידָה לָהּ, רַכָּה בְּשָׁנִים,	Vaaní yeḥidá la, raká beṣaním,
וְנַחַל אַכְזָר לְפָנַי —	Venáḥal aḥzár lefanáy—
לְאָן הוּא נוֹשֵׂא אֶת פָּנַי הַקְּטַנִּים?	Leán hu nosé et panáy haktaním?
לָמָּה הוּא קוֹרֵעַ אֶת עֵינַי?	Láma hu koréa et eynáy?

The river as "Time" is associated in our second poem with ideas of "no return." Here a little girl looks into the river and sees her face distorted and carried away from her childhood home.

(1) *To where will the stream carry my small face?* (2) *Why is he opening (tearing) my eyes?* (3) *My home is far away in a grove of pines,* (4) *Sad is the swishing of my pines.*

(5) *The river seduced me with a gay song,* (6) *Caroled and called me by name,* (7) *I went to him, following the sound,* (8) *I abandoned my mother's house.*

(9) *I am her only [child], tender in years,* (10) *And a cruel river [is] before me—* (11) *To where is he carrying my small face?* (12) *Why is he opening (tearing) my eyes?*

If we are struck by the simple, Verlainian quality of the diction, we can also hear echoes of East European folksongs, whose naturalness makes a reader feel that he has heard the song before. Except for line 2. The idiom *likróa eynáyim* can mean merely "to stretch (the) eyes in wonderment," but the literal meaning— "to tear the eyes"— carries an ominous suggestion associated with distortion and aging and inseparable from the child's awareness that the river is not only "gay" with its song but also irresistible and undeniable and—as line 10 suddenly discovers—cruel. The questions asked in lines 1 and 2 and and repeated in lines 11 and 12 remain unanswered.

The opening of stanza 2 carries a gleeful, seductive, dance-like movement: (5) ∪ — ∪ / ∪ — ∪ / ∪ — ∪ / —; (6) ∪ — / ∪ ∪ — / ∪ —. In line 6, the word *rinén*, which sometimes means "to gossip," possibly gives a slight hint of guilt. In the final quatrain, the rhythm and rime of the opening return, to enhance the folksong effect of the whole poem.

— EZRA SPICEHANDLER

Lea Goldberg

FROM MY MOTHER'S HOME · MIBÉYT IMÍ · מִבֵּית אִמִּי

מֵתָה אִמָּהּ שֶׁל אִמִּי	Méta imá ṣel imí
בַּאֲבִיב יָמֶיהָ. וּבִתָּהּ	Baavív yaméha. Uvitá
לֹא זָכְרָה אֶת פָּנֶיהָ. דְּיוֹקְנָהּ הֶחָרוּט	Lo zaḥrá et panéha. Dyokná heḥarút
עַל לִבּוֹ שֶׁל סָבִי	Al libó ṣel saví
נִמְחָה מֵעוֹלַם הַדְּמוּיוֹת	Nimḥá meolám hadmuyót
אַחֲרֵי מוֹתוֹ.	Aḥaréy motó.
רַק הָרְאִי שֶׁלָּהּ נִשְׁתַּיֵּר בַּבַּיִת,	Rak hare'í ṣelá niṣtayér babáyit,
הֶעֱמִיק מֵרֹב שָׁנִים בְּמִשְׁבֶּצֶת הַכֶּסֶף.	Heemík meróv ṣaním bemiṣbétset hakésef.
וַאֲנִי, נֶכְדָּתָהּ הַחִוֶּרֶת, שֶׁאֵינֶנִּי דּוֹמָה לָהּ,	Vaaní, neḥdatá haḥivéret, ṣeeynéni domá la,
מַבִּיטָה הַיּוֹם אֶל תּוֹכוֹ כְּאֶל תּוֹךְ	Mabitá hayóm el toḥó keél toḥ
אֲגַם הַטּוֹמֵן אוֹצְרוֹתָיו	Agám hatomén otsrotáv
מִתַּחַת לַמַּיִם.	Mitáḥat lamáyim.
עָמֹק מְאֹד, מֵאֲחוֹרֵי פָּנַי,	Amók meód, meaḥoréy panáy,
אֲנִי רוֹאָה אִשָּׁה צְעִירָה	Aní roá iṣá tseirá
וְרֻדַּת לְחָיַיִם מְחַיֶּכֶת.	Vrudát leḥayayím meḥayéḥet.
וּפֵאָה נָכְרִית לְרֹאשָׁהּ.	Ufeá noḥrít leroṣá.
הִיא עוֹנֶדֶת	Hi onédet
עָגִיל מָאֳרָךְ אֶל תְּנוּךְ אָזְנָהּ. מַשְׁחִילַתְהוּ	Agíl mooráḥ el tnuḥ ozná. Maṣḥiláthu
בְּנֶקֶב זָעִיר בַּבָּשָׂר הֶעָנֹג	Benékev zaír babasár heanóg
שֶׁל הָאֹזֶן.	Ṣel haózen.
עָמֹק מְאֹד, מֵאֲחוֹרֵי פָּנַי, קוֹרֶנֶת	Amók meód, meaḥoréy panáy, korénet
זְהוּבִית בְּהִירָה שֶׁל עֵינֶיהָ.	Zehuvít behirá ṣel eynéha.
וְהָרְאִי מַמְשִׁיךְ אֶת מָסֹרֶת	Vehare'í mamṣiḥ et masóret
הַמִּשְׁפָּחָה:	Hamiṣpaḥá:
שֶׁהִיא הָיְתָה יָפָה מְאֹד.	Ṣehí haytá yafá meód.

A girl looks into her grandmother's mirror—the setting of the poem is familiar, the words and the images unexalted. Disarmed by the quietness of the key, the reader may at first be unaware of the curious depths into which he will be drawn. The poetic devices are minimal; the rhythm is rambling and free, marked with only an occasional strong alliteration (e.g., lines 1, 8, 13).

(1) *My mother's mother died* (2) *In the spring of*

her days. And her daughter (3) *Did not remember her face. Her portrait, engraved* (4) *Upon my grandfather's heart,* (5) *Was erased from (wiped off) the world of images* (6) *After his death.*

(7) *Only her mirror remained in the home,* (8) *Sunken (deepened) with age into the silver frame.* (9) *And I, her pale granddaughter, who does not resemble her,* (10) *Look into it today as into* (11) *A pool which conceals its treasures* (12) *Beneath the waters.*

(13) *Very deep (down), behind my face,* (14) *I see a young woman* (15) *Pink-cheeked, smiling.* (16) *And a wig on her head.* (17) *She puts* (18) *An elongated earring on her ear-lobe, threading it* (19) *Through a tiny hole in the dainty flesh* (20) *Of her ear.*

(21-22) *Very deep (down), behind my face, the bright goldness of her eyes sends out rays,* (23) *And the mirror carries on the tradition of* (24) *The family:* (25) *That she was very beautiful.*

Line 9, with its regular anapest, focuses upon the main statement: the speaker, a disappointed child-woman, does not look like *and* is not like—both meanings are in the Hebrew words—her grandmother. This line acquires telling significance with the closing suggestion: Grandmother was very "beautiful." Grandmother, unlike both mother and daughter, epitomizes the beauty of the tradition—to which the poet elsewhere has shown ambivalent attitudes.

Although she was born and reared in Kovno, a famous center of talmudic learning, Lea Goldberg rarely alluded to traditional Jewish life in her early poetry: her commitment was Western in outlook. In the wake of Hitlerian persecution, however, a change occurred. In the forties, for example, she devoted an entire book to the country of her birth (*From My Old Home*)—"I departed never to return/ Never wanting to return;/ The past which I did not love/ Has become my beloved past."

The speaker in "From My Mother's Home," though not like her grandmother, is nevertheless her direct descendant and her heir: the child-woman must focus upon this *Gestalt* of the past and all that it stands for. Beginning with the image of the wig, which orthodoxy required the women to wear (16), the speaker gazes upon her grandmother's earring. The long earring is lengthened sonally by the intentionally suffixed *maṣḥiláthu*, an agglutinated word which is both biblical and oldfashioned. Further lengthening is created in the enjambments of lines 17-18-19-20 and in the extending of this stanza beyond the six-line limit of the first two. The effect is one of arrested motion, in which the image of the grandmother becomes fixed.

In her only published play, *The Lady of the Manor*, Lea Goldberg allows her main character to assert that "the past has many things which watchmakers' sons should also know and even love." Would such a statement have relevance to the attitude of the speaker in the poem? After one accepts the main statement—that the child-woman neither looks like nor is the grandmother—it becomes difficult to read it without awareness of underlying ironies. One may ask, with the girl, as she gazes at this picture of the past, how much of it she would wish to call her own and to admire and envy. The full import of the poem, then, may depend as much upon the answer of the reader as upon the thought of the child-woman, whose tongue says no more than what family tradition insists: that Grandmother was very beautiful.

— EZRA SPICEHANDLER

Lea Goldberg

TEL AVIV 1935 · TEL-AVÍV 1935 · **תֵּל־אָבִיב 1935**

הַתְּרָנִים עַל גַּגּוֹת הַבָּתִּים הָיוּ אָז	Hatraním al gagót habatím hayú az
כְּתָרְנֵי סְפִינָתוֹ שֶׁל קוֹלוּמְבּוּס	Ketornéy sfinató ṣel kolúmbus
וְכָל עוֹרֵב שֶׁעָמַד עַל חֻדָּם	Veḥól orév ṣeamád al ḥudám
בִּשֵּׂר יַבֶּשֶׁת אַחֶרֶת.	Bisér yabéṣet aḥéret.
וְהָלְכוּ בָּרְחוֹב צִקְלוֹנֵי הַנּוֹסְעִים	Vehalḥú barḥóv tsiklonéy hanos'ím
וְשָׂפָה שֶׁל אֶרֶץ זָרָה	Vesafá ṣel érets zará
הָיְתָה נִנְעֶצֶת בְּיוֹם הַחַמְסִין	Haytá nin'étset beyóm haḥamsín
כְּלַהַב סַכִּין קָרָה.	Keláhav sakín kará.
אֵיךְ יָכוֹל הָאֲוִיר שֶׁל הָעִיר הַקְּטַנָּה	Eyḥ yaḥól haavír ṣel haír haktaná
לָשֵׂאת כָּל כָּךְ הַרְבֵּה	Lasét kol kaḥ harbé
זִכְרוֹנוֹת יַלְדוּת, אֲהָבוֹת שֶׁנָּשְׁרוּ,	Ziḥronót yaldút, ahavót senaṣrú,
חֲדָרִים שֶׁרוֹקְנוּ אֵי־בָּזֶה?	Ḥadarím ṣeroknú ey-bazé?
כִּתְמוּנוֹת מַשְׁחִירוֹת בְּתוֹךְ מַצְלֵמָה	Kitmunót maṣḥirót betóḥ matslemá
הִתְהַפְּכוּ לֵילוֹת חֹרֶף זַכִּים.	Hithapḥú leylót ḥoref zakím,
לֵילוֹת קַיִץ גְּשׁוּמִים שֶׁמֵּעֵבֶר לַיָּם	Leylót káyits gṣumím ṣemeéver layám
וּבְקָרִים אֲפֵלִים שֶׁל בִּירוֹת.	Uvkarím afeylím ṣel birót.
וְקוֹל צַעַד תּוֹפֵף אַחֲרֵי גַּבֵּךְ	Vekól tsáad toféf aḥaréy gabḥá
שִׁירֵי לֶכֶת שֶׁל צְבָא נֵכָר,	Ṣiréy léḥet ṣel tsvá neḥár,
וְנִדְמֶה — אַךְ תַּחְזִיר אֶת רֹאשֵׁךְ וּבַיָּם	Venidmé—aḥ taḥzír et roṣḥá uvayám
שָׁטָה כְּנֵסִיַּת עִירֵךְ.	Ṣatá kneysiyát irḥá.

Tel Aviv in 1935 was a small town which changed its character with every arrival of shiploads of refugees. Many of these newcomers were Europe-weary Jews who had seized hold of Zionism out of despair and who were often assailed by doubts as to whether Zionism's goals could ever be realized. The cruel brilliance of the landscape—so strange to East European eyes—exposed every doubt, enlarged every illusion, and, above all, aggravated the frightening strangeness of the Mediterranean city:

(1) *The masts on the house-roofs were then* (2) *Like the masts of Columbus' ship* (3) *And every crow (raven) standing on their pinnacles* (4) *Announced a different shore.* The ocean does not stop at this shore. Like the sensation of motion that often stays with a seafarer after

he has disembarked, the sense of wandering persists in the speaker even though he has landed—at "home." Moreover, this new city has no fixed character—so the lines suggest in the allusion to the raven-crow that Noah had sent out to discover whether the flood had receded and which had come back with a negative reply. Each raven brings back tidings of a different shore:

(5) *And the travelers' knapsacks walked down the street* (6) *And the language of a foreign land* (7) *Was plunged into the Ḥamsín (sirocco) day* (8) *Like the blade of a cold knife.*

(9) *How could the air of the little city* (10) *Bear so many* (11) *Memories of childhood, of loves which dropped away,* (12) *Of rooms which were emptied somewhere?*

(13) *Like pictures blackening in a camera,* (14) *[They] were reversed: clear winter nights,* (15) *Rainy summer nights [of] overseas,* (16) *And dark mornings in (of) Capitals.*

Loves that withered (on the way to the new homeland) and "rooms that were emptied somewhere" (11-12) suggest far more than family and familial love. The semi-tropical climate of the strange new city inspires feelings of nostalgia, for the "clear winter nights," for the "dark mornings in [foreign] Capitals" (14-16)—far from the provincial sunny settlement—and for "rainy summer nights" (15). At the period of this poem, newly arrived artists and writers frequently complained of the paradoxical sense of foreignness that their new homeland aroused in them, with its disconcerting landscape and the brillant light almost painful to their eyes. As the poet David Shimoni once lamented, the snows obscure the deserts.

The effort to adjust one's vision to the strange new world inevitably produces a distortion of old-world images as they flash upon the memory. It is as though the pictures are darkened and reversed (13) by the new context in which they are recalled.

(17) *And the sound of a footstep drummed behind your back* (18) *Marching songs of a foreign army,* (19) *And it seems—if you would only turn your head—that in the sea* (20) *Your city's church is floating.*

Try as he will to avoid them, the remembered sights of the abandoned country follow him like a nemesis. How safe can he feel when the symbols of European civilization—of the army and of the church—are now pursuing him on the very shores of the city of refuge? According to an old legend, at the time of the Messiah all the synagogues of the Diaspora will return to the Holy Land. The last line of the poem, read in the light of this legend, adds a final note of danger to the series of contrasts and reversals that precede it.

— EZRA SPICEHANDLER

Gabriel Preil

LAKES · AGAMÍM · אֲגַמִּים

אֲגַם הַקֶּרַח מָחוּץ שָׂרָטוֹת מַלְבִּינוֹת.	Agám hakéraḥ maḥúts saratót malbinót.
נָעוֹת וְקוֹפְאוֹת עָלָיו דְּמֻיּוֹת עַלִּיזוֹת־חֹרֶף,	Naót vekof'ót aláv dmuyót alizót-ḥóref,
פְּלָטָן אֵי־מִשָּׁם הַזְּמַן הָעִוֵּר	Platán ey-miṣám hazmán haivér
הַבּוֹעֵר וְקַיָּם.	Haboér vekayám.
הָאֲגַם הַשֵּׁנִי שֶׁמִּמַּעַל, עֲבָרוּהוּ פִּצְעֵי אוֹר וְעָנָן.	Haagám haṣení ṣemimáal, avarúhu pits'éy or veanán.
וְהוּא שֶׁהָיָה עֵדוֹ הַנִּצְחִי שֶׁלַּזְּמַן, עִמּוֹ לָן, —	Vehú ṣehayá edó hanitsḥí ṣelazmán, imó lan,—
מַפְתִּיעֵהוּ הֹד מָטוֹס חָג, אוֹ יָרֵחַ אַ חֵ ר	Maftiéhu ḥod matós ḥag, o yaréaḥ *aḥér*
בּוֹקֵעַ גַּלָּיו.	Bokéa galáv.
הַסַּכִּינִים הַכְּחֻלִּים שֶׁל הַקֶּרַח	Hasakiním hakḥulím ṣel hakéraḥ
יִהְיוּ כִּפְרָחִים בַּזִּכָּרוֹן,	Yihyú kifraḥím bazikarón,
גּוֹנֵי שֶׁלֶג יִגְלְשׁוּ בוֹ	Gonéy ṣéleg yigleṣú bo
כַּכֶּסֶף וְכַצֶּמֶר:	Kakésef veḥatsémer:
בְּטֶרֶם תִּדְעַךְ מַנְגִּינָה עַל אֲגַם	Betérem tid'áḥ manginá al agám
וְהָעוֹלָם הַנִּכָּר יֵאָסֵף.	Vehaolám hanikár yeaséf.

Though Palestine-Israel has been the undisputed center of Hebrew literature since the 1920's, the career of Gabriel Preil serves as a reminder that Hebrew poetry still extends beyond the geographical limits of Israel. Preil, born in Dorpat, Estonia, in 1911, has lived in New York since 1922, writing Hebrew (and also Yiddish) verse against a background of American experience.

While many of the surviving American Hebrew poets seem like ghostly vestiges of the vanished world of Bialik and Tchernichovsky, Preil has managed to become a living presence in contemporary Hebrew literature. His poems appear in a variety of Israeli periodicals, from the established literary monthlies to the most recent *avant-garde* publications. He is the only American Hebrew poet who can be regarded in some sense as an "influence" on the younger Israeli poets. One important affinity between Preil and the younger generation of Israeli writers is a shared interest in American and English poetry. Among the poets Preil has translated are Frost, Sandburg, and Jeffers, and his own verse has shown how elements from these and other English-language poets can be assimilated into Hebrew verse.

Almost all Preil's poems are brief: typically his verse is a purely lyric response to a moment of things seen and felt, to a passing memory, to the nuances of a mood or the suggestiveness of an image. Even when he deals with a historical event, as in "Lakes," which is a kind of meditation on the appearance of a man-made satellite in the sky, the event and its implications are rendered in terms of images.

(1) *The lake of ice is lacerated with whitening scratches.* (2) *Winter-merry figures move and freeze upon it,* (3) *[Figures] that blind time spewed out from somewhere,* (4) *[Time] that burns and exists.*

The unnamed lake is seen from a distance, like everything else in the poem. This perspective, by reducing human beings to miniscule figures, makes visually clear the contrast between the merriment of the skaters moving over the ice and the vast indifference of the frozen winter all around them. Time casts people from "somewhere" into being because it has nothing to do with man; it "spews" him out (*platán*, 3), splendid in its imperviousness to man, who changes and passes away. Time is eternal (*kayám*, 4, the Hebrew for "exists," is less dryly scientific than its English equivalent, being often associated with eternality). Time, seen through the image of this bright, cold day, burns, like Moses' bush, but is not consumed.

The first stanza is relatively traditional in juxtaposing transient man and eternal time. But there is a little shock in the physical violence of *maḥúts* ("smashed," "wounded") of line 1. The meaning of that shock will become clearer in the next stanza:

(5) *The second lake that is above has been crossed over with wounds of light and cloud* (6) *And that* [the second lake] *which has been the eternal witness of time, dwelling with it—* (7) *The nose [*lit. *sharp point] of a circling airplane or another (different) moon surprises it,* (8) *Cleaving its waves.*

The sky, "the second lake above," seems at first to be a mirror-image of the lake below, but we quickly discover that the inverted elements of the "reflected" image have been disturbingly transformed. Just as the frozen lake surface is smashed to a fine white powder by the skate blades (1), the sky is crossed over with "wounds"—deeper than scratches—of light and cloud. The sky is time's witness because, like time, it seems to exist perfectly and eternally beyond the world of change. In the logic of the poem's images, the sky is not merely the eternal witness of time, "dwelling with it" (the phrase has a biblical loftiness), but it is also a visual equivalent of time, representing it concretely in the action of the poem.

The crucial difference between the human encounters with the lake below and the lake above is suggested by the images of penetration that dominate the second stanza. In the traditional winter scene, man's playthings "lacerate" the frozen lake, but without really affecting it, merely scratching its surface. And the lake in any case is, like man, outside eternal time, part of the world of change. The encounter with the second lake, on the other hand, is one in which man is at work, not at play, using the portentous instruments of modern technology. Man upsets the eternal aspect of things, thrusts himself upon time's inviolable witness. With his machines—the nose of the speeding plane, the hurtling satellite—he rapes the sky, and the images of the stanza trace the act of violation in a quick movement from the initial "wounds" to the final "splitting through" the waves of the sky.

(9) *The blue knives of the ice* (10) *Will be like flowers in the memory (remembrance),* (11) *Shades [hues] of snow will glide down in it [the memory]* (12) *Like silver and like wool:*

(13) *Before melody flickers out on a lake* (14) *And the familiar world is gathered in [to death].*

The free-verse line is noticeably shorter in the last two stanzas as the narrative movement of 1-8 yields to an elegiac rhythm. Lines 9-12 are a kind of ironic summary or poetic parody of the experience of nostalgia. The skaters' winter merriment will soon be part of not only a personal past but of the past of man as well. While this kind of beauty is in the process of vanishing, the ordinary response will be to cherish a simplified, idealized image of it. The dangerously jagged loveliness of ice will be transformed into blue flowers of sentimental recollection; the remembered colors of snow will be those of precious substance (silver) or even of something warm and soft (wool). The gliding figures of the realistic first stanza become gliding hues. This entire humanly contrived harmony of nostalgia is echoed in the musicality of the four lines, with frequent alliteration of *k* and hard *g* and the assonances of *ṣéleg* (11), *késef* (12), *tsémer* (12).

The nostalgic music of the verse leads naturally to "melody" in line 13, the only word in the poem that refers directly to sound and not sight. But even the melody is imagined visually; it "flickers out" on the lake like a candle. The definite article has now been dropped from "lake"—the lake at the end of the poem is not a particular lake but any lake in the world.

That familiar, recognizeable world (14) is threatened not merely with change but perhaps even with apocalyptic destruction under the new signs man set in the sky—jet, satellite, hydrogen bomb. The poem conveys this idea of irrevocable, frightening change with artful restraint. The speaker evokes the passing of the familiar world through the starkly simple statement about the flickering out of melody, and the poem concludes on a note of quiet dignity, with *yeaséf* ("is gathered in"), the common biblical euphemism for dying.

— ROBERT ALTER

· · III · ·

Amir Gilboa

ISAAC · YITSḤÁK · יִצְחָק

לִפְנוֹת בֹּקֶר טִיְּלָה שֶׁמֶשׁ בְּתוֹךְ הַיַּעַר
יַחַד עִמִּי וְעִם אַבָּא
וִימִינִי בִּשְׂמֹאלוֹ.

כְּבָרָק לֶהָבָה מַאֲכֶלֶת בֵּין הָעֵצִים.
וַאֲנִי יָרֵא כָּל־כָּךְ אֶת פַּחַד עֵינַי מוּל דָּם עַל הֶעָלִים.

אַבָּא אַבָּא מַהֵר וְהַצִּילָה אֶת יִצְחָק
וְלֹא יֶחְסַר אִישׁ בִּסְעֻדַּת הַצָּהֳרַיִם.

זֶה אֲנִי הַנִּשְׁחָט, בְּנִי,
וּכְבָר דָּמִי עַל הֶעָלִים.
וְאַבָּא נִסְתַּם קוֹלוֹ.
וּפָנָיו חִוְּרִים.

וְרָצִיתִי לִצְעֹק, מְפַרְפֵּר לֹא לְהַאֲמִין
וְקוֹרֵעַ הָעֵינַיִם.
וְנִתְעוֹרַרְתִּי.

וְאָזְלַת־דָּם הָיְתָה יַד יָמִין

Lifnót bóker tiylá ṣémeṣ betóḥ hayáar
Yáḥad imí veím ába
Viminí bismoló.

Kevarák lahavá maaḥélet beyn haeytsím.
Vaaní yaré kol-káḥ et páḥad eynáy
[mul dam al healím.

Ába ába mahér vehatsíla et yitsḥák
Veló yeḥsár iṣ bis'udát hatsohoráyim.

Ze aní haniṣḥát, bní,
Uḥvár damí al healím.
Veába nistám koló.
Ufanáv ḥivrím.

Veratsíti lits'ók, mefarpér lo lehaamín
Vekoréa haeynáyim.
Venit'orárti.

Veazlát-dam haytá yad yamín

Amir Gilboa was born in Volhinya (Ukraine) in 1917. His first Hebrew poems were written before he came to Palestine in 1937, as an illegal immigrant. For several years he roamed the country, working for short spells in a collective settlement, an orange grove, a quarry; at building roads; and with British army camps. In 1942 he volunteered for service in the Hebrew Unit of the British Army, and, as a member of the drivers' section, shared the ordeal of the Eighth Army in Egypt and North Africa and in the siege of Malta, eventually joining the ranks of the "Jewish Brigade" in Italy. The poems of his second volume (*Ṣéva Reṣuyót, Seven Domains*, 1949) bear witness to the innumerable desert stops and besieged towns. He was demobilized in 1946, only to serve soon after in the Israeli War of Independence. His collected poems were issued in 1963.

By virtue of its highly individual blend of traditional elements and colloquial usages, Gilboa's poetry broke with the Shlonsky-Altermann tradition (see pp. 74 ff., 106 ff.). It set the stage for the group of poets who matured during the war years and especially for the younger writers now emerging into prominence.

"Isaac" was published in Gilboa's third book, *Ṣirím Babóker Babóker* (*Songs in Early Morning*, 1953). It belongs to the opening section, entitled "Kḥulím Vaadumím" ("Blue and Red" in plural form). The reference seems to be to the blue and red shapes that appear upon the screen of the inner lid when the eyes are shut tight. This quality of inventive revery—sometimes extremely playful, sometimes verging upon nightmare, but almost always bearing overtones of a child's voice—characterizes the poems of the group.

Both "Isaac" and "Moses" (p. 138) are part of a subsection sequence entitled "An Ancient War," which includes several other elaborations of biblical themes. But unlike earlier writers, who had used the Bible with a kind of objective deliberateness to make moral or nationalistic statements, Gilboa tends not so much to write about as to identify himself completely—and in a very special manner—with his biblical figures. A poem such as "Isaac" owes its effectiveness to this direct imaginative identification with the protagonist in the biblical drama.

(1) *Early in the morning the sun took a walk in the forest* (2) *Together with me and with Father* (3) *And my right hand in his left.*

(4) *Like lightning a knife flamed between the trees.* (5) *And I fear so the terror of my eyes facing blood on the leaves.*

(6) *Father, Father hurry and save Isaac* (7) *And no one will be missing at lunchtime.*

(8) *It is I who am being slaughtered, my son,* (9) *And my blood is already on the leaves.* (10) *And Father's voice was stifled.* (11) *And his face pale.*

(12) *And I wanted to cry out, writhing not to believe* (13) *And tearing open the eyes.* (14) *And I woke up.*

(15) *And bloodless* [lit. *helpless-of-blood*] *was the right hand.*

The poem begins as a woodland idyll told by the child—he and his father and the sun took a walk in the forest. Happily, proudly, he goes hand in hand with his father (referring here to *ába*, "daddy," rather than to *aví*, "my father"). Their handclasp itself bespeaks a blissful intimacy, with its strong evocation of the Song of Songs (2:6): "His left hand is beneath my head, and his right hand doth embrace me."

Suddenly a knife flashes between the *eytsím*—the word meaning both trees and the wood used by Abraham in the burnt offering. The child cries out: "And I fear so the terror of my eyes facing blood on the leaves." The hideous sight and the intimation of blood on the leaves make him shut his eyes in terror, but the very sentence is garbled as the child strives to express an emotion far beyond his powers.

In lines 6-7 the child's supplicating voice is heard, reminding his father that Mother might be worried by her son's absence at noon. At the same time, his words imply that not his father but some alien power is the executioner—for it is his father who is to save him. This homely reference to the luncheon meal (7) sets the anti-heroic tone of the poem.

Abraham, who in Genesis is portrayed, for all his tenderness, as an archetype of single-minded faith verging on the inhuman, is transformed in lines 8-11 of Gilboa's poem. The contrast between his sorrowful assertion that the spilled blood is his own and the child's earlier plaintive cry grows overwhelming. Note also the child's pained awareness of the "stifling" of the father's voice and of the fact that his father's face was pale.

Like one enmeshed in a desperate nightmare, the child "wanted to cry out" (12), but fear overpowers him: he is now stifled as his father was stifled (10). His "writhing not to believe" calls to the reader's mind not only the binding of Isaac to the sacrificial altar but also the attempt of the poet to free himself in this poem from the unendurable emotion of a nightmarish memory. This curiously twofold quality appears again when the poet-as-Isaac declares that by disbelieving in the reality of what has happened he is trying to make it disappear.

But the full reality of the knife and the flame is ineradicable—"tearing eyes" (5), "bleeding eyes," "wounded eyes," "torn eyes," are recurring images in Gilboa's work —and the only possible release at this point is total loss of consciousness. This is strongly implied in the sharp break between lines 12-13 and 14.

It is not only Isaac, a character in the poem, but the poet himself who has wakened: the poet has been witness and participant and speaker throughout the nightmare experience. Now the opening line, "the sun took a walk in the forest," emerges as a surrealistic dream image and the poem as a whole takes on the quality of dream. "Tearing eyes" (13) becomes the attempt of the dreamer to escape the nightmare by forcing open his eyes. And the final line refers to the speaker's own awakening from the experience to find that his right hand is *azlát-dam*, "bloodless," a poetic construction based on the common idiom *azlát-yad*, meaning "scarcity of hand," i.e., "helplessness." The poet's own right hand (which in Hebrew is literally also "mainstay and power") is now corpse-like. The dream's horror thus carries over into waking reality. The loss has been real: blood has actually been shed.

The destruction of European Jewry, one of Gilboa's pervasive themes, lies at the core of the experience. The knife flashing between the trees threatens both father and son; the blood on the leaves refers directly to the Nazi massacres in the forests of Eastern Europe. But the poem has completely reversed the biblical account, for the protagonists—the poet, his family, his people—are victims of something that is hardly comprehensible as a trial of faith. And the language of the re-enactment has been bent and torn to fit the nightmare.

— ARIEH SACHS

Amir Gilboa

MOSES · MOṢÉ · מֹשֶׁה

As in our opening poem, "Moses" depends on a dream quality, a highly individual use of biblical material, and a counterpointing of adult and childhood experience. But there all likenesses end.

In the opening stanza the speaker imagines himself a child who is imagining himself an adult. In this role, he approaches the great general to offer him some strategic advice.

(1) *I went up to Moses and said to him:* (2) *Place the armies thus and thus.* (3) *He looked at me* (4) *And placed them as I told him to.*

(5) *And who did not see me then in my glory?* (6) *Sara from childhood was there* (7) *In whose name I had planned to build a city.* (8) *The long-legged one from the girl-workers' farm was there.* (9) *And Melvina from Rabbat in Malta.* (10) *Dina from the Italo-Yugoslav border.* (11) *And Ria from the Lowlands in the North.*

(12) *And very proud, I hurried to Moses* (13) *To show him the right way* (14) *When suddenly it became clear to me* (15) *That she who within my name* (16) *Is carved and rightly (firmly) emplaced* —(17) *Was not [present].*

(18) *Moses Moses lead the people.* (19) *Look, I am so tired and I wish to sleep some more* (20) *I am still a boy.*

The tone in which all this is recounted is playful, and the effect is not simply that of a child seriously telling about a fantasy of

נִגַּשְׁתִּי אֶל מֹשֶׁה וְאָמַרְתִּי לוֹ:	Nigáṣti el moṣé veamárti lo:
עֲרֹךְ אֶת הַמַּחֲנוֹת כָּךְ וְכָךְ.	Aróḥ et hamaḥanót kaḥ veḥaḥ.
הוּא הִסְתַּכֵּל בִּי	Hu histakél bi
וְעָרַךְ לְפִי שֶׁאָמַרְתִּי.	Vearáḥ lefí ṣeamárti.
וּמִי לֹא רָאָה אָז בִּכְבוֹדִי!	Umí lo raá az biḥvodí!
הָיְתָה שָׁם שָׂרָה מִן הַיַּלְדוּת	Haytá sam sára min hayaldút
שֶׁעַל שְׁמָהּ תִּכַּנְתִּי לִבְנוֹת עִיר.	Ṣeál ṣma tikánti livnót ir.
הָיְתָה שָׁם אֲרֻכַּת־הָרַגְלַיִם מֵחַוַּת־הַפּוֹעֲלוֹת.	Haytá ṣam arukát-haragláyim [meḥavát-hapoalót.
הָיְתָה מֶלְוִינָה מֵרַבַּת אֲשֶׁר בְּמַלְטָה.	Haytá melvína merabát aṣér bemálta.
דִּינָה מֵהַגְּבוּל הָאִיטַלְקִי־הַיּוּגוֹסְלָבִי.	Dína mehagvúl haitalkí-hayugoslávi.
וְרִיָּה מֵהַשְּׁפֵלָה שֶׁבַּצָּפוֹן.	Veríya mehaṣfelá ṣebatsafón.
וְגֵאֶה מְאֹד מִהַרְתִּי אֶל מֹשֶׁה	Vege'é meód mihárti el mosé
לְהוֹרוֹתוֹ הַדֶּרֶךְ הַנְּכוֹנָה	Lehorotó hadéreḥ hanḥoná
וְהָחְוַר לִי לְפִתְאֹם	Vehoḥvár li lefit'óm
כִּי זוֹ אֲשֶׁר בְּתוֹךְ שְׁמִי	Ki zo aṣér betóḥ ṣmi
חֲרוּתָה וּנְכוֹנָה —	Ḥarutá unḥoná—
אֵינֶנָּה.	Eynéna.
מֹשֶׁה מֹשֶׁה הַנְחֵה אֶת הָעָם.	Moṣé moṣé hanḥé et haám.
רְאֵה, אֲנִי כָּל־כָּךְ עָיֵף וְרוֹצֶה לִישֹׁן עוֹד	Re'é, ani kol-káḥ ayéf verotsé liṣón od
אֲנִי עוֹדִי נַעַר.	Aní odí náar.

glory, but of a man recognizing the child alive within him and adopting the voice appropriate to that child. For the adult *is* the child—and yet the disarming naïvete is paradoxically mixed with a detachment that is present not only in the initial playfulness but also in everything that follows.

This double point of view—of naïvete and detachment, of childlikeness and maturity—gives the special flavor to the listing of girlfriends; they are invoked in order to witness the man-child's influence over his hero. Not only is the tone adult in its playfulness; the catalogue itself could hardly have been compiled by an inexperienced youth. Ranging from the childhood sweetheart to the "long-legged one from the girl-workers' farm" (*ḥavát poalót*: the pioneer farms which trained women for agricultural work)—whose name has evidently slipped from the speaker's memory—the parade of amatory experiences is both considerable and varied. References to Malta, the Italo-Yugoslav border, and the Netherlands Plain indicate that the speaker has spent a good deal of his life in wandering homelessly from one part of the globe to another, specifically from the North down to the Mediterranean.

Although the recollections hardly recount an easy or secure existence, the tone throughout the poem is bright and exultant. There is joy in this piling of memory upon memory and in the mere enumeration of all these figures from the past who are now to admire the exploits, prowess, and wisdom of their lover-turned-child.

With the third stanza, the tone changes abruptly. Now that he has gathered his throng of female worshippers to witness his influence over the demi-god Moses, the child proudly hastens to the leader to show him the right way in which to continue the journey, when he realizes—suddenly become an adult—that the woman whom he truly desires is "not present" (17). The sudden and intense evocation of this unique Beloved has diminished all the others. If the previous glory is that of a dream, the speaker has now awakened into the overpowering truth of adult awareness.

The first words of the last stanza—"Moses Moses"—set the new, disenchanted tone, and a total reversal of roles concludes the poem, dramatizing the shift from joyous dreaming to sorrowful waking. Whereas at the outset the voice was that of an adult talking as if he were an exuberant child, it is now that of a child talking as if he were a tired adult: "I am so weary . . . I am still a boy." It is as if the speaker were saying: "Waking reality is too much for me; I wish to sleep some more."

— ARIEH SACHS

Amir Gilboa

IN THE DARK · BAḤÓṢEḤ · בַּחֹשֶׁךְ

שָׁלַחְתִּי אֶת יָדַי לְפָנַי, אֶל תּוֹךְ הַחשֶׁךְ		Ṣaláḥti et yadáy lefanáy el toḥ haḥóṣeḥ
וְהָאֶצְבָּעוֹת בִּקְשׁוּ אוֹר	2	Vehaetsbaót bikṣú or
רוֹעֲדוֹת מֵאֵימַת אִי הַוַּדָּאוּת.		Roadót meeymát i-havadaút.
אָסַפְתִּי, לָכֵן, אֶת הָאֶצְבָּעוֹת		Asáfti, laḥén, et haetsbaót
פְּנִימָה אֶל תּוֹךְ הַכַּף		Pníma el toḥ hakáf
וּפָתְחוּ הֵן בִּנְהִימָה חֲמִימָה	6	Ufatḥú hen binhimá ḥamimá
כְּגוּרֵי כַּלְבָּה עַל הַדַּדִּים		Keguréy kalbá al hadadím
וְקֵץ לֹא הָיָה לְבִטְחוֹנָן		Vekéts lo hayá levitḥonán
בִּצְוַת הָאֶגְרוֹף הַקָּמוּץ.	9	Bitsvát haegróf hakamúts.
אַחַר כָּךְ עָלָה הַשַּׁחַר.		Aḥár kaḥ alá haṣáḥar.

With its tightly knit metaphors, "In the Dark" takes the reader on a journey of the spirit from darkness to light (1, 10). The journey is one of withdrawal from the outer to the inner world.

(1) *I put out (sent forth) my hands before me*

into the darkness (2) *And the fingers sought light* (3) *Trembling out of (with) the fear of uncertainty.*

(4) *I therefore gathered the fingers* (5) *Inward into the palm* (6) *And they began to growl warmly* (7) *Like a bitch's cubs at the teats* (8) *And there was no end to their security* (9) *In the team of the clenched fist.*

(10) *Afterwards the dawn rose.*

The initial image "groping in the dark" is of course more than a realistic description. Fingers do not literally seek for light. But the concentration throughout the poem on the organs of touch gives reality to the absoluteness of the dark and, by implication, to the spirit's alienation and terror. Here the usual means for "seeing" the world are useless.

With the second stanza, the uncertainty is replaced by a kind of security, one that becomes possible as the spirit recoils from the world. Utterly lost in the initial darkness and in the meaninglessness it had encountered in surrounding reality, the soul no longer tries to find the source of light (2) and so discovers strength. As in Gilboa's poem "Moses" (p. 138), where it wished to save itself by shutting out reality, here it succeeds —but not through sleep.

The image of fingers goes through surprising elaborations. In the first stanza they strained, spreading out to find their object, each finger trembling (3) and uncertain in its separation from the central part of the hand, the metaphorical parent. But now, recoiling from the outer world into close, self-protective union—the clenched palm (5)—together they find sustenance and warmth. The "warm growl" (6) of satisfied security emitted by the puppy-fingers—*binhimá ḥamimá*—is onomatopoetic to the Hebrew ear. As to the faithfulness of the image of suckling, the reader has only to spread out his fingers and then note their appearance when reclenching them—the continuous shape formed by the thumb and the mound of flesh below it seems to resemble an animal, and the fingers four nestling cubs. Moreover, like cubs, the fingers are blind, and so their seeking for light (2) takes on an added dimension.

As we have noted, the fingers find warmth and sustenance in the parental bosom, and also as a result of their being closely united. But their unification also brings power, and this inner force of union becomes associated with the outer strength signified in the stereotype of the clenched fist. Hence it can defend itself against the dark rather than continue to grope in trembling. But has security really been found? The word *tsvat* (9) when spelled with a *bet* means "a pair of tongs," and when the final *t* sound is written with a *tet* instead of a *tav*, it means "pinch." The word, then, which in the poem means literally "team of," carries an immediate association of tension. Though the spirit has found strength within itself, it remains on guard against some possible terror, for it is still alone and surrounded by unknown forces.

The speaker's experience out of which the poem arose is never made explicit. At the most, it is intimated by the silence that extends between the clenching of the fist at the end of stanza 2 and the coming of dawn in the last lines. An extremely long pause follows line 9, to prepare for the conclusion, which comes as either anticlimax or climax. The speaker's night has been seemingly endless as he waits alone, in self-defense, for the resolving dawn.

But in another sense, the coming of day springs directly from the adventures sustained during the night. The initial uncertainty and trembling fear (stanza 1) is succeeded by the gathering of forces (2) to make possible the discovery of the light originally sought or of a different light: "Afterwards the dawn rose."

— ARIEH SACHS

Amir Gilboa

JOSHUA'S FACE · PNEY YEHOṢÚA · פְּנֵי יְהוֹשֻׁעַ

וִיהוֹשֻׁעַ מֵעָל אֶל פָּנַי מַבִּיט. וּפָנָיו זָהָב	Vihoṣúa meál el panáy mabít. Ufanáv zaháv
שָׁחוּט. חֲלוֹם קַר. חֲלוֹם חָנוּט.	Ṣaḥút. Ḥalóm kar. Ḥalóm ḥanút.
וּלְרַגְלַי הַיָּם מַכֶּה נְצָחִים אֶל הַחוֹף.	Uleragláy hayám maké netsaḥím el haḥóf.
אֲנִי חוֹלֶה נְהִיָּתוֹ. דּוֹמֶה, אֲנִי עוֹמֵד לָמוּת.	Aní ḥolé nehiyató. Domé, aní oméd lamút.
אַךְ מֻכְרַחֲנִי, מֻכְרַחֲנִי לְחַכּוֹת חַי	Aḥ muḥraḥáni, muḥraḥáni leḥakót ḥay
אֶל־תָּמִיד.	El-tamíd.
אָחִי מֵעָל פָּנָיו עוֹלִים בָּעָב	Aḥí meál panáv olím baáv
לְהַגִּיד עִקְּבוֹתַי בַּחוֹל הַנִּשְׁטָף.	Lehagíd ikvotáy baḥól haniṣtáf.
הַיָּם מַכֶּה וְנָסוֹג. מַכֶּה וְנָסוֹג.	Hayám maké venasóg. Maké venasóg.
מִלְחָמוֹת אֵיתָנִים מֻתְנוֹת בַּחֹק.	Milḥamót eytaním mutnót baḥók.
אֲנִי. בָּרוּחַ. אַחֵר. בּוֹרֵחַ. רָחוֹק.	Aní. Barúaḥ. Aḥér. Boréaḥ. Raḥók.
גַּם יְהוֹשֻׁעַ עַכְשָׁיו נָח מִמִּלְחָמוֹת.	Gam yehoṣúa aḥṣáv naḥ mimilḥamót.
שֶׁהִנְחִיל נַחֲלָה לְעַמּוֹ,	Ṣehinḥíl naḥalá leamó,
אֲבָל קֶבֶר לֹא חָצַב לוֹ	Avál kéver lo ḥatsáv lo
בְּהָרֵי אֶפְרָיִם.	Beharéy efráyim.
עַל כֵּן לַיְלָה לַיְלָה הוּא יוֹצֵא	Al ken láyla láyla hu yotsé
לָשׂוּחַ בַּשָּׁמַיִם.	Lasúaḥ baṣamáyim.
וַאֲנִי חוֹלֶה, דּוֹמֶה עוֹמֵד לָמוּת	Vaaní ḥolé, domé oméd lamút
מְיַחֵף בְּחוֹל יָרֵחַ קַר	Meyaḥéf beḥól yaréaḥ kar
בְּשׁוּלֵי הַמָּיִם	Beṣuléy hamáyim
וְהוֹמֶה בִּי, הוֹמֶה בִּי סוֹף	Vehomé bi, homé bi sof
הַמַּכֶּה לְרַגְלַי אֶת מוֹתִי	Hamaké leragláy et motí
גַּל אַחַר גָּל	Gal aḥár gal—
עַל פְּנֵי חַיִּים רַבִּים	Al pney ḥayím rabím
יִתְרוֹמֵם וְיִתְגַּדֵּל.	Yitromám veyitgadál.

"Joshua's Face," from Gilboa's volume of collected verse (1963), is a recent poem. (1) *And Joshua from above looks at my face. And his face is beaten gold.* (2) *A cold dream. A mummified dream.* The gentle music of the first line has been jarred suddenly by the harsh *ṣaḥút* ("beaten") which opens line 2. (3) *And at my feet the sea beats eternities toward the shore.* (4) *I am sick with its lament. It seems I am about to die.* (5) *But I must, I must await alive* (6) *The "Always."* (7) *Above, my brother's face rises in the cloud.* (8) *To tell [foretell] my footsteps in the [sea]washed sand.*

"Joshua's face" looking at the speaker, who is standing on the seashore at night, has a threefold implication which gradually unfolds. It is the moon shining over the shore and the rising tide (1-3)—reminiscent of the talmudic phrase "The face of Moses is like the face of the sun and the face of Joshua like the face of the moon." It is also the face of the speaker's dead brother Joshua (7)—the dedicatory note to the volume reads: "With me are my father and mother Haim and Frieda and my brothers and sisters Bella and Joshua and Brunia, Moses and Sara and Esther" (slaughtered members of his family who appear in many of the poems and often in terms of their biblical namesakes). It is also the face of the biblical hero and conqueror (12).

The strange, moonlit seascape points to a removal from the land of the living: both moon and sea appear in images of death. The brother's memory is implicitly summoned in line 2: the moon's face is *zaháv ṣaḥút* (I Kings 10: 16-17), literally "gold beaten," but the primary meaning of *ṣaḥút* is "slaughtered." The moon's cold face is like a mummified dream, transfixed, yellow with age. The lamenting sea is no less death-like, being both within and beyond time, "beating eternities toward the shore" (3). And the lament is the sea's as well as the moon's. The word *nehiyá* (4) means both "longing" and "lament"—Gilboa's *ḥolé nehiyá* ("sick with lament") being patterned on *ḥolát ahavá* ("sick with love") from the Song of Songs.

In lines 4-6 thoughts of suicide arise only to be suppressed, and the music of this conflict is no less savage, no less guttural, than it was in line 2, which set the lunatic landscape as it beat out the gutturals *ṣaḥút—ḥalóm—ḥanút* which move like an undertow throughout the poem.

As if in answer to the speaker's decision (5-6), the brother (now explicitly named) rises above him. The apparition's "spiritualistic" nature is made clear by the choice of words: *olím baáv* ("rises above in the cloud") echoing *maalím baóv* ("raise an apparition from the dead"). Line 8 extends this suggestion, for *lehagíd* means not only "to tell" but also "to divine, to prophesy," so that the brother's ghost rising in the cloud also foretells the speaker's footsteps by the signs in the sea-washed sand.

(9) *The sea beats (attacks) and retreats. Beats and retreats.* (10) *Elemental wars conditioned by law.* (11) *Me (myself). In the wind. Different (other). Escaping. Distant.* (12) *Joshua too is now resting from wars.* (13) *For he left an estate (heritage) to his people,* (14) *But did not hew himself a grave* (15) *In the mountains of Ephraim.* (16) *Therefore he goes out night after night* (17) *To walk in the sky.* (18) *And I am sick, it seems I am about to die* (19) *Walking barefoot in cold moon-sand* (20) *At the water's edge* (21) *And murmuring within me, murmuring within me is the end* (22) *Which beats my death at my feet* (23) *Wave after wave—*

(24) *Upon [the faces of] many lives* (25) *May he be raised and glorified.*

The sea, which had "beaten eternities toward the shore" (3), now attacks in a death-bearing manner that is also a manifestation of the laws of nature (9-10). The very immutability of these laws seems to spur the speaker into a frenetic outburst as of a man shouting against the elements: "Myself. In the wind. Different. Escaping. Distant."—five stacatto Hebrew words whose rasping gutturals and internal rimes echo the sounds of line 2.

But the war-like waves of the sea also call to mind the human wars: the bloody battles of both the Book of Joshua and of World War II, in which his brother was murdered. The brother's spiritual legacy is referred to in line 13. Here "he" is only the brother, for Joshua the successor of Moses was buried in his extreme old age "in the border of his inheritance . . . in Mount Ephraim" (Joshua 24: 29-30). The speaker's brother Joshua, though he also left an inheritance, was not allowed to live out his life nor did he "hew himself a grave in Mount Ephraim." And that is why his ghost, the moon, is homeless and must haunt the skies (16).

The atmosphere of the poem is reminiscent of *Hamlet* in several respects. Not only is the moon seen as a restless ghost which haunts the protagonist with memories of the terrible murder of his closest of kin: the sublunar world of the poem in general, symbolized by the sea and the shore, resembles the universe of *Hamlet* in its being the scene of unpunished crime, vain mutability, and death.

The life-weary speaker, obsessed with death, walks "barefoot in the cold moonsand" (19), answering his brother's nightly call. The determination to live (5-6) and the frantic attempt to escape (11) are followed by the recognition that wave after wave inexorably bring him his death (21-23).

The conclusion is an acceptance of this fact in an affirmation of death which is unique in Gilboa's poetry. The phrase *ḥayím rabím* ("much life" or "many lives") carries the association of *máyim rabím* ("many waters"), harking back to the image of the sea. And the final line makes the whole poem a kind of dirge, for it is a variation on the opening words of the *Kadíṣ* (a prayer recited in memory on the dead): *Yitgadál veyitkadáṣ* ("magnified and sanctified . . .").

— ARIEH SACHS

Amir Gilboa

These two poems appear in Gilboa's volume, *Songs in Early Morning*, of 1953. They are part of a section subtitled "Songs of Just Like That" (*Ṣirím Kaéle*).

In "Moses" (p. 138), the speaker imagined himself a child who was imagining himself an adult. In "If There Were a Hundred Hats" the two figures fuse in an exuberant fantasy:

(1) *If there were a hundred hats on my head* (2) *A hundred hats   A hundred colors* (3) *A hundred hats   A hundred colors and shades of color* (4) *A hundred hats   A shower of colors*

(5) *If there were a hundred hats on my head* (6) *I would go out to the square in the market* (7) *Clearing a path for myself through the square in the market* (8) *And throw them upwards with joy*

(9) *If there were a hundred hats on my head* (10) *I would go out to the square in the market* (11) *And all the people would clear a path for me* (12) *Awaiting the moment of the waving of the hats*

(13) *If there were a hundred hats on my head* (14) *A hundred hats   A hundred colors and shades of color* (15) *If there were a hundred hats   And a tall sun* (16) *Straight at my head   Straight at my colors*

(17) *[And] oh the People   Cries of admiration all readied in its throat* (18) *And its great heart beating in the square* (19) *The heart of the people waiting*

(20) *For the waving of a hundred hats   A hundred colors and shades of color.*

Having a hundred hats is in itself a great joy. Managing to get them all on his head is a still greater joy for the speaker. That each hat is differently shaded, that the sun brings out all the colors, that the hats can be tossed into the sky with a gesture of complete irresponsibility, and above all, that the speaker's "heroic" feats are properly appreciated by the populace—all these delights can be uttered only in repeated child-like phrases. (In a later poem, "Israel," the voices of the people crying *El, El, Yisraél!* sound to the speaker as though they were cheering on their favorite soccer team.)

IF THERE WHERE A HUNDRED HATS

LU MEÁ KOVAÍM LEROṢÍ · לוּ מֵאָה כּוֹבָעִים לְרֹאשִׁי

לוּ מֵאָה כּוֹבָעִים לְרֹאשִׁי	Lu meá kovaím leroṣí
מֵאָה כּוֹבָעִים מֵאָה צְבָעִים	Meá kovaím meá tsvaím
מֵאָה כּוֹבָעִים מֵאָה צְבָעִים וּבְנֵי צֶבַע	Meá kovaím meá tsvaím uvnéy tséva
מֵאָה כּוֹבָעִים מְטַר צְבָעִים	Meá kovaím metár tsvaím
לוּ מֵאָה כּוֹבָעִים לְרֹאשִׁי	Lu meá kovaím leroṣí
הָיִיתִי יוֹצֵא אֶל כִּכַּר הַשּׁוּק	Hayíti yotsé el kikár haṣúk
מְפַנֶּה לִי דֶּרֶךְ בְּכִכַּר הַשּׁוּק	Mefané li déreḥ beḥikár haṣúk
וְזוֹרְקָם עַל מִשִּׂמְחָה	Vezorkám al misimḥá
לוּ מֵאָה כּוֹבָעִים לְרֹאשִׁי	Lu meá kovaím leroṣí
הָיִיתִי יוֹצֵא אֶל כִּכַּר הַשּׁוּק	Hayíti yotsé el kikár haṣúk
וְכָל הָאֲנָשִׁים מְפַנִּים לִי הַדֶּרֶךְ	Veḥól haanaṣím mefaním li hadéreḥ
מְצַפִּים לְרֶגַע נִפְנוּף הַכּוֹבָעִים	Metsapím leréga nifnúf hakovaím
לוּ מֵאָה כּוֹבָעִים לְרֹאשִׁי	Lu meá kovaím leroṣí
מֵאָה כּוֹבָעִים מֵאָה צְבָעִים וּבְנֵי צֶבַע	Meá kovaím meá tsvaím uvnéy tséva
לוּ מֵאָה כּוֹבָעִים וְשֶׁמֶשׁ גְּבֹהָה	Lu meá kovaím veṣémeṣ gevohá
יָשָׁר אֶל רֹאשִׁי יָשָׁר אֶל צְבָעַי	Yaṣár el roṣí yaṣár el tsvaáy
הוֹ הָעָם קְרִיאוֹת הִתְפַּעֲלוּת בִּגְרוֹנוֹ נָכוֹנוּ	Ho haám kriót hitpaalút bigronó naḥónu
וּמִתְפָּעֵם לִבּוֹ הַכַּבִּיר בַּכִּכָּר	Umitpaém libó hakabír bakikár
לֵב הָעָם הַמְצַפֶּה	Lev haám hamtsapé
לְנִפְנוּף מֵאָה כּוֹבָעִים מֵאָה צְבָעִים וּבְנֵי צֶבַע	Lenifnúf meá kovaím meá tsvaím [uvnéy tséva

Excitement is worked up by these repetitions and then, in line 17, the voice rises to a pitch of delirium.

In other "poems of wish-fulfilment" by Gilboa (and again "Moses" comes to mind), reality intrudes ominously. The very movement of these lyrics involves a kind of "joy" or delirium of language, yet adult sobriety remains ever present, and the result is a counterpoint of innocence and experience.

JOY · SIMḤÁ · שִׂמְחָה

כָּל אֶחָד בָּרְחוֹב שָׁאַל מָה אַתָּה שָׂמֵחַ
וַאֲנִי לֹא שָׁמַעְתִּי כִּי הָיִיתִי שָׂמֵחַ
עַד שֶׁהִגַּעְתִּי כִּמְעַט לְסוֹף הָרְחוֹבוֹת.
נִמְצָא לִי יֶלֶד קָטָן שֶׁשִּׂחֵק בַּחוֹל בְּסוֹף הָרְחוֹבוֹת

אָמַרְתִּי לוֹ בּוֹא הֱיֵה גַּם אַתָּה שָׂמֵחַ
אָמַר לִי אַתָּה נִמְצָא בְּסוֹף הָרְחוֹבוֹת.

כָּל אֶחָד בָּרְחוֹב שָׁאַל מָה אַתָּה שָׂמֵחַ
וַאֲנִי לֹא שָׁמַעְתִּי כִּי הָיִיתִי שָׂמֵחַ
עַד שֶׁהִגַּעְתִּי כִּמְעַט לְסוֹף הַשִּׂמְחָה.
נִמְצֵאתִי לִי יֶלֶד קָטָן שֶׁאֵינוֹ בָּא לְסוֹף הַשִּׂמְחָה

אָמַרְתִּי לִי אַתָּה עוֹד וְעוֹד תִּהְיֶה שָׂמֵחַ
וּלְעוֹלָם לֹא תָבוֹא עַד סוֹף הַשִּׂמְחָה.

כָּל אֶחָד בָּרְחוֹב שָׁאַל מָה אַתָּה שָׂמֵחַ
וַאֲנִי לֹא שָׁמַעְתִּי כִּי הָיִיתִי שָׂמֵחַ
וְגַם אֵינִי שׁוֹמֵעַ בִּשְׁעַת הַשִּׂמְחָה.
נִמְצָא לִי יוֹם אָרֹךְ שֶׁלֹּא הָיִיתִי שָׂמֵחַ
וְתָמַהְתִּי עַל כָּל אֶחָד שֶׁאָז שָׁאַל לַשִּׂמְחָה
וְתוּגָה אֲכָלָה בַּלֵּב גְּדוֹלָה כַּשִּׂמְחָה.

Kol eḥád barḥóv ṣaál ma atá saméaḥ
Vaaní lo ṣamáti ki hayíti saméaḥ
3 Ad ṣehigáti kim'át lesóf harḥovót.
Nimtsá li yéled katán ṣesiḥék baḥól [besóf harḥovót

Amárti lo bo heyé gam atá saméaḥ
Amár li atá nimtsá besóf harḥovót.

7 Kol eḥád barḥóv ṣaál ma atá saméaḥ
Vaaní lo ṣamáti ki hayíti saméaḥ
Ad ṣehigáti kim'át lesóf hasimḥá.
Nimtséti li yéled katán ṣeeynó ba [lesóf hasimḥá

11 Amárti li atá od veód tihiyé saméaḥ
Uleolám lo tavó ad sof hasimḥá.

Kol eḥád barḥóv ṣaál ma atá saméaḥ
Vaaní lo ṣamáti ki hayíti saméaḥ
15 Vegám eyní ṣoméa biṣ'át hasimḥá.
Nimtsá li yom aróḥ ṣeló hayíti saméaḥ
Vetamáti al kol eḥád *ṣeáz* ṣaál lasimḥá
Vetugá aḥlá balév gdolá kasimḥá.

The second poem from "Songs of Just Like That," entitled "*Simḥá*" ("Joy, Happiness, Rejoicing"), works through random-like repetitions of lines and through variations upon phrases. The substitution of one word for another suddenly introduces shades of meaning, all of which lead to the "sorrow as great as joy" at the conclusion.

(1) *Everyone in the street asked what are you happy about* (2) *And I hadn't heard that I was happy* [and: *I didn't hear, for I was happy*] (3) *Until I came almost to the end of the streets.* (4) *I chanced upon* [lit. *was found to me*] *a little child playing in the sand at the end of the streets* (5) *I said to him come, be happy too* (6) *He said to me you are* [lit. *found*] *at the end of the streets.*

(7) *Everyone in the street asked what are you happy about* (8) *And I hadn't heard that I was happy* [and: *I didn't hear, for I was happy*] (9) *Until I came almost to the end of the happiness (rejoicing).* (10) *I found myself to be a small child who does not reach the end of happiness* (11) *I said to myself you will be joyful again and again* (12) *And never will you reach the end of joy.*

(13) *Everyone in the street asked what are you happy about* (14) *And I hadn't heard that I was happy* [and: *I didn't hear, for I was happy*] (15) *And besides I don't hear* [*at all*] *in moments of joy.* (16) *It happened* [lit. *was found to me*] *one*

long day that I wasn't happy (18) *And I was perplexed about everyone who* THEN *asked about the joy* (19) *And a sorrow as great as the joy ate at the heart.*

Child and adult keep changing roles. The word *nimtsá* ("was found") occurs in varying contexts in each of the stanzas (4, 6, 10, 16), pointing to the shifting discoveries of identity —always in terms of child-adult—that the speaker undergoes. In stanza 1, it is the adult who roams the streets whereas the child whom he "finds" points out to him that they are "at the end of the streets"—which is to say: (a) that this is the end of the child's world of all that is familiar and (b) that there is really nothing to be so joyful about.

In stanza 2, the adult nearly exhausts his fund of joy but suddenly discovers ("was found to me," 16) that he himself is really a child, and so his happiness is renewed, coupled with the hope of unending joy. In the third stanza sorrow replaces joy with finality. By now the stage has been set for the replacement of joy by the earlier references to "the end of streets" and "the end of joy." It may be noted that all the adventures in the poem occur in an isolated world of introspection. Not only are "the people in the street" uncomprehending; the "joy" itself is so engrossing that it prevents the speaker from hearing what goes on outside himself (15).

The poem began with a very simple colloquial statement. But in the very next line two different readings press themselves upon the listener. The speaker hadn't heard that he was happy and, at the same time, he couldn't hear the question because he was happy. Such ambiguous play is present throughout the poem, culminating in the misinterpreted sorrow of the final line.

— ARIEH SACHS

Abba Kovner

OPENING · PTIḤÁ · פְּתִיחָה

בְּאֵרוֹת־קְדוּמִים נִקְווֹת לְפֶתַע בָּעֵינַיִם
כָּל נַהֲרוֹת דָּמַי עֵרִים כִּפְולֵי־אָפִיק.
וְלֵב נָעוּל אָז. מִצֵּאת. מִבּוֹא. מִגֶּשֶׁת.
וְרַק שִׁכְשׁוּךְ שֶׁל מַיִם אַדִּירִים וְקוֹל עַתִּיק:

אַל תִּפְסַע, רֵעִי, מוּזָרוֹת רַגְלֵינוּ כָּאן
וְהוּא, רֵעִי, פּוֹסֵעַ. וְרַגְלֵינוּ — מְיֻתָּרוֹת.
הִנֵּה צְעָדֵינוּ כָּבִים. לֹא אַתָּה הוּא כָּאן
הַהֵלֶךְ־הַגָּדוֹל, רֵעִי —
פָּשַׁט רֵעִי חָפְנָיו, רָכַן, מַגַּע כַּפּוֹת
וְהָאֲדָמָה בָּאָה.

עֲדָרִים־עֲדָרִים מֵהֶמָּה הִיא אֶת רַגְלֶיךָ
בְּאוֹר בּוֹזֵז. וְרַגְלָיו נוֹתְבוֹת־וְלֹא־נוֹתְבוֹת.
« רֵעִי, נִפֹּל » — אוֹ־אָז כֻּלָּהּ תָּבוֹא
בְּגַל אֶל זְרוֹעוֹתֶיךָ
הָאֲדָמָה הַזֹּאת.

Beerót-kdumím nikvót leféta baeynáyim
Kol naharót damáy erím kfuléy-afík.
3 Velév naúl az. Mitsét. Mibó. Migéṣet.
Verák ṣiḥṣúḥ ṣel máyim adirím vekól atík:

Al tifsá, reí, muzarót ragléynu kan
Vehú, reí, poséa. Veragléynu—meyutarót.
7 Hiné tseadéynu kavím. Lo atá hu kan
Hahéleḥ-hagadól, reí—
Paṣát reí ḥofnáv, raḥán, magá kapót
Vehaadamá báa.

11 Adarím-adarím mehamá hi et ragléḥa
Beór bozéz. Vegragláv notvót-veló-notvót.
"Reí, nipól"—o-áz *kulá* tavó
14 Begál el zrootéḥa
Haadamá hazót.

Born in the Crimea in 1918, Abba Kovner grew up in Vilna, where he was graduated from a modern Hebrew *gymnasium* and became a student at a Polish university. He played a leading role in a Zionist youth movement, while also devoting himself to sculpture and to Hebrew poetry. In 1943 he assumed command of the United Partisan Organization of the Vilna ghetto, and when the ghetto fell and small groups broke through to the forests, he served as the commander of the Jewish "Vengeance" battalion. Not long after the defeat of Germany, he settled in a kibbutz in Palestine (1946), only to take up arms again, in the War of Independence.

As one would expect, Kovner's poetry is interwoven with his tragic and heroic experiences as a fighter in Europe and in Israel. His long modernist poems attempt a fusion of personal and historical materials in the broad genre of Alexander Blok's "The Twelve." "Until-No-Light" ("Ad-Lo-Or," 1947) recreates in lyric-dramatic narrative the life of the partisans in the forests and swamps. "The Key Drowned" ("*Hamaftéaḥ Tsalál,*" 1951) gives symbolic expression to the tragedy of the ghetto fighters who knew they could not save the mass of the people then clinging to life and unwilling to believe they were doomed.

The War of Independence, however, provides the specific background for Kovner's prose trilogy *Face to Face* (*Paním el Paním*, 1953) and the verse sequence entitled *A Parting from the South* (*Pridá Mehadaróm*, 1949). Varied in tone and theme, the latter projects a complex vision of the War, unified by recurring images and leitmotifs, through the perspectives of a soldier's experiences.

"Opening," the second poem in the section "Night March," revolves on the double confrontation of the soldier: with death and with the strange desert. The antiquity of the landscape, echoing, as it does, a national past, suddenly overwhelms the intruder:

(1) *Wells of old gather suddenly in the eyes* (2) *All the rivers of my blood are alert in double [river] beds.* (3) *And the heart is then locked. Nothing shall go out of it, nothing come into it, nothing approach it* [lit. *From leaving. From entering. From approaching*]. (4) *And only the clamor of mighty waters and an ancient voice:*

The soldier's eyes are flooded by "wells of old"—*beerót kdumím*, an expression patterned on *náḥal kdumím*, "rivers of old," from Deborah's war song (Judges 5:21)—much as the dry desert rivers of the Negev are suddenly overrun by powerful streams from the mountains. By the use of the word *afík* ("river bed," 2) the image is placed in its traditional context, for it clearly recalls the simile of Psalm 126:4: "Turn again our captivity, O Lord, as the streams *(afikím)* in the Negev (South)."

The awakened "rivers of blood" (2) move in both directions: to and from the heart, but they are double in another sense also; they now stream here as once they streamed "there."

The sudden surge of "ancient wells," the alerted "rivers of blood," virtually place the heart in a state of siege: cut off from the outside world—within and without at the same time—belonging and not belonging—it can only listen to a warning voice from the past. The clamor of "mighty waters" (4)—again a biblical phrase; from Moses' victory song (Exodus 15:10)—and the "ancient voice" *both* seem to rise from within the depths of the speaker, addressing himself and at the same time describing his own reactions. (In the Hebrew, the poet speaks to himself in the second person and of himself in the third.)

(5) *Don't step, my friend, our feet are strange (alien) here* (6) *And he, my friend, steps. And our feet—[are] superfluous.* (7) *Here (now) our footsteps are being extinguished. You are not the one here [who is]* (8) *The great walker (wanderer), my friend—*(9) *My friend stretched forward the hollows of his hands, bent down, a touching of palms* (10) AND THE EARTH CAME [*toward him*].

The ancient voice, welling up from the individual and historical depths of the soldier-speaker, warns him that he is alien to this unchanging landscape that "extinguishes" his steps and those of his comrades as water extinguishes fire. This desert earth, in the image of the "great walker-wanderer," streams constantly under his ephemeral steps; he is transient and he is an intruder. In an attempt to make the earth respond to him, to create actual, physical contact, he "stretches forth his palms" (9)—*paṣát yad* also means "to beg"—to the earth.

(11) *Herd upon herd, she* [the earth] *murmurs softly about your feet* (12) *With plundering light. And his feet [both] trace and do not trace [a path].* (13) *"My friend, we shall fall"—Oh then* ALL OF HER [*the earth*] *shall come* (14) *In a wave to your arms:* (15) *This earth.*

The moving "herds" of sand dunes, upon which the speaker is borne, enfold his steps with a constant soft rush of light. Kovner produces a striking effect here (11) by using the intransitive verb *hamá* (denoting a soft, longing sound, as of pigeons) in a transitive manner—the sense is that the earth enfolds, covers your feet with a soft noise, envelops them in soft sound. But this is done with a "plundering light"—a light that overwhelms the speaker's very existence, threatening him with extinction. In this light, his feet leave hardly any imprint upon the ground (12)—and here, again, Kovner produces an unusual image in the word "trace": a neologism made from the noun *nativ*, "path"; literally "he paths and does not path."

This fear of personal annihilation, of leaving no trace, is voiced abruptly by someone near the speaker, perhaps another soldier experiencing the same anguish: "My friend, we shall fall." And the poet's reply to the sudden voice and to himself is the poem's conclusion, both tragic and exultant. Only in death—the first gesture, a touching of the palms (9) was not sufficient—will this earth in her entirety, like a flooding wave or an encompassing mother—come to one's arms.

— BENJAMIN HRUSHOVSKI

Abba Kovner

SOUNDS FROM NEARBY · TSLILÍM MIKARÓV · צְלִילִים מִקָּרוֹב

קָנִיתִי לִבְנִי פַּעֲמוֹן קָטָן.		Kaníti livní paamón katán.
בְּנִי, אִטֵּר־יַד־יְמִינוֹ,		Bni, itér-yad-yeminó,
נָטַל בְּיָדוֹ אֶת הַפַּעֲמוֹן הַקָּטָן	3	Natál beyadó et hapaamón hakatán
וְצִלְצֵל בִּשְׂמֹאלוֹ.		Vetsiltsél bismoló.
פַּעֲמוֹנִים יֶשְׁנָם בְּכָל הָעוֹלָם.		Paamoním yeṣnám beḥol haolám.
צְפַרְדְּעִים מְקַרְקְרוֹת, לֹא לַטֶּרֶף.		Tsfardeím mekarkerót, lo latéref.
כְּשֶׁבְּנִי מְצַלְצֵל בַּפַּעֲמוֹן הַקָּטָן,	7	Kṣební metsaltsél bapaamón hakatán,
נֶאֱנָחִים אַמְנוֹן־וְתָמָר עִם עֶרֶב.		Neenaḥím amnón-vetamár im érev.
וּבַלַּיְלָה רָאִיתִי יַעַר מוּזָר —		Uvaláyla raíti yáar muzár—
מַה יָּפוּ עֵינָיו הַנְּבוֹכוֹת שֶׁל הָאַיִל!		Ma yafú eynáv hanvuḥót ṣel haáyil!
וּמְצַלְצֵל מְצַלְצֵל פַּעֲמוֹן עַל צַוָּאר —	11	Umtsaltsél metsaltsél paamón al tsavár—
וְדוֹלְקוֹת אַחֲרָיו גִּדְרוֹת־תַּיִל.		Vedolkót aḥaráv gidrót-táyil.
וְכָל הַכְּתָלִים אֲטוּמִים. וְהַבָּתִּים אִלְּמִים כְּמוֹ סֵפֶר.		Veḥól haktalím atumím. Vehabatím ilmím
אוּלַי שׁוֹמֵעַ הַיָּם הַכָּחֹל	14	Uláy ṣoméa hayám hakaḥól [kmo séfer.
אֵיךְ נוֹבֵט בָּעֲרָבָה הָאֵפֶר.		Eyḥ novét baaravá haéfer.
אַל תִּבְכֶּה, בְּנִי, גֵּא הָיָה הָאַיִל.		Al tivké, bni, ge hayá haáyil.
צַלְצֵל בִּימִינְךָ בַּפַּעֲמוֹן הַקָּטָן —	17	Tsaltsél *biminḥá* bapaamón hakatán—
אִתְּךָ אֲנִי, עַד לַיִל.		Itḥá aní, ad láyil.

The first section of "Night March," from which our first Kovner poem was taken, ends upon the verge of a military attack. At this point the dramatic tension is interrupted for a slow, song-like lyric entitled "Sounds from Nearby."

Characteristically, this poem is not tightly linked to the other sections. Perhaps it recalls a short visit home between nights of combat, perhaps it echoes the reference in the poem that precedes it to the soldiers as "children of my life." Like "Opening," it has a mirage-like quality in which memories of the past clash with or fuse with the present moment.

(1) *I bought my son a little bell.* (2) *My son, left-handed* [lit. *whose right hand is bound*] (3) *Took the little bell in his hand* (4) *And rang with his left.*

(5) *There are bells all over the world.* (6) *Frogs croak, not for prey.* (7) *When my son rings the little bell,* (8) *Amnon and Tamar sigh as evening falls.*

The helplessness of the child deprived of the use of his right hand (2, *itér yad yeminó,*

Judges 3:15) is expressed in the simplest of words. Nature echoes his innocent joy—in the voices of frogs and in the sighing of Amnon and Tamar, the biblical lovers who gave their names to the pansy.

But the naïve negation of "not for prey" (6) has already set the scene for the intrusion of another landscape—swamps, forests, partisans—of other fateful bells of which the father now tells his son:

(9) *And at night I saw a strange forest—* (10) *How beautiful were the bewildered eyes of the ram!* (11) *And a bell on the neck is ringing, ringing—* (12) *And the barbed-wire fences chase (burn) after him [the ram].*

(13) *And all the walls are opaque. And the houses are mute as a book.* (14) *Perhaps the blue sea can hear* (15) *How the ashes sprout in the desert.*

(16) *Don't cry, my son, the ram was proud.* (17) *Ring the little bell with your* RIGHT *(hand)—* (18) *I am with you, till night (falls).*

In that "strange forest" there was a hunt for prey—a Chagallian ram, the sacrificial ram of the Abraham-Isaac episode, was being pursued by fire (12) amidst indifference and treason—the indifference of a deaf world and the betrayal of words and "books," of humanist ideals (13). Note that the Hebrew word used for "chase" in line 12, in referring to the barbed-wire fences, also means "burning *(dolkót)* after him."

The two worlds—that of the burning ghetto and partisans' forests, and that of the Israeli desert in which the poem is set—now fuse into one. "Perhaps the blue sea can hear..."—only in this place where the desert stops at the edge of the water can the ashes of that burning sprout; moreover, the desert cannot come to life again without them.

Though helpless and doomed, the ram was not without dignity—so the soldier-father reassures his son. "I am with you, till night falls," he adds, for he cannot promise to remain longer; night is the time of combat (the next poem in the section is entitled "Battle"). But here, in the different war on the soil of their native land, the child will be ringing the bell with his right hand—the traditional symbol of power ("thy right hand hath holden me up"—Psalms 18:35; "thy right hand is full of righteousness"—Psalms 48:10; etc., etc.).

"Sounds from Nearby" is straightforward, lilting, story-like. Its simple words, elementary images, and almost helpless rimes—*téref-érev* (6-8), *áyil-táyil-láyil* (10-12-16-18), *séfer-éfer* (13-15), etc.—contrast powerfully with the dense texture and multiple allusions of our first Kovner poem. But like all of this poet's verse, this poem is extremely difficult to approach and to discuss in isolation. Basic motifs and images—the burning ghetto; the ram who represents both the slaughtered "flock" and the proud revolt; the act of battle and death seen in erotic terms; the soldiers looked upon as children ("faces, faces in a thousand cradles")—recur and are elaborated throughout Kovner's work, and their full impact can be grasped only in this context.

— BENJAMIN HRUSHOVSKI

Tuvya Rübner

SPRING IN THE WORLD · AVÍV BAOLÁM · אָבִיב בָּעוֹלָם

הַפְּרָחִים גְּדוֹלִים, כְּאִלּוּ	Hapraḥím gdolím keílu
אֶפְשָׁר לָגוּר בְּתוֹכָם,	Efṣár lagúr betoḥám,
עֲנָנִים שְׁקוּפִים בַּתְּכֵלֶת,	Ananím ṣkufím batḥéylet,
כְּאִלּוּ הַלֵּב רֻחַם,	Keílu halév ruḥám,
פַּרְפָּרִים מִתְפָּרְצִים, כְּאִלּוּ	Parparím mitpartsím, keílu
לֹא רָאוּ אֶת הָאוֹר מֵעוֹדָם,	Lo raú et haór meodám,
גּוּפִי עִם גּוּפֵךְ, כְּאִלּוּ	Gufí im guféḥ, keílu
אֵין גְּבוּל בֵּין דָּם לְדָם,	Eyn gvul beyn dam ledám,
לַהֲבוֹת צִפֳּרִים, כְּאִלּוּ	Lahavót tsiporím, keílu
הַשַּׁחַק לְבַסּוֹף נִשְׁלַם,	Haṣáḥak levasóf niṣlám,
צִיצֵי צְחוֹקִים, כְּאִלּוּ	Tsitséy tsḥokím, keílu
אָבִיב בָּעוֹלָם.	Avív baolám.

Tuvya Rübner, unlike most of the contemporary poets in this volume, is a member of a kibbutz, which he joined soon after his arrival in Palestine at the age of twenty. Born in Czechoslovakia, he grew up under the influence of German literature. Translations from medieval and modern German poets are interspersed in his books.

Rübner's poetry blends contemporary Hebrew with elements of classical Hebrew, resulting in a distinctively individual idiom. His work as a whole exhibits what amounts to an obsession with time and with the need for retaining values in a world of crumbling security. Hence, it is no accident that the title of his second book *Ṣirím Limtsó Et—Poems to Find Time* (1960)—is an inversion of the Hebrew meaning and word-order of *Ṣirím Leét Metsó*, "occasional poems" (literally, "Poems for Time Found"). Here the forms are often free, the colloquialisms frequent. In some poems the statements are not only fragmentary but they verge on stream-of-consciousness. Though clearly the work of a contemporary, many of the poems retain classical or folkloristic elements, some of which may be seen in our selection.

(1) *The flowers are big, as if* (2) *[It were] possible to live inside them,* (3) *[There are] transparent clouds in the blue,* (4) *As if the heart had been comforted (pitied).*

(5) *Butterflies [are] bursting (out), as if* (6) *They had never seen the light,* (7) *My body [is] with your body, as if* (8) *[There were] no boundary between blood and blood.*

(9) *Flames of birds, as if* (10) *The sky had been completed at last,* (11) *Buds of laughters, as if* (12) *[There were] spring in the world.*

The poem delicately interweaves exultation with delusion. On the one hand, "Spring in the World" recalls a traditional, merry spring-song, with its images of flowers, clouds in blue sky, heart, butterflies, birds, and with its simple and clear pattern. Each pair of lines deals with a single image, introduced by the first line and commented upon by the second.

On the other hand, these introductory images are constantly qualified by *keilu* ("as if"). While the opening of the poem seems to be an exultant hyperbole, the succeeding lines raise a doubt in the reader's mind: the second "as if" (4) appears to imply that there is no genuine comfort; that the speaker knows that he has surrendered to an illusion.

This doubt is held in suspense in lines 5-6, which at first seem to reassert exuberant belief. But as the lines go on, it becomes obvious that "as if" is not used as a means of comparison, as an extended "like" linking two seemingly disparate phenomena: it is a phrase of contrast, employed to divide. The lovers are ready to simulate a complete union but the boundary is not to be overcome. (Line 8, incidentally, echoes a passage from Deuteronomy 17:8: "between blood and blood, between plea and plea.")

Doubt is intensified in lines 9-10. Here the "flames of birds" (*lahavót tsiporím*)—a play on the common expression for "flocks of birds" (*lahakót tsiporím*)—arouse the comment in line 10 implying that creation is in fact not "completed." "At last" even suggests that the speaker was always aware of the fundamental flaw or blemish in the created world.

The subtle yet surprising conclusion turns everything upside down. "Buds of laughters" —*tsitséy tsḥokím*, with its sparkling alliterative sound—is a generalizing image which encompasses all the elements that preceded. The speaker denies the very existence of spring. Everything now appears to have been a deception. And the final line, restating the title but following a final "as if," sheds ironical light, by implying: "there is spring in the world, as if there were spring in the world." Thus even the exultation of lines 5-6 seems to falter: the butterflies had already seen the light and their bursting out is perhaps a meaningless act rather than one of ecstasy or rebirth.

The key word *keílu* ("as if"), which checks every new image of spring while introducing each line of reflection, gains added emphasis from the cesura that precedes it. And the somewhat free anapestic (or amphibrachic) trimeter always drops an unstressed syllable before the cesura (before *keílu:* for example, line 5—*parparím mitpartsím, keilu . . .*).

The refrain-like structure, the variations on the basic rime (*ḥam-ḥam, dam-dam, lam-lam*), the elaboration of the spring similes, all contribute to the poem's cohesiveness and charmed song-like quality—which is, in a way, as misleading as the spring of which it sings. Yet the irony is sad rather than harsh: the poem is anything but a sardonic parody.

– DAN PAGIS

Haim Gury

ODYSSEUS · ODÍSES · אוֹדִיסֶס

Haim Gury was born in Tel Aviv in 1926, and the outlines of his biography—agricultural training at school, apprenticeship in a kibbutz, active service at home and abroad in the Haganah, and in the commando troops during the War of Independence—are, to a large extent, typical of his generation. His first impassioned war poems (*Flowers of Fire*, 1949) were immediately acclaimed, recited, and sung as a poignant expression of the war generation. Gury felt himself to be the representative of a time when "people spoke in the first person plural." But the post-war years, which ushered in the inevitable emotional anticlimax together with a host of socio-economic problems, did much to destroy the mood of national unity that had nourished Gury's verse. The "first person plural" gave way to the primacy of the individual.

The sense of estrangement, disillusion, and loneliness (which characterizes much of Gury's later poetry) pervades "Odysseus" (1960), though the poem is not to be read allegorically:

(1) *And upon returning to his native town, he found a sea* (2) *And various fish and grass floating on the slow waves,* (3) *And a sun weakening on the rim of the sky.*

(4) *Error always recurs [returns], said Odysseus in (to) his tired heart,* (5) *And he returned to the crossroads that are near the neighboring town* (6) *To find the road to his native town which was not water.*

(7) *A wanderer tired as a dreamer and full of longing* (8) *Among people who spoke different Greek.* (9) *The words he had taken with him as provision on the path of his voyages had died meanwhile—*

(10) *For a moment he thought he had been (fallen) asleep for many days* (11) *And had returned to people who did not wonder upon seeing him,* (12) *And did not stare wide-eyed [*lit. did *not tear eyes open].*

(13) *He asked them with gestures and they tried to understand him* (14) *From beyond the distances.* (15) *Purple grew into violet on the rim of the same sky* [i.e., as in line 3].

(16) *Then the adults arose and took the children who were standing round him in a circle* (17) *And drew them away.* (18) *And light after light grew yellow in house after house.*

(19) *Dew came, and fell upon his head.* (20) *Wind came, and kissed his lips.* (21) *Water came, and bathed his feet, like old Euryclea,* (22) *And did not see the scar, and continued down the slope as water does.*

Classical Greek and traditional Hebraic elements merge into a pattern which is unmistakably modern. The wanderer returns after many years; but this time-span is conceived in a manner essentially different from that of the classical tale, which grants its heroes everlasting youth and timelessness and makes possible a complete recognition and reconciliation. In the world of Gury's Odysseus, changes are irrevocable. Odysseus is not a hero but a "tired wanderer" (7) with a "tired heart" (4) who, having been oblivious to time's passing, finally reaches his native town only to find himself utterly alien (10 ff.). Perhaps he even implies that he himself is a recurring "mistake" (4), using the actual words of an everyday proverb.

Homer's Odysseus was brought while asleep to his native island and on waking at first did not recognize it. But Gury's reference is to an old Hebrew legend about a famous sage, Ḥoni the Circle-Maker. In pondering a well-known verse on the Babylonian exile —"When the Lord brought back those who returned to Zion, we were like them that dream" (Psalm 126)—Ḥoni wondered: Is it possible for a man to dream for seventy years? Some time later Ḥoni actually fell asleep only to awake seventy years later and to learn that his son had long been dead.

וּבְשׁוּבוֹ אֶל עִיר מוֹלַדְתּוֹ מָצָא יָם
וְדָגִים שׁוֹנִים וְעֵשֶׂב צָף עַל הַגַּלִּים הָאִטִּיִּים
וְשֶׁמֶשׁ נֶחֱלֶשֶׁת בְּשׁוּלֵי שָׁמַיִם.

טָעוּת לְעוֹלָם חוֹזֶרֶת, אָמַר אוֹדִיסֵס בְּלִבּוֹ הֶעָיֵף
וְחָזַר עַד פָּרָשַׁת־הַדְּרָכִים הַסְּמוּכָה לָעִיר הַשְּׁכֵנָה
לִמְצֹא אֶת הַדֶּרֶךְ אֶל עִיר מוֹלַדְתּוֹ שֶׁלֹּא הָיְתָה מַיִם.

הֵלֶךְ עָיֵף כְּחוֹלֵם וּמִתְגַּעְגֵּעַ מְאֹד
בֵּין אֲנָשִׁים שֶׁדִּבְּרוּ יְוָנִית אַחֶרֶת.
הַמִּלִּים שֶׁנָּטַל עִמּוֹ כְּצֵידָה לַדֶּרֶךְ הַמַּסָּעוֹת, גָּוְעוּ
בֵּינְתַיִם.

רֶגַע חָשַׁב כִּי נִרְדַּם לְיָמִים רַבִּים
וְחָזַר אֶל אֲנָשִׁים שֶׁלֹּא תָּמְהוּ בִּרְאוֹתָם אוֹתוֹ
וְלֹא קָרְעוּ עֵינַיִם.

הוּא שָׁאַל אוֹתָם בִּתְנוּעוֹת וְהֵם נִסּוּ לְהָבִין אוֹתוֹ
מִתּוֹךְ הַמֶּרְחַקִּים.
הָאַרְגָּמָן הִסְגִּיל וְהָלַךְ בְּשׁוּלֵי אוֹתָם שָׁמַיִם.

קָמוּ הַמְּבֻגָּרִים וְנָטְלוּ אֶת הַיְלָדִים שֶׁעָמְדוּ סְבִיבוֹ
בְּמַעְגָּל
וּמָשְׁכוּ אוֹתָם.
וְאוֹר אַחַר אוֹר הִצְהִיב בְּבַיִת אַחַר בַּיִת.

בָּא טַל וְיָרַד עַל רֹאשׁוֹ.
בָּאָה רוּחַ וְנָשְׁקָה לִשְׂפָתָיו.
בָּאוּ מַיִם וְשָׁטְפוּ רַגְלָיו כְּאֶבְרִיקְלֵיָה הַזְּקֵנָה.

וְלֹא רָאוּ אֶת הַצַּלֶּקֶת וְהִמְשִׁיכוּ בַּמּוֹרָד כְּדֶרֶךְ הַמַּיִם.

Uvșuvó el ir moladtó matsá yam
Vedagím șoním veésev tsaf al hagalím haitiyím
Veșémeș neheléșet beșuléy șamáyim.

Taút leolám ḥozéret, amár odíses belibó heayéf
Veḥazár ad paraṣát- hadraḥím hasmuḥá laír hașḥená,
Limtsó et hadéreḥ el ir moladtó ṣeló haytá máyim.

Héleḥ ayéf keḥolém umitgaagéa meód
Beyn anaṣím ṣedibrú yevanít aḥéret.
Hamilím ṣenatál imó ketseydá ledéreḥ hamasaót, gav'ú beyntáyim.

Réga ḥasáv ki nirdám leyamím rabím
Veḥazár el anaṣím ṣeló tamhú bir'otám otó
Veló kar'ú eynáyim.

Hu ṣaál otám bitnuót vehém nisú lehavín otó
Mitóḥ hamerḥakím.
Haargamán hisgíl vehaláḥ beṣuléy otám ṣamáyim.

Kámu hamvugarím venatlú et hayladím ṣeamdú svivó bemaagál
Umaṣḥú otám.
Veór aḥár or hitshív beváyit aḥár báyit.

Ba tal veyarád al roṣó.
Báa rúaḥ venaṣká lisfatáv.
Báu máyim veṣatfú ragláv keevrikléa hazkená.
Veló raú et hatsaléket vehimṣíḥu bamorád kedéreḥ hamáyim.

Encountering only strangers, he told them: "I am Ḥoni." They did not believe him and they scoffed at him. In his loneliness, he asked God for mercy and he died.

Gury's allusions to the legend appear in the Hebrew as early as line 7. Three lines later Odysseus is clearly identified with Ḥoni and a further allusion is perhaps found in 16, contrasting the circle that Ḥoni is said to have fixed around himself when he prayed for rain with the quickly dispersing circle of children who surround Odysseus. But the surest links are in the situation and tone. The people Odysseus meets speak "different Greek." He cannot recognize anything as he looks about him—except the sky. Though the curious children draw close to him, the adults, quite unconcerned with his fate, draw them away; all the human beings abandon him, to retire to their lighted homes.

But Odysseus shows no bitterness. He finds momentary consolation in dew, water, and wind (19-20), and meets with seeming hospitality: "Water came, and bathed his feet, like old Euryclea," (21) the nurse of Homer's account, who while bathing his feet recognized him by his old scar. But Gury's Odysseus, like the legendary Ḥoni, never experiences recognition. The water, "as water does," rushes by and down the slope, never "seeing" the old scar of his suffering.

A restrained tone of resignation pervades the poem. Most of the words and expressions are conversational and the style is closer to the simplicity of the Legends than to the loftiness of biblical poetry. The lines vary in length; there is no fixed meter. Structure derives from syntactic patterns, repetitions, alliterations (as in line 3), and a subtly balanced rime scheme. The first two lines of each stanza are unrimed but the third rimes throughout (the assonance in line 18 has the value of a rime). The reader of the Hebrew cannot escape the particular emphasis placed upon these rimes—sky, water, meanwhile, eyes, sky, house—even though they are separated. — DAN PAGIS

Haim Gury

[IT SEEMS TO ME · NIDMÉ LI · נִדְמֶה לִי]

Similar in feeling to "Odysseus," this untitled poem makes a direct personal assertion of the speaker's disillusion and of his incapacity—perhaps even unwillingness—to cope with violent change.

(1) *It seems to me that I guard the walls of a city* (2) *That died a long time ago.*

(3) *Lights which now illumine me* (4) *Are the (last-will-and-) testaments of a light which went out years ago.*

(5) *I walk between the things that time has abandoned,* (6) *Pass on.* (7) *And they live without time, which gradually disintegrates in clocks.*

(8) *They come back to me, come back to me to live more slowly,* (9) *Next to ashtrays,* (10) *Next to cups of coffee growing cold.*

(11) *I walk a great deal and guess (a great deal)* (12) *And enjoy the benefit of the doubt.*

(13) *But I guard the walls of a city that died years ago.*

The imagery suggests the ruined remains from a remote age. The speaker himself is, anachronistically enough, "guarding" a city long dead, or so "it seems." The many lights (*orót,* 3) he now observes are weak, dispersed reflections of a single source (*or,* "light," 4) that has ceased to exist—such as the light of a long-vanished star that shines down to us through space. Thus the comparatively narrow time-span in which social and cultural changes occurred (*ṣaním,* "years," rather than "ages" [4]) has been metamorphosed into the immensity of "light years."

A feeling of emptiness attaches itself even to those things that "disintegrating" time has not affected. These "things" (*dvarím* is an unspecific, even blurred category) are "abandoned" by time and the speaker also passes them by. They come back to him devoid of any urgency of action: they live without time. They live a slow existence alongside ashtrays and cups of coffee growing cold (8-10), petty everyday objects that are all the witnesses that remain to the memory of a great past.

But there is nothing here of revolt. Indeed,

נִדְמֶה לִי כִּי אֲנִי שׁוֹמֵר חוֹמוֹת שֶׁל עִיר
2 אֲשֶׁר גָּוְעָה לִפְנֵי זְמַן רַב.

אוֹרוֹת הַמְּאִירִים אוֹתִי כָּעֵת
4 הֵם צַוָּאוֹת שֶׁל אוֹר אֲשֶׁר כָּבָה לִפְנֵי שָׁנִים.

אֲנִי הוֹלֵךְ בֵּין הַדְּבָרִים אֲשֶׁר הַזְּמַן עָזַב אוֹתָם,
6 עוֹבֵר.
וְהֵם חַיִּים בְּלִי זְמַן הוֹלֵךְ וּמִתְפּוֹרֵר בַּשְּׁעוֹנִים.
הֵם שָׁבִים אֵלַי, שָׁבִים אֵלַי לִחְיוֹת יוֹתֵר לְאַט.
9 לְיַד מַאֲפֵרוֹת,
לְיַד סִפְלֵי קָפֶה מִצְטַנְּנִים.

אֲנִי מַרְבֶּה לָלֶכֶת וּלְנַחֵשׁ
12 וְנֶהֱנֶה מֵהַסָּפֵק.

אֲבָל אֲנִי שׁוֹמֵר חוֹמוֹת שֶׁל עִיר אֲשֶׁר גָּוְעָה לִפְנֵי שָׁנִים.

Nidmé li ki aní ṣomér ḥomót ṣel ir
2 Aṣér gav'á lifnéy zman rav.

Orót hameirím otí kaét
4 Hem tsavaót ṣel or aṣér kavá lifnéy ṣaním.

Aní holéḥ beyn hadvarím aṣér hazmán
[azáv otám,
6 Ovér.
Vehém ḥayím bli zman holéḥ umitporér
[baṣeoním.
Hem ṣavím eyláy, ṣavím eyláy liḥyót yotér
[leát.
9 Leyád maaferót,
Leyád sifléy kafé mitstanením.

Aní marbé laléḥet ulnaḥéṣ
12 Venehené mehasafék.

Avál aní ṣomér ḥomót ṣel ir aṣér gav'á
[lifnéy ṣaním.

the speaker can actually enjoy the "benefit of doubt" (12). The legal phrase makes it clear that his status and his rights are undecided, as though he had been acquitted through lack of evidence. But the phrase may also be understood as the speaker's own enjoyment of a doubtful situation, in which he is under no compulsion to make decisions or to take any other action—he is free simply to walk around a great deal and to do a lot of guessing (11) . . . perhaps at the same time wondering—as Gury remarks elsewhere in the same volume from which our poem comes (*Windrose*, 1960)—"What, in fact, had we wanted to say? / Where and when did the error begin?"

The final line of our poem repeats the first two lines, compressing them into one but significantly omitting the qualification: "It seems to me." Thus there remains only one certainty: that the speaker is a guardian of the dead past—not only of his own but also of the dead past of a once-living society, of an entire "city" which has crumbled to pieces. Anachronistic and superfluous though he be, nevertheless he guards the walls that remain.

The almost pained contrast between a once-thriving "walled city"—the biblical overtones are inescapable—with the pettiness of modern "ashtrays" is a familiar phenomenon in Gury's poetry. Often the effect is achieved stylistically by the opposition of biblical rhetoric to colloquial directness, as for example, in the line from an untitled poem in the same volume: *hiné yamim baim ṣel zéhu ze*, literally "Behold the days shall come of that's that."

From the point of view of poetic form, "It Seems to Me" gives an impression of looseness. As opposed to the conventional structures in Gury's first volume, looseness of pattern is frequently found in his later writing, and there is also a pronounced tendency toward simplicity and colloquialism in the choice of words and phrases. In "It Seems to Me" an almost hidden, sporadic rime (*-ním*) links several of the stanzas or sections. Although upon closer analysis an iambic pattern can be discerned, the effect of a regular meter is quite lacking because of the great variations in line length (from 1 to 9 iambic feet) and of the tired "crumbling" tone.

— DAN PAGIS

Haim Gury

HIS MOTHER · IMÓ · אִמּוֹ

לִפְנֵי שָׁנִים, בְּסוֹף שִׁירַת דְּבוֹרָה,
שָׁמַעְתִּי אֶת דוּמִיַּת רֶכֶב סִיסְרָא אֲשֶׁר בּוֹשֵׁשׁ לָבוֹא,
מַבִּיט בְּאִמּוֹ שֶׁל סִיסְרָא הַנִּשְׁקֶפֶת בַּחַלּוֹן,
אִשָּׁה שֶׁפַּס כֶּסֶף בִּשְׂעָרָהּ.

שְׁלַל צְבָעִים רִקְמָה,
צֶבַע רִקְמָתַיִם לְצַוְּארֵי שָׁלָל, רָאוּ הַנְּעָרוֹת.
אוֹתָהּ שָׁעָה שָׁכַב בָּאֹהֶל כְּנִרְדָּם.
יָדָיו רֵיקוֹת מְאֹד.
עַל סַנְטֵרוֹ עִקְּבוֹת חָלָב חֶמְאָה וָדָם.

הַדּוּמִיָּה לֹא נִשְׁבְּרָה אֶל הַסּוּסִים וְאֶל הַמֶּרְכָּבוֹת,
גַּם הַנְּעָרוֹת שָׁתְקוּ אַחַת אַחַר אַחַת.
שְׁתִיקָתִי נָגְעָה בִּשְׁתִיקָתָן.
אַחַר זְמַן־מָה שָׁקְעָה הַשֶּׁמֶשׁ.
אַחַר זְמַן־מָה כָּבוּ הַדִּמְדּוּמִים.

אַרְבָּעִים שָׁנָה שָׁקְטָה הָאָרֶץ. אַרְבָּעִים שָׁנָה
לֹא דָּהֲרוּ סוּסִים וּפָרָשִׁים מֵתִים לֹא נָעֲצוּ עֵינֵי
זְכוּכִית.
אֲבָל הִיא מֵתָה, זְמַן קָצָר אַחַר מוֹת בְּנָהּ.

Lifnéy ṣaním, besóf ṣirát dvorá,
Ṣamáti et dumiyát réḥev sisrá aṣér boṣéṣ lavó,
Mabít beimó ṣel sisrá haniṣkéfet baḥalón,
Iṣá ṣepás késef bis'ará.

Ṣlal tsvaím rikmá,
Tséva rikmatáyim letsavréy ṣalál, raú [hanearót.
Otá ṣaá ṣaḥáv baóhel kenirdám.
Yadáv reykót meód.
Al santeró ikvót ḥaláv ḥem'á vadám.

Hadumiyá lo niṣberá el hasusím veél hamer- [kavót,
Gam hanearót ṣatkú aḥát aḥár aḥát.
Ṣtikatí nag'á biṣtikatán.
Aḥár zman-má ṣak'á haṣémeṣ.
Aḥár zman-má kavú hadimdumím.

Arbaím ṣaná ṣaktá haárets. Arbaím ṣaná
Lo daharú susím ufaraṣím metím lo
[naatsú eynéy zḥuḥít.
Avál hi méta, zman katsár aḥár mot bna.

Characters mentioned only in passing in the Bible have often been a source of inspiration for later Hebrew literature. From ancient Jewish legends to recent poetry and prose, such minor figures have been elaborated upon and sometimes used as means for expressing present-day attitudes. Gury's poem, for example, centers in the character of Sisera's mother, who is mentioned only briefly, if perhaps strikingly, in the famous "Song of Deborah" (Judges 5: 28-30), with which every Israeli schoolboy is familiar.

Sisera, the leader of a Canaanite army, fought against Israel and was defeated by Barak and by the prophetess Deborah. After deserting the battlefield, he was lured into the tent of Jael, a chieftainess, who offered him milk and butter. He quenched his thirst and fell into a deep sleep; then Jael drove a wooden nail through his head and killed him. The "Song of Deborah" triumphantly celebrates these deeds and goes on to describe the dead enemy's mother as she awaited her son in vain:

"The mother of Sisera looked out at a window, And cried through the lattice: Why is his chariot so long in coming? Why tarry the wheels of his chariots? Her wise ladies answered her, yea, she returned answer to herself: Have they not sped? have they not divided the prey; to every man a damsel or two; to Sisera a prey of divers colors, A prey of divers colors of needlework, Of divers colors of needlework on both sides, meet for the necks of them that take the spoil?"

Gury's poem follows the biblical text in its general argument and in some details, but it reverses the point of view. The poet takes the part of the defeated leader and of his bereaved mother:

(1) *Years ago, at the end of the Song of Deborah,* (2) *I heard the quiet of Sisera's chariots, which were late in coming,* (3) *As I looked at Sisera's mother watching at the window,* (4) *A woman whose hair is a streak of silver.*

(5) *A prey of divers colors of needlework* (6) *Divers colors of needlework on both sides meet for the necks of them that take the spoil* [Judges 5:30], *the maidens saw;* (7) *At that very moment he lay like a sleeper in the tent;* (8) *His hands [were] very empty.* (9) *On his chin, traces of milk, butter, and blood.*

(10) *The quiet was not shattered by [*lit. *to] the horses and the chariots;* (11) *The maidens also fell silent, one after the other.* (12) *My silence touched their silence.* (13) *After a while, the sun set.* (14) *After a while, the twilight went out.*

(15) *Forty years—the land was calm. Forty years* (16) *Horses did not gallop and dead horsemen did not stare with glassy eyes.* (17) *But she died a short time after her son's death.*

The variation on the biblical passage has a distinctly subjective tone, for the poet speaks for himself in the first stanza and in his identification with the maidens' silence (11). But his departure from Scripture is even more pronounced in the imaginatively descriptive passages. The image of the mother's "silver-streaked hair" (4) creates the emotional tone for what follows: the enemy's mother, an aging woman, is waiting, like every mother, for the safe return of her son; but all she hears is the silence of his absence. While the maidens in her entourage (the biblical "wise ladies") see in their imagination Sisera's booty, the son himself lies dead. And since the poem conceives Sisera not as an enemy but as a lamented son, it suggests that Jael behaved treacherously, violating the elementary code of hospitality.

The biblical hymn does not describe the moment when the mother learns of her son's death, and neither does the poem. The poet passes from the mournful scene of silence and of slowly fading light (12-13) to the conclusion, carefully omitting all reference to the triumphant cry of the "Song of Deborah"—"So let all thine enemies perish, O Lord," etc. The poem reproduces only the last few words of the chapter that tells, in the dry tone of the chronicle, that after the victory there came forty years of peace and security.

Note that the poet minimizes the outcome of that war. On the contrary, by changing the word order of the quotation ("And the land had rest forty years" (Judges 5: 31), and by repeating the time phrase in the same line (15), he stresses "forty years"—a long period of peace in a war-ridden country—and continues to praise the peace in affirming the absence of horrors (16). But these positive results seem to be diminished as they lie enclosed in the mood of tragedy and human loss suffered by the aging woman who herself died soon after her son's death.

Although the poem is close to the Bible in vocabulary, the syntax and poetic forms are modern. The subdued tone avoids both sentimentality and rhetoric. It is almost an improvisation on a familiar theme, with utterly changed emphasis, in lines of varying length, which seem to be independent rhythmic segments.

— DAN PAGIS

Yehuda Amihai

OF THREE OR FOUR IN A ROOM

MIṢLOṢÁ O ARBAÁ BAḤÉDER · מִשְׁלשָׁה אוֹ אַרְבָּעָה בַּחֶדֶר

מִשְׁלשָׁה אוֹ אַרְבָּעָה בַּחֶדֶר	Miṣloṣá o arbaá baḥéder
תָּמִיד אֶחָד עוֹמֵד לְיַד הַחַלּוֹן.	Tamíd eḥád oméd leyád haḥalón.
מֻכְרָח לִרְאוֹת אֶת הָעָוֶל בֵּין קוֹצִים	Muḥráḥ lir'ót et haável beyn kotsím
וְאֶת הַשְּׂרֵפוֹת בַּגִּבְעָה.	Veét hasreyfót bagiv'á.
וְכֵיצַד אֲנָשִׁים שֶׁיָּצְאוּ שְׁלֵמִים	Veḥeytsád anaṣím ṣeyats'ú ṣleymím
מֻחְזָרִים בָּעֶרֶב כְּמַטְבְּעוֹת עֹדֶף לְבֵיתָם.	Muḥzarím baérev kematbeót ódef leveytám.
מִשְׁלשָׁה אוֹ אַרְבָּעָה בַּחֶדֶר	Miṣloṣá o arbaá baḥéder
תָּמִיד אֶחָד עוֹמֵד לְיַד הַחַלּוֹן.	Tamíd eḥád oméd leyád haḥalón.
שְׂעָרוֹ הָאָפֵל מֵעַל לְמַחְשְׁבוֹתָיו.	Searó haafél meál lemaḥṣevotáv.
מֵאֲחוֹרָיו הַמִּלִּים.	Meaḥoráv hamilím.
וּלְפָנָיו הַקּוֹלוֹת הַנּוֹדְדִים בְּלִי תַּרְמִיל,	Ulfanáv hakolót hanodedím bli tarmíl,
לְבָבוֹת בְּלִי צֵידָה, נְבוּאוֹת בְּלִי מַיִם	Levavót bli tseydá, nevuót bli máyim
וַאֲבָנִים גְּדוֹלוֹת שֶׁהוּשְׁבוּ	Vaavaním gdolót ṣehuṣvú
וְנִשְׁאֲרוּ סְגוּרִים כְּמִכְתָּבִים שֶׁאֵין	Veniṣ'arú sgurím kamiḥtavím ṣeéyn
לָהֶם כְּתֹבֶת וְאֵין מְקַבֵּל.	Lahém któvet veéyn mekabél.

When the late George Santayana declared that no poet can be great unless he writes in the language of the lullabies that his mother sang to him, he could not, of course, have been taking into account modern Hebrew poetry, which affords many examples that contradict him. Yehuda Amihai, born in Würzburg in 1924, is one of a number of Israeli poets who have achieved greatness or great distinction in spite of the fact that Hebrew is not their mother tongue. In Amihai's çase, his mother tongue was German. Although he entered the government-sponsored Israelitische Volkschule at the age of six and learned to read and to write Hebrew, he did not begin to speak the language of Israel until 1936, when he settled in Jerusalem.

Amihai's influence upon contemporary Hebrew verse has been widely acknowledged. The traditionalists would attribute his influence largely to the "foreign" flavor of his poetry, with its affinities to both English and German, whereas others might point to the fact that Amihai has made usefully assimilable such writers as Rilke and Auden. In any event, his coming late to spoken Hebrew may have impressed him with the freshness and richness of the colloquial. More, perhaps, than most of his contemporaries, Amihai has availed himself of the rhythms and idioms of daily speech, enriching his own verse and, through it, the work of younger writers.

"Of Three or Four in a Room," from *Two Hopes Away* (1958), offers his conception of the poet's role. As Amihai sees him, the poet is a special creature, living in two worlds but not quite welcome in either. And it is because of this ambiguous state that he is able to serve as intermediary.

(1) *Of three or four in a room* (2) *[There is] always one [who is] standing by the window.* (3) *[He] must see injustice among the thorns* (4) *And the fires (burning) on the hill.* (5) *And how men who departed whole* (6) *Are brought back to their homes in the evening like small change.*

(7) *Of three or four in a room* (8) *[There is] always one [who is] standing by the window.* (9) *His dark hair above (upon) his thoughts.* (10) *Behind him, words.* (11) *And before him voices that wander without a knapsack,* (12) *Hearts without provisions, prophecies without water,* (13) *And large stones that have been returned* (14) *And remain unopened like letters that have no* (15) *Address and no recipient.*

Of the poet's two worlds, one is the room—by its very nature a protected place, at a seemingly safe remove from the world of direct experience outside. The other world is the stony landscape of the Judean hills seen through the window as a place of injustice, destruction, waste, and unfulfilled longing. Hearing the words in the room, he turns his back on them (10), to travel in thought to the world outside.

But though he does not actually go outside, his vision enables him to bring back to those within the room something of that place of thorns and conflagration (3-4) and defeat. Men go out into this world in the morning of their lives, whole in spirit (5) and ready to offer in exchange everything they have, with the whole coin which is their selves. But the evening of their lives finds them diminished; their whole coin has been broken down into the "small change" (6) that they have become—wholeness shattered into compromise, emptiness, frustration. The breakdown is further indicated by their manner of departure and return: they set forth on their own feet but when returning they are "brought" back (6).

The contemporary sense of frustration is emphasized by contrasts. In the ancient days those who went out into the waterless lands were prophets and when their journeys were fulfilled, they returned with God's word, for He is the source of living waters (Jeremiah). Their hearts had already been provided (11-12) with life-giving waters of faith, so that in a sense they found what they had already possessed. But the faithless today set forth with a hope that is hopeless. No wonder, then, that they cannot read the "large stones" (13)—the tablets of God—that He has strewn everywhere.

The poet might long to be a prophet; but, not a true inhabitant of the waste places, he observes them from his comfortable and safe post at the window. What "words," then, could he in fact bring back to the talkers around him, that might assuage their thirst for the waters of the spirit?

A reader may hear in the poem's incomplete personifications—in its abstract voices, hearts, and prophecies—the tones of Rilke. Line 11 adds another poetic quality that in a sense reflects a certain absence of materiality: the phrase *hakolót hanodedím* ("wandering voices") is a play on *haḥolót hanodedím* (which means "quicksand"). This twofold evocation suggests the danger that the individual can be sucked into the desert outside as well as into the desert within.

— ROBERT FRIEND

Yehuda Amihai

THE TWO OF US TOGETHER, EACH OF US ALONE

ṢNÉYNU BEYÁḤAD VEḤÓL EḤÁD LEḤÚD · שְׁנֵינוּ בְּיַחַד וְכָל אֶחָד לְחוּד

״שניהם ביחד וכל אחד לחוד״...
[מתוך חוזה שכירות]

Ṣneyhém beyáḥad veḥól eḥád leḥúd.

יַלְדָּה שֶׁלִּי, עוֹד קַיִץ עָבַר		Yaldá ṣelí, od káyits avár
וְאָבִי לֹא בָּא לַלּוּנָה־פַּרְק.		Veaví lo ba lalúna-park.
הַנַּדְנֵדוֹת מוֹסִיפוֹת לָנוּד.	3	Hanadneydót mosifót lanúd.
שְׁנֵינוּ בְּיַחַד וְכָל אֶחָד לְחוּד.		Ṣnéynu beyáḥad veḥól eḥád leḥúd.
אֹפֶק הַיָּם מְאַבֵּד סְפִינוֹתָיו —		Ófek hayám meabéd sfinotáv—
קָשֶׁה לִשְׁמֹר עַל מַשֶּׁהוּ עַכְשָׁו.		Kaṣé liṣmór al máṣehu aḥṣáv.
מֵאֲחוֹרֵי הָהָר חִכּוּ הַלּוֹחֲמִים.	7	Meaḥoréy hahár ḥikú haloḥamím.
כַּמָּה זְקוּקִים אָנוּ לְרַחֲמִים.		Kamá zkukím ánu leraḥamím.
שְׁנֵינוּ בְּיַחַד וְכָל אֶחָד לְחוּד.		Ṣnéynu beyáḥad veḥól eḥád leḥúd.
יָרֵחַ מְנַסֵּר אֶת הֶעָבִים לִשְׁנַיִם —	10	Yaréaḥ menasér et heavím liṣnáyim—
בּוֹאִי וְנֵצֵא לְאַהֲבַת בֵּינַיִם.		Bói venetsé leahavát beynáyim.
רַק שְׁנֵינוּ נֹאהַב לִפְנֵי הַמַּחֲנוֹת.		Rak ṣnéynu noháv lifnéy hamaḥanót.
אוּלַי אֶפְשָׁר עוֹד הַכֹּל לְשַׁנּוֹת.	13	Uláy efṣár od hakól leṣanót.
שְׁנֵינוּ בְּיַחַד וְכָל אֶחָד לְחוּד.		Ṣnéynu beyáḥad veḥól eḥád leḥúd.
אַהֲבָתִי הָפְכָה אוֹתִי כַּנִּרְאֶה		Ahavatí hafḥá otí kanir'é
כְּיָם מָלוּחַ לְטִפּוֹת מְתוּקוֹת שֶׁל יוֹרֶה;		Keyám malúaḥ letipót metukót ṣel yoré;
אֲנִי מוּבָא אֵלַיִךְ לְאַט וְנוֹפֵל.	17	Aní muvá eyláyiḥ leát venofél.
קַבְּלִינִי. אֵין לָנוּ מַלְאָךְ גּוֹאֵל.		Kablíni. Eyn lánu mal'áḥ goél.
כִּי שְׁנֵינוּ בְּיַחַד. כָּל אֶחָד לְחוּד.		Ki ṣnéynu beyáḥad. Kol eḥád leḥúd.

The title "The Two of Us Together, Each of Us Alone" (1955) comes, as the epigraph tells us, "from a lease contract," meaning "Both of them jointly and severally." It is highly characteristic of Amihai to take words or phrases from legal documents, nursery rimes, folk-sayings, popular tunes, as well as from the Bible and the Book of Daily Prayer, and to set them in a new context or alter them slightly. The new context may reaffirm a tradition, deplore it, or mock its absence or perversion. Usually a deflationary device, the slight change is sometimes merely playful; but at other times the playfulness has serious intent.

(1) *My girl [darling], another summer has gone by* (2) *And my father hasn't come to the amusement park* [lit. Luna Park]. (3) *The swings continue to swing.* (4) *The two of us together and each of us alone.*

Everything is directed towards freshness and simplicity. The words are such as any child will understand, the rhythm as easy as a 15th-century English ballad. Even the awkwardness of the rimes (*avár-park*, 1-2) adds to the ballad-like effect, charming the reader with the naïve offness. Line 2 echoes a children's song popular when the poem was written: *Ábale bo lalúna-park*, "Daddy, come to the amusement park." Amihai's references to his father in his early poetry are frequent almost to the point of obsession. Here the poet regards the amusement park of his childhood as a lost Eden. Though the scene is apparently unchanged (3), everything now is different. For it is no longer a child who enters the park accompanied by his father but a grown man with a girl, the new object of his love. And, as line 4 remarks, the two of them form part of the total human condition of separateness and loneliness.

(5) *The horizon of the sea loses its boats*— (6) *Hard to keep (hold onto) anything now.* (7) *Behind the hill the soldiers waited.* (8) *How much in need of mercy are we.* (9) *The two of us together and each of us alone.*

Though the scene is that of the lost Eden of his childhood, its meaning has been totally altered. The boats disappearing beyond the horizon not only suggest loss and transitoriness but, as line 7 makes clear, they are sailing off to war. And some of the erstwhile children have turned into soldiers, adults who lie in ambush and who kill. To many readers familiar with the smallness of the territory of Israel, the first three lines of this stanza may convey the sense of an entire country transformed (from sea and coastal plains to hills of the border) into a state of war.

(10) *The moon is sawing the clouds in two*— (11) *Come, let's go out to a joust of love.* (12) *Only the two of us will [make] love between (before) the two [armed] camps.* (13) *Perhaps it is still possible to change everything.* (14) *The two of us together and each of us alone.*

Though everything, even the sky, is striving toward divisiveness, perhaps an act of love, publicly performed, may yet redeem the world: "change everything" (*hakól leṣanót*). The phrase *ahavát beynáyim*—"joust of love" is an invention of Amihai's based on *milḥémet beynáyim* meaning simply "duel" or "joust." But it has an echo of *iṣ beynáyim* with its two meanings: "champion" and "go-between." Hence, the "joust of love" implies that the two lovers are champions whose individual "war" will obviate the need for a general armed struggle. They are also conciliators, intermediaries, and their love the arbitrating act that may bring about peace. And yet the word *uláy* ("perhaps," 13) dominates the stanza.

Even the affirmation that follows is essentially a cry. The poet asks little more of his love than help to endure. He knows, though he pretends for a moment that it has performed its transforming miracle, that it will not redeem. (15) *My love, it would seem, has changed me* (16) *As the salt sea [is changed] into the sweet drops of the first rains.* (17) *I am brought to you slowly and [I] fall.* (18) *Receive (accept) me. We have no redeeming angel.* (19) *Because the two of us are together. Each of us is alone.*

If the opening affirmation—"My love apparently has changed me"—is clearly qualified by the third word, the transforming miracle as a whole has inherent limitations as well. For in a world without transcendence, how can two people save themselves from all that surrounds and engulfs them, capable as they are of no more than personal, individual action? Line 17 tells us that the speaker has been "brought" to his beloved and that he "falls." The latter verb describes more than the human body in its movement toward an embrace. It tells also of a descent from a world of faith in which angels might have redeemed (18) two lovers and a world in strife.

The change in punctuation of the refrain deepens the impact of the irony, as the two half-sentences—"the two of us together, each of us alone"—divide. The first half declares (it is a complete statement only grammatically) that the lovers are together; but an isolated and chilling counterstatement follows: "Each of us is alone."

— ROBERT FRIEND

Yehuda Amihai

HALF OF THE PEOPLE IN THE WORLD

MAḤATSÍT HAANAṢÍM BAOLÁM · מַחֲצִית הָאֲנָשִׁים בָּעוֹלָם

In this unrimed free-verse poem, the speaker is once again a private individual confronting the "adversary." This is now seen to be the entire public world of ceaseless endeavor, a world essentially destructive, which achieves its maximum of destructiveness in the form of war. "Half of the People in the World" love the other half, but the obverse side of this collective love is hate. Where, then, can the private person go in hope of finding a viable place between these two halves that so perfectly complement each other (29)? The poem is a pervasive questioning, interwoven with complex references whose totality creates the poet's answer.

(1) *Half of the people in the world* (2) *Love the other half.* (3) *Half of the people* (4) *Hate the other half.* (5) *Must I because of these [people] and those [people]* (6) *Go and wander and change unceasingly,* (7) *Like rain in its cycle, and sleep among the rocks,* (8) *And be rough like olive trunks,* (9) *And hear the moon barking over (at) me,* (10) *And camouflage my love with worries,* (11) *And sprout like frightened grass between the railroad tracks,* (12) *And live in the earth like a mole,* (13) *And be with roots and not with branches,* (14) *And not with my cheek upon the cheek of angels,* (15) *And love in the first cave,* (16) *And marry my wife under a canopy* (17) *Of beams which hold up (support) the earth,* (18) *And act out (play) my death, always* (19-20) *To the last breath and the last words and without understanding,* (21) *And add to [*lit. *make for* or *in] my house flagpoles above* (22) *And a (bomb) shelter below. . .*

Must the individual, to save himself, suffer a reduction of his humanity if he is to exist at all—much as the grass manages to survive miserably between railroad tracks (11)? Must he live an underground existence cut off from the life of the spirit (12, 14)? Must he flee into the wilderness?— (22) . . . *And go forth on roads* (23) *Made only for returning and undergo (pass)* (24) *All the terrible stations—* (25) *Cat, stick, fire, water, (ritual) slaughterer,* (26) *Between the kid and the angel of death:*

The traditional canopy under which the Jewish marriage ceremony is performed (16) is referred to in the same breath with the posts of an air-raid shelter. And the "terrible stations" (24) suggest that individual suffering at the hands of the enemy world is the inescapable condition of human existence. The agent or agency may change in the course of history—crucifixion, animal ritual slaughter—but the important fact is its continuity.

Everyone must now endure the fourteen stages of the Passion or suffer one of the deaths described in another tradition—the one, for example, commemorated in the Aramaic children's song that ends the Passover service: "Then came the most Holy, blessed be He, and slew the angel of death, who had slain the slaughterer, who had slaughtered the ox, which had drunk the water, which had extinguished the fire, which had burnt the stick, which had beaten the dog, which had bitten the cat, which had

מַחֲצִית הָאֲנָשִׁים בָּעוֹלָם	Maḥatsít haanaṣím baolám
אוֹהֲבִים אֶת הַמַּחֲצִית הַשְּׁנִיָּה,	Ohavím et hamaḥatsít haṣniyá,
מַחֲצִית הָאֲנָשִׁים	Maḥatsít haanaṣím
שׂוֹנְאִים אֶת הַשְּׁנִיָּה,	Son'ím et haṣniyá,
הַאִם בִּגְלַל אֵלֶּה וְאֵלֶּה עָלַי	Haím biglál éyle veéyle aláy
לָלֶכֶת וְלִנְדֹּד וּלְהִשְׁתַּנּוֹת בְּלִי הֶרֶף,	Laléḥet velindód ulehiṣtanót blí héref,
כְּגֶשֶׁם בַּמַּחֲזוֹר, וְלִישׁוֹן בֵּין סְלָעִים,	Kagéṣem bamaḥzór, veliṣón beyn slaím,
וְלִהְיוֹת מְחֻסְפָּס כְּגִזְעֵי זֵיתִים,	Velihiyót meḥuspás kegiz'éy zeytím,
וְלִשְׁמֹעַ אֶת הַיָּרֵחַ נוֹבֵחַ עָלַי,	Veliṣmóa et hayaréaḥ novéaḥ aláy,
וּלְהַסְווֹת אֶת אַהֲבָתִי בִּדְאָגוֹת,	Ulehasvót et ahavatí bid'agót,
וְלִצְמֹחַ כְּעֵשֶׂב הָרָהוּי בֵּין פַּסֵּי הָרַכֶּבֶת,	Velitsmóaḥ kaésev harahúy beyn paséy
וְלָגוּר בָּאֲדָמָה כַּחֲפַרְפֶּרֶת,	Velagúr baadamá kaḥafarpéret, [harakévet,
וְלִהְיוֹת עִם שָׁרָשִׁים וְלֹא עִם עֲנָפִים,	Velihiyót im ṣoraṣím veló im anafím,
וְלֹא לֶחְיִי עַל לְחִי מַלְאָכִים,	Veló leḥyí al leḥi mal'aḥím,
וְלֶאֱהֹב בַּמְּעָרָה הָרִאשׁוֹנָה	Veleehóv bameará hariṣoná
וְלָשֵׂאת אֶת אִשְׁתִּי תַּחַת חֻפַּת	Velasét et iṣtí táḥat ḥupát
הַקּוֹרוֹת הַנּוֹשְׂאוֹת אֲדָמָה,	Hakorót hanos'ót adamá,
וּלְשַׂחֵק אֶת מוֹתִי, תָּמִיד	Ulesaḥék et motí, tamíd
עַד הַנְּשִׁימָה הָאַחֲרוֹנָה וְהַמִּלִּים	Ad hanṣimá haaḥaroná vehamilím
הָאַחֲרוֹנוֹת וּבְלִי לְהָבִין,	Haaḥaronót uvlí lehavín,
וְלַעֲשׂוֹת בְּבֵיתִי עַמּוּדֵי דְּגָלִים לְמַעְלָה	Velaasót beveytí amudéy dgalím lemála
וּמִקְלָט לְמַטָּה. וְלָצֵאת בַּדְּרָכִים	Umiklát lemáta. Velatsét badraḥím
הָעֲשׂוּיוֹת רַק לְשִׁיבָה וְלַעֲבֹר	Haasuyót rak leṣivá velaavór
אֶת כָּל הַתַּחֲנוֹת הַנּוֹרָאוֹת —	Et kol hataḥanót hanoraót—
חָתוּל, מַקֵּל, אֵשׁ, מַיִם, שׁוֹחֵט,	Ḥatúl, makél, eṣ, máyim, ṣoḥét,
בֵּין הַגְּדִי וּבֵין מַלְאַךְ־הַמָּוֶת?	Beyn hagdí uvéyn mal'áḥ-hamávet?
מַחֲצִית הָאֲנָשִׁים אוֹהֲבִים,	Maḥatsít haanaṣím ohavím,
מַחֲצִיתָם שׂוֹנְאִים.	Maḥatsitám son'ím.
וְהֵיכָן מְקוֹמִי בֵּין הַמַּחֲצִיּוֹת הַמֻּתְאָמוֹת כָּל־כָּךְ,	Veheyḥán mekomí beyn hamaḥatsiyót
	[hamot'amót kol-káḥ,

devoured the kid, which my father bought for two *zuzím* ("tuppence"): *ḥad gadyá, ḥad gadyá* ("only one kid, only one kid").

The enemy world bears down upon the individual with relentless power, forcing him almost unconsciously to resort to his own war (as "camouflage" indicates in line 10); driving him back into the caves of Stone Age existence (15), until he resembles an automaton blindly obeying the rules of some game or an actor in a meaningless play (18 ff.).

(27) *Half of the people love,* (28) *Half of them hate.* (29) *And where is my place between the halves that are so suited* [lit. *fitted*] *(to each*

וְדֶרֶךְ אֵיזֶה סֶדֶק אֶרְאֶה אֶת	Vedéreḥ éyze sédek er'é et
הַשִּׁכּוּנִים הַלְּבָנִים שֶׁל חֲלוֹמוֹתַי,	Haṣikuním halvaním ṣel ḥalomotáy,
וְאֶת הָרָצִים הַיְחֵפִים עַל הַחוֹלוֹת	Veét haratsím hayeḥefím al haḥolót
אוֹ לְפָחוֹת אֶת נִפְנוּף	O lefaḥót et nifnúf
מִטְפַּחַת הַנַּעֲרָה, לְיַד הַתֵּל?	Mitpáḥat hanaará, leyád hatél?

other), (30) *And through what crack shall I see* (31) *The white housing projects of my dreams,* (32) *And the barefoot runners on the sands* (33) *Or at least the waving* (34) *Of a young girl's handkerchief, beside the mound?*

There is some tender mockery in the fact that the beleaguered young man of the poem (with no doubt the socialist leanings of Amihai, the young soldier, and of his contemporaries) can conceive of no more ideal dwelling place than a housing project. Even as the speaker imagines his ideal world (30 ff.) in which he is in possession at last of his own peaceful home and of a body able to express itself freely in love, the vision is compromised. For if the young girl waves to him, she is doing so from "beside the mound"—the *tel* of the archaeologist, who values these mounds (found all over the countryside of Israel) because they contain the artifacts and the shards of vanished civilizations—constant reminders of another destructiveness: time's. And yet, both time and war recede as the speaker sees the girl standing there, the embodiment of the love that can, if only for a fleeting moment, redeem.

— ROBERT FRIEND

Yehuda Amihai

[MY FATHER · AVÍ · אָבִי]

This sonnet, the first in a cycle "We Loved Here," from Amihai's first volume, *Now and in Other Days* (1955), combines two of the poet's pervasive subjects: his father and war. The poem begins with the experience of the older man as a German soldier in World War I. It ends with a sudden reference to the poet's own experiences as a Lance Corporal in the British Army in World War II and as a member of the Infantry in the Israeli War of Independence.

(1) *My father was (took part) four years in their war,* (2) *And he didn't hate his enemies or love [them].* (3) *But I know that already there [on the battlefield]* (4) *He was building (forming) me daily out of his tranquillities*

(5) *So few, which he had gleaned (gathered)* (6) *Between the bombs and smoke,* (7) *And [which he] put into his ragged knapsack* (8) *With the leftovers of his mother's hardening cake.*

(9) *And with his eyes he gathered (collected) the nameless dead,* (10) *The many dead he gathered for my sake,* (11) *So that I should know them with (in) his glances and love them*

(12) *And not die like them in terror . . .* (13) *He filled his eyes with them and he erred:* (14) *I depart for all my wars.*

The attitude of the son towards his father is one of veneration and tenderness. He is deeply moved by his father's having preserved, in the midst of "the bombs and smoke" (6), his inner peace; by his devotion

אָבִי הָיָה אַרְבַּע שָׁנִים בְּמִלְחַמְתָּם,		Aví hayá arbá ṣaním bemilḥamtám,
וְלֹא שָׂנֵא אוֹיְבָיו וְלֹא אָהַב.		Veló sané oyváv veló aháv.
אֲבָל אֲנִי יוֹדֵעַ, כִּי כְּבָר שָׁם		Avál aní yodéa, ki kvar ṣam
בָּנָה אוֹתִי יוֹם־יוֹם מִשַּׁלְווֹתָיו	4	Baná otí yom-yóm miṣalvotáv
הַמְּעָטוֹת כָּל־כָּךְ, אֲשֶׁר לָקַט		Hamuatót kol-káḥ, aṣér lakát
אוֹתָן בֵּין פְּצָצוֹת וּבֵין עָשָׁן,		Otán beyn ptsatsót uvéyn aṣán,
וְשָׂם אוֹתָן בְּתַרְמִילוֹ הַמְּמֻרְטָט		Vesám otán betarmiló hamemurtát
עִם שְׁאֵרִית עֻגַת־אִמּוֹ הַמִּתְקַשָּׁה.	8	Im ṣeerít ugát-imó hamitkaṣá.
וּבְעֵינָיו אָסַף מֵתִים בְּלִי שֵׁם,		Uveeynáv asáf meytím bli ṣem,
מֵתִים רַבִּים אָסַף לְמַעֲנִי,		Meytím rabím asáf lemaaní,
שֶׁאַכִּירֵם בְּמַבָּטָיו וְאוֹהֲבֵם	11	Ṣeakirém bemabatáv veohavém
וְלֹא אָמוּת כְּמוֹהֶם בַּזְּוָעָה...		Veló amút kmohém bazvaá . . .
הוּא מִלֵּא עֵינָיו בָּהֶם וְהוּא טָעָה:	13	Hu milé eynáv bahém vehú taá:
אֶל כָּל מִלְחֲמוֹתַי יוֹצֵא אֲנִי.		El kol milḥamotáy yotsé aní.

in gathering with his eyes "the nameless dead" (9) for his son's sake. For the father hoped to transmit this truth to defeat terror; that all men, whether they wear the "names" of friend or foe, or whether they are anonymous (not only without a name but also without a national label), are to be loved. But neither this wisdom nor his tranquillities can avail the son, for they were the fruit of a war accurately described as "theirs." However, such events as the Nazi holocaust have intervened, bringing with them the necessity to fight wars for spiritual as well as for physical survival. The son has no alternative but to go out to fight his war, rejecting the father's "truth" and his tranquillities, which were—it must be noted—put into the knapsack "with the leftovers" of the "mother's hardening cake" (8). By the time the son has inherited them, they have—like the cake—grown stale—poor crumbs that cannot nourish, though prepared with loving care.

In poem after poem in his early work, Amihai writes about his father; and the poet himself has suggested much of the cause. When at the age of fifteen he ceased to believe in a deity, he felt overcome by a complex sense of guilt, for this was more than a rejection only of God. It was a betrayal also of the father he loved—and there was yet another "father" to whom he was proving unfaithful: the Jewish people, which had kept itself alive through the centuries by its faith. If the feelings of guilt persist, Amihai has sought in his poetry to fill the void created by his threefold rejection with endless references to Him and to His Book and to traditional Jewish ceremonies and customs. In the sonnet above, however, there are few such specific allusions. The father seems rather the integral symbol rising out of the actions of a living man.

The sonnet is Shakespearian in the octet but not in the sestet (riming *aba ccb*). Amihai takes greater freedom with meter (lines 1, 7, 11 are hexameters) and with rime (lines 6 and 8 rime assonantly). The straightforward syntax, everyday vocabulary, and occasional enjambments (3-4, 4-5, 5-6) contribute to the effect of ease and informality not usually found in this strict poetic form.

— ROBERT FRIEND

T. Carmi

TO THE POMEGRANATE · EL HARIMÓN · אֶל הָרִמּוֹן

לֵךְ, לֵךְ מִכָּאן.	Leḥ, leḥ mikán.
לֵךְ אֶל עֵינַיִם אֲחֵרוֹת.	Leḥ el eynáyim aḥerót.
אֲנִי כְּבָר כָּתַבְתִּי עָלֶיךָ אֶתְמוֹל.	Aní kvar katávti aléḥa etmól.
אָמַרְתִּי יָרֹק	Amárti yarók
לַעֲנָפֶיךָ הַקְּדִים בָּרוּחַ	Laanaféḥa hakadím barúaḥ
וְאָדֹם אָדֹם אָדֹם	Veadóm adóm adóm
לְאֶגְלֵי פֶּרְיְךָ.	Leegléy peryeḥá.
קָרָאתִי אוֹר לְשָׁרְשְׁךָ	Karáti or leṣorṣeḥá
הַלַּח וְהָאָפֵל וְהָעִקֵּשׁ.	Haláḥ vehaafél vehaikéṣ.
עַכְשָׁו אֵינְךָ.	Aḥṣáv eynḥá.
עַכְשָׁו אַתָּה מַסְתִּיר לִי אֶת הַיּוֹם	Aḥṣáv atá mastír li et hayóm
וְהַיָּרֵחַ שֶׁעוֹד לֹא עָלָה.	Vehayaréaḥ ṣeód lo alá.
בּוֹאִי,	Bói,
(כָּתַבְתִּי עָלַיִךְ שִׁלְשׁוֹם	(Katávti aláyiḥ ṣilṣóm
וְזִכְרֵךְ הַצָּעִיר	Veziḥréḥ hatsaír
מְלַהֵט אֶת יָדַי כְּסִרְפָּד)	Melahét et yadáy kesirpád)
בּוֹאִי וְתִרְאִי אֶת הָרִמּוֹן הַמְשֻׁנֶּה:	Bói vetir'í et harimón hameṣuné:
דָּמוֹ בְּנַפְשִׁי, בְּרֹאשִׁי, בְּיָדַי,	Damó benafṣí, beroṣí, beyadáy,
וְהוּא עוֹדֶנּוּ שָׁתוּל בִּמְקוֹמוֹ!	Vehú odénu ṣatúl bimkomó!

Born in the City of New York in 1925, Carmi was brought up in one of a small number of families in America that used Hebrew as the spoken language of the home, so that his Hebrew preceded his English. For the first three years of his schooling, his family had lived in Palestine. The years following were spent in New York. The year preceding his settlement in Israel in 1947, Carmi worked with Jewish war-orphans in France, an experience recorded in his second book, *There Are No Black Flowers* (1953), a series of dramatic monologues. His experiences on the Jerusalem front during the War of Independence are the subject of many of the poems in his first book, *Blemish and Dream* (1951).

"To the Pomegranate" (from *The Brass Serpent*, 1961) is written in the person of the poet. He is ordering the objects of his world, arranging them by command according to the needs of his poetry and, more important, of his personal bias. The poem, then, is about poetry, not in the broad manner of

Wallace Stevens (whom Carmi has translated) but in a more private and active sense. The poem has even a time—it is a poem by daylight—and the time in part dictates the mood and the movement of the line:

(1) *Go away, go away from here.* (2) *Go to other eyes.* (3) *I already wrote about you yesterday.*

(4) *I said green* (5) *To your branches bowing in the wind* (6) *And red red red* (7) *To the drops of your fruit.* (8) *I cried light to (I released into the light) your root,* (9) *The moist and dark and stubborn.*

(10) *Now you are not [you don't exist].* (11) *Now you block [my view of] the day from me* (12) *And [of] the moon that hasn't yet risen.*

(13) *Come!* (14) *(I wrote about you* [the feminine pronoun] *the day before yesterday,* (15) *And your young memory* (16) *Inflames my hands like nettle.)* (17) *Come and see the strange (odd) pomegranate:* (18) *His blood [is] in my soul, on [in] my head, on [in] my hands* (19) *And still he is emplanted in his place.*

The poet orders the tree away (1-3) much as Donne, in "The Sunne Rising," commands the sun ". . . goe chide/ Late schoole boyes, and sowre prentices,/ Goe tell Court-huntsmen" etc. The opening line carries the force of "Scram!"; the poet has already dealt with the pomegranate—as far as he is concerned, he has done with it. Once having had his say, it would be best if the tree would actually vanish, leaving behind only the fullness of his statement.

"I said green" (4) and "I cried light" (8) are parallel constructions in the Hebrew and there is a play on the idiom *karáti dror* ("I freed"), which becomes *karáti or* ("I released into the light"), thus suggesting both meanings (8). It is this reading that makes possible the wishful formula "Now you are not" (10). For the poet as creator-magician should ideally have such absolute powers over his creation.

In line 6, the threefold repetition *adóm adóm adóm* ("red red red") echoes the praise of the seraphim in the heavenly spheres: *kadóṣ, kadóṣ, kadóṣ* ("Holy, holy, holy is the Lord of Hosts") of the Hebrew Prayerbook. "To the drops of your fruit" (7), however, is Carmi's own turn of phrase. The Hebrew *égel* ("drop") is generally used in describing the dew.

If in the opening stanzas the poet-as-mover is emphasized, the last two stanzas insist upon the stubborn autonomy of the object. *Aḥṣáv eynḥá* (9): "Now you don't exist" for me any more, declares the speaker (10), which is true enough for him in his role as poet. Nevertheless, he goes on, you are obstructing my view of the day with your insistence upon yourself as an object, so much so that I cannot even see the moon that hasn't yet risen (12).

With the last stanza, "Go!" (twice repeated in the first two lines) changes to "Come," and the tree is replaced, swiftly and without warning, by the parenthetical lines (14-16) introducing the girl. She in her own way is also something of a problem, with her gentle insistence by which her presence demands to be recognized (the mild irritant of nettle, 16). With the last lines, she is invited to look at the tree, the "odd pomegranate" (17), though it might well have been the other way around: the tree could have been called to witness the equally perplexing uniqueness of the girl, whose "young memory" burns and stings.

"His blood" (18) not only is literal for the pomegranate fruit but also initiates a series of Hebrew idioms meaning "his blood endangers my life, I am responsible for his blood and shall pay the penalty," and "the deed is mine." However, the literal sense of the first—"his blood is in my soul" (which echoes the biblical "for the blood is the soul") —clearly implies: the object is perceived so fully that its life-force now flows also in the soul and in the body of the poet. And so, in one sense, the poem might be read as a tribute to the stubborn immovability of the tree (19), to the irreducibility of the object.

A word should be said about the confident and natural musical line that Carmi has developed from simple colloquial phrases. This use of colloquialism is built upon the peculiar pace and movement of spoken Hebrew, so that the phrases take their place as lyrical units. A reader with a knowledge of spoken Hebrew would, for example, feel the quickening pace of *adóm adóm adóm* (6) and the pauses that follow each of the three adjectives at the end of line 9: *haláḥ, vehaafél, vehaikéṣ*. This rhythmical insistence, this adherence to the native qualities of Hebrew, distinguish Carmi's poems from those in which colloquialism and the homely or contemporary object is used as flat area.

— HAROLD SCHIMMEL

T. Carmi

SHE IS ASLEEP · HI YEṢEYNÁ · הִיא יְשֵׁנָה

הִיא יְשֵׁנָה; אֲבָל יָדָהּ עֵרָה		Hi yeṣeyná; avál yadá eyrá
יוֹתֵר מִכַּף־יָדוֹ שֶׁל הַמְנַתֵּחַ		Yotér mikáf-yadó ṣel hamnatéaḥ
לָרוּחַ וְלַדֹּפֶק וְלָרֵיחַ,	3	Larúaḥ veladófek velaréaḥ,
לְרַחֵשׁ הַקִּינָה הַמְּסֻתָּרָה.		Leráḥaṣ hakiná hamsutará.
הִיא יְשֵׁנָה; אֲבָל אָזְנָהּ פְּקוּחָה		Hi yeṣeyná; avál ozná pkuḥá
לְקִישׁ מַתֶּכֶת קְרִירָה וְנִיד		Lekíṣ matéḥet krirá veníd
עַפְעַף כָּבֵד. הִיא עֲרוּכָה תָּמִיד	7	Af'áf kavéd. Hi aruḥá tamíd
לְדוּמִיַּת־פִּתְאֹם וְלַמְּבוּכָה.		Ledumiyát-pit'óm velamvuḥá.
הִיא יְשֵׁנָה; אֲבָל בְּךָ עֵינָהּ,		Hi yeṣeyná; avál beḥá eyná,
בְּפַחַז הָאָבִיב וּבַשַּׁלֶּכֶת,		Befáḥaz haavív uvaṣaléḥet,
בַּמֵּת הַבָּא, וּבְנִשְׁמַת־כָּל־חַי...	11	Bamét habá, uveniṣmát-kol-ḥay...
שָׁלוֹם לַחֲלוֹמָהּ, הִיא יְשֵׁנָה.		Ṣalóm laḥalomá. Hi yeṣeyná.
אֲבָל יָדָהּ הָאֱמוּנָה חוֹתֶכֶת		Avál yadá haemuná ḥotéḥet
עַד בּוֹא הַשֶּׁמֶשׁ בַּבָּשָׂר הַחַי.	14	Ad bo haṣémeṣ babasár haḥáy.

The sonnet "She Is Asleep" (from *The Last Sea*, 1958) is quite regular in form and presentation. The first line of each quatrain repeats the haunting *hi yeṣeyná; avál* ("she is asleep; but . . .") and a terse couplet clinches the controlled, determined tone without dissolving any of the poem's strangeness:

(1) *She is asleep; but her hand is awake* (2) *More than a surgeon's palm* (3) *To breath, to*

pulse and odor, (4) *To the whisper of the hidden dirge.*

(5) *She is asleep; but her ear is alert (open)* (6) *To the clink of cold metal and the quiver* (7) *Of a heavy eyelid. She is prepared always* (8) *For the sudden silence and confusion.*

(9) *She is asleep; but her eye is on [in]* YOU, (10) *On the recklessness of spring and on the leaf-fall,* (11) *On the death* [lit. *dead man*] *to come, and on the breath of every living creature . . .* (12) *Peace to her dream. She is asleep.*

(13) *But her skilled hand cuts* (14) *Till sundown in the living flesh.*

In the opening line the willful distortion of a well-known verse from "The Song of Songs" (5:2)—"I am asleep and my heart is awake"—at once alerts the reader that this is no ordinary lover's aubade. The emergence in the next line of "the surgeon" followed by the word "odor" introduces a harsh tone, which is insisted upon by the rime *hamnatéaḥ-réaḥ* ("surgeon-odor"). This sinister operating-room context is steadily enforced—both musically and visually—as the poem progresses from "the hidden dirge" (4) to "the clink of cold metal and the quiver of a heavy eyelid" (6-7), and finally to "death" (11), and the stark recognition of the closing couplet.

Hebrew has the poetic advantage of being rich in delicately accurate onomatopoetic words. *Lekíṣ matéḥet krirá* ("to the clink of cold metal," 6) is, appropriately, hard-edged in Hebrew; the battery of strong accents breaks the regular musical pattern. In 7, the dead-stop *d* sound of the monosyllable *nid* ("quiver") is repeated in *kavéd* ("heavy") and *tamíd* ("always"). The internal rime *aruḥá* (7) strengthens the final rime of the second quatrain (*velamvuḥá*). This helps to create a unit of the first two parallel quatrains.

This break in the sonnet (despite the latent third repetition "She is asleep; but") is essential, for the third quatrain introduces direct address: "but her eye is on you"—or, more literally, since the syntax places the stress: "but upon you is her eye." *Beḥá* ("upon you") implies, of course, the speaker himself, involved in his monologue. But it also carries the implication: "and upon you too"—that is, upon all of us.

The woman has powers akin to the uncanny vision of some street beggar, into whose cup (5-6) one drops a coin, with fear and respect for the vigilance of that dark mind. Unmoving, she seems, perhaps because of it, strangely knowledgeable, even to the extent of divining "who will be the next to die" (11). "The breath of every living creature" (11)—an opening phrase of great beauty from a prayer in the Sabbath service—*niṣmát kol ḥay*—is under the watchfulness of her closed eyes. "Peace to her dream" (12) is not said with sweetness; it echoes the Hebrew idiom "Peace to her dust," which is used when speaking of the dead.

The musical pattern of the entire sonnet dictates the closing couplet and it is only with the satisfaction of the two suspended rimes—*ṣaléḥet* (10) and *ḥay* (11) with *ḥotéḥet* (13) and *haḥáy* (14)—that the ending can be complete. The power of the closing couplet lies both in its lyrical conciseness and in its full-circle return to the opening image of the surgeon's hand. What was originally metaphorical and figurative, here becomes pointedly accurate—descriptive of the actual course of a living relationship. The fourth and final *avál* ("but") is made to hang longest, following as it does both the period and the stanza break. It is also the most terrible, the speaker having at last moved to direct and committing statement.

— HAROLD SCHIMMEL

T. Carmi

AWAKENING · YEKITSÁ · יְקִיצָה

בּוֹאִי, הַעֲבִירִי אֶת יָדֵךְ עַל פִּי.
אֲנִי אֵינִי רָגִיל בָּאוֹר הַזֶּה.

עֲטַלֵּפִית אַהֲבָתֵנוּ, סְחוֹר וַאֲפֵלוֹת,
וְלֹא תַחֲטִיא. פָּנַיִךְ מַסְבִּירוֹת לִי
אֶת יָדַי. מָה אָבִין בָּאוֹר?
קוּמִי, הַעֲבִירִי אֶת יָדֵךְ עָלַי.

שְׁנָתִי (מָה הַשָּׁעָה?) חָבְקָה אֶת יַלְדוּתֵךְ.
עֶשֶׂר בֵּין יָם לְלַיְלָה, חֲצוֹת בֵּינִי
לְבֵינֵךְ, שֶׁבַע בֵּין חֲרַכֵּי־הַשַּׁחַר.
הוֹ לֹא, אֵינִי רָגִיל בָּאוֹר הַזֶּה

הַבָּא לִפְקֹחַ אֶת עֵינַי כַּחֲרִירִים
קָרִים. בְּמֹאזְנֵי־הַכַּוֶּנֶת אֶשְׁקֹל
אֶת עִוְרוֹנִי וּפַחַד־עֲפָרֵךְ.
קוּמִי, הַעֲבִירִי בִּי יָדֵךְ.

פָּנִים־אֶל־פָּנִים, הַאִם עוֹד יִהְיוּ לִי?
אֲנִי עָלוּל לִשְׁתֹּק, אוֹ לְדַבֵּר.
בּוֹאִי, הַעֲבִירִי אֶת יָדֵךְ עַל פִּי.
אֲנִי אֵינִי רָגִיל בָּאוֹר הַזֶּה.

Bói, haavíri et yadéḥ al pi.
Aní eyní ragíl baór hazé.

Atalefít ahavaténu, sḥor vaafelót,
Veló taḥatí. Panáyiḥ masbirót li
Et yadáy. Ma avín baór?
Kúmi, haavíri et yadéḥ aláy.

Ṣnatí (ma haṣaá?) ḥavká et yaldutéḥ.
Éser beyn yam leláyla, ḥatsót beyní
Leveynéḥ, ṣéva beyn ḥarakéy-haṣáḥar.
Ho lo, eyní ragíl baór hazé

Habá lifkóaḥ et eynáy kaḥarirím
Karím. Bemoznéy-hakavénet eṣkól
Et ivroní ufáḥad-afaréḥ.
Kúmi, haavíri bi yadéḥ.

Paním-el-paním, haím od yihiyú li?
Aní alúl liṣtók, o ledabér.
Bói, haavíri et yadéḥ al pi.
Ani eyní ragíl baór hazé.

The love-poem, here, is unusual: it is a voice overheard—talk beginning in darkness, and so (for the silence that darkness imposes on animals) almost in whispers.

(1) *Come, touch* [lit *pass*] *your hand across my mouth.* (2) *I'm not accustomed to this light.*

(3) *Bat-like* [*is*] *our love—roundabout and* [*of*] *darknesses*— (4) *And does not miss its aim. Your face explains to me* (5) *My hands. What can I understand by light?* (6) *Come* [lit. *rise*], *pass your hand over me.*

(7) *My sleep (what time is it?) hugged your childhood.* (8) *Ten between sea and night, midnight between me* (9) *And you, seven between the slits of dawn.* (10) *Ah no, I'm not accustomed to this light*

(11) *That comes to pry* [*open*] *my eyes like needle-eyes*— (12) *Cold. In the scales of the gunsights I'll weigh* (13) *My blindness and your clay's fear.* (14) *Come* [lit. *rise*], *pass your hand through me.*

(15) *Face to face, will I still have* [*a face*]*?*

(16) *I may keep silent, or speak.* (17) *Come, pass your hand across my mouth.* (18) *I'm not accustomed to this light.*

The poem is both specifically masculine and specifically romantic. Romantic, in the terrible split between the night-world of the lovers and the world of clearly defined possibilities and impossibilities which full light will impose. And masculine in that the night-time movements of impulse and desire, which "do not miss" (4), are hampered (here, blinded) by the inhibitions of daylight and the different responsibilities it implies. "Face to face" (15), in full light, the speaker doesn't know whether he'll still have a face. In his role of lover, he is only a night-creature; her fear (13) that the coming of daylight will be her end is therefore justified. And whether he will speak or remain silent will not really matter—for both, he knows, are inadequate.

The poem's opening line is borrowed from the *Zohar* passage that describes the visit of Rabbi Hiya to Simeon ben Yohai. Rabbi Hiya's mouth falls as he sees the "curtain of fire"; he drops his eyes and lowers his head. Simeon ben Yohai then directs his son: "Pass your hand across his mouth, for he's not accustomed to this." What may have interested Carmi, in addition to the sound of the Hebrew phrase, is ben Yohai's direction "across his mouth" and not, as would be expected, "his eyes."

By re-setting the phrase in the context of a love-poem, Carmi has further underlined its tactile emphasis. The speaker can understand only by touching (4-5). It is not the woman ("you") that can explain his hands to him but the touch of her face upon his hands (*panáyiḥ*, "your face," 4). His only assurance is the certainty of her touch. And this accounts for his increasingly more urgent requests: that she pass her hand "across" his mouth, "over" him, and finally "through" him (1, 6, 14).

This progression marks the dramatic organization of the lyric. Spoken at the morning hour, it traces the speaker's preoccupation with the coming of the light; the transformations of "across" to "over" and "through" are the stages of his rising terror. Even his sleep (7) is not free of the intruding question: "(What time is it?)". Time becomes the intermediate body that is constantly "between" (*beyn*, *beyní*, *beyn*). "Midnight" (*ḥatsót*, 8) carries the added overtone of *laḥatsót*, "to divide in half," "to cross between" or "through."

The final division of the lovers occurs when the first breaking of the sky at dawn—*ḥarakéy haṣáḥar*, "slits of dawn" (9)—brings also the image of early light streaming through the blinds. The cry *ho lo* ("Ah no," 10) marks his fear of full light. The impetus of the cry is carried over to the next stanza (the only run-on line in the poem), where the image of slits reappears as "cold needle-eyes of gunsights," and in its final transformation (12) as "scales"—the form of a gunsight resembling the balance of scales—*kavénet* ("gunsights") is derived from the verb *kavén* ("to intend" or "to aim"). *Eṣkól* ("I'll weigh," 12) conveys also the sense of "I'll consider" or "think," as the speaker weighs the fact of his blindness-in-light against her dependent fear (*páḥad afaréyḥ*, "the fear of your clay," her fear of becoming dead clay).

In a sense, the whole poem has been an elaboration of the various implications of the opening request. The element central to both the *Zohar* passage and the love-poem is the reassurance implicit in the offered or requested touch. This goes back to Adam's loneliness and the efficacy of Isaac's blessing —"Come near, I pray thee, that I may feel thee, my son..." (Genesis 27:21)—tied to touch.

— HAROLD SCHIMMEL

Ayin Hillel

THE EAGLE · HANÉṢER · הַנֶּשֶׁר

בִּמְלֹאת לִי שִׁבְעִים שְׁנוֹתַי	Bimlót li siv'ím snotáy
וְכָל שְׁעָרַי שְׁלָגִים	Veḥól searáy ṣlagím
אָמַרְתִּי; הִנֵּה יוֹם אֵצֵא לָרְכָסִים וְלַשִּׂיאִים	3 Amárti; hinéy yom etsé larḥasím velasiím
לָבוֹא אֶל מַלְכִּי הַנֶּשֶׁר.	Lavó el malkí hanéṣer.

לַשַּׁחַר אָחַזְתִּי מַקֵּל הַשָּׁקֵד לִסְמֹךְ יְמִינִי וְתִקְווֹתַי	Laṣáḥar aḥázti makél haṣakéd lismóḥ [yeminí vetikvotáy
וָאֶטּוֹשׁ נָשַׁי עִם יְלָדַי וְיֶתֶר מוֹעֲצוֹת רֵעַי	6 Vaetóṣ naṣáy im yeladáy veyéter moatsót [reáy
וָאָבוֹא חוּצוֹת וְחַתְחַתִּים וְאֵשׁ־חֲמָסִים שׁוֹטֵי.	Vaavó ḥutsót veḥatḥatím veéṣ-ḥamasím [ṣotáy.

הִכּוּ קוֹצִים פָּנַי וַעֲרוּצִים כַּפּוֹתַי,	Hikú kotsím panáy vaarutsím kapotáy,
הָלוֹךְ וּבָכֹה נְתִיבוֹתַי	9 Halóḥ uvaḥó netivotáy
עָשִׂיתִי דַּרְכִּי בַּסֶּלַע.	Asíti darkí baséla.
רָאֲתָה מִמָּרוֹם הַשֶּׁמֶשׁ	Raatá mimaróm haṣémeṣ
כּוֹכָבִים מִמְּסִילוֹתָם.	12 Koḥavím mimsilotám.

כִּי מָלֵאתִי שִׁבְעִים שְׁנוֹתַי וְנַפְשִׁי נִבְקְעָה לַנֶּשֶׁר.	Ki maléti siv'ím ṣnotáy venafṣí [nivkeá lanéṣer.

שֻׁסְפוּ מִנְעָלַי בַּדֶּרֶךְ	Ṣusfú min'aláy badéreḥ
אַהֲבוֹתַי כָּבוּ בָּעַרְבַּיִם,	15 Ahavotáy kavú baarbáyim,
מֵיטַב שְׁנוֹתַי וּפְעָלַי רוּגְזוֹת גַּם נִשְׁפּוֹת הַשְּׂחוֹק	Meytáv ṣnotáy ufealáy rugzót gam [niṣpót haṣḥók
כָּלוּ בָּעֵמֶק אַחֲרַי	Kalú baémek aḥaráy
בְּאֵלֶם נִסְכָּם וְחָכְמָתָם.	18 Beélem niskám veḥoḥmatám.
כִּי קָרָא מִמְּרוֹמִים הַנֶּשֶׁר	Ki kará mimromím hanéṣer
וְנַפְשִׁי מָלְאָה!	Venafṣí mal'á!

Born in 1926 in a kibbutz (agricultural collective) in the Valley of Jezreel, Ayin Hillel imbibed its twofold ideal of socialist justice fused with a yearning for national liberation. Like Gury, Hillel spent his youth in "the movement," later serving in the Palmach, the elite revolutionary military organization that bore the brunt of the fighting during Israel's War of Independence. As poets of the "Palmach Generation," they celebrated—"in the first person plural" (see p. 154)—its collectivist and nationalist ideals.

Once the War of Independence had been won, feelings of exaltation gave way to a painful, often desperate, probing of everyday realities. By the mid-fifties, Hebrew poets began to voice the doubts and disillusions besetting an entire generation "on the road back" from the war. In Hillel's first volume (1950) a number of symbols and poems foreshadowed a questioning, pessimistic mood. In "To the Eagle," from his *Niṣrá* (1962), this mood is forcefully expressed.

(1) *When I was filled with my seventy years* (2) *And all my hair, snow [*lit. *hairs, snows]* (3) *I said: this day I shall go out to the ridges and to the peaks* (4) *To come to my king the eagle.*

(5) *At dawn I grasped the almond staff to support my right hand and my hopes* (6) *And I abandoned my wives and my children and the rest of my councils of friends* (7) *And went out into the marketplace (the open) and the pitfalls, and fires of violence whipped me on [*lit. *were my whips].*

(8) *Thorns struck my face and ruts [of earth struck] my feet* (9) *Treading and bewailing [I made] my paths* (10) *I made my way in the rock.* (11) *The sun saw from above,* (12) *The stars from their courses.*

(13) *For I was filled with my seventy years and my soul longed for [*lit. *was split open to] the eagle.*

(14) *My sandals were hacked on the road* (15) *My loves burnt out at twilight,* (16) *My best years and deeds, angers as well as revels of laughter* (17) *Ended (were dispelled) in the valley behind me* (18) *In the muteness of their* [i.e. years' and deeds', etc.] *libation and their wisdom.* (19) *For the eagle had called from on high* (20) *And my soul was filled.*

צָהֳרַיִם עֶרֶב וָלַיִל רַק מַקֵּל הַשָּׁקֵד עִמִּי	21	Tsohoráyim érev valáyil rak [makél haṣakéd imí
צָמֵתִי לְלֶחֶם וּמַיִם, קֹרַע מְעִילִי וּבְשָׂרִי		Tsámti leléḥem umáyim, korá meilí uvsarí
כִּי קָרָא מִמְּרוֹמִים הַנֶּשֶׁר!		Ki kará mimromím hanéṣer!
לַיְלָה הָלְמוּ רַקּוֹתַי	24	Láyla halmú rakotáy
בֹּקֶר נְטָשׁוּנִי חֲיָלֵי כּוֹחַי		Bóker netaṣúni ḥayaléy koḥáy
חֹשֶׁךְ רָץ בָּרָק		Ḥóseḥ rats barák
רְעָמִים חָרְשׁוּ פְּעָמַי	27	Reamím ḥarṣú peamáy
וְעִמִּי רַק מַקֵּל שָׁקֵד		Veimí rak makél ṣakéd
וְהַנֶּשֶׁר עֶלְיוֹן כַּנֵּד.		Vehanéṣer elyón kanéd.
וּבַיּוֹם הַשְּׁבִיעִי בִּזְרוֹחַ שֶׁמֶשׁ	30	Uvayóm haṣvií bizróaḥ ṣémeṣ
בִּגְאוֹת דְּמָמַת עוֹלָם		Big'ót dimemát olám
בָּאתִי;		Báti;
בָּאתִי עָדֶיךָ, הוֹ מַלְכִּי הַנֶּשֶׁר,	33	Báti adéḥa, ho malkí hanéṣer,
לִפּוֹל בָּעוֹרְבִים הַטּוֹרְפִים נִבְלָתֶךָ.		Lipól baorvím hatorfím nivlatéḥa.

(21) *Noon, evening, and night only the almond staff with me* (22) *I hungered for bread and [thirsted] for water, my coat and my flesh were torn* (23) *For the eagle had called from on high!*

(24) *At night my temples pounded* (25) *At morning the troops of my strength abandoned me* (26) *Lightning ran (in) darkness* (27) *Thunders plowed my steps* (28) *And only the almond staff with me* (29) *And the eagle supreme as a column.*

(30) *And on the seventh day when the sun shone* (31) *As the world's silence swelled* (32) *I came;* (33) *I came unto you, O my king the eagle,* (34) *To fall among the ravens devouring your corpse.*

European influences in Hillel's writings are minimal. He rarely follows their verse forms or metrical devices, turning instead to biblical prosody. Lyrical economy is sacrified for rhythmic and dramatic effect, verbal precision for sweep of phrase. His obsession with biblical diction often expresses itself in his use of archaic or obsolescent words.

Whatever European flavor his poetry possesses comes indirectly—through the medium of Hebrew literature. The exotic metaphors and synesthesia in his early work in all likelihood came out of his encounter with Alterman rather than with Continental modernism. His declamatory recitative, Whitmanesque though it often sounds, probably grew out of his reading of Uri Zvi Greenberg.

Israeli poets often find their link to the soil and their national past in the Hebrew Bible, but a "de-theologized" Bible read as the nation's literary masterpiece. In the poem before us Hillel not only draws on biblical themes, symbols, and diction but he also makes use of biblical versification. As pointed out in the Note on Prosody (p. 211), such verse embodies two main structural elements. First, the line is usually divided into two half-lines, one of which parallels or contrasts with the phrasing of the other. Second, the rhythmic pattern consists of a "beat" falling within each half-line upon the significant words only. Hillel follows these patterns skillfully (note, for example, line 2, with its parallel half-lines of three "beats" each).

Hillel also produces a drum-like effect in the terminal line of the stanza by reducing the number of stresses (4, 12, 20, 23), clashing a rime (28-29), introducing assonance (6-7), or using a feminine ending (4, 13, 23, 34). Note also the heavy emphasis on *hanéṣer* (4, 23), *ṣnotáy* (7), *haséla* (10), *mimsilotám* (12), *mal'á* (20), *kanéd* (29). Though the rimes make no discernible scheme, the frequently repeated *ay* rime (1, 5, 6, 7, 8, 9, 17, 24, 25, 27) with its doleful effect reverberates throughout the poem.

If the biblical cadences reinforced by the archaic texture of the diction give the poem a timeless, epic dimension, its austere symbolism also accords with its ancient setting. The prophet-pilgrim sets out in conquest of his ideal, the eagle, grasping the almond staff, a symbol of eternal hope as well as of persistence (Jeremiah 1:11-12); he climbs to the hills and is mercilessly strafed by the elements (26-27). The pilgrimage is begun in old age, after the speaker has been disillusioned with the ordinary experiences of life (17). But the quest is not the result of voluntary decision; the pilgrim is impelled by some inner force to give up the security of the valley and to ascend the hills (23). The journey ends on the seventh day, the Sabbath, the day of fulfilment—which turns out to be the day of failure.

Having attained his goal, the pilgrim finds that the eagle—the ideal that had sustained him in the valley, compelled him to abandon family and friends (6), and to endure hunger, pain, and loss of strength—is a corpse. He "falls among the crows" who are devouring the dead eagle, but not to join them in desecration. His fall is the final fall of despair, death, obliteration. There is no suggestion that he might find nourishment of any kind in the lifeless remnants of what was once his overpowering ideal.

— EZRA SPICEHANDLER

Dan Pagis

THE LOG BOOK · YOMÁN HAṢÁYIT · יוֹמַן הַשַּׁיִט

בְּעוֹד הָרוּחַ שֶׁעַל פְּנֵי הַמַּיִם חוֹזֶרֶת
לְמִי שֶׁנְּתָנָהּ וְהַדֶּגֶל
נִשְׁמָט מֵרֹאשׁ הַסְּפִינָה, וּמֶרֶד
עָמוּם בְּבִטְנָהּ מְאַיֵּם — יָדַעְנוּ לִבְסוֹף:
הַמַּפּוֹת שִׁקְּרוּ, וּקְלִילִים כְּשַׁעַם
נִלְכַּדְנוּ בְּרִשְׁתָּן וְצַפְנוּ
כְּאִלּוּ נָסַעְנוּ.
אֵיךְ נִקְלַעְנוּ לְאִי הַמַּטְמוֹן? מִן הָעֹמֶק עוֹלוֹת
פְּנִינֵי הָאֲוִיר הַיָּפוֹת כְּמוֹ שֶׁל טוֹבֵעַ
וּבְתֵבַת גֻּלְגֹּלֶת פְּתוּחָה מִתְגַּלִּים
יַהֲלוֹמֵי הַמֶּלַח. לֹא נוֹתַר לָנוּ אֶלָּא
לִכְרוֹעַ עַל פְּנֵי הַסִּפּוּן וּלְהוֹדוֹת
לְשָׁמַיִם וּלְיָם מְנֻמְנָם שֶׁנָּתְנוּ לָנוּ כֹּחַ:

הֵן אָנוּ, שֶׁכְּלָל לֹא הִפְלַגְנוּ, הִגַּעְנוּ.
יֵשׁ לַעֲגוֹן וְלִשְׁכֹּחַ.

Beód harúaḥ ṣeál pney hamáyim ḥozéret
Lemí ṣentaná vehadégel
Niṣmát meróṣ hasfiná, uméred
Amúm bevitná meayém—yadánu livsóf:
Hamapót ṣikrú, uklilím keṣáam
Nilkádnu beriṣtán vetsáfnu
Keílu nasánu.
Eyḥ niklánu leí hamatmón ? Min haómek olót
Pniney haavír hayafót kemó ṣel tovéa
Uvteyvát gulgólet ptuḥá mitgalím
Yahalomey hamélaḥ. Lo notár lánu éla
Liḥróa al pney hasipún ulhodót
Leṣamáyim uleyám menumnám ṣenatnú
[lánu kóaḥ:

Hen ánu, ṣeklál lo hiflágnu, higánu.
Yeṣ laagón veliṣkóaḥ.

Dan Pagis was born in Bukovina in 1930 and grew up in a German-speaking environment. During the Second World War he was interned for several years in a Ukranian concentration camp, from which he escaped in 1944. Two years later he came to Israel. He now teaches Medieval Hebrew Literature at the Hebrew University in Jerusalem.

His first volume of verse, *Ṣeón Hatsél* (*Shadow Dial*, 1959), consisted in the main of short, tightly knit poems, which often concentrate upon a single image. The poems in *Late Leisure* (1964) are broader in scope and much freer in structure. Our selection, which appears in this volume, is part of a sequence entitled "Five Conclusions"—meditations on unsentimental leave-takings ("Epilogue to Robinson Crusoe," "Bill Quits the Theatre," etc.).

"The Log Book," with its ironic title, is built upon two basic symbols which suggest a variety of literary associations as well as reminiscences of adventure stories: the first (lines 1-7) is a ship of the dead which floats pilotless in the sea; the second (8-14), a treasure island, suddenly and unexpectedly discovered. There is no ostensible narrative link between the two sections; they even seem at first to contradict each other. But this apparent impression dissolves once we realize that the entire poem is built on a series of negations in which each new statement cancels the very existence of the one that preceded it.

(1) *While the wind upon the face of the waters*

was returning (2) *To him who had given it and the flag* (3) *Drooped from the topmast* [lit. *head*] *of the ship, and mutiny,* (4) *Muted, threatened in her belly—we knew at last:* (5) *The maps had lied, and weightless as cork* (6) *We were trapped in their net and were floating* (7) *As though we had traveled.*

The speaker, one of the passengers, has no identifiable characteristics; indeed his lack of individuality reinforces the impression that he incarnates the spirit of the ship and her voyage. He records the dangers facing the ship, the first of which was "external": the wind (*rúaḥ*, which also means "spirit, breath of life") has been removed at the command of the higher power that had released it (2). The reader may recognize the obvious allusion to Ecclesiastes 12:7 (". . . and the spirit [*rúaḥ*] shall return unto God who gave it") which, in its biblical context, is part of an elaborate description of death. The second danger to the becalmed ship is "internal" and its agency is human: the muted rumble of a mutiny (3-4) in the hold, which has not yet erupted.

All these detailed portents of catastrophe—dying wind, drooping flag, repressed mutiny—"at last" give rise to the awareness that no voyage has really taken place. The helpless voyagers were deluded by false maps (5) and snared in their "nets"—an image which also calls to mind the grid patterns of a map. From the very outset, then, the sailing was only imagined—"as if we had traveled" (7). The sense of expectancy generated by this new awareness is further heightened by the surprising question that introduces the second section:

(8) *How did we happen on to the treasure island? From the depths ascend* (9) *The beautiful pearls of air as if of a drowning man* (10) *And in an open skull-box are discovered* (11) *The diamonds of salt. Nothing remains for us but* (12) *To kneel upon the deck and thank* (13) *Heaven and a drowsy sea which had given us strength:* (14) *For we, who did not set forth at all, have arrived.* (15) *One must cast anchor and forget.*

The voyagers have reached the island out of chance. Though the existence of the treasure island is now a certainty, the manner in which it was reached remains mysterious. Moreover, its "treasure" is seen to consist in the voyagers' heightened consciousness of the pervasiveness of death, both recent (9) and ancient (10-11).

The emblems of death—air-bubbles, salt-corroded skull—do not repel them; on the contrary, they are attracted by their uncommon beauty. And now there is nothing left for them (11-13) but to offer a prayer of thanks, which they do in words that echo an ancient Hebraic Adoration: "Let us praise the master of the world . . . we bend the knee, bow down and thank the Lord. . . ."

Thus, the supernatural powers which had frustrated the journey are exalted for having given the voyagers the strength to achieve the final and most radical realization: "For we, who did not set forth at all, have arrived" (14).

This last and as it were total reversal negates the very title of the poem. It now becomes clear that the voyagers not only did not float (6) but had never even set out. They have "arrived" where they have actually been all along—at the island of death's treasures. And they are thankful—if not joyful—for having finally discovered this.

The discovery of their true "place" gives rise to a tone of impersonal resolution: "One should cast anchor and forget" (15)—forget the deception, the bitterness, the very desire to set sail.

The poem has a controlled, almost elegiac tone. It moves unobtrusively from one negation to another in a free amphibrachic pattern, making rich use of sound clusters (e.g., *leṣamáyim ulyám menumnám*, "to heaven and a drowsing sea" (13). The scattered end-rimes (1-3, 13-15) and the few internal rimes and assonances (e.g., *sefiná*, 3; *bitná*, 4) are delicately interwoven. They reinforce the sinuous development of the poem, which opens on a spell and mystery that is gradually illuminated until the final, conscious surrender is achieved.

— DALIA RAVIKOVITCH

Nathan Sach

[I SAW · RAÍTI · רָאִיתִי]

רָאִיתִי צִפּוֹר לְבָנָה בַּלַּיְלָה הַשָּׁחוֹר		Raíti tsipór levaná baláyla haṣaḥór
וְיָדַעְתִּי כִּי קָרוֹב לִכְבּוֹת אוֹר	2	Veyadáti ki karóv liḥbót or
עֵינַי בַּלַּיְלָה הַשָּׁחוֹר.		Eynáy baláyla haṣaḥór.
רָאִיתִי עָב קְטַנָּה כְּכַף יַד אִישׁ		Raíti av ktaná keḥáf yad iṣ
וְיָדַעְתִּי כִּי אֶת הַגֶּשֶׁם שֶׁאֲנִי מַרְגִּישׁ	5	Veyadáti ki et hagéṣem ṣeaní margíṣ
עוֹד לֹא הִצְלַחְתִּי לְסַפֵּר לְאִישׁ.		Od lo hitsláḥti lesapér leíṣ.
רָאִיתִי עָלֶה אֲשֶׁר נָפַל, אֲשֶׁר נוֹפֵל.	7	Raíti alé aṣér nafál, aṣér nofél.
הַזְּמַן קָצָר. אֲנִי אֵינִי קוֹבֵל.		Hazmán katsár. Aní eyní kovél.

"I Saw" is taken from the *Early Poems* (1956) of Nathan Sach, a poet who was born in Berlin in 1930 and came to Israel six years later. He is one of the country's most effective young writers, his influence extending beyond the impact of his verse, which in itself is highly original. With his critical writing he has attempted a revaluation of Hebrew poetry, deflating established reputations and pointing to virtues in others (such as Steinberg [pp. 54-57], Fogel, and Lensky). Sach has also made a number of translations for the Hebrew stage—of Frisch, Brecht, Dürrenmatt, and others—in which his individual use of the rhythms of spoken Hebrew is unmistakable.

Like many of Sach's poems, "I Saw" has a starkness of feeling which is complemented by an economy of expression. The imagery is simple and bare. Sentimentality is avoided, banality admitted with irony. The colloquial syntax and forthright rimes give the poem a quality of spontaneity and directness.

"I Saw" embodies an insight into the mystery, into the terror and alienation of human existence. In each of its three sections, some sharply perceived image leads toward a conclusion concerning the speaker's ultimate identity:

(1) *I saw a white bird in the black night* (2) *And I knew that soon would be extinguished* [lit. *close to extinction is*] *the light* (3) *Of my eyes in the black night.*

(4) *I saw a cloud small as a man's palm* (5) *And I knew that the rain that I feel* (6) *I haven't succeeded in telling about to anyone.*

(7) *I saw a leaf that fell, that is falling.* (8) *Time is short. I am not complaining (grieving).*

The "black night" in the opening line provides the setting for the "white bird," a symbol for vision. By line 3, the "black night" has become the night of the speaker's death. The haunting, sharp contrast of black and white is thus interpreted as an intimate awareness of the fragility of sight and of life itself, engulfed as it is by extinction.

The "cloud small as a man's palm" (4) calls to mind I Kings 18: 44-45—"Behold, there ariseth a little cloud out of the sea, like a man's palm . . . and there was a great rain." The speaker is led to the reflection that the rain, felt before its falling, cannot be described, conveyed, told about to others. Fragility of human sight is compounded, as it were, by the human inability to communicate what is experienced as ineffable feeling. The speaker's existence is thus defined implicitly as an irreducible awareness of subjectivity, of a walled-in separateness from both the world of nature and of people.

The third image, of the leaf (7), is, like the two that preceded, a small thing set in desolation—a leaf that fell. But immediately the speaker tells about another leaf, now falling slowly before his very eyes. The unexpected shift to the present tense refocuses the entire poem.

The repeated structure of the first two stanzas—"I saw . . ." and "I knew . . ."—has conditioned the reader to expect in the third a highly personal and elegiac reflection on mutability, but instead he is arrested by the reference to time and by the shrug of the shoulders implied in "I do not complain (grieve)." The last stanza, unlike the others, has only two lines, as if there were nothing more to be said.

Perhaps the outstanding characteristic of Sach's poetry is his individual manner of playing a strong emotion against a canceling irony. The effect of "I Saw," for example, issues from the detached resignation—if it can be said to be entirely such—of its curt conclusion. All the emotion built up in the first six lines turns upon itself critically. It is as though everything that has been said must now be unsaid, since nothing can ever be "told" or indeed even "felt" for very long.

— ARIEH SACHS

Nathan Sach

FROM YEAR TO YEAR IT · MIṢANÁ LEṢANÁ ZE · מִשָּׁנָה לְשָׁנָה זֶה

מִשָּׁנָה לְשָׁנָה זֶה נַעֲשָׂה יוֹתֵר מְעֻדָּן,
זֶה יִהְיֶה כָּל כָּךְ מְעֻדָּן בַּסּוֹף, —
הִיא אָמְרָה וְהִתְכַּוְּנָה לָזֶה.

אֲבָל לִי יֵשׁ לִפְעָמִים הַרְגָּשָׁה שֶׁאֲנִי טוֹבֵעַ בַּזְּמַן,

יֵשׁ לִי הַרְגָּשָׁה שֶׁאֲנִי טוֹבֵעַ מִזְּמַן,
הִסֵּס.

זֶה הַכֹּל מִפְּנֵי שֶׁאַתָּה שׁוֹקֵעַ, הֵשִׁיבָה.
זֶה הַכֹּל מִפְּנֵי שֶׁאַתָּה שׁוֹקֵעַ, אַתָּה יוֹדֵעַ.

אֵינֶנִּי יוֹדֵעַ. לִפְעָמִים אֲנִי חוֹשֵׁב שֶׁכֹּחִי שׁוּב לֹא אִתִּי.

מְעֻדָּן, אַתְּ יוֹדַעַת, זֶה צַד אַחֵר שֶׁל שְׁלִילִי.

אֲנִי יוֹדַעַת וַאֲנִי מְבָרֶכֶת אוֹתְךָ עַל גִּלּוּיֶיךָ,
אֲנִי מְבָרֶכֶת אוֹתְךָ עַל צֶבַע עֵינֶיךָ,
שׁוּם דָּבָר אֵינְךָ מַשְׁאִיר אַחֲרֶיךָ.

וּבְכֵן זֶהוּ בְּדִיּוּק מַה שֶּׁמַּדְאִיג אוֹתִי,
וּבְכֵן זֶהוּ בְּדִיּוּק מִי שֶׁמַּסְפִּיד אוֹתִי,
וּבְכֵן זֶהוּ מַה שֶּׁאֲנִי מַרְגִּישׁ.

שׁוּב אַתָּה טוֹעֶה: אַתָּה מַרְגִּישׁ בְּטוֹב וְהַטּוֹב מַקִּיף
אוֹתְךָ.
הוּא כְּבָר מִסָּבִיב, עַל כְּתֵפָיו הוּא מַרְכִּיב אוֹתְךָ,
אִם תִּהְיֶה סַבְלָנִי, הוּא עוֹד יְחַבֵּק אוֹתְךָ,
בְּסוֹפוֹ שֶׁל דָּבָר הוּא חַיָּב לְנַשֵּׁק לְךָ.
אַתָּה יוֹדֵעַ אֵיךְ דְּבָרִים כָּאֵלֶּה קוֹרִים.

Miṣaná leṣaná ze naasá yotér meudán,
Ze yihiyé kol kaḥ meudán basóf,—
Hi amrá vehitkavná lazé.

Avál li yeṣ lif'amím hargaṣá ṣeaní tovéa
[bazmán,

Yeṣ li hargaṣá ṣeaní tovéa mizmán,
Hisés.

Ze hakól mipnéy ṣeatá ṣokéa, heṣíva.
Ze hakól mipnéy ṣeatá ṣokéa, atá yodéa.

Eynéni yodéa. Lif'amím aní ḥosév ṣekoḥí
[ṣuv lo ití.

Meudán, at yodáat, ze tsad aḥér ṣel ṣlilí.

Aní yodáat vaaní mevaréḥet otḥá al giluyéḥa,
Aní mevaréḥet otḥá al tséva eynéḥa,
Ṣum davár eynḥá maṣ'ír aḥaréḥa.

Uvḥén zéhu bediyúk ma ṣemad'íg otí,
Uvḥén zéhu bediyúk mi ṣemaspíd otí,
Uvḥén zéhu ma ṣeaní margíṣ.

Ṣuv atá toé: atá margíṣ betóv vehatóv
[makíf otḥá.
Hu kvar misavív, al ktefáv hu markív otḥá,
Im tihiyé savlaní, hu od yeḥabék otḥá,
Besofó ṣel davár hu ḥayáv lenaṣék leḥá.
Atá yodéa eyḥ dvarím kaéle korím.

This is a dramatic dialogue: a man and woman between whom no real communication is possible are engaged in a painfully intimate conversation. Their topic is *ze* ("it") referred to in the title in varying contexts throughout the poem. This "it" is what is most significant and crucial in the man's life, probably his existence as an artist.

The woman is impatient but she is also encouraging, her encouragement probably springing from a helpless, desperate kind of love.

(1) *From year to year it becomes more refined,* (2) *It will be so very refined in the end—* (3) *She said, and she meant it* [the *it* of the title and of line 1].

(4) *But I sometimes have a feeling that I'm drowning in time,* (5) *I have a feeling that I've been drowning a long time—* (6) *He hesitated.*

(7) *It's all because you're sinking—she answered.* (8) *It's all because you're sinking, you know.*

(9) *I don't know. Sometimes I think my strength has gone from me* [lit. *is no longer with me*]. (10) *Refined, you know, is another side (aspect) of [the] negative.*

(11) *I know and I congratulate (bless) you for your revelations.* (12) *I congratulate (bless) you for the color of your eyes;* (13) *You leave nothing behind you.*

(14) *Well, that's exactly what's worrying me,* (15) *Well, that's exactly who's mourning (eulogizing) me,* (16) *Well, that's what I feel.*

(17) *You're wrong again: you feel good and the good surrounds you.* (18) *He [the good] is already around [you], He [the good] is carrying you on his shoulders;* (19) *If you'll be patient, he [the good] will embrace you yet;* (20) *Ultimately he [the good] must kiss you.* (21) *You know how such things happen.*

The man's remarks are plaintive, hesitant, tentative; the woman's grow assertively optimistic. But her optimism is ironically exposed as obtuseness. Her insistence that the man in reality is blessed (11-13) serves as a foil for his own inner conviction that "from year to year" he is becoming more sterile and hopeless.

The poetic effect of this laconic exchange depends entirely on the value and the tone of the words used by both speakers. In fact, the dramatic setting is no more than an excuse for Sach's typical exposition of an inner despair through the laconic use of extremely charged language peppered with casual rimes (e.g., lines 1-4, 9-10, 11-12-13).

The speakers talk at cross purposes. The woman begins by remarking upon the growing "refinement" of "it" (1-2), but the man turns her insistence into nonsense by his feeling that he is "drowning" with the years (4-5), for the word "drowned" is on an entirely different level of seriousness from the word "refined." To which she can only reply that he is allowing himself to sink into self-doubt and perhaps self-pity (7-8).

This time he answers that he is losing the powers he once possessed and that sophistication ("refinement," 1-2, 10) may well be in itself an aspect of sterility. There is a constant playing with the tentativeness of the exchange: *I have a feeling . . . You know . . . I don't know . . . You know . . . I know . . . I feel . . . You are wrong . . . You know.*

The dialogue reaches a climax when the man plaintively interprets the woman's irrelevant compliments. The fact that *aní mevaréḥet* (12) means both "I congratulate" and "I bless" is significant here as an exact response to his distress. And the woman's ambiguous "You leave nothing behind you," offered as a term of praise, gives him the negative element on which to seize. For, as he emphasizes, that is precisely what is worrying him. It is this absence of a viable achievement "who" is lamenting his failure (15).

But she must assure him that he is quite wrong. Her final, hurried statements, hedged with conditions, insist that the "Good"—an abstraction personified as a kind of loving father or uncle—really has him in its care. But her final assurance—that in the end this "Good" is sure to kiss him—carries an echo in Hebrew of "kiss my arse." The mounting exaltation of this last speech is crushingly offset by the weary banality of the closing line: "You know how such things happen."

— ARIEH SACHS

Nathan Sach

FAILURE · KIṢALÓN · כִּשָּׁלוֹן

שֶׁבַע פְּעָמִים אָמַר הַזְּאֵב לַגְּדִי,	Ṣéva peamím amár hazeév lagdí,
חֲדַל. רַק אַחַר כָּךְ טָרַף.	Ḥadál. Rak aḥár kaḥ taráf.
מַה הִכְרִיחַ אוֹתִי לְהִמָּשֵׁךְ כָּךְ	3 Ma hiḥríaḥ otí lehimaṣéḥ kaḥ
אֶל מַה שֶּׁהַלֵּב נִמְשָׁךְ.	El ma ṣehalév nimṣáḥ.
מַה הִכְרִיחַ אוֹתִי לְנַסּוֹת לְהַפְרִיד	Ma hiḥríaḥ otí lenasót lehafríd
בֵּין מַיִם לְמַיִם	6 Beyn máyim lemáyim
שֶׁאִי־אֶפְשָׁר לְהַפְרִיד	Ṣeí-efṣár lehafríd
וְרַק בַּשָּׁמַיִם	8 Verák baṣamáyim
הֵם נֶהְפָּכִים לַאֲוִיר.	Hem nehepaḥím leavír.
בֵּינְתַיִם	10 Beyntáyim
נִשְׁאַר רַק הַלֵּב, שָׁבִיר	Niṣ'ár rak halév, ṣavír
כְּדַרְכּוֹ,	Kedarkó,
וְכָל מַה שֶּׁלֹּא עָלָה	13 Veḥól ma ṣeló alá
בְּחַכָּתוֹ.	Beḥakató.

"Failure" may give the reader the feeling that it sprang from an initial image which then moved forward primarily in terms of the musical word-values of the Hebrew language. It is almost as though the poem's paraphraseable meanings developed out of the sounds of the words rather than vice versa. Although the reader, like the author, seems to be carried along from rime to rime and through the associations arising from the images, the progression is only apparently haphazard. The rimes serve to heighten the effect of spontaneity and of improvisation. And the reader is taken almost by surprise as the meanings emerge and coalesce out of a seemingly aimless drift of images:

(1) *Seven times the wolf said to the lamb (the kid):* (2) *Stop it. Only after that did he devour.*

(3) *What forced me to be thus drawn* (4) *To (by) whatever the heart is drawn (to)?*

(5) *What forced me to try to separate* (6) *Water from water*

(7) *Which one cannot separate;* (8) *And only in the sky (heavens)*

(9) *Are they* [lit. *is it*—the waters] *changed into air?* (10) *In the meantime*

(11) *Only the heart remains, fragile* (12) *As ever (as is its wont),* (13) *And all that has not come up* (14) *On its hook (fishing rod).*

This poem, like "From Year to Year It," and a good many others by Nathan Sach, elaborates a theme of estrangement, frustration, and futility from a point of view that is somehow beyond despair. The manner is deceptively quiet, the tone very close to that of ordinary, unexcited conversation.

The speaker—the "I" of the poem—knew in advance that his attempts would end in failure, having been warned by previous experience (1-2). Nevertheless he persisted, like a silly lamb, in provoking the wolf. It was he, after all, who picked the fight. The wolf was satiated. He kept trying patiently to ward off the lamb, but finally he had to lose patience.

It was the speaker's own recklessness that made his destruction inevitable. When translated into action, the compulsive desires of the human heart are sure to culminate in disaster (3-4). And the stronger the desire, the more certain the ultimate failure to attain satisfaction.

I attempted, reflects the speaker (5 ff.), to distinguish and to choose where distinction is pointless and choice futile. In a world of immutable laws, I tried to achieve what could be brought about only by some miraculous reversal of nature. God was able to create a world by "dividing waters" (Genesis, 1: 6), and His prophet Moses had no difficulty in dividing the waters of the Red Sea, turning it into dry land for the passage of the Children of Israel. Water loses its density only in the sky (8-9), where it can move about unimpeded: there are no substances that resist in the heavens, for all is pure spirit there. But as for me, I am neither God nor one of His prophets, nor am I in Heaven. I am down here, on earth, a creature of flesh and blood. My heart is as "fragile as always" and "as is its wont"—it can be broken again and again.

The last two lines of the poem derive especial force from the Hebrew idiom *lo lehaalót beḥaká*, which means literally "not to bring up with one's fishing rod." Used in everyday conversation, the phrase signifies lack of success in any endeavor. Here the idiom takes on added vividness through its recall of the earlier reference to "divided" waters (5-6). The heart is like a persistent angler constantly bringing up his rod only to discover that he has caught nothing. There is probably not a single fish in the stream.

— ARIEH SACHS

Dalia Ravikovitch

CLOCKWORK DOLL · BUBÁ MEMUKÉNET · בֻּבָּה מְמֻכֶּנֶת

בַּלַּיְלָה הַזֶּה הָיִיתִי בֻּבָּה מְמֻכֶּנֶת
וּפָנִיתִי יָמִינָה וּשְׂמֹאלָה, לְכָל הָעֲבָרִים,
וְנָפַלְתִּי אַפַּיִם אַרְצָה וְנִשְׁבַּרְתִּי לִשְׁבָרִים
וְנִסּוּ לְאַחוֹת אֶת שְׁבָרַי בְּיָד מְאֻמֶּנֶת.

וְאַחַר־כָּךְ שַׁבְתִּי לִהְיוֹת בֻּבָּה מְתֻקֶּנֶת
וְכָל מִנְהָגַי הָיָה שָׁקוּל וְצַיְתָנִי,
אוּלָם אָז כְּבָר הָיִיתִי בֻּבָּה מִסּוּג שֵׁנִי
כְּמוֹ זְמוֹרָה חֲבוּלָה שֶׁהִיא עוֹד אֲחוּזָה בִּקְנוֹקֶנֶת.

וְאַחַר כָּךְ הָלַכְתִּי לִרְקֹד בְּנֶשֶׁף הַמְּחוֹלוֹת
אַךְ הִנִּיחוּ אוֹתִי בְּחֶבְרַת חֲתוּלִים וּכְלָבִים
וְאִלּוּ כָּל צְעָדַי הָיוּ מְדוּדִים וּקְצוּבִים.

וְהָיָה לִי שֵׂעָר זָהָב וְהָיוּ לִי עֵינַיִם כְּחֻלּוֹת
וְהָיְתָה לִי שִׂמְלָה מִצֶּבַע פְּרָחִים שֶׁבַּגָּן
וְהָיָה לִי כּוֹבַע שֶׁל קַשׁ עִם קִשּׁוּט דֻּבְדְּבָן.

Baláyla hazé hayíti bubá memukénet
Ufaníti yamína usmóla, leḥól haavarím,
Venafálti apáyim ártsa venişbárti lişvarím
4 Venisú leaḥót et şvaráy beyád meuménet.

Veaḥár-kaḥ şávti lihiyót bubá metukénet
Veḥól minhagí hayá şakúl vetsaytaní,
Ulám az kvar hayíti bubá misúg şeyní
8 Kemo zmorá ḥavulá şehí od aḥuzá
[biknokénet

Veaḥár-kaḥ haláḥti lirkód benéşef hamḥolót
Aḥ hiníḥu otí beḥevrát ḥatulím uḥlavím
11 Veílu ḥol tseadáy hayú medudím uktsuvím.

Vehayá li seár zaháv vehayú li
[eynáyim kḥulót
13 Vehaytá li simlá mitséva praḥím şebagán
Vehayá li kóva şel kaş im kişút duvdeván.

Dalia Ravikovitch's first book of poems, *The Love of an Orange* (a deliberate play on the name of Prokofief's burlesque-opera), established her when it appeared in 1959 as one of Israel's leading younger poets. Her verse conveys a strong feeling of disorientation and loss, and a complaint about the injustice that the poet finds inherent in existence itself. But in many of her poems, the deeply personal hurt assumes the impersonal forms of myth and hallucination. It is this restraining of strong emotion in the very act of expressing it by means of impersonal visionary symbols that gives impact to such a poem as "Clockwork Doll."

The speaker in this poem is recounting a vivid dream. The doll embodies the total loss of self which follows some traumatic excess of feeling. A sense of thwarted eroticism runs through the poem. But the dehumanized doll is no mere figure of speech: there is a total identification between the human being and the mechanical toy.

(1) *That night I was a clockwork [*lit. *mechanical] doll* (2) *And I turned to the right and to the left, in all directions,* (3) *And I fell [on my] face to the ground and was broken to bits.* (4) *And they tried to join my broken bits expertly [*lit. *with an expert hand].*

During "that night" the speaker felt she

was a clockwork doll. Drained of her human self, she had become an emotional robot. The doll is inanimate, yet it moves. It resembles a pretty girl but is quite sexless and incapable of feeling. Its face is a blank surface of paint, its movements angular and mechanical. Though it is remote from life, its very life-likeness is uncanny and disturbing. The image of the toy spread out suddenly in broken bits evokes utter desolation. The quatrain ends with an ironical reference to a lover's or a doctor's "expert" attempt to put the doll together again; his very "expertness" makes him appear domineering and incapable of being loved.

(5) *And after that I became again a complete (mended, proper) doll,* (6) *And my whole manner was balanced (deliberate) and obedient,* (7) *But then I was already a doll of a second (another) type* (8) *Like an injured twig held by a tendril.*

The doll in the second quatrain turns out to be even more "mechanical" than before. She has been made to conform (*metukénet* in line 5 means both "repaired" and "proper"). Whereas before the breakdown she had "turned in every direction" with at least a show of independence, she has now become a doll of "another kind," lacking all volition, completely passive, "decorous and obedient." The image of the broken twig forlornly hanging by a tendril—a simile surprisingly drawn from organic nature—reinforces both the idea of a precarious existence that is only partly alive and of the absolute dependence and passivity ("held by a tendril") described in the previous lines.

(9) *And afterwards I went to dance at the ball,* (10) *But they put (left) me in the company of cats and dogs* (11) *Whereas all my steps were measured and rhythmical.*

The recollected dance reflects the speaker's feeling of alienation from the world of the living. At the ball, she has been "left" in the company of cats and dogs—creatures unlike her in that they are moved by the principle of vitality and not by clockwork. But at the same time the reference to these animals is derogatory. The speaker is really estranged from these "indecorous" creatures because her remoteness and her beauty make her unique. Her own movements are properly "measured and rhythmical," and this is, after all, as it should be at a dance. It is implied that she really should have been allowed to associate with something better than "cats and dogs." The complexity of the speaker's attitude towards herself becomes dominant here: the doll is not only terrifying in its combination of motion and lifelessness, it is also fascinating in its remoteness—a surrealistic quality that may recall the doll Olympia in E. T. Hoffmann's "The Sandman."

(12) *And I had golden hair and I had blue eyes* (13) *And I had a dress the color of flowers in the garden* (14) *And I had a hat of straw with a cherry ornament.*

The wistful final tercet brings to the fore a certain childlike quality that has been present throughout the sonnet—the tone of an infant coquette fascinated by her own appearance and quite oblivious of all else. The poem ends in a voice that stops without giving the feeling that she has finished, a conclusion in which nothing is concluded.

But it is a doll, not a human being, who has been speaking to us. Its childish voice and its detached manner produce a flat blend of naïveté and adult objectivity. There is a kind of disturbing innocence in its straightforward narration (that night I was . . . and then I became . . . and then I went to dance . . . and I had . . . and I had . . . and I had . . .). The sonnet form, appropriate precisely because of its rigidity, is used with control and originality, combining a prose technique with full rimes. The declarative flatness of the entire poem produces quite the opposite of a flat effect.

— ARIEH SACHS

· · · APPENDIX · · ·

· · · APPENDIX · · ·

HOW TO READ THE PHONETIC TRANSCRIPTIONS OF THE POEMS

This essay is addressed primarily to the English reader who cannot read Hebrew yet wishes to know how to pronounce the poems presented in this volume. Accordingly, section I below contains an explanation of the method used in the phonetic transcription that accompanies each of the poems. Once the reader has mastered the consonants, vowels, and other material in section I, he may wish to read through sections II and III, which introduce a number of details of specialized interest.

The great majority of the poems in this volume were written by and for speakers of contemporary Israeli Hebrew, and hence reflect current Israeli pronunciation.[1] The poems distinguished by an asterisk after the title were composed by poets who used the traditional Ashkenazi pronunciation, which was current in Eastern Europe before the revival of Hebrew as a spoken language. In using the phonetic transcriptions, however, the reader need not be concerned with the differences between the two types of pronunciation. (These differences are discussed in section III of this essay.)

I

The phonetic transcription should enable the English reader to approximate the pronunciation of the Hebrew original. Although accurate pronunciation can not be learned otherwise than by steadfast aural and oral practice, an attentive reading of the following directions should go a long way toward giving the English-speaking reader some idea of the sounds intended; and although a certain effort is involved, that effort will be far smaller for Hebrew than for most other languages.

We begin with the consonant symbols representing sounds so close to their English parallels as to require practically no comment. The table gives, on the left, the symbol used in our poem transcriptions; on the right, an English word containing the sound intended. The reader will find at the end of this essay a table listing the Hebrew letters corresponding to these sounds.

b	*b*ad
p	*p*ut
d	*d*og
t	*t*ea
g	*g*ood
k	*k*in
s	*s*ad
z	*z*oo
f	*f*ar
v	*v*oid
l	*l*ove
m	*m*ad
n	*n*ot
h	*h*ot
y	*y*es, bo*y*
ş	*sh*ot

[1] The term "Sephardic pronunciation" is sometimes used as a rough equivalent of "Israeli pronunciation." However, the two are, strictly speaking, not interchangeable, and the pronunciation described here (for details, see below) is best referred to simply as "Israeli."

Only the last symbol (*ṣ*) is unfamiliar, but the sound it represents is the familiar one written *sh* in English. Note that the symbols above *always* have the sound indicated in the table: *g* is never as in English *gem*, *s* never as in *boys*. With respect to *l*, the normal American *l* will do, but Israeli pronunciation prefers the "light" or "clear" variety as in French, German, or Spanish.

We now come to the only two consonant symbols for sounds which have no equivalent in most varieties of English, and which therefore require a special effort:

r	French g*r*and, Spanish to*r*o
ḥ	Scottish lo*ch*, Spanish *j*unta

The *r* is produced either by a trill or friction at the back of the mouth (as in French or German) or by a flap or trill at the front of the mouth (as in Spanish or Russian); the normal American *r* should be avoided, though the flap often heard in British pronunciations of *very*, *America*, is quite acceptable. The *ḥ* is a rasped sound made at the back of the mouth, either as in the German *ch* in *Achtung* and *Bach*, or as in the Russian *kh* in *kolkhoz*, or as in the Spanish and Scottish examples indicated; it must never be confused with a plain *h* (as in English *hot*).

The vowel symbols (vowels in Hebrew are indicated by vowel points written below, above, or next to the letter, as shown in the table at the end of this essay) and their approximate English equivalents are as follows:

a	f*a*ther
e	b*e*t
i	mach*i*ne
o	sh*o*re
u	s*ou*p

Hebrew vowels are much more similar to their Spanish equivalents than to the English parallels given above. A rough approximation can nevertheless be achieved, provided that care is taken always to give the vowels the value indicated, and never to yield to the temptation to pronounce *o* as in *low*, *u* as in *cute*, *i* as in *fine*, *a* as in *cat* or in *cape*, *e* as in *me*, etc.

The diphthongs are formed by adding the sound of *y* to each of the foregoing vowel sounds. Thus, with English equivalents:

ay	m*y*, m*i*ne
ey	gr*ey*, n*ei*gh
oy	b*oy*

The diphthong *uy* is closer to that of the German *pfui* or that of the French *fouille* than to that of the English *hooey*. The diphthong *iy* is closer to the sound of the French *fille* than to that of the English *fee*.

Over and above this inventory of consonants, vowels, and diphthongs, the following points must be borne in mind:

(1) The symbol ʹ (acute accent) placed above a vowel shows where the word is to be stressed. Thus: *bánu* ("we came") is stressed on the first syllable, whereas *banú* ("they built") is stressed on the second.

(2) When two vowels adjoin, they are pronounced separately, so that each is given its true value. Thus *meód* is pronounced as *me* followed by *od* (which is stressed); *taím* as *ta* followed by *im;* *keév* as *ke* followed by *ev;* *páam* as *pa* (which is stressed) followed by *am*. The separation is often made particularly clear by the occurrence of an audible "catch" or slight pause between the vowels (especially when the second vowel is stressed). This separation is not generally marked in the transcription, though the symbol ' (apostrophe) has occasionally been used to prevent possible confusions: *si'á* ("a faction").

(3) The same symbol (') is regularly introduced between a consonant and a vowel whenever these belong to different syllables and are to be pronounced with the audible "catch" separating them. Thus: *kav'á* ("she determined") is pronounced as *kav* followed by *a*, with an audible separation

between them, whereas *kavá* ("he determined") is pronounced simply as *ka* plus *va*. This "catch" is very similar to that heard in English between the two halves of *uh-uh* meaning "no."

(4) When two consonants adjoin, they are pronounced without any intervening vowel sound. English speakers should pay careful attention to this, particularly at the beginning of words: *któvet* ("address"), *pkak* ("cork"), *psólet* ("rubbish"), *tsav* ("turtle"), *tslav* ("cross"). The combination *ts* is especially frequent in Hebrew, and it is often followed by another consonant: *ratsá* ("he wanted"), *ratstá* ("she wanted"), *tsmigím* ("tires"). (Some further details connected with the combination *ts* are given in section II, paragraph 9.)

II

Of the several varieties of Israeli pronunciation (hereafter referred to as IP) the one reflected by our transcriptions may be characterized as "native, Europeanized, moderately formal, and non-puristic." There are other varieties of IP, hence other ways in which the poems can be read—for example, in a puristic or highly formal style, in the fairly widespread "Arabicized" or "Middle Eastern" pronunciation, in one of a number of non-native pronunciations, etc. The type of pronunciation selected for our transcriptions appeared to the writer and to the editors as the one most suited for a volume of this sort, and it is to this variety only that the abbreviation IP refers in the remainder of this essay. Some consequences of this choice, together with additional details on the method of transcription, are listed below.

(1) The symbol *ḥ* has been used to designate the sound of the Hebrew letter ח (*ḥet*) as well as that of כ (ך at the end of a word) (*ḥaf*), since IP does not distinguish between them; thus *paḥ* for both פַּח ("a can") and פַּךְ ("a flask"). Similarly, with א (*alef*) and ע (*ayin*), which our transcription renders identically: by nothing at all when they represent no sound, or by ' when they represent the audible separation described in section I above. Thus: *or* for both אוֹר ("light") and עוֹר ("skin"), *kar'á* for both קָרְאָה ("She read") and קָרְעָה ("she tore"). These distinctions (their exact nature need not detain us here) are, however, maintained by speakers using other Hebrew pronunciations, and even IP speakers occasionally introduce them for stylistic purposes.

(2) Informal pronunciation, and even moderately formal pronunciation, tends to "drop" the *h* sound rather frequently. Our transcription retains *h* wherever it would be sounded in carefully enunciated speech, but not at the end of certain words, where it is a feature of puristic pronunciation only: thus we write *góva* ("height"), not *góvah*.

(3) We write double consonants only in the rare cases where IP actually has them: *dannu* ("we discussed") pronounced *dán-nu*, as opposed to *dánu* ("they discussed"). (The dot placed at the center of a consonant often indicates that the consonant was traditionally pronounced double. Though that tradition has, to some extent, been retained by a number of non-IP speakers, it has been lost in IP except in a very few instances, such as the form *dannu* just referred to.)

(4) A special problem for transcription is created by the alternation between *b* and *v*, *p* and *f*, *k* and *ḥ*. The rules of formal grammar governing the choice are fairly well defined, but actual usage is far more complex. For example, *po* ("here"), *ba* ("he came"), *kol* ("all"), when preceded by the negative *lo*, may be read either as *lo po* or *lo fo* ("not here"); as *lo ba* or *lo va* ("he did not come"); as *lo kol* or *lo ḥol* ("not all"). In each case the first variant is the informal, everyday one, the second the strictly formal one. In transcribing, decisions as to which variant to use had to be based, in each case, on the general tone of the poem, the rime scheme, and the like.

(5) There is often a choice between *e* and *ey* in many words spelled with .. or י.. ; Thus: the word for "son" can only be pronounced *ben;* the word for "between," on the other hand, is pronounced *ben* by some and *beyn* by others. In cases where there are two possible pronunciations, the present transcription usually writes *ey*, viz. *beyn* for "between," and so on.

(6) There is often a choice between *e* and no sound at all, especially where the Hebrew spelling has the sign ְ below the first letter of a word: one can say either *kemó* or *kmo* ("as, like"). Our transcription follows the meter; when the two alternatives are both prosodically acceptable, we usually omit the *e*.

(7) In given cases, there is optional or stylistic variation in the place of the stress, e.g. *káma* ("she rises")—ordinary usage, or *kamá* —very formal usage. In our transcription the choice is governed either by the meter or, when both are prosodically possible, by considerations of style.

(8) Words are transcribed as separate, joined, or hyphenated according to the Hebrew spelling. No stress mark is placed on monosyllables, and polysyllabic words are stressed according to the place of the stress in the isolated word.

(9) In the great majority of cases, the combination *ts* corresponds to the Hebrew letter צ (ץ at the end of a word) (*tsádi*). It also represents the Hebrew sequences טְס and תְס so that our transcriptions do not differentiate between הוּצָא ("he was taken out") and הוּטְסָה ("she was flown"), both being rendered by *hutsá*. This non-differentiation is adequate for our purposes. (The English reader may be interested in learning that the two kinds of *ts* are not entirely equivalent. First, there is a difference of syllabic division, though this is rarely heard in actual speech: הוּצָא is *hu-tsá*, whereas הוּטְסָה is *hut-sá*. Accordingly, there is an "inseparable" *ts* [corresponding to צ] and a "separable" *ts* [corresponding to טְס and תְס]. Inseparable *ts* corresponds to a single consonant not only in spelling but in the structure of the language as a whole; separable *ts* corresponds to two consonants. For these reasons, Hebrew speakers think of the two kinds of *ts* as being quite distinct, and one consequence of this is that *hu-tsá* [הוּצָא] is unlikely to rime with anything but another *tsa* [צָ], whereas *hut-sá* might rime with words ending in *sá*.)

III

It has already been mentioned that not all the poems in this book were written by speakers of IP. Those poems marked by an asterisk (e.g., pp. 25, 60) were originally meant to be read in the so-called "Ashkenazi pronunciation" (hereafter referred to as AP), traditionally used in Central and Eastern Europe. The chief differences between AP and IP are: (a) AP tends to stress the syllable before the last, IP more often the last: AP *kálbi* vs. IP *kalbí* ("my dog"); (b) some differences in the vowels, e.g., AP *baḥlóymo* vs. IP *baḥalomá* ("in her dream"); (c) AP often has *s* where IP has *t*, e.g., AP *kóyseyv* vs. IP *kotév* ("writing").

Now these AP poems, if read in AP, would be unintelligible to most Israelis. Instead, they are read today either in ordinary IP, which has the effect of obliterating both rime scheme and meter, or they are read in a slightly modified IP—one that keeps the AP stress patterns and hence has the effect of retaining at least the essentials of the meter. In transcribing the AP poems in this book, the editors decided to follow the latter practice, i.e., to use IP vowels and consonants but to retain AP stresses. Thus, a line which originally sounded something like *miḥtov kóton li kosóvo*
("she wrote me a little letter") now reads:

miḥtav kátan li katáva

in our transcription (but not

miḥtáv katán li katáva

as it would in ordinary IP). The reader may wish to compare the poem by Bialik, which is here given in the original Ashkenazi pronunciation, with the transcription on p. 20, which, along with all our other AP poems, is a combination of IP sounds and AP stresses.

Bisṣuvósi

Suv lefónay: zókeyn bóle,
Pónim tsóymkim umtsoyrórim,
Tseyl kaṣ yóveyṣ, nod keóle,
Nod vonó al-gábey sfórim.

Ṣuv lefónay: zkéyno bólo,
Óyrgo, sóyrgo puzmekóoys,
Pího móley ólo, klólo,
Usfosého tómid nóoys.

Uḥmeyóz loy moṣ mimkóymoy
Ḥsul beyséynu—óydoy hóyze
Beyn kiráyim, uvaḥlóymoy
Im-aḥbórim yáas ḥóyze.

Uḥmeyóz boóyfel mṣúḥim
Kúrey éreg haakóviṣ
Mléyey fígrey zvúvim nfúḥim
Ṣom bazóvis hamaróvis . . .

Loy ṣunéysem mikadmásḥem,
Yóṣon nóṣon, eyn ḥadóṣo;—
Óvoy áḥay, beḥevrásḥem!
Yáḥdov nírkav ad-nivóṣo!

The table that follows summarizes, for convenient reference, the essentials of IP. On the left are the symbols used in the transcription, in the center an approximate equivalent sound given, wherever possible, in an English word; on the right, the Hebrew character corresponding to the given sound in Israeli pronunciation. Hebrew letters in parentheses denote that the given character does not always correspond to the sound indicated and that details are to be looked for in the body of the essay.[2] The vowel points are, for convenience, all written below or next to the letter ב (*vet*).

[2] The sign ָ almost always represents the sound *a*, but stands for *o* in a few words.

SYMBOL	EQUIVALENT	HEBREW CHARACTER	NAME OF CHARACTER
b	*b*ad	בּ	*bet*
v	*v*oid	ו, ב	*vet, vav*
g	*g*ood	ג	*gímel*
k	*k*in	ק, כּ	*kaf, kof*
d	*d*og	ד	*dálet*
t	*t*ea	ת, ט	*tet, tav*
p	*p*oor	פּ	*pe*
f	*f*at	פ	*fe*
ts	ca*ts*	ץ, תְס, טְס, צ (final)	*tsádi*
s	*s*ad	שׂ, ס	*sámeḥ, sin*
z	*z*oo	ז	*záyin*
h	*h*ome	ה	*he*
y	*y*ou, bo*y*	י	*yod*
l	*l*ove	ל	*lámed*
m	*m*ad	ם, מ (final)	*mem*
n	*n*oise	ן, נ (final)	*nun*
ṣ	*sh*oe	שׁ	*ṣin*
r	Fr. *r*at, Sp. to*r*o	ר	*reṣ*
ḥ	Ger. Ba*ch*, Sp. *j*unta	ך, כ, ח (final)	*ḥet, ḥaf*
’	(see sec. II	(ע, א)	*álef, áyin*
a	f*a*ther	בַ בֲ (בָ)	
e	b*e*t	בֶ בֱ (בֵ) (בֵי) (בְ)	
i	mach*i*ne	בִ בִי	
o	sh*o*re	בוֹ בֹ בֳ (בָ)	
u	tr*u*e	בוּ בֻ	
ay	*my*	בַי בָי	
ey	*grey*	(בֵי) (בֵ)	
iy	Fr. *fille*	בִי	
oy	b*oy*	בוֹי	
uy	Ger. pf*ui*	בוּי בֻי	

—HAIM BLANC

AN OUTLINE HISTORY OF MODERN HEBREW POETRY

The modern period in Hebrew poetry dates from the end of the 18th century, when European Jews were beginning to emerge from their ghettos and to enter into the modern world. Although by the close of the biblical period, Hebrew had all but ceased to be a spoken language, Hebrew verse continued to be written. The apocryphal literature and the recently discovered Dead Sea Scrolls preserve many examples from the late- and post-biblical periods. The ensuing five centuries, however, seem to have been almost devoid of poetry, for this talmudic period (circa 70-500 A.D.) contains within its extensive literature only occasional dirges and a few fragments of folk-rimes. A resurgence in poetic activity occurred in Byzantine Palestine (6th-8th centuries)[1] and in Iraq (8th-10th centuries). In both countries a number of hymn-writers composed intricate baroque-like hymns and didactic verses, many of which came to be included in the liturgy of the synagogue.

Medieval Hebrew poetry flourished in Spain, reaching its zenith during the so-called "Golden Period" (10th-15th centuries), when a group of gifted writers produced secular as well as religious verse. Readers of the Bible are aware that not all of ancient Hebrew literature need be described as exclusively religious. The Song of Songs, for example, despite the various allegorical interpretations that both Jewish and Christian exegetes have read into it, was essentially a series of love- and marriage-poems whose plain meaning contains little which could be regarded as sacred. The love-songs and the wine-songs of the Spanish and Provençal Hebrew poets continued this non-sacral strain.

Though such secular poetry was of course regarded as secondary to the great corpus of religious literature composed in the biblical age, it was written, preserved, and read throughout Jewish history. The Spanish Hebrew poets adapted the verse forms, metrics, and many of the conventions of Arabic poetry—Samuel Hanagid (993-1056), Solomon Ibn Gabirol (1021-1058?), and Judah Halevi (1075?-1141?) are important in the annals of medieval European poetry—and their example was followed in Provence, Italy, even in remote Yemen. By contrast, the medieval Hebrew poets of Central Europe produced only religious poems, following the style of the Byzantine Palestinians (whose meter was determined by the number of words per line). To this day the Ashkenazi (German-Polish) liturgy has preserved a great number of these medieval hymns composed in Germany and in France.

Until its modern period, therefore, Hebrew poetry was predominantly sacred. Even in Spain and Provence, and later in Italy, the quantity of religious verse far exceeded that of secular verse. Only with the breakdown of the religious tradition in Central and Eastern Europe during the 18th and 19th centuries were the roles reversed: in this modern period, secular poetry becomes the main occupation of the Hebrew writer and only occasionally does he deal with religious themes. Yet paradoxically, modern Hebrew poetry not only marks a break with a very long tradition of sacred poetry but actually continues it. The secularity of modern

[1] Some scholars would put the date of the development of this type of liturgical verse several centuries earlier. (See, for example, p. 212).

Hebrew verse sets it apart from ancient and medieval verse at the same time that its language, symbols, figures of speech, and allusions generally bridge the gap between them. This interplay of the old and the new in Hebrew poetry constitutes one of the fascinating aspects of the literature before us.

Although some distortion inevitably results when one attempts to divide a literary tradition into neat periods, a chronological framework should prove helpful to readers unfamiliar with the course of modern Hebrew poetry. The outline that follows is divided into three periods which, though overlapping to some degree, reflect in general the major developments: I. The European (1880-1924), II. The Palestinian (1920-1947), and III. The Israeli (1948-).

I. The European Period (1880-1924)

Our volume begins with Chaim Nachman Bialik (1873-1934), the greatest figure in modern Hebrew literature. He arrived on the scene at the culmination of a development begun at the end of the 18th century and which was called *Haskalah*, "The Enlightenment". This was the name given to the ideology of the new Jewish merchant class that rose to prominence with the industrialization of Central and Eastern Europe and which adopted with enormous enthusiasm the new values of the rising European bourgeoisie. Taste and reason were to replace the restricting, legalistic, tradition-bound Jewish orthodoxy of the old order. The Enlighteners (*maskilim*) called for the secularization of Jewish life, the Europeanization of Jewish taste, and the reformation of the traditional system of education. By modernizing and reforming Jewish society, they believed, Jews would win acceptance by the gentile world and attain both political and social emancipation. For them—as for their gentile counterparts—education was the key to social and economic amelioration. The Enlighteners looked upon literature as a didactic, propagandistic tool for disseminating their program.

They wrote their propaganda in Hebrew because Hebrew was the literary language of the audience they wished to arouse. During the earlier stages of the Enlightenment, Yiddish was out of the question despite the fact that it was the spoken tongue of Jewry in the Central and East European areas. For to most Enlighteners and particularly those living in Prussia (the center of the new Hebrew literature until about 1820), Yiddish was a quite undignified patois of German, Hebrew, and Slavic elements, fit for only the ignorant, the women, and the servants. Many of the early Enlighteners would have preferred to write in "civilized" German but their parochial audience knew no German. They favored Hebrew also because in non-Jewish circles it had the status of a classical language—and the Enlighteners took their standards from the gentile world. But they also had a genuine love for the classical language, as many of their verses "in praise of Hebrew" make clear.

If these early poems were translated into English, they would call to mind the elaborate and affected style of Euphuistic writers of Britain. The diction was turgid and imitative, the lines were a mosaic of biblical phrases and verses. German was the predominantly literary influence upon these writers—literally thousands of poems were written, and even labeled "*nach Schiller*" ("in the manner of Schiller"). For almost a century such versifying continued, and ultimately a few poets of talent appeared, but whatever gifts they possessed were impeded by the Hebrew of that time which lacked the vocabulary and flexibility of a living language.

By the 1860's, the Enlightenment had

taken on a romantic-nationalist coloration. This change was to some degree a result of the rise of Romanticism in European literature and the concomitant growth of nationalism throughout the continent. It was also caused in part by developments within the Jewish community. The second generation of Enlighteners had begun to react against the extreme cosmopolitanism of their predecessors. Moreover, there was an increasing disappointment with a European civilization which was clearly not prepared to fulfil its promise to grant full emancipation to its Jews. At the same time, the center of the movement now shifted to Eastern Europe, where a much larger and far less assimilable Jewish population lived, for the most part in the self-contained "Jewish" town (*shtetl.*)[2] Their political and sociological stituation preserved a sense of *folk* which was rapidly being diluted in the more dispersed and emancipated Jewish communities of Germany. This new nationalism in Eastern Europe expressed itself in professions of love for the Jewish people and the Hebrew language, in a romanticization of Jewish historical experience, and in a profound nostalgia for ancient Palestine. Ultimately it found its organizational form in the Zionist movement which was to sweep over East European Jewry in the wake of the Russian pogroms of the 1880's.

Bialik always acknowledged his debt to the gifted authors within the Enlightenment, particularly to Judah Lev Gordon (1830-1893), the most gifted of all. Their experiments in theme, language, and form prepared the way for the Bialik generation; nevertheless, even Gordon's achievement could be described as "a little honey and a great deal of sweat . . . the aesthetic-psychological basis, that which gives flavor to poetry, was almost completely absent." In the same essay Bialik concluded that only in his own generation did a genuinely modern Hebrew poetry emerge. The classical literature was now assiduously searched to rediscover an adequate vocabulary and where none was forthcoming, Hebrew writers invented acceptable words. "With their mighty strength and amazing patience, they sifted the sands and found pearls . . . The reign of *melitsá* [Hebrew Euphuism] declined. The biblical verse no longer walked before them like a blind man's staff, but ran after them playfully."

In terms of viable accomplishment, modern Hebrew poetry begins with Bialik and his contemporaries. Although this group was far from homogeneous in literary and ideological views, its members had much in common. They were almost all East Europeans, whose mother tongue was Yiddish. They were usually products of the tradition-bound *shtetl* where they had received an orthodox religious education from which all secular subjects had been excluded. Except for a very few, they learned no European languages (not even the various Slavic dialects of their neighbors) until adulthood, for they had been brought up in the isolated, ghettoized world of the Jewish town. It was not until their adolescence that they came into contact—through the Enlightenment literature—with the new and exciting "outside" world of Europe and proceeded to experience agonizing conflicts.

Bialik's generation marks the transition; for while it freed Hebrew poetry from the didacticism and the rhetoric of the past, it could not free itself completely from the parochial concerns of East European Jewry. Born into a tradition-centered world, its

[2] In Russia the Jewish population was for the most part confined by law (1790's) to certain provinces which already contained a large number of Jews. Broadly speaking, these constituted what was called the Pale of Settlement. Within the Pale, a minority of Jews lived in large cities; the overwhelming number resided in the *shtetl*, the small town which served as the market center for the predominantly agricultural economy, the peasantry and local gentry living in the surrounding area.

writers were suddenly wrenched into the harsh, non-believing milieu of pre-Revolutionary Russia. They were able to accept secularism and a modern view of man intellectually, but emotionally they remained tied to their Jewish experience. Little wonder that they gravitated toward the program of Achad Haam (1857-1927), a positivist-utilitarian essayist and editor who proposed an ethico-nationalist interpretation of both Judaism and Jewish history. But Achad Haam's basic conservatism had a limiting effect on Hebrew literature. Though the writers did not entirely share his view that they should confine themselves to Jewish problems and Jewish themes (some of them actively opposed this view), many of them limited their poetry, in the main, to the new cause of nationalism. And their readers, also, seemed to prefer such subject matter.

The pogroms that took place in Eastern Europe beginning with the 1880's did much to disabuse the Enlighteners of their illusions about the prospects for amelioration. Modern Russia demonstrated its unreadiness and unwillingness to assimilate its masses of Jews. But even if the non-Jewish society were to change and accept Jews as social and political equals, would not this very acceptance require the destruction of Jewish distinctiveness and the unique culture that accompanied it? Would it be worth the price? The new Zionist program answered both the physical need for a state free from economic, social, and political discrimination as well as what Achad Haam had described as the need for a spiritual center where a secularized Jewish culture could maintain itself and even flourish. Before long, Hebrew writers found themselves rallying to the nationalist cause whose goal was a Jewish state in Palestine.

In common with many other "small" literatures, the Hebrew poetry of Bialik's generation suffered from "culture lag." Russian literature had become the dominating influence, but the new Hebrew writers ignored the Russian *avant-garde*, in their preference for such established figures as Pushkin, Krilov, and Lermontov. Note also that at a period when Symbolism was spreading throughout Europe, the two leading Hebrew poets, Bialik and Tchernichovsky, were translating Homer and Shakespeare, Schiller and Shelley.

Bialik was hailed as the herald of a new epoch the moment he had launched upon his literary career, in the 1880's. Although his earliest poems were largely reworkings of Enlightenment themes and not quite free from Hebrew Euphuism, he soon introduced new subjects and began to forge a modern idiom which, while grounded in the tradition, was capable of expressing the thought of a 19th-century poet.

Throughout his life Bialik was torn between two roles. On the one hand, he viewed himself as the genius of his people who, in a disintegrating world, must give voice to its longings and frustrations and to its aspirations for national rebirth. On the other, he saw himself as a sensitive poet who owed his allegiance to the inner call of art. It was of course Bialik as "National Poet" who excited the imagination and admiration of the Hebrew reading public of his day. His lengthy rhetorical poems were appropriate vehicles for this type of public verse and their powerful periods spoke to the hearts of an entire generation. But the Hebrew reader of our day, like his English-reading contemporary, seems to shy away from such oratorical poetry in favor of briefer, more lyrical verse. Bialik often chose the purely personal vein. Such poems were frequently given an allegorical "nationalist" reading by Bialik's generation. Poems about autumn and spring were, they insisted, really about the death and rebirth of the Jewish nation. Today we read them as we read other lyrics, with concern for the poem itself. And we may note that Bialik in his late period seemed to favor a type of poetry simpler in statement and non-rhetorical in mode.

As happens often in the course of literature, a dominant figure may not only obscure his contemporaries but overwhelm them. Bialik's language, techniques, and even his themes were widely imitated—and as a consequence the last part of the European period of Hebrew poetry has been called "The Age of Bialik." Nevertheless a group of important writers came on the scene during his lifetime. Foremost among them was Saul Tchernichovsky (1875–1943), who—unlike Bialik and most of their contemporaries—was not a product of the Jewish Pale of Settlement. A native of the "New" Russia, which had been annexed from the Turks in the 19th century, Tchernichovsky spent his childhood in a region where the Czarist regime deliberately used a comparatively liberal Jewish policy so as to attract new settlers. Here they spoke Russian, lived closer to nature than was possible in the Pale, and entered into closer relationships with their gentile compatriots. They were not burdened by the terrible oppressiveness of "exile" then prevalent throughout the rest of Russia. Unlike Bialik, Tchernichovsky received a systematic European education, studying at the universities of Heidelberg and Lausanne. What he lacked in traditional lore he made up for in European taste and in a thorough familiarity with the classics of Western literature. This atypical experience led him to introduce many European verse forms into Hebrew literature and to enrich it in other ways.

Accepting the view of a number of the Enlighteners that Judaism was too otherwordly, he called for a liberation from its moral puritanism and extolled pre-biblical Hebrew paganism. But his nature myth was more pantheistic than pagan (while living in Germany, he had come under the influence of Nietzscheism) and he filled it with a vibrant *joie de vivre* hitherto absent from Hebrew letters. More lyricist than thinker, he was temperamentally responsive to certain positive elements of the tradition, as in his series of good-humored portrayals of the less rigid aspects of Jewish folk life in his native Crimea. His Jews seem natural and healthy and free from the sorrowing pain—the *Judenschmerz*—that we normally associate with Russian Jewry.

Whereas Bialik's encounter with Palestine had little influence on him as a writer, Tchernichovsky was profoundly affected. Among his last works is a lengthy poem "Golden Folk" which deals with rural life in Russia and in the new homeland. Tchernichovsky describes bee-culture in rich and knowing detail—he often delighted in displaying his scientific training (and in the process enriched the language with numerous botanical and zoological words). Although he probably used this theme to comment on the Palestine collectives and their "bee-like" existence, the poem stands in its own right as a remarkable literary achievement whose keen observation and wit are irresistible.

In Bialik's day, Zalman Schneur (1887-1959) ranked as the third member of the "great triumvirate," but this judgment no longer seems valid. He introduced the motifs of urban ennui and modern sexuality into Hebrew letters, attacking the accepted bourgeois morality of his readers and demanding a freer and earthier attitude. At the close of his career he published a volume in which he too sought to rediscover pagan and primitive naturalness in biblical and pre-biblical ancestors. Schneur's works for the most part tend to be talky and somewhat contrived; they lack the conciseness and power of Bialik and Tchernichovsky at their best.

Bialik had, at one point in his career, called for a shift from theological and nationalist themes to a personal, lyrical poetry and two of his younger contemporaries followed this direction—and in doing so, foreshadowed some of the poets of the succeeding period. Jacob Steinberg (1887-1947) produced highly individual, melancholy, and meditative poems, particularly after his final settlement in Palestine in 1925. Because he had avoided national themes in a period of national struggle, his work did not, until recently, receive the critical attention it merited. His terse sentences, ambiguous phrasing, and introspective pessimism have proved unusually appealing to readers today.

Like Steinberg, Avraham Ben Yitshak (1883-1950) favored the brief poem, but his diction is much less complex and his work more accessible. He wrote in free verse, with carefully constructed lines unmarred by rhetorical flourishes. Both his language and imagery reflect his affinity for the poetry of Stefan George and Rainer Maria Rilke. Indeed, together with David Fogel (1891-1943), he introduced what Hebrew critics have called "European Modernism" into Hebrew poetry. Their brief, subjective, "imagistic" poems, cast in the melancholy lyric mode that prevailed in post-war Europe, were harbingers of developments that were to emerge in both the Palestinian and Israeli periods.

II. The Palestinian Period (1920-1947)

In the wake of World War I and the Russian Revolution, the literary centers of Hebrew literature in Eastern Europe collapsed. The Communist regime declared Hebrew to be a religious, bourgeois language and jailed many Hebrew writers. Through the intercession of Maxim Gorky, Lenin agreed to release most of them and to allow them to leave Russia. For a few years the center shifted to Berlin, where Bialik had fled, but Berlin proved a temporary refuge. A seemingly inevitable process was propelling Hebrew writers toward Palestine, which was then ruled by Britain under a League of Nations mandate for the establishment of a Jewish National Homeland.

To be sure, immigration to Palestine had been going on for forty years and even in the 1880's its small Zionist community had included a number of Hebrew writers. However, it was during the days of the so-called Second Migration (1905-1914—"Second *Aliyah*," literally "Ascent"), when sizeable groups of immigrants made their way into Palestine, that a number of Hebrew writers established a small literary center in Jaffa. Their magazine, *Hapoël Hatsaír* ("The Young Worker"), bore a title indicative of a new trend in Palestinian Jewish life. The new settlers no longer dreamt of the small privately owned farm. They thought of themselves as pioneers (*ḥalutsím*) and they developed various socialist-zionist philosophies which were to become the dominant ideology in the reconstructed homeland. By and large, the new pioneers had broken with the Jewish religion; their new "religion" was a socialist nationalism.

Almost all the pioneers of the Second Migration were committed to the revival of Hebrew and it was virtually by an act of will that they succeeded in turning the classic tongue into a spoken language. Having given themselves to agricultural and manual occupations, they now extended the social context of Hebrew far beyond the petit-bourgeois purview characteristic of its use in Russia. Jewish workers and farmers in Russia spoke Yiddish; in Palestine, Hebrew became the language of the street, the workshop, the farm, the school, and the home.

Both in prose and verse the influence of the spoken word began to be felt. Rachel (1890-1931), a young pioneer poetess whose works are still popular among Israel's teenagers, was the first to write conversational poems (Bialik had used "conversational asides" derived from Yiddish in some of his verse). To the classically oriented readers and writers of the earlier generation, Rachel's lines looked thin, untraditional, superficial. The poems, short stories, and articles of *Hapoël*

Hatsaír and other periodicals were often read with learned contempt by the former students of rabbinical colleges—but the spoken language had arrived and with it had come the shift of pronunciation and stress, from the Ashkenazi to that of spoken Sephardic.[3]

The encounter with the actual earth of Palestine gave rise to a considerable amount of landscape and local-color poetry. To the Jew living in Europe, his idealized homeland was as familiar as his Bible and Prayerbook; but the country he was now experiencing at first hand—with its brilliant sunlight and exotic landscape—suddenly seemed alien to his northern eye. Alien and also "his own." Poets began to sing paeans to the "New Jew," the pioneering worker and farmer who, having turned his back on Europe, was seeking—and often found—a new life-purpose and meaning in the rebuilding of Zion. David Shimoni (1886-1956), one of the early Palestinian poets, concentrated on these themes, and they are to be found in the verses of almost all the poets who arrived on the scene at this period. Jacob Fichman (1881-1958), for example, a member of Bialik's circle who migrated to Palestine in 1912, combined a romantic temperament with a strong gift for visual portrayal. Note also Abraham Shlonsky's poems about the Mt. Gilboa region ("Ámal, p. 74) and Lea Goldberg's retrospective "Tel-Aviv 1935" (p. 130). Among the very early writers who produced landscape poetry soon after migrating to Palestine was Judah Karni (1885-1949); and his work is notable not only for its almost mystical quality but also for its early use of the Sephardic accent.

A peculiar tension between social and asocial attitudes emerged in the poetry of this period. On the one hand, the writers expressed disillusion with established Jewish and bourgeois values and even skepticism about a socialist-humanist ethic. (The work of such a poet as Shlonsky, for example, is saturated with despair and ennui; note some of the titles of his books or poems: "Pain," "Stones of the Abyss," "Songs of Collapse and Reconciliation.") On the other hand, there was an overpowering desire to find an ideology and to cling to it despite its flaws. A stirring and extremely popular work of the 1920's was Isaac Lamdan's (1899-1954) *Masáda*, which became the manifesto poem of the *ḥalúts* ("pioneer") who, disillusioned by wars, pogroms, revolutions, and ideologies, flees to the Homeland to make his last stand, clinging desperately to the hope of national rebirth. Lamdan spoke of dancing over the abyss with closed eyes. Pioneerism (*ḥalutsiyút*) becomes an almost mystical act of faith bound up with the exciting, exotic new landscape yet also connected to the fervor of a no-longer-accepted religious tradition. Despite his new secularism, the poet remained in various degrees bound to the Jewish past by links of language and images drawn from traditional literature and by childhood memories of a milieu steeped in orthodox piety.

Second only to the theme of Pioneerism, and often linked to it, was the poetry of lament composed in the wake of the ever-increasing catastrophes that were visited upon Europe's Jews in the first half of our century. The biblical *Lamentations* was only the beginning of a vast threnodic literature (*kiná*). With Chaim Nachman Bialik (p. 32), the secularized *kiná* becomes a major genre in modern Hebrew verse. The poets of the Palestinian period continue to record the grievous experiences of their people—in the Ukraine of the early 1920's and in all of Europe during the Hitlerian period. The "Holocaust" occupies a central position in the work of Uri Zvi Greenberg (see p. 64) and no poet ignores it. In the later (Israeli) period, echoes of the same tragedy resound, not only in the work of poets like Kovner and Gilboa (see pp. 148, 142) but also in that of a writer

[3] See pp. 194 f.

such as Carmi who was geographically removed from the scene.

Migrating as they did from various parts of Europe, the Hebrew poets brought with them a rich variety of literary traditions and backgrounds. Rarely in the entire course of literature has there occurred such a fecund process of literary cross-fertilization. Moreover, it differs from the usual manner by which foreign influences exert themselves upon another literature. Most Hebrew authors had strong roots in the European culture and were often as fluent in its idiom as in that of their own. These factors give Hebrew literature of the Palestinian period a distinctive and often enchanting quality. They also explain why it is difficult to characterize its poetry.

The Russian Revolution made an overpowering impact upon Hebrew literature soon after World War I—during the Third Migration. Even the Hebrew poets who rejected communism were affected by the bold rhetoric of Yesenin and Mayakowsky. At the same time, the more subdued tones of Russian Symbolists were audible in some of the new Hebrew poets, and sometimes both influences appeared in the work of the same writer. From France, Austria, and Germany, where many poets of the Palestinian period had lived and studied, other elements were taken over—from Freud's psychology, Bergson's views of art and of time, the experiments of French Symbolists, the German Expressionists, the "imagism" of George and Rilke.

It was natural for the new generation of Hebrew writers soon to come into open conflict with Bialik and the establishment. Abraham Shlonsky was the leader, openly attacking Bialik, his literary and political conservatism, and his Achad Haamism. Shlonsky called for the liberalization of Hebrew syntax and the legitimization of the new spoken idiom as the proper resource for poetic language. He inveighed against the classicism and parochialism still prevalent in diction, idiom, and subject matter. The new "nation" must accept, he argued, all the consequences that secularism and modernism implied. A circle called *Yaḥdáv* ("Together") formed around Shlonsky and began to publish the new poets along with literary journals which propounded their views.

Of the key figures of the Palestinian period —Greenberg, Shlonsky, Alterman, Ratosh, Goldberg—Greenberg (1895-) is in many respects the most "Jewish." An ultra-nationalist, he preaches a quasi-messianic mysticism of blood and race, whose harshness is mollified by the fact that to him the ethic of the Prophets is a genuinely Jewish product. He is able to bolster his anti-European, anti-Christian prejudices by insisting that "they" of the West are in fact unbiblical and that Christianity is only a façade behind which lurks the European "beast." For Greenberg, the Jew and Judaism are the antithesis of Europe and Christianity; hence, of the two camps there can be no synthesis. Strongly influenced by German Expressionists and Yiddish poets, Greenberg achieves his effects with bold rhetorical flourishes, overwhelming his subject with words. His lines are rarely metrical; they are frequently unrimed and usually dependent on an almost biblical cadence. He chooses this form because he believes it to be authentically Jewish and not an alien borrowing from a gentile culture, which he finds so utterly "other."

Abraham Shlonsky (1900-), on the other hand, turns to European humanism and socialism. In his early poetry, the despair, loss of faith, and ennui of modern existence appear to hold out little promise for "salvation," and yet he finds meaning in the pioneering effort of the *ḥalutsím* and in the exotic Palestinian earth. From Russia's revolutionary poets he adopts the exuberant, troubadour, celebrant rhetoric of the Revolution. Like them, he draws on the tradition for striking imagery—and like them, he secularizes it. He often patterns his poems on Russian meters and forms. Shlonsky's work is replete with bold images and bold lines, but there are moments when lyric contemplation prevails and the Symbolism of his Russian mentors takes over. Of all the poets of the period, Shlonsky is the great advocate of the syntax of the spoken idiom and his is undoubtedly the most musical ear.

Nathan Alterman (1910-), the mentor of the succeeding generation, extended Shlonsky's experimentation with the rhythm and syntax of spoken Hebrew. He also enjoyed enormous popularity as a result of both the hundreds of political verse satires that he wrote during the final years of the British Mandate and his lyrical work as well. Alterman makes great use of the European ballad. If in his first period Shlonsky had been something of a troubadour-poet, Alterman became the Hebrew troubadour-poet par excellence, producing imagery that was often wild and at times almost outlandish. Alterman is the creator of Israel's new urban myth. Against the boredom and decadence of the European city, he often projects the new Israeli city a-building: Tel Aviv, vibrant with vitality. Some of Alterman's finest work is permeated with the love and death themes of the romantic agony. The returning dead lover, often the rejected lover, the inconstant woman, the poet-as-wanderer viewing the world-as-inn are motifs which recur in his poetry.

Greenberg tried to relate to the past through a mystic, messianic poetry that would give heroic dimensions to the reconstituted homeland. For Shlonsky and Alterman, the past became a storehouse of images and memories that provides a valid mythology for the contemporary age. For Yonatan Ratosh (1908-), however, the emergence of the New Palestine marks not only a clear break with the past but is diametrically opposed to it. In his view, Bialik and his generation are "Jews," not authentic "Israelis" or "Palestinians." Judaism, moreover, is the antithesis of the New Palestinian World, and all that Jewish culture produced in the Diaspora was "decadent." What holds significance for him is pre-biblical Canaanite and biblical Israelite literature, written and composed within the native terrain.

As a contemporary man, Ratosh does not call for a return to Canaanism or to Biblicism but rather for the adaptation of its literary forms and rhythms. This, in his view, is the language of the "race"—even more, it is a language of the Middle East; and if the New Palestinian is to become at home in his area, he must turn his back on past Jewish culture. Ratosh's literary concerns send him back not only to the Bible but also to ancient Canaanite poetry, which he has studied carefully. With notable skill he tries to create a contemporary poetry in the verse forms, images, rhythms, and archaic words of ancient Hebrew and Canaan. (He does not, however, eschew certain European verse forms.) Involved in this primitivism is a sensual sexuality—which he often equates with pre-Israelite ritual. Some critics see in his work a continuation of the so-called paganism and Canaanism of Tchernichovsky, but the older poet used materials in an allegorical way, to attack his contemporaries for their overconcern with ethics.

Lea Goldberg (1911-), of all the poets of the Palestinian period, is the least ideological. Like Ben Yitshak, she usually disregards nationalist and Jewish subjects in favor of the more universal concerns typical of the mainstream of modern world poetry. In her early career she followed the Russian Symbolists—Blok, Akhmatova, Gomilov, and others; her verse was lyrical, conversational, disarmingly simple. Under the influence of German Neo-romantics her lines grew more complex; they became redolent with ambiguities. One of her central themes is the Lithuanian world of her childhood, which perhaps led her to study and adopt various forms and motifs of Slavic and Lithuanian folk poetry.

The Russian landscape has even greater appeal for Yocheved Bat-Miriam (1901-). Manifestly influenced by Russian Futurism, she is first and foremost a poetess of eerie imagery, nostalgic temper, and sudden associative leaps which give her work a unique dreamlike quality. Though she also wrote a number of Palestinian poems, she is at her best when she invokes the psychological and material landscapes of her northern childhood.

During this 1920-1947 period, a minor center of Hebrew literature arose in New York, where British and American elements were grafted onto a Hebrew poetry rooted in the school of Bialik. Some of its younger members, however, were also influenced by the Palestinian poets. Ultimately most of the gifted New York poets moved to Israel, among them Simon Halkin (1899-), Israel Efrat (1891-), and Abraham Regelson (1896-).

Halkin's work is unmistakably American in both choice of subject and technique—much of it is inspired by the American terrain. Steadily seeking a mystical union with the universe, he embodies his quest in delicately wrought landscape poetry. Although his diction is far removed from the conversational mode so prominent in the contemporary idiom, Halkin's use of metaphor is clearly modern in its kinship with Anglo-American imagism.

Of the poets still residing in New York, Gabriel Preil (1911-) is by far the most impressive. Like Halkin, he represents the encounter of Hebrew poetry with its modern English-language counterpart; but unlike Halkin, he generally turns away from formal techniques. Each poetic idea, he seems to suggest, creates its own rhythms and patterns. Most of his verse might be described as painterly—landscape poetry of a highly visual type, often dreamlike in effect.

Any discussion of the Palestinian period should at least make mention of five other poets: Shin Shalom (1905-), a neo-romantic whose work reflects the influence of Freudian and Rankian psychoanalysis; Jacob Cahan (1881-1963), a prolific writer in the Bialik tradition; Hayim Lensky (1905-?), who continued to write vital Hebrew poetry despite the fact that as a citizen of the Soviet Union he was of course denied access to the literary center; Jacob Rimon (1903-1959), one of the few moderns who wrote religious verse; and Esther Rab (1899-), the only native Palestinian of the period who has produced some fine and authentic landscape poetry.

Most of the poets of the period are still productive. Some, like Shlonsky, and Lea Goldberg, show indications of an effort to write in the idiom of the younger poets, and surely no clear-cut line can distinguish the later work of a writer such as Ratosh from the poets in their thirties. Nevertheless, the poets of the Palestinian period tend to continue within the purview of their generation, as the focus shifts to their younger contemporaries.

III. The Israeli Period (1948-)

The year 1948, when Israel won political independence, approximates the time that a new group of writers, the so-called "Native School," began to publish. The designation should not be taken literally: although some of its members were born in Palestine, a considerable number were not. The latter, however, either were brought there in their childhood and educated there, or were so deeply involved in Zionist and Hebrew youth movements that they had been "culturally Palestinian" regardless of where they happened to live.

With the rise of this Israeli school, Hebrew literature finally produced a generation of writers who were born into both the language and the landscape of Israel. The aim of their predecessors to create an idiom out of a living, spoken language was now fulfilled as the colloquialisms and the conversational rhythms embedded in contemporary Hebrew verse lost the somewhat forced ring that they once had. The landscape has taken on reality—it is no longer something idealized in the Zionist dreams of an immigrant poet from the Diaspora, nor is it an earth viewed with pained ambivalence by an artist whose childhood memories were rooted in the North. The ecstasy and loneliness have almost disappeared, although they sometimes survive in poems about the Negev, Israel's last frontier.

The receding of the Diaspora from the consciousness of the Hebrew poet has had its effect on both the texture of language and the range of symbols. Echoes of Yiddish along with the luxuriant sentimentality and nostalgia of the small Jewish town fade away. The secular schooling of the contemporary Israeli poet has also affected his vocabulary and his imagery. While the Bible remains a central element of the educational system of the new culture, rabbinic literature is no longer taught with the intensity that had formerly accompanied it in the religiously oriented schools of the Diaspora. If some of the Israeli poets still draw on these sources, it is because they came from religious families which had sent them to traditional schools. Others, lacking such background, set out to study the tradition after their initial publications.

The removal of the poets from Europe has also affected the role that Western poetry plays in their work. Unlike the Palestinian generation, which could draw directly from a variety of literary traditions, many of the younger Israeli poets have acquired their European languages in school. Often they become acquainted with European literary trends through translations or critical articles published in Hebrew. In contrast to their predecessors, who were influenced by Eastern Europe (where most of them were born) or Central Europe (where many of them lived or studied), the poets of the Israeli period look to British and American literatures. English is now the dominant foreign tongue in Israel. This does not mean that other literatures are not read or that they do not affect contemporary Hebrew writers: a considerable number of them still read East European languages. Moreover, for the first time in almost a century, a number of writers of German-Jewish origin have achieved prominence in Hebrew letters. (The Palestinian period could claim only one such poet, Ludwig Strauss.) Coming from German-speaking homes, they continue to read German. Other poets have also made contact with French and Italian literatures as a result of travel and temporary residence abroad. But the overwhelming influence, increasingly among writers under thirty-five, comes from Britain and America. One can readily find traces in most of their work of Eliot and Auden and of the ironic element in contemporary English verse.

The crisis in ideology that bore down upon European literature in the wake of World War II reached Israeli literature somewhat later—the national struggle for independence and the visions of socialist-Zionism held off the disenchantment that swept over the intellectual circles of Western Europe. Thus at the very time when Existential *angst* was spreading through Europe, many of Israel's young poets were fighting for the national and social ideals of the War of Liberation. Coming as many of them did either from collective settlements (*kibutsim*) or from the various left-wing Zionist groups, they retained the enthusiasm of the ideologist. Literature was to serve as an instrument of the struggle for national independence and of the new society that would arise. It was in this period that war hymns such as Gury's "See Our Bodies Cast" and Whitmanesque odes such as Gilboa's "Early Morning Poem" formed a large part of the literary output.

It would, however, be false to think that what was happening in Europe had no effect in Israel even in these earlier years. Disillusion, *angst*, and irony often take over in the work of poets imbued with the enthusiasm of Israel's rebirth. Thus Gilboa, for example, was able to write optimistic, life-affirming verse at one moment and at another to sink into a pensive, world-weary mood. In one poem he can sing of the joy in existing things and of the need to "Wrap the barren rocks of silent life in the youthfulness of their greenery." In another he can lament: "When all is said and done, we haven't said a thing; / We haven't yet said ourselves. / A great fire once was flaming in the face, we shall say. / Great waters and their mighty rushing swept us, we shall say. / We shall surely be silent and shall not be able to say more. / And then our sons learning the arithmetic of the day will sharpen their pencils. . . ."

Following the War of Independence, the crisis in ideology became pronounced. It was inevitable that the fulfilment of the dream of national independence would usher in the realization that not all problems has been resolved. The egoisms that had been harnessed during the struggle now broke loose. The new realities in economics and politics pushed aside the theories.

The transition to non-ideological poetry marks what Halkin calls "the disappearance of the vital ideal from Hebrew poetry." In the Palestinian period tendentious verse and poetry-for-poetry's sake seemed to have flourished side by side. If Shlonsky and his contemporaries attacked Bialik's Achad Haamism in the name of Art, they too, to some degree, subjected their writing to a non-artistic, "objective" standard: the hopes, the aspirations, of the new nation of workers and farmers returning to the historic homeland. In the present—post-Independence—society, the earlier ideologies lose their relevance. Neither the religious tradition nurtured in the Diaspora nor the cultural nationalism of Bialik and Achad Haam nor the pioneering nationalism of the Palestinian poets seems to answer the needs of the contemporary artist.

Yet for the very reason that he finds himself detached from the past, the Israeli poet must seek his values: within the subject itself, not outside it—in the inner experience of the artist and within the scope of the art itself. Such subjectivism leads paradoxically to a more universal poetry. Moving away from parochially Jewish concerns as well as ready-made answers of ideologists, the contemporary Israeli poet is compelled to face both man and art directly.

He must face his language also. Now that Hebrew has lost its classical character and has acquired the flexibility of common speech, the poet is impelled to work with its new rhythms and its new sound patterns. Some of the verse of Gilboa, Sach, and Amihai has the quality of a musical étude. The poet seems to be beating against the boundaries of language in order to expand its possibilities and to say what has not yet been said—sonally.

Two poets of the Palestinian period, Shlonsky and Alterman, may be regarded as the chief mentors of the Israeli generation. Their modernism, their ear for the rhythms of speech, and their musicality had the greatest appeal to the first generation of Israeli poets. It took the new generation several years to overcome their aversion to Diaspora poets such as Bialik. Yet within a decade, they rediscovered Bialik along with the more consistently aesthetic members of his circle. Ideological considerations also caused them for some time to overlook the achievements of such poets as Ratosh and Greenberg. Only after the revolt against ideology in the 1950's did these poets receive full recognition.

As personal lyric poetry moves to the center of the new literature, the long poem characteristic of the Age of Bialik and significant in the Palestinian period becomes a rarity, though writers like Abba Kovner (1918-) and Avot Yeshurun (1904-) sometimes produce long poems of a different type. The tendency already discernible in the Palestinian period toward the concise poem and the condensed line grows ever stronger. Nevertheless, the expansive, rhetorical line has not quite disappeared. Biblical verse, Bialik's long poems, and Greenberg's rhetoric and free verse still have their effect, sometimes even on poets who favor compactness of expression.

Within the Israeli period a natural division occurs between the older and younger members. The older, now in their late thirties or forties, lived through the War of Independence and were more strongly affected by the socialist-Zionist youth movements. Many of them (like the Palestinian poets) were also subject to a variety of foreign traditions. The younger writers, on the other hand, having arrived on the scene in the post-ideological world of the late 1950's and 1960's, never experienced the conflict that some of their older contemporaries went through as they moved from "ideology to subjectivity." In addition, the younger group differs from the older in being more consistently responsive to American and British poetry.

Another kind of distinction should also be made: between writers of exclusively Palestinian education and those who were exposed to European or American culture. Among the older group, such poets as Carmi and Amihai brought with them a knowledge of Western poetry and from the very beginning composed lyrical, melancholy, and tightly constructed verse—and while they too faced the ideological "crisis," it was far less intense for them than for such poets as Gury and Hillel. However, as the Palestinian-educated group came into prominence, most of its members were directly exposed to European poetry: Gury, to take one example, lived in Paris for some time and this contact with French literature had a discernible effect upon his writing.

Although Yehuda Amihai (1924-) belongs to the older group, his work has set the tone for many of his younger contemporaries. His use of daily speech, his irony, his "metaphysical" metaphors and Existential ennui have become hallmarks of contemporary writing. Some of his titles contain the word *aḥṣáv* ("now"); the "here and now" is in fact a leitmotif in his work as well as in that of a good many other writers. Eternal values and experiences no longer have meaning for them. Only the intensity of the experienced moment, always doomed to be lost, retains a redeeming element.

T. Carmi (1925-), another member of the older group, has a smaller range but a far more disciplined line. His poems are taut, his metaphors precise and replete with irony and with visual and tactile richness. Both his verse translations for the theater and his original poetry reflect the rigorousness of a writer who has mastered his art.

By contrast, Amir Gilboa's (1917-) work has an unmistakably surrealistic air. His imaginative blending of dream fragments with patches of early childhood memories give his poetry a highly individual and, at times, an almost playful quality. Gilboa has been one of the major poetic influences of his generation. Many of his lines are rich with multiple meaning. His experiments in rhythm at times achieve the power of incantation.

It is worth noting that although these three poets are non-religious, because of their traditional upbringing they employ a full arsenal of religious referents. These include not only symbolic and metaphorical elements but also certain rhythmic and verbal associations that echo verses and phrases from the Hebrew classics.

The work of Tuvya Rübner (1921-)—like that of Yehuda Amihai and Nathan Sach—reflects the influence of German neo-romanticism. His poems distil the details of landscape and human activity into a single poetic experience. Unlike his German masters, Rübner has a penchant for surrealism and verbal experimentation.

Abba Kovner (1918-) arrived in Palestine

in 1946. His early poems grew out of his experiences as a partisan in Nazi-occupied Poland; his later work uses the War of Liberation as background. Kovner's writings are the subjective and lyrical verse of a man who has lived through the "moment of truth." His free rhythms are lashed together with wild associative leaps.

Avot Yeshurun (1904-) tries to capture the Middle-Eastern landscape and mood not so much by incorporating biblical rhythms and archaisms (as Shlonsky, for example, did in "End of Adár," p. 78) as by introducing phrases and cadences from spoken Arabic. These he often counterpoints against traditional Hebrew and even Yiddish phrases to point up the contradictions between the old and the new milieux—and at times even the fusion of the two. Like his contemporaries, Yeshurun tends to shatter his syntax in order to reflect the ambiguities and absurdities which exist in his world.

Only a word need be said of the poets within the younger group who are included in this volume. Both Nathan Sach (1930-) and Dan Pagis (1929-) show an affinity for Existentialism, but here the similarities end. Pagis' lines are denser and less conversational than Sach's, some of whose work reflects his response to German and American poetry. Dalia Ravikovitch (1935-) skillfully blends a delightful girlish naïvete and a simple, almost biblical, style with surrealistic statement.

Anthologies cannot, of course, include all poets of talent, and some among the younger generation who do not appear in this volume must at least be mentioned: Yechiel Mar (1921-), Ozer Rabin (1921-), Benjamin Galai (1921-), Rina Shani (1937-). These are but a few of the most promising poets in an extremely prolific milieu. The reader should bear in mind that the extraordinarily active literary productivity of which we have given only a hint occurs in a country with a population of little more than two million more than half of whom are recent immigrants.

Although it would be fruitless to speculate on the new directions that modern Hebrew poetry might take, the current trend toward a non-ideological poetry of a character more universal than that of the preceding generations seems likely to continue. If some critics lament that contemporary poets are detached from the "great tradition" of classical religious literature, that tradition is still strongly evident insofar as the formal aspects of poetry are concerned. Allusions to classical phrases, metaphors, and rhythms abound, and it is no accident that in the Israeli period in this anthology there are several poems directly drawn from biblical motifs. Thus modernism and tradition somehow still merge to form the peculiarly fascinating blend that constitutes contemporary Hebrew poetry.

— EZRA SPICEHANDLER

A NOTE ON HEBREW PROSODY

The modern Hebrew poet, when approaching his language, is confronted with a *musée imaginaire* (to use Malraux's expression) in which more than three thousand years of Hebrew verse live concurrently. Of the few ancient poetries that have continued uninterruptedly, the Hebraic is surely the most variegated and versatile in its forms, having interacted in its wanderings with quite different systems of language and poetry. But since the canonization of the Bible, Hebrew verse has retained—through all ages, countries, pronunciations, and changes of tone, genre, poetic language, and prosodic system—its close tie with a basic text and tradition. Moreover, Hebrew—as a semi-"dead" tongue—has never changed the core of its vocabulary or the written form of its words, its basic morphology, certain patterns of syntax and of idiomatic formulations, or the fundamental frame of its historical, semantic, and mythological allusions. Thus a Hebrew poet of whatever generation who knows "the beginning and the end"—that is, his Bible and the Hebrew verse of his own time—can understand the language of all intervening periods. For these reasons even the most cursory note on modern Hebrew poetry must take at least a glimpse at the historical gallery of forms that are omnipresent to the contemporary Hebrew poet.

I. BIBLICAL VERSE

Though it includes writings ranging over nearly a thousand years, the Bible has been viewed by later ages as primarily a unified work with a basically common language. Whatever may have been the developments in phonetics and prosody during the time of its creation, the Bible for post-biblical readers has meant what the canonized text presented, with its system of stresses, intonation marks, and punctuation. This text has exerted an overpowering influence on Hebrew writers in all ages; its rhythmic character has even been felt within quite contrary metrical systems.

Scholars have battled for years over the secrets of biblical prosody and there have also been attempts to correct the text in order to make it conform to pseudo-classic ideas of rhythm, requiring strict numbering of some kind—regularized "feet," equalized hemistichs, or stanzas of recurring numbers of lines. Today all such attempts seem pointless, for rhythm by no means needs to be "based" upon numerical regularity.

In principle, biblical poetry (like most "primitive" poetries) is irregular with respect to number. Disregarding differences of genre, period, and style, we may say, first, that the meter of biblical verse is *accentual* (or "tonic"); that is, it is based upon stress. In Hebrew, as in English, stress is a conspicuous element; it organizes the word and it may distinguish its meaning (as it distinguishes the English *cónduct* from *condúct*). But stress is not the only determinant. The other major principle of biblical verse is parallelism. A "verse" consists of 2 (or 3 or 4) parts or hemistichs. Each such part is a phrase, a basic rhythmical and logical unit, composed of 2 or 3 or 4 words. Since the Hebrew language sums up each independent idea in a strongly accented word—often complex—there is an overlapping of "logical rhythm" and "phonetic rhythm." The hemistichs are usually parallel—completely or in part—not only in the numbers of words but also in their meaning and/or syntax, in a variety of ways: synonymous, antithetic, etc. The following simple example is from Psalm 24:3:

mi-yaalé behár adonáy
umi-yakúm bimkóm kodsó

Here we have 3 stressed units in each hemistich; the whole line is thus a 3:3 pattern of rhythm. But this number is not kept consistently in the sequel. (In fact, the next verse of this psalm has 3 hemistichs with a varying number of stresses in each.) Note that in our example each stress-unit is a single Hebrew word but in an English word-for-word translation each stress-unit becomes a phrase:

Who shall go up / to the mountain / of the Lord
And who shall rise / in the place / of His holiness

But it is important to note that the number of unstressed syllables between any two stresses, though free in principle, is also regulated: usually one, two, or three. Since each stressed element is thus related to its counterpart, parallelism emphasizes (or "doubles") the impact. Moreover, because of the smallness and compactness of the hemistich, each stress has conspicuous force. The condensed, laconic nature of Hebrew also contributes to the prominence of each word within the line. This is supported by the fact that biblical syntax favors parallelism rather than subordination of clauses and phrases and the long periodic sentences frequent in certain Indo-European languages.

To the reader accustomed to English and European verse, biblical poetry seems "free," its rhythmical patterns determined by meaning alone. And he feels no tension or conflict between the rhythm of meter and the rhythm of meaning: the two coincide (as they do only rarely in English verse, for example). This relative freedom from numerical determination combined with the rhythmical role of meaning-patterns and the symmetry of the basic units helped make possible the translation of biblical verse into other languages without serious loss of rhythmical effect.

II. THE MIDDLE AGES

The Middle Ages saw the emergence of two major traditions in Hebrew poetry: the liturgical tradition (the *piyút*) and the quantitative metrics developed in Spain. Both were used throughout the Diaspora and both were included in the Prayerbook.

The liturgical verse, evolved in the land of Israel in the first centuries of the Christian era, used complex structures of interlocking patterns of all types: semantic, syntactic, sonal, allusive, etc. Whereas repetition in biblical verse was based on parallelism and symmetry, liturgical poetry made use of formalized, multiple repetitions of its elements. Acrostic, end-rime, and internal rime, recurring formulas, words, refrains, and allusions occurred often in long chains of distinct stanzaic structure. The meter was founded on a more or less regular number of words per line. Many types of liturgical poems were written throughout the ages for occasions in the religious and national life of the people—prayers, holiday songs, litanies, elegies, etc.

The secular and religious verse that flourished in Spain from the 10th to the 15th centuries was quantitative (similar to Greek meter). Developed under Arabic influence, it disregarded stress entirely while bringing into prominence another feature of the language: the difference in the amount of time required to pronounce a schwa (or "half-syllable"),[1] considered as short and all other syllables regarded as long. The poets then patterned the short and long syllables in strict meters. In most cases, the poems used a single rime throughout, but stanzaic forms with complex riming also emerged.

Another type of prosody developed first in Italy, then in the Portuguese community of Amsterdam. Hebrew sonnets were written in hendecasyllables (11 syllables per line) which also observed the short-and-long system

[1] viz., the "mobile schwa," a brief vowel sound, indicated in Hebrew by ְ below the letter.

mentioned above—a hybrid of Arabic and Italian metrics. Later, the poets, especially in 19th-century Central and Eastern Europe, dropped the quantitative distinctions to write purely syllabic verse (fixed number of syllables per line). The disregard of stress seemed strange, considering the role of stress in the Bible and in the metrics of the immediate environment (German, Russian, Yiddish). But stress often emerged unconsciously. Owing to the length of the line used, there was a more or less regular number of words, often in parallel units; thus this strictly syllabic verse also echoed rhythms of the Bible.

III. MODERN HEBREW METER

Some seventy-five years ago Hebrew writers adopted the poetics of 19th-century German and Russian verse. For prosody this meant full attention to the dynamic stress of the language itself. The new Hebrew meter came to resemble that of English, German, Yiddish, and Russian poetry. It takes into account not only accent (as in the accentual meter of the Bible) or number of syllables (as in the syllabic verse of the 19th century) but both; that is, it is an *accentual-syllabic* system. Only the quantitative principle (length of syllables) is disregarded.

In modern Hebrew poetry, a meter means a permanent order of stressed (—) and unstressed (∪) syllables. As in English, the five basic meters are: iamb (∪ —) and trochee (— ∪); anapest (∪∪ —), amphibrach (∪ — ∪), and dactyl (— ∪∪). But only rarely is the abstract metrical pattern given in the language of every line of a poem. For example, this is a typical Hebrew stanza of four iambs:

∪ — ∪ — ∪ — ∪ — ∪
Tsaḥút hatsémer haṣoféa.
∪ — ∪ — ∪ — ∪ —
Lavnút haléḥem hanivtsá.
∪ — ∪ — ∪ — ∪ — ∪
Irí poréṣet et-noféha
∪ — ∪ — ∪ — ∪ —
Umizdakéfet merivtsá.

("Purity of the flowing wool. / Whiteness of the broken bread. / My city spreads out its vistas. / And rises from its crouching. /" —Abraham Shlonsky).

The number of syllables is regular but there are only three or two accents (indicated by ′) in each line. This fact is due to the large number of polysyllabic words in Hebrew. Of course, an expressive reading will sound only the actual accents and the actual rhythmical divisions (between words and phrases). Nevertheless the meter is there, perhaps subsiding into the background of such an expressive, meaningful reading, since the text *can* be scanned or performed mechanically (in this instance, 4 iambs, with an extra syllable at the end of lines 1 and 3). It can be scanned because the text complies with the general rule: any word may be given two or more metrical stresses according to an abstract pattern, provided that at least one such stress falls upon the syllable that is normally accented. To put it differently: an iambic line in Hebrew means a line in which the accents of words fall on the even syllables (second, fourth, sixth, etc.) though not, of course, on all of them.

This rule is incomparably more relevant for Hebrew with its superabundance of polysyllabic words than it could be for English, with its very high proportion of monosyllabic words. Hebrew meters are much more similar to their Russian than to their English counterpart, not only because of the direct influence of Russian upon Hebrew verse but also because of the large number of polysyllabic words in both languages. This characteristic quality has been the primary source of rhythmical variation in Hebrew.

In order to avoid monotony of meter, every language employs specific resources which allow for deviations from the abstract scheme. Thus English will use its monosyllables for this purpose, e.g., place accented syllables in unstressed positions ("To be or not to be, thát is the question" or the so-called "spondaic foot," as in Milton's "Rocks, Caves, Lakes, Fens, Bogs, Dens, and shades of Death") and rely on the changing, asymmetrical rhythms of its phrasal divisions. One has only to compare, for example, the changing length of the phrase in Shakespearean iambic pentameter with the example given above, from Shlonsky. An English-speaking reader may miss such effects in Hebrew verse and think that it is rhythmically too "smooth." But it is simply a matter of the difference in the ways in which variation is achieved. In Hebrew meters, rhythmical expression is felt when stresses are omitted (and they are omitted in a variety of ways) and when word-boundaries contradict metrical boundaries ("feet"). In the stanza quoted above, Shlonsky "skips" stresses and also avoids symmetrical division of his lines by using penultimately stressed words in the middle of each line, thus inhibiting a rest after the second iamb. The English reader must understand that such lines, when read in their own tradition, are much less monotonous than is iambic tetrameter in English, for example. But when Hebrew verse moved recently out of the Russian influence into the tone of English poetry and the "melodic" manner of reading verse gave way to a prosy, matter-of-fact approach, rhythm also moved away from the symmetrical lines and moved toward the interplay of phrase-groups characteristic of English.

Metrical patterns which stress every third syllable are much more common in Hebrew than in English, for two reasons: the external influence of Russian and Yiddish and their natural "fitness" to the language, (since there is, on the average, one accent to three syllables in Hebrew). It is as easy to write anapests in Israeli Hebrew (or amphibrachs in Ashkenazi) as iambs in English. But obviously the advantage of these meters is also their disadvantage in terms of rhythmical variation—the more so in Israeli Hebrew, where most of the words are accented on the last syllable. Thus in an anapest, in most cases, the end of a word and the end of a foot, the metrical stress and the tonic accent, *all* coincide. This creates an effect of very strong cuts in the line—ta-ta-tá | ta-ta-tá | ta-ta-tá—which subdues all semantic subtleties in the words.

Aside from such non-metrical means as sound orchestration and patterns of syntax and of meaning that "disagree" with the units of meter, the possibilities for rhythmical variation in these meters are rather limited. Hence the poets have resorted to changes in the metrical scheme itself, as we shall see in our discussion of free rhythms.

IV. CHANGES IN PRONUNCIATION

In the first decades of this century, when the cultural center of Hebrew moved to Palestine, it suffered the shock of losing its sound-basis. Unlike the changes in pronunciation which influenced euphony and prosody in other languages, this change was not gradual—it was produced by a sudden confrontation. The 19th-century Hebrew poetry written in Eastern Europe was based on the Ashkenazi pronunciation (with its several sub-dialects) that had been used there since the Middle Ages. The new "dialect" which Hebrew poets faced in Palestine—the "Sephardic" or "Israeli"—was no longer a semi-living language confined to prayer, learning, and letter-writing, but a full-scale spoken Hebrew of a modern society alive to all aspects of changing existence. Most "disturbing" of all: Israeli vocabulary and grammar did not differ considerably from the Ashkenazi except in pronunciation. Suddenly the perfect Lithuanian Ashkenazi rime רְתֵת־עֹז: *rseys-eyz* ("trembling-strength"), for example, became *rtet-oz*, a pair of words without a single sound in common.

In the accenting of words, the major change was from the penultimate to the ultimate (עִבְרִית, "Hebrew," changed from *Ívris* to *Ivrít*). This was not a different language, then, but a different way of reading the same signs. Hence, to read the (Ashkenazi) poetry of the flourishing period in the beginning of our century in accordance with the (Israeli) pronunciation that one uses naturally today is to deprive it of its metrical effects and its sound orchestration and to place it at the mercy of its ideas. This break in the field of sound and of poetic immediacy contributed to the gap between generations. It reinforced the usual break with the past of a modernist movement (which overtook Hebrew poetry in the twenties) and magnified the change in background from the North, the Diaspora, the Small Town, to the South, the Land of Israel, the New Society, the Modern World.

In the work of some poets (Shlonsky, Greenberg, for example) the phonetic change was achieved toward the end of the twenties. But the poets of the older generation could not adapt their verse so easily to the new pronunciation of the street (even though they might consider it to be the "right" one, since it was closer to the accents marked in the Bible). Some poets were unwilling to consign all that they had written to oblivion. Some at first fought against the change only to give in later, pressed by the reality of living speech; others kept stubbornly to the Ashkenazi as being more "melodious." Still others switched to Israeli Hebrew for their more "impersonal" (declamatory, ballad-like) poems, returning to Ashkenazi for verse that reinvoked the world of their childhood, with which the new sounds did not somehow associate (Tchernichovsky, in his "Idylls"). And, finally, some poets tried to translate their own poetry from Hebrew to Hebrew, involving themselves in a reshuffling of sound-meaning relationships that rarely succeeded.

In the process of change there were several stages and a series of mixed phenomena. Thus, for example, "bilingual" poems emerged, such as Greenberg's in which the poet writes in Ashkenazi but the workers talking use Israeli Hebrew. And matters became even more confounded—and, on the contrary, resolved—by the spread of free verse.

V. FREE RHYTHMS

Under the impact of European modernist poetry, especially after World War I, a great variety of free verse appeared in Hebrew. Of course there is always a rhythmical pattern of some kind which, in most cases, uses metrical form as at least a framework from which to deviate or as a background against which the rhythm is constructed. Since the possibilities, tendencies, intermediate forms, etc., are too numerous and since they are based on combinations of elements too complex to be analyzed in these brief remarks on prosody, we may content ourselves with merely hinting at certain kinds of free verse that are common in Hebrew, especially those unfamiliar to English-speaking readers.

The most widely used pattern since World War I—and the least "free" one—has been the so-called anapestic "net," adapted from such Russian poets as Blok, Yesenin, and Akhmatova. (In different varieties, it was a favorite with Bat-Miriam, Alterman, Lea Goldberg, and others.) This "net" may be described as a rhythm based on more or less regular numbers of stresses per line with a limited freedom regarding the number of unstressed syllables lying between any two stresses. This may call to mind Coleridge's "Rime of the Ancient Mariner," but the freedom in the anapestic "net" is much more restricted. Usually the anapestic flow is established—in Hebrew it sounds less artificial than in English because of the larger distance between accents in Hebrew words—and then the effect of deviation or "frustrated expectation" is achieved by the unexpected absence of an unstressed syllable here and there. Thus, the abstract pattern resembles a net with some holes in it. In reading, of course, the effect of these "holes" will vary, since a missing syllable may be compensated for either by a pause (to emphasize a syntactic rest or an emotive gesture) or by a lengthening of the remaining syllables (in order to make them conform to the established rhythmical expectation). Or, if the tone of the poem happens to be rather prosaic, the reader may not compensate for the missing syllable, thus emphasizing the prose-like irregularity of time intervals between stresses. Since this type of verse is not merely a matter of freedom, permitting one or two unstressed syllables, but of concrete and purposeful skips, within an established pattern, there are subtle variations in the use of this mode of rhythmical expression.

Some poets used no preestablished framework for an entire poem but still relied on meter, using different metrical segments (iambs, anapests, etc.) in particular lines. In the youngest generation, especially under the impact of English influence—and supported also by its misreading of Ashkenazi verse—we find poems quite close to prose. The development of spoken Hebrew has encouraged this tendency. The rhythm is based largely on groups of phrases and the tension between phrasal division and lines. Word-groups are often used in ways reminiscent of biblical verse, though the syntax differs, being frequently more complex and Indo-European rather than Semitic.

To be sure, long before the advent of modernism, the Bible had exerted a liberating effect on Hebrew meter, similar to the effect of Greek meters on such German poets as Klopstock and Hölderlin. As early as Bialik, in his poems with a biblical tone, freedom from metrical strictness is evident. A similar effect had been produced by the Yiddish folksong and, in the case of Tchernichovsky, by the Greek dactylic hexameter. But freedom—even of a single syllable—was confined only to such specific genres.

VI. RIME

After making some sporadic use of rime, post-biblical Hebrew poetry, around the 5th or 6th centuries, developed end-rime as a permanent and obligatory feature of a poem.

Owing to its presence in the liturgy of the Prayerbook, rime has been an everyday experience of Jews throughout the world. Moreover, it has been actively used by Jews of all generations: in rimed fiction, rabbinical letters, birthday songs, grave inscriptions, book introductions, chronicles, and, above all, in religious and secular verse.

The norm of modern Hebrew rime is parallelism of final sounds from the last stressed vowel onwards. As in English, rimes are called either "masculine"—when the final syllable is stressed: *bake-rake;* Hebrew: *ṣor-ḥamór* ("ox-donkey")—or "feminine"—when a stressed syllable is followed by an unstressed syllable: *heaven-seven;* Hebrew: *méleḥ-héleḥ* ("king-wanderer"). An English rime such as *latitude-gratitude*, however, is found practically only in Ashkenazi Hebrew (*gálela-tsálela*, "she spread-she dived", for, as we have already noted, Israeli words are usually stressed on ultimate or penultimate syllables).

Some of the conventions of Hebrew riming may be of interest to English-speaking readers. For example, at least one consonant is required when the rime ends on a stressed vowel: *koRÁ-dibRÁ* (capital letters show identical sounds).

Rime based on a repeated suffix is not favored. Thus *nehagÍM-korÍM* ("drivers-miners") is frowned upon as a merely "grammatical" rime which lacks a root-consonant. But *koRÍM-dvaRÍM* ("miners-things") is a satisfactory rime, for *RÍM* contains not only the pluralizing suffix *IM* but also the consonant R which in both words is part of the root.

The tradition of writing verse with alternate masculine and feminine rimes and the scarcity of "feminine" Israeli Hebrew words encouraged the use of inexact rimes. Such a rime is identical in the stressed vowel but different in the final sound. Usually it compensates for this difference by repeating the sound that precedes the identical vowel. Thus, the rime *gÉṢER-nÉṢER* ("bridge-eagle") is exact, but *GÉṢEr-laGÉṢEt* ("bridge-to approach") is inexact: instead of an identical final consonant, we have r and t, but the consonant G preceding the stressed vowel E is identical; cf. in English: CÁNNOn-CÁNNOt.

Such a modernist rime may actually involve more sounds than are required—as, for example, in Alterman's *LeḤ uṢMÁ-haḤaṢMÁL* ("go and listen—the electricity") and KoS HaMÁyIm-KSuMÁ HI ("glass of water—she is charmed"). In addition to the stressed vowel and the consonant preceding it (*ṢMÁ* and *MÁ*), these two rimes repeat additional consonants, though not necessarily in identical order. Hence this type of inexact rime may be called "discontinuous." It is based primarily on the consonants, which alone carry lexical meaning in Hebrew (*odér-adár*, for example, are merely two forms of the same verb ["he digs—he dug"], whereas *either-other* are two entirely different words in English). Although this tendency was undoubtedly encouraged by the rich inexact rimes of modern verse in other languages (Mayakowsky's, for example), it is matched by a similar phenomenon in the early stages of Hebrew rime: "discontinuous" rime, involving several consonants (though exact in its endings), is favored in early liturgical poetry.

Medieval Hebrew rime, in all its varieties, was not stress-bound but based on the final syllable and the preceding consonant—*géṢER-koṢÉR* ("the bridge—he ties"). It was in a way similar to Wyatt's fourfold rime "harbor-banner-suffer-displeasure," riming the final sounds *ER* without regard for stress; but unlike English rime, it required an additional preceding consonant—like the French *rime riche: homMAGE-iMAGE*. This additional consonant, obligatory in liturgy, and easy to achieve in a language with most words stressed ultimately, is favored—though not required—in Israeli poetry too.

Thus, from even these brief remarks, the English-speaking reader can see that Hebrew rime, like Hebrew prosody, is a multitude of voices, patterns, associations, traditions, and fresh responses.

— BENJAMIN HRUSHOVSKI

NOTES ON CONTRIBUTORS

ROBERT ALTER Department of English, Columbia University; Author: *Rogue's Progress: Studies in the Picaresque Novel;* introduction to *Israeli Stories;* Contributor: *Commentary*, etc.

HAIM BLANC Department of Linguistics, Hebrew University; Author: *Studies in North Palestinian Arabic, Communal Dialects in Baghdad, Intensive Spoken Israeli Hebrew*, etc.; Contributor: *Language, Word, Orbis*, etc.

ARNOLD BAND Department of Hebrew and Near Eastern Languages, University of California at Los Angeles; Author: *Hare'i Boér Baéṣ (The Mirror Burns with Fire);* Contributor: *Midstream, Judaism, Jewish Social Studies, Molád*, etc.

ROBERT FRIEND Department of English, Hebrew University; Author, *Shadow on the Sun; Now* (with Harold Schimmel and Dennis Silk); *Salt Gifts;* Contributor: *Poetry, Atlantic Monthly, Partisan Review, The New Yorker, London Magazine, Hortulus*, etc.

LEA GOLDBERG Chairman, Department of Comparative Literature, Hebrew University; Author: *Al Hapriḥá (On Bloom), Barák Babóker (Lightning in the Morning), Mukdám Umeuḥár (Early and Late); Baalát Haarmón (Lady of the Manor)*, etc.; Translator: *As You Like It, War and Peace, Peer Gynt, Poems of Petrarch*, plays by Goldoni, Pirandello, Brecht, Wilder, etc.

BENJAMIN HRUSHOVSKI Department of Comparative Literature, Hebrew University; Translator: *Poems of A. Sutskever; Poems of Moshe Leib Halpern* (with A. Sivan); Contributor: *Style in Language, Field of Yiddish*, etc.

ABRAHAM HUSS Department of Meteorology, Hebrew University; Contributor: *Poetry, Hortolus, Molád, Kéṣet, Gazít, Orót, Masá*, etc.

DAVID MIRSKY Associate Professor of English and Dean of Admissions, Yeshiva University; Contributor: *Harpers Bible Dictionary, Herzl Year Book; Jewish Life; Horizon*, etc.

DAN PAGIS Department of Hebrew Literature, Hebrew University; Author: *Ṣeón Hatsél (The Shadow Dial), Ṣahút Meuḥéret (Late Leisure);* Translator: stories by A. L. Strauss *(Hakád Haatík);* texts for music *(Pierrot Lunaire, Bastien et Bastienne*, etc.); Editor: *Collected Poetry of David Fogel, Collected Works of Levi ibn Altabban;* Contributor: *Amót, Molád, Moznáyim, Hortulus*, etc.

DALIA RAVIKOVITCH Author: *Ahavát Tapúaḥ Hazaháv (Love of an Orange); Ḥóref Kaṣé (Hard Winter);* Translator: *The King Must Die;* Contributor: *Amót, Molád, Moznáyim, Kéṣet*, etc.

TUVYA RÜBNER Author: *Haéṣ Baéven (The Fire in the Stone), Ṣirím Limtsó Et (Poems to Find Time);* Editor *Studies in Literature* by A. L. Strauss; Contributor: *Hortulus, Moznáyim, Molád*, etc.

ARIEH SACHS Department of English, Hebrew University; Contributor: *Medieval Studies, Journal of English and Germanic Philology, Cambridge Review, Modern Language Review, Studies in English Literature, Romanica et Occidentalia, Cambridge Opinion, Southern Review, English Studies*, etc.

DAVID SARAPH Translator: *Jews and Antisemitism* by Peretz Bernstein; Contributor: *Transatlantic Review, Haárets, Jerusalem Post, Jewish Quarterly*, etc.

HAROLD SCHIMMEL Department of English, Hebrew University; Author: *Now* (with Robert Friend and Dennis Silk).

STANLEY BURNSHAW Lecturer in Literature, New York University (1958-1962); Author: *Early and Late Testament, Caged in an Animal's Mind, The Sunless Sea*, etc.; Translator: *André Spire and His Poetry;* Editor: *The Poem Itself; Varieties of Literary Experience*, etc.; Contributor: *Sewanee Review, Poetry, Partisan Review, the Saturday Review, Columbia Dictionary of Modern European Literature*, etc.

T. CARMI Author: *Mum Vaḥalóm (Blemish and Dream), Eyn Praḥim Ṣhorím (There Are No Black Flowers), Ṣéleg Biruṣaláyim (Snow in Jerusalem), Hayám Haaḥarón (The Last Sea), Neḥáṣ Haneḥóṣet (The Brass Serpent);* Translator: *Midsummer Night's Dream*, plays by Sophocles, Brecht, Ghelderode, Behan, Albee, etc.; Contributor: *Poetry, Encounter, Midstream, Hortulus*, etc.

EZRA SPICEHANDLER Professor of Hebrew Literature, Hebrew Union College (Cincinnati); Co-editor: *Prakím Beyahadút (Chapters in Judaism);* Contributor: *Israel Argosy, Hadóar, Moznáyim, Commentary, Midstream, Judaism, Hebrew Union College Annual, Journal of the Oriental Society, Studies in Jewish Bibliography and Booklore, Jewish Book Annual, Historia Judaica*, etc.